MYTHS AND MYSTERIES
OF SAME–SEX LOVE

Christine Downing

Continuum • New York

1996

The Continuum Publishing Company
370 Lexington Avenue, New York, N.Y. 10017

Printed in the United States of America

Library of Congress Cataloging-in-Publication Data

Downing, Christine, 1931-
  Myths and mysteries of same-sex love/Christine Downing.
    p. cm.
  Includes index.
  ISBN 0-8264-0918-0 (pbk)
    1. Homosexuality. 2. Freud, Sigmund, 1856–1939—Views on
homosexuality. 3. Jung, C.G. (Carl Gustav), 1875–1961—Views on
homosexuality. 4. Homosexuality—Mythology. 5. Mythology, Greek.
6. Homosexuality in literature. I. Title.
HG76.25.D68 1989
306.7′66-dc20   89-7231
                                                                 CIP

"In a lyrical celebration of same-sex love that charts a course away from established notions of homosexuality. Downing appeals to Freud to illuminate an alternative path that validates pleasure and recognizes that *all* sexuality is both infinitely diverse and flawed and wounded. . . . Writing 'in a time when lovemaking and deathmaking have become so painfully confused,' Downing's book offers us new myths to live by, myths that are rooted in our psychic depths and cultural past."

—*Religious Studies Review*

"A remarkable book . . . offering important accounts of gay/lesbian experiences rarely explored and a vision of not one homosexuality but many. Its explorations of the links between men's fear of femininity and their fear of death sheds new light on the psychology of sexism and homophobia. And while it acknowledges the traumatic impact of AIDS on the gay/lesbian communities, the book's predominant image is not one of loss but of infinite possibilities."

—*Women's Review of Books*

"Part personal reminiscence, part exegesis of classic Greek myth, part critique of Freud's and Jung's psychiatric studies, this foray into the lore of homosexuality is an ambitious work. . . . offering freshly perceived insights and a finely tuned sensitivity."

—*Kirkus*

"A massive work of remarkable scholarship, which reads as easily as an historical novel, and draws together depth psychology and classical mythology, Freud and Plato's Phaedrus."

—*Journal of Psychology and Christianity*

Front cover: Zeus and Ganymede. Clay group of the severe style (470 B.C.E.). Olympia Museum.

Back cover: Women gossipping. Made at Myrina. Unknown provenance. Late second century B.C.E. British Museum.

*For many
and especially for Peter*

These are the lesser mysteries of love, into which even you, Socrates, may enter; but to the deepest mysteries of the complete vision, to which the former, if you take the right path, will lead, I know not whether you will be able to attain.

Diotima to Socrates in Plato's
Symposium

Contents

List of Illustrations

Acknowledgments

I want to thank:

Peter Downing for building the cabin in the canyon to which I have retreated to write this book.

River Malcolm, this book's first and most important reader, for her questions, suggestions, appreciation, and love.

The students at the Jung Institut in Zurich and the participants in the Gay and Lesbian Forum at the San Diego campus of the California School of Professional Psychology for their response to the lectures in which I first presented the material which has issued in this book.

A long list of friends—male and female, gay and straight, students and colleagues, old friends and new—whose encouragement of this project has been essential to me during the time devoted to its completion: Peter Barchi, Christopher Beck, Karen Brown, David Cohen, Carol Christ, Marea Claeesen, Eric Downing, William Doty, Adria Evans, Miles Frieden, Yitz Gefter, Alan Hamm, David Highnam, Gail Hornstein, Delores Jacobs, Estella Lauter, Philip Loftus, John McConnell, Dave Malcolm, Sherry May, Christopher Mead, Dan Noel, Kelley O'Neel, Margaret Pavel, Al Rabil, Steven Schaber, Sabine Scheffler, Kay Turner, Dick Underwood, Suzanne Valery, Peter Wayson, Ted Warren, Pamela Weeks, Merida Wexler, Martin Worman, Sharon Young, Bonnie Zimmermann.

My editors at Continuum, George Lawler and Frank Oveis, for their critical acumen and affectionate support.

Bill Whitehead, who was an editor at Dutton when they published my first book though he was not my editor. Bill was among the first to encourage me to write this book but died of AIDS before I managed to do so.

Elaine Estwick for the innumerable letters and memos she has written on my behalf, for the telephone calls she has made and answered, the inquiries she has pursued, the mysteries she has resolved, and most especially for her sustained good humor and equanimity.

PROLOGUE

A PERSONAL FOREWORD

I am a lesbian.

Many of my closest male friends are homosexual. Some have AIDS. Some have died.

This book grows out of my wish to reflect on the inner meaning of my own life choices and out of my love for these men.

It is not an AIDS book, though because of AIDS it is inevitably different from the book it would have been had I written it seven years ago, when I first contemplated doing so. AIDS has added a new urgency to my writing, a new depth to my reflections. It seems even more important now than it did then to look at the inner meaning of love directed toward others of the same gender as oneself. We all need support for confronting the confusion and dread, the anger and suffering, that the conjunction of desire and death implicit in the AIDS epidemic arouses in us.

This book is written for men and women, for homosexuals and for heterosexuals. I am persuaded that the particular joys and difficulties, needs, hopes, wounds, and blessings that shape the lives of those whose love is primarily directed toward same-sex others are relevant to the self-understanding of *all* of us, irrespective of our own conscious sexual orientation. To acknowledge that none of the ways we live our gendered lives is fully satisfying, that all of us are to some degree wounded in our sexuality, that none of us can live out all our fantasies, be all we dream of being, have all we long for, is to recognize that others who choose different paths from our own do so on our behalf. They live for us, as well as for themselves.

Yet so often those of us who direct our love and sexuality primarily to others like ourselves, who have become who we are primarily through relationships based on analogy rather than contrast, on mirroring rather than the complementation of opposites, are met with fear and hate from those who make the more traditional choice.

To search after an understanding of the soul meaning of same-sex love—an understanding of the deep longings that such love expresses, assuages, frustrates, engenders—will help those of us who live as homosexuals to know ourselves more richly, more complexly, more honestly. I hope it might also help heterosexuals to understand not just us but themselves better, to see more clearly in what ways their and our most profound wishes and fears are really different and in what ways the same. I hope it might encourage them to explore the roots of their denigration and fear of homosexuality and to recognize how their negative feelings cripple them as well as us.

Most of this book's reflections on how depth psychology and classical mythology illuminate what same-sex love means to the psyche, the soul, might have been voiced long before AIDS. Even the last section of the book, which explores how insight into the intimate interrelationship between Eros and death might help us in a time when lovemaking and deathmaking have become so painfully confused—even that section could perhaps have been written earlier, though the imperative to do so was lacking. But the inescapable reality of AIDS has lent an added intensity to every page. It deepens my sense of the particular power and beauty, the particular pains and confusions, of same-sex love. It enhances my awareness of the fear that this love arouses in some and of the new compassion it has awakened in others.

Thus it seems more important than ever to look at the meanings we ascribe to the love of another who is of the same gender as ourself—not only at the conscious meanings but at the meanings at work in the less accessible strata of our psyches, the meanings discovered by depth psychology, the meanings communicated in those ancient myths that helped shape the substrata of our culture and of our own souls. To bring these more unconscious meanings into view is to be helped toward a more polyphonic, more richly imaged, more poetic, and more soulful, a *deeper* understanding of same-sex love.

The longing for such a depth understanding has led me to look anew at what the depth psychologists have written about homosexuality—and to discover in them, particularly in Freud, a view very different from that usually associated with the psychoanalytical perspective, and much more illuminating, much more supportive. It has also led me to return to the myths about homosexual desire that were told and retold in ancient Greece, a culture where same-sex loving was validated as part of everyone's normal eroticism—as well as to what two of Greece's most gifted writers, Sappho and Plato, had to say about the homoerotic.

All of these sources speak more explicitly about male than about female homosexuality—which, of course, raises two problems. First, because male and female homosexuality are not isomorphic, I cannot simply extrapolate from male experience in trying to understand lesbian love. So I shall mine as much as I can from my texts that is relevant to women, and when I have gone as far as "discovery" takes me, I will (as Monique Wittig encourages us to do) "invent." Second, I, a woman, in much of this book try to articulate an understanding of male homosexuality that will seem relevant to gay males. So I will dare to say as much as *I* can about male experience—and leave it to men to determine in what way it speaks to them.

IN DIOTIMA'S LINEAGE

I feel encouraged in this project by Diotima, the ancient woman of wisdom whom my epigraph invokes. For it was from her, Socrates tells us, that he learned all that he knows about Eros. I also feel sistered in my undertaking by such powerful contemporary female reimaginers of male homosexual love as Mary Renault, Colette, and Marguerite Yourcenar.[1] Like them, I feel there is a sense in which I know male homosexuality from within.

For I have not always been a lesbian, and the path that led from my being a woman with some homosexual experience whose primary orientation was clearly heterosexual to my being a woman deeply committed to the woman lover with whom I share my home and my life is a complexly meandering one. It includes seven years during which my most important relationships were with gay men, some of whom became lovers. I believe those years gave me a more intimate access to an inner view of male homosexuality than is available to most women, though I know it is, of course, nonetheless a *woman's* view.

It was during those years that I wrote most of the studies that were eventually gathered together in my book *The Goddess: Mythological Images of the Feminine*. When I had completed that book several of my gay friends urged me to address myself next to a study of mythological images of homosexuality. At about the same time I also had several dreams that encouraged me in the same direction.

In response to these inner and outer urgings, my present project was begun but then soon laid aside—as I became involved with the woman with whom I now live and as understanding male homosexuality no longer seemed to be *my* task. Now I find myself pulled to return to the topic, in part out of a longing for a deeper understanding of my own homosexuality (which has issued in a broadening of the study as originally conceived to include lesbianism), and in part out of a resurgence of my love for gay men as I watch them wrestle with death. That has changed my project even more profoundly—for, as Freud discovered, in the light of death our sexuality looks different, appears under a new name, becomes Eros.

As I review what I had imagined writing then—an encomium to sexual exploration and diversity, a celebration of individual integrity and courage, a validation of a pleasure-oriented sexuality, a critique of conventional gender roles and definitions—it seems painfully inadequate. It is difficult to believe that only seven years have passed; so much has changed. How well I understand Fran Leibowitz's comment that coming to terms with the impact of AIDS on the homosexual world has meant recognizing that it is no longer possible to write the book for which she had for years been hoarding material, unless she were to write it "as a historical novel because it's about a world that in the last few years has disappeared almost entirely."[2] Yet I also know that my experience of that now-gone world still inevitably helps shape my relation to the one that replaced it. It still seems right to begin by reflecting on what I learned with and from those men I loved and love.

MALE MYSTERIES: A WOMAN'S WITNESS

To speak of myself as a "fag hag" during the years when I was intimately involved with gay men may seem exaggerated, masochistic, and in poor taste to some, but I have come to embrace this supposedly derogatory term for women who become part of the male homosexual world—because I have learned to celebrate "faggots" and "hags." Most of the gay men I know well would never choose to call themselves faggots, but the few who do have taught me to understand that they intend thereby to express their kinship with the homosexuals of medieval and early modern Europe who, like witches, were burned as heretics on bundles of sticks called faggots. (Later the victims themselves were by extension referred to as faggots.) Indeed, heresy and homosexuality were at that time regarded as so interchangeable that those accused of heresy would sometimes attempt to prove their inno-cence by establishing their heterosexuality. The men I know who consider themselves faggots use the label in order to acknowledge their continuity with this history of oppression. They would argue that there is a sense in which homosexuality is indeed a heresy, for it represents a profound critique of "heterosexism," of all patriarchal institutions, including Christianity. To them the term also provides a way of emphasizing the *bonds* among gay men—for faggots are separate entities closely bound together. Self-styled faggots are homosexuals who affirm their deep bond with the feminine, who choose themselves as antimasculine. They perceive how the hyper-masculinity of some gay men makes impossible what those men themselves most want: an intimate connection with a man. Fags are men who affirm the hag within themselves.[3]

Like many other feminists, I have come to embrace the term *hag* as a designation for a woman who has endured and come to celebrate her own courage, strength, and wisdom. Her very in-herself-ness makes her ugly and frightening to those who fear female-identified women. Hecate and Artemis are the goddesses of hags (as Artemis was often also the goddess worshiped by medieval gay men). Hags aren't necessarily old, but they are "haggard": willful, intractable, wanton, unyielding—survivors.[4]

So, although no one (to my face at least) has ever called me a "fag hag," I enjoy applying the term to myself, especially to the self of those years in which so much of my energy was devoted to relationships with gay men. I was moved by their feminism and, perhaps oddly, moved toward my own.

At about the time that I began the later-aborted version of this study, I had a dream of being involved in a moonlit menopausal ritual: I found myself immersed in a herb-infused bath, participating in a ritual presided over by a wizened, fearsome crone. The unknown elements that the old woman had added to the water had a strange effect: their scent opened my mind, but they also were stimulating a strange growth in my body. I could feel the cells in my genital area rearranging themselves; to my female organs were now added a penis and testicles.

Like many dreams, this one had plural significations—but I take one of its meanings to be that my relation to male homosexuality is an inner issue and not just an outer one. (I sense a parallel between what this dream means to me and what the dream of conceiving or giving birth to a child means to some of my male homosexual friends.) As I reflected on the dream, "fag hag" came to have a new sense, to refer to a woman who in some way *is* a fag, someone who loves gay men because they are *like* her in a way that straight men are not, rather than because they are different. Earlier I had tended to see my pull to gay men as a pull to particular individuals. Now I began to suspect that there was an archetypal meaning to my relation to male homosexuals. This helped me to see more clearly why their homosexuality was part of my way to my own homosexuality, my lesbianism. It was as though I needed first to free myself from an inner heterosexism, from the fantasy of contrasexuality, from a focus on *otherness*.

To the degree that one can date such things, I would say that my move away from a taken-for-granted heterosexism began about twenty years ago as I was returning from a sabbatical that I consciously experienced even then as an interlude between two lives. The familiar way of being myself had died with the traumatic ending of a love affair just before my leave. I no longer believed in the fantasy that wholeness and happiness were inevitably and necessarily connected to heterosexual pairing.

During the next few years (in the late 1960s and early 1970s) something magic, confusing, transformative was in the air, which none of us touched by it wholly understood. The old rules and definitions about sexual relationships and gender identity seemed to be suspended. It was a time when I and many of my women friends, both students and contemporaries, were discovering the importance of our love for one another. I understood our bonds with the homosexual men who often clustered around us as a function of our shared longing to be free, internally as well as externally, of oppression by the prevailing conventions about masculinity and femininity. Women's liberation, sexual liberation, homosexuality—all were interfused. It seemed quite natural to me that several of my male students would come to me for support as they went through the initial stages of "coming out," first to themselves and then to others, and that a female student who had never had an explicitly sexual involvement with a woman might fantasize me as her initiator.

During this period, although still married to the man I had wed when I was twenty, I was, as I said above, no longer living in the "marriage fantasy" and knew that when our children were grown I would no longer want to live in the marriage at all. So, seven years after the return from the sabbatical, I came to California—alone. When I left my husband it was because it seemed time to explore my own in-oneself-ness, my capacity for solitude and for creative work. Though I was frightened by her, I knew I wanted to come to terms with Artemis and the kind of self-sufficiency she represents. I was also drawn to what she models about the kind of respect and trust, passion and commitment, women can share with one another. I wanted a deeper connection with women and with my own feminine being.

I was not at all prepared for the discovery that suddenly, shortly after the move to California, a friendship with a gay man seemed to be at the center of my life. I had thought to stay free for a while of any deeply entangling relationships; I had imagined that later I might find a woman lover. Instead I found myself immediately and intensely drawn to a much younger homosexual man. We were soon involved in a relationship whose oft-changing shape has significantly informed the lives of both of us ever since. That might have been an isolated incident, but a few years later I found myself deeply involved with another gay man. In retrospect I see each of these relationships as having both liberating and self-protective aspects. I am sure that part of my pull to homosexual men derived from my knowledge that they were not fully available, that there was no danger of these becoming loves in which I would lose myself.

What happened between me and the gay man with whom I fell in love immediately upon my arrival in California was what I would have expected to find only in a relationship with a woman. I responded to him as though *he* were *my* anima—and only thus discovered how long I had coveted a relationship in which another would figure as anima for me, instead of my carrying that for him. He was my connection to soul, to the imaginal, to the intuitive and poetic, the dark and hidden, in myself. He was muse, affirming my creativity and nurturing it. The aspects of me I had hoped to cultivate, to bless, to live from in coming here were what he saw and loved and encouraged. As time went on I learned from him that these aspects are intimately and integrally related to my vulnerability and woundedness, my fearfulness and neediness. At long last I was able to begin to live without denying these hitherto denied and feared parts of myself. (It says much of who this man was to me if I acknowledge that I was sleeping with him when I had the dream that inspired my book on Greek goddess traditions, a dream in which I found myself in a dark underground cave in which the goddess was palpably but invisibly present.)[5]

I found that his femininity brought me more in touch with my own—whereas I had feared that loving someone "feminine" (male or female) would make me more "masculine." Our ways of being together gave me a new sense of the polymorphous possibilities of any relationship; for there were times when I was also anima or muse to him, Lou Salomé to his Rilke, Persephone to his Hades. Though in many ways our love was like that of one woman for another, there were also times when we *knew* we had been boys together in ancient Greece—and times when we celebrated the ways in which our relationship echoed the incestuous bond between mother and son.

Our love was complicated (and enriched) from its onset because we did not assume that his being gay meant that we would never become lovers in the literal physical sense. Rather, almost from the beginning that possibility was present as a question, as a fear, as a numinous possibility. We discovered that our being together evoked the beauty, power, and terror of a gay male's deeply ambivalent relation to the feminine, particularly to the feminine in its Great Mother aspects. When eventually we did become lovers, our lovemaking, especially the first time but often later as well, retained some of the awesomeness of the primordial connection of a male and a female—of how it was originally in the mythological time when the sons became the lovers and then the sacrificial victims of the mother goddess. (Though sometimes an entirely different loving occurred, reminiscent of Hades' taking of Persephone.)

I recall how important between us was an evening we spent with two other gay male friends, which to the surprise of all of us moved into serious and intense sexual contact. I felt enormously privileged to be so included in this male mystery and deeply touched by the gentleness, the slow-paced-ness, the unselfishness, the polymorphousness of the lovemaking. That evening meant many things to me and to each of the other participants, but among them was that my lover and I experienced it as our celebrating together that he loved men and was loved by them and that that was beautiful.

I remember, too, another occasion, several years later, which took place one sun-filled afternoon on my patio. We had each taken a psychedelic drug as part of a ritual celebration of my move into my present home. I felt myself approached by Dionysus and made love to by him. I was only dimly aware of my human lover's presence some feet away, as priestess and witness. I did not touch myself and my companion never came close enough to touch me, but I felt myself touched by a lover who knew me utterly, who touched every surface with delicate and absolute assurance, who made me entirely alive, who opened me up as I had never been opened, who entered me and found a deeper within-ness than there had been until then. All that happened seemed to happen between the god and myself. But my lover was present, the only person I can imagine being present who would not have made such an experience impossible and the only one who would have known imme-diately what was transpiring. Later that evening we, too, made love and some weeks later I discovered I was pregnant. As soon as I realized that, it seemed clear to me that the child belonged to the god and was to be ritually sacrificed to him. I feared that might mean having to arrange for an abortion; instead I aborted spontaneously on the morning of the summer solstice, Dionysus's birthday. It felt as though the god himself had come to take the child away.

This strange conception, with its intermingling of fantasy and fact, which meant so much symbolically but was so out of place in the everyday world, has always seemed the perfectly appropriate expression for our love. It seems not irrelevant that this man whose homosexuality was so central to what gave our relationship its unique power and meaning, was the first important male lover with whom I had never longed for a child. The love between us seemed to carry some of the same energy and significance that homosexual love carries—a transcendence of reproductive love, a commitment to a different kind of co-creation.

The image of the child also played an important role in my other intimate relationship with a gay man. This man and I had found ourselves drawn to each other at several summer parties because both of us were fascinated by the topic of involvements between gay men and women. He because he had only recently left a heterosexual marriage and as a therapist hoped to learn how to help others moving through the same transition do so with less pain and confusion. I because of how mysterious I felt my bond with my young lover to be. In the fall he and I decided to spend an evening together. Over dinner we began a slow, serious telling of our stories, including some of the painful ones not usually told so early in a friendship. I dreamt that night of being with him in my home as though it were *our* home and of being visited by my family and some close friends. In the dream I was carrying on my hip a child whom even in the dream I recognized as *the* child of my dreams. As always she was a joy-filled, joy-giving presence. Several times in the midst of the dream's comings and goings I had stopped to nurse her and as I was about to do so again, I suddenly realized, as I held her buttocks in my left hand and stroked the head nestled against my shoulder with my right, that, albeit happy and healthy, she hadn't been growing. Though by now eight or nine months old, she was no bigger than she'd been months before. I understood this to be because she had never had any nourishment other than my milk and that it was past time now for her to begin receiving solid food. When I awoke I realized that though this child had often been in my dreams before, she had never before appeared outside the nursery to which I alone had access. I wondered what it meant that this man whom I barely knew would in my dream have the power to get me to trust bringing the child openly into the world of others, to get me to acknowledge it needed nourishment beyond what I could myself provide.

We began to meet quite often; we soon became occasional lovers; we began to work together as co-therapists for a group of lesbians and gay men. We spent one evening together with my other lover, which led into so mutual a lovemaking among the three of us as none of us had ever imagined. Again, and much more deeply, I had a sense of being included in what was essentially a male mystery—and *fully* included. There was true caring and intense desire flowing in every possible direction. We all three woke up the next morning with an awareness of the sacredness of what had happened.

During the course of that year the new man and I began to spend more and more time with each other, more time than either of us was spending with anyone else. We became for each other *the* person to turn to with our hurts and our impasses, with confusing dreams, with our puzzles about our other relationships. The one thing we rarely spoke of was our own relationship. We both accepted that he was gay. Affirming that and reordering his life to acknowledge it had been a long and traumatically painful process. To risk putting his sexual orientation into question again was too scary. He was gay. I knew that. I myself had seen that his sexual pull to men and the fullness of his response to them was more intense than anything that had ever happened between us. On my side, to acknowledge that I was in love with a man who was really longing for a male lover was also too scary. But a time came when I could no longer bear not saying, "I love you," when he could no longer keep himself from saying, "Yes, I know and I love you." We admitted how long we had each evaded that acknowledgment. We wouldn't have chosen it, but the fact was it had happened: we were in love. What a release to affirm that at last! To choose now to live our love, consciously and honestly, without evading the fact that he was still a gay man.

The relationship that developed was very different from the one with the much younger lover, which had, despite its power, always remained peripheral to our ongoing day-by-day lives. This man and I were clearly, for now, the most important persons in each other's lives. We did not live together or ever seriously consider doing so. He continued his sexual involvements with men, with some old friends and some new acquaintances. I, too, occasionally spent time with other lovers, both male and female. I loved him enough to hope for him that someday he would find a man whom he would love and trust in as rich and multidimensional a way as he loved me. I loved him enough to know that when that happened I would experience it as a terrible loss and probably not be as "good" about it as I would want to be. We spent much of our time in the gay world; many of our mutual friends were gay men; we went dancing at gay discos, explored gay San Francisco and New York together. Our closest friends were a lesbian couple whose honesty with each other and trust in the strength of their bond seemed to match ours in a way that was true of no other couple we knew. We often drew to us gay men, as individuals or sometimes as couples, who saw us as able to help them sort through some of the more painful puzzles in their lives. We spent much of our private time together talking about the mysteries of sexual orientation—childhood beginnings, adolescent confusion, adult struggles, the false myths and the true.

Paradoxically, my lover's being homosexual seemed to have much to do with the strength of our bond. Because we knew that, although for the time being we were focused on each other, this was not likely to remain true—we were able to be honest and vulnerable with each other as neither of us had ever been able to be with anyone else. There was no point, ever, in dissembling today for the sake of insuring some putative tomorrow. Thus hurt, disappointment, preferences, fears, hopes could all be voiced. We were not as good at voicing anger. I was able to share my most frightened, most self-doubting moments—and in doing so to experience their full power in my life for the first time. I felt him doing the same and was awed at his courage in revealing the really raw and scabrous wounds. I felt trusting and trusted. Though there were times when our intimacy was too intense, when he would withdraw; and also times when the other's *otherness* was too overwhelming, when one of us would be disappointed that the other was different from what we'd imagined or hurt that we weren't fully accepted as our real selves after all.

After two years of intensely focused involvement, the anticipated, dreaded time came. My lover fell in love with a man I knew well and had already come to care for deeply. They seemed beautifully suited to each other; indeed, I had more difficulty in understanding the things that didn't go well between them than in understanding the attraction. I was happy for him, and also painfully unhappy, as I had known I would be. I felt more abandoned than I had expected. We had spoken of this eventuality so often, but had always imagined we would in large measure meet it together. Instead I felt my lover's lover to be more attuned to my pain than my lover himself. We still spent time together, but it seemed always to focus on his struggles in the new relationship. And I was less brave and honest than earlier, less able to acknowledge (even to myself) how radically abandoned I felt (since my objective conscious self knew that to be an exaggerated response). I tended to interpret all the changes that were occurring in our relationship as due to the new involvement. I did not see how some of the strains and understandings that had surfaced between us had actually begun earlier.

Nor did I see how much I myself had needed the relationship to become less absorbing than it had become, how much I needed to recover the sense of in-myself-ness that I had assumed would be inviolate in this relationship but wasn't. While struggling with the redefinition of our relationship, we took a vacation together during which I wrote the Artemis chapter of my Goddess book. The writing reminded me of the oft-recurring struggle in my life between devotion to Aphrodite and to Artemis and showed me how important it was at this point in my life to honor Artemis. I felt (again!) that perhaps I was done with Aphrodite for good.

That turned out to be a misapprehension. But I did seem to be done with gay men as the most important figures in my life for good. When I fell in love again it was with a woman, the woman with whom I still live and hope to live for the rest of my life. But those years with these two men remain figural in my life—part of my way, not a deviation from it. And what I know of male homosexuality comes at least as much from my relationships with them as from anything I have learned from psychology or mythology.

MY LOVE FOR WOMEN

I have not always been a lesbian, though to say when I became one would not be easy. That depends so much on what we take the term to mean—

which is part of what I want to explore, not to decide on beforehand. Some might want to deny me the designation even now, though it is important to me to claim it. Again it seems right to begin by rehearsing the history, telling the stories, in order to make evident the perspective from which my later reflections on psychological and mythological reflections on lesbian love issue.

When I was in college I was deeply in love with a woman. Our relationship was sustained over several years; it was intense, passionate, sexual—but neither of us then, almost forty years ago, ever thought of ourselves as lesbian. We took it for granted that someday we would marry and have children—as we did. I have long ago lost track of what became of her, though I sometimes wonder.

During the early years of my marriage there was again one close woman friend. We read poetry and depth psychology together, we encouraged each other's art, we shared our dreams—and, very rarely, our bodies. Sometimes our intimacy seemed to summon that expression, but mostly both of us directed our sexuality toward men. Sometimes to the same man—which, after one painfully disruptive outburst of jealousy between us, seemed like yet another way of being close.

It wasn't until after my return from my European sabbatical that loving women became a *conscious* issue in my life. I came home to discover that suddenly during my year away my female students had become feminists—and that for some of them this meant being lesbians as well. Really valuing and loving themselves as women meant loving women, not only in the sense of political identification and commitment but with all their being—personally, emotionally, sexually. Although they used the rhetoric of the time—"the personal is the political," "sisterhood is powerful," "freedom from compulsory heterosexism"—they also spoke with clear, persuasive, poetic, individual voices. These young women became my teachers as I learned from them to see so much that until then had been invisible to me, about the world within which I lived and about myself. I loved them—for their passion and courage, their integrity and hopefulness, for their iconoclasm and creativity. Some of them loved me; some of them even dared to tell me that they desired me. I knew that it wasn't appropriate to accede to their fantasies, but I discovered that I was stirred and began to wonder about my own sexual orientation, to question what my earlier involvements with women really signified. I knew that this group of lesbian students and young lesbian faculty had come to constitute my "home" within the university.

Sexually I was still involved with men. Yet it wasn't quite that simple. I had gone to Europe in part to work through the guilt of how my love for another woman's husband had shattered her life—and while there had discovered that I could never again let love for a man lead me to betray a "sister," a woman. In some sense I already knew that my bond to women took precedence over any relationship to men. One of the things that made possible the heterosexual relationship that began a few years after my return from Europe was that this man's wife blessed our affair. Indeed, we became very close. Occasionally—the old pattern—we even became lovers. By the time I moved to California I felt my bond to her to be more intimate and more focal than my bond to her husband.

As I have already said, when I came to live here I expected that my next lover would be a woman. It turned out otherwise. First there were those years during which my most important ongoing love affairs were with gay men—though I had close women friends and several brief affairs with women, and though my gay male lover and I spent much of our time in the company of lesbian women. During this time I began to think of myself as a "bisexual" in terms of how I actually *lived* my sexuality, and as a "lesbian" in terms of my commitment to women.

Then I took a trip around the world that became my "journey through menopause."[6] On the other side of that I began the relationship with the woman with whom I now live. For me the love of women as the central commitment of my life has blossomed only in these postmenopausal years. But it *has* blossomed.

We moved into acknowledging our love slowly. Much of our courtship, our first tentative admitting of affection and longing, was conducted through letters, though we lived in the same city. After we first made love and discovered how many fantasies of a life together that had stirred in each of us, we cried—as we mourned together the child my lover had still hoped she might one day have (though long a lesbian, she had begun thinking about men, marriage, children), as she then mourned that I would in all likelihood die many years earlier than she. Though our relationship had really hardly begun, we were already so in touch with its costs. We were both so used to living alone, so shy of commitment, so wary of failure—it was a year before we were ready to live together, another year before we decided that we would like to try to have a child. That decision made us aware of how much we wanted our relationship to have the recognition, the support, the blessing accorded to heterosexual couples when they marry, and so we invited our families and friends to a celebration during which we exchanged vows naming our hope to stay together, fruitfully, creatively, honestly, lovingly. Though we tried for two years, my lover did not conceive and we agreed that it was time to adopt a different dream for our life together. Though I don't believe we have ever questioned that choice, the sense of loss is real, sometimes painfully intense, especially for her. My granddaughters help, but it is not the same as a child of our own.

Among the things that first drew us to each other was that we were both writers, that we valued the other's writing, that we imagined a relationship in which our writing would flourish. But for the first few years our creative energies seemed all to be channeled into the relationship itself and neither of us wrote. Now what we hoped for at the beginning has begun to happen. I am filled with a resurgence of Eros for my work that I know is fueled by our life together. She, too, is pulled back to her writing and has undertaken a new career in which she can use her gifts of naming and evoking, empathy, intuition, image creating, healing. The relationship is fruitful—though we have no child, though we are much less sexual now than we were at first.

I bless the passion that smoothed our early struggles. I mourn its passing. Reflecting on the diminished sway of sexuality in our lives, we sometimes jokingly ask if we are still real lesbians. But because there is no other word that communicates the depth of our commitment to each other and of our bond to other women who have defined their lives by their love for women, we continue to rediscover the importance of claiming the name.

PSYCHOLOGY'S MYTHS

· 1 ·

THE MYTH
OF HOMOSEXUALITY

That *we* choose to call ourselves lesbians, that we decide what this designation means to us, is itself a challenge to how same-sex loving has most often been defined in our culture. For by and large we have been the defined not the self-definers, the object of others' mythmaking rather than the creators of our own mythology. In this chapter we will explore the language and images through which same-sex love is most often viewed in our time. This language inevitably shapes how all of us feel and think about such love—even if we consciously reject some of its implications and connotations. We will seek in later chapters to expand and deepen these perspectives, but they represent our necessary starting points.

During this century it has become customary to bring women who love women and men who love men together under the same rubric: homosexuality. This term collapses into one word the myth about same-sex love that has largely shaped both how we are viewed and how we view ourselves. Although our attempt to reach a depth understanding of same-sex loving must take us beyond that myth, must lead us to a look at how such loving was imaged earlier (especially in classical Greece), we must begin with our culture's myth.

As we examine the currently dominant conception, we quickly discover that homosexuality has a *very* short history—that is, that the term *homosexual* appeared in English less than a hundred years ago and that the way of construing human sexuality, which the introduction of the term implies and which we tend to take for granted, is very recent. The creation of this hybrid Greek-Latin neologism coincides with the rise of depth psychology and with the beginnings of a new tendency to understand sexuality primarily in psychological terms. There is a sense, then, in which homosexuality is a myth created by clinical psychology.

The word *homosexual* was evidently coined in 1869 by a German physician, brought into more popular usage in Germany around 1880, and

3

introduced into English in 1892. Recent as it is, however, it antedates the term *heterosexual*, which was (so the *Oxford English Dictionary* tells us) not used until eight years later.[1] Obviously this does not mean that there was no same-sex or contra-sex loving until then; and yet just as obviously the introduction of the terms suggests that there is something new in how such loving is being understood. The new language may not have created the new identities, but it certainly validated and substantiated them.

HOMOSEXUAL IDENTITIES

What was new was the notion that personhood might be defined by whether one's sexuality was primarily directed toward persons of the same gender as oneself or toward persons of the other gender. Earlier in the nineteenth century a different term, *sexual inversion*, had been in vogue. Its meaning was different—though it, too, was applied to both women and men. Then the emphasis had fallen not on deviant "sexual object" choice but on deviant gender behavior. "Inverts" were effeminate men, men who adopted feminine sex roles, who felt themselves to be women in male bodies, or women who acted in masculine ways. The "inversion" was understood to be manifest in every aspect of one's life, in aberrant "tastes, conduct, character, feelings and behavior."[2] "Inversion" was closely associated with transvestism, with cross-dressing, as well as with a preference for the "sexual aim" appropriate to the other gender. Male inverts were assumed to prefer adopting a passive "feminine" role in their sexual engagement, as their female counterparts were expected to manifest an aggressive, active "masculine" sexual desire. Thus inversion might be *expressed* by sexual involvement with "normal" members of one's own gender, but it was *not defined* by such behavior.

When we say that "homosexuality" does not exist until the end of the nineteenth century, we of course do not mean that no one before then engaged in sexual activity with persons of their own gender, but simply that in earlier periods such behavior was understood in a different context. The notion of "inversion" differed from the later notion of "homosexuality" in emphasizing a broad range of gender-deviant behavior, but it prepared the way for the presently dominant understanding in its assumption that our sexuality determines our personhood, our consciousness, our entire life. Both inversion and homosexuality are construed as constituting specific identities. That is, in the nineteenth century some individuals were labeled inverts, as some are now considered to *be* homosexuals; whereas earlier, though there were homosexual *acts*, temporary aberrant behaviors in which presumably anyone might engage, there were no homosexual *persons*. At least not persons who were identified by society or themselves as such.

The antithetical categorization of persons as either heterosexual or homosexual is clearly recent. In earlier periods sexual behaviors were classified along different "fault lines," not on the basis of whether one's preferred partners were members of the same or opposite sex as oneself. In the medieval world the most important distinction was between procreative and nonprocreative practices. Anal or oral sex was condemned even within marriage, and regarded as more sinful than rape or incest because nonreproductive. Among the Greeks, as we shall see, significance was attached primarily to whether one played the active or the passive role; a free adult male might appropriately be sexually involved with both male and female partners, but it was essential that with both he be the penetrator. Among the Romans, the important dichotomy was that between givers and receivers "of seed"; it was acceptable for an adult male citizen to be fellated or to penetrate a male or female but not to himself suck another's penis or to allow his anus to be entered.[3] Clearly all the behaviors that we associate with homosexuality were recognized and practiced in each of these societies, but they were ordered within a different schema, interpreted differently, valued differently.

Michel Foucault suggests that what is most distinctive in the nineteenth century's designations is their *psychological* emphasis; both "inversion" and "homosexuality" are believed to refer to a distinct *subjectivity*. He sees the psychologist and the homosexual as forming a dyadic unit: the psychologist is fascinated with motives and fantasies, the hidden, inner life of the other; the attention he gives to the confessions he elicits is a voyeur's attention, is itself a sexual activity.[4] This attention objectifies, solidifies, reifies; it creates sexual heterogeneities: permanent, visible particular sexualities. The new labels imply that you as a person are essentially either heterosexual or homosexual.

Their conviction that specific identities are the creation of specific cultures leads Foucault and Guy Hocquenghem to see the idea of "the homosexual" as an artifact of bourgeois society. They reaffirm the close association posited by Engels between the institution of private property and the valorization of the patriarchal family and recapitulate his analysis of how under capitalism all expressions of sexuality that do not serve to perpetuate the family are repressed. Yet, they assert, because from the bourgeois perspective the family is seen as the source of all the vicissitudes of sexuality, even homosexuality is brought *within* the family by being "explained" in terms of family dynamics. The homosexual (along with the infant and the hysteric) is *as-*

signed the social role of representing the denied aspects of the sexuality of all of us. "The establishment of homosexuality as a separate category goes hand in hand with its repression."

What is most fascinating in this analysis is its description of how the definition of homosexuality as deviant sexuality comes to constitute the basis for the definition of normal sexuality—which helps explain why the term *homosexual* antedates the term *heterosexual.* Homosexuality, once defined, "becomes the center of everyone's haunting nightmare," the clue to the full truth about the sexuality of all of us.

They also show how the dominant cultural assumptions come to inform the self-perception of those who engage in the castigated behaviors. Because the prevailing view of sexuality makes polymorphous, unfocused sexuality terrifying to everyone, those who act in response to homosexual desire are ready to surrender to the "recuperative" interpretation that this constitutes their sexuality per se, are ready to accept a homosexual identity. Better this identity than none. They themselves fail to recognize what Hocquenghem takes to be the *truth* about homosexual desire: that it "represents an arbitrarily frozen frame in an unbroken and polyvocal flux."[5]

The interpretations put forward by Foucault and Hocquenghem invite "homosexuals" to recognize how the label both distorts and shapes their own experience; they offer the beginnings of an alternative myth. They seek to remind us that the "myth of homosexuality" was created by heterosexuals, from outside not within. The homosexual was, by definition, "the Other." The "secondary gains" that Simone de Beauvoir describes as persuading women to accept being "the Other," the objectified, as a social role affect this *other* "Other," the homosexual, as well.[6] Many of us, men and women, have accepted the homosexual label, for doing so provides us not only with a *self*-definition but also with a *group* identity.

It is, of course, always difficult to see through one's own culture's assumptions. Yet it is important to recognize the degree to which these assumptions, less than a century old, shape our view of ourselves and our behaviors—and how they may not really fit. Thus in looking at how same-gender relationships are viewed in other cultures, it is important not to interpret them anachronistically, on the basis of contemporary perspectives—as it may also be helpful to ask if these different views might not challenge and expand our own.

The presently dominant myth implies that "homosexuality" is a uniform category, that the history, the experience, the self-understanding of those whose love is directed to members of the same gender can be subsumed within the same definition, the same explanatory paradigm. Whereas in actuality, as many recent studies have acknowledged, even as they still use the word, we would do better to speak in the plural, to speak of "homosexualities."

LESBIAN IDENTITY

One highly questionable implication of the "myth of homosexuality," as we have already noted, is the way it lumps together lesbians and male "homosexuals"—and implies that female experience can adequately be understood in relation to a model based on a male paradigm.[7] Again, it may be difficult for us to realize how recent this amalgamation is—to recognize that the contemporary lesbian protest that our experience must be set within the context of the specific history of female sexuality rather than within the context of same-gender object-choice as modeled by men is in some respects like a call for a return to more traditional assumptions.

Erotic or sexual relations between women seem always to have received less attention than such relations among men. There are, for example, hardly any accounts of ecclesiastical or lay prosecutions of women sexually involved with women in medieval or early modern Europe. Although there are occasional condemnations of women "committing shameful deeds with women" by influential theologians, beginning with the Apostle Paul and including Augustine, Ambrose, Anselm, Abelard, and Thomas Aquinas, there are no references to such practice in either Dante or Boccaccio, whose writings offer descriptions of so many other forms of sexual expression. Indeed, a noncoital sexuality seems to have been so relatively invisible, almost unimaginable, to male writers that there was no agreed-upon language to refer to what we think of as lesbian sexuality. It was "the sin that cannot be named" or "the silent sin." The phrase "female sodomy," though sometimes used, was felt to be inadequate because sodomy meant not just *penetration*, which might be accomplished through mutual masturbation or the use of "material instruments," but penetration by a genital organ, and was therefore something that only women with extraordinarily large clitorises could be imagined to engage in. The most common appellation was that of "fricatrices" or "tribades"—women who rub each other. The women themselves, whose lives were confined to the private familial sphere, had (as far as we know) no sense that their sexual practices bestowed a distinct social identity.

The word *lesbian* seems to have been used once in the modern sense in the sixteenth century, but this definition did not gain currency until late in the nineteenth century. Indeed, in the 1928 edition of the *Oxford English*

Dictionary "lesbian" is still defined as applying to the Aegean island, to a particular kind of mason's rule, and to a principle of judgment that is pliant and accommodating—but not to female eroticism. Nor is there an entry under "lesbian" in the more recent *Supplement*. (The entry under "Sapphic" mentions only the Greek poet and a meter used by her.) Even when "lesbian" was used in a more erotic sense, it was taken to connote sensuality, sexual indulgence, rather than a distinctively female sexuality. It may be difficult for us to realize that when Sappho's poetry was rediscovered in the mid-sixteenth century its focus on same-sex loving was largely ignored. It is only as in the modern world identities have come to be defined by sexual orientations that the word *lesbian* has come to have as its primary meaning: female homosexuality.[8]

Many feminists have argued that it is inappropriate to apply the term *homosexual* to women's love of women because of the word's focus on the sexual expression of that love. They prefer the term *lesbian*, which, they say, "describes a relation in which two women's strongest emotions and affections are directed toward each other" whether or not sexual contact is part of the relationship,[9] and would reserve the phrase "female homosexual" as an accurate description of women who relate genitally to women but "give their allegiance to men and male myths, ideologies, styles, practices, institutions, and professions."[10]

The emphasis some contemporary lesbians put on emotional commitment rather than physical intimacy recalls earlier periods when women's *love* of women was culturally affirmed—while the very possibility that the love might have a genital dimension was denied. For, as Lillian Faderman has shown, before the modern era not only lesbian sexuality but female sexuality itself was well nigh invisible. Faderman's historical account reveals how— because of the phallocentric assumptions about sexuality held by most males—the most intimate physical contact between women was in earlier centuries not viewed as sexual. As we noted above, sex without a penis was considered an impossibility. Thus in the Renaissance and in the early modern world it was only when a woman challenged the culture's gender restrictions by claiming male prerogatives, usually by trying to dress and pass as a man, that she was liable to the sanctions and punishments directed against sexual deviance. Even in the nineteenth century "Sapphic sexuality" was assumed to depend on one woman's being "masculine," not only in terms of her psychical characteristics but physically; she would have an enlarged clitoris or, failing that, would necessarily make use of a dildo. Krafft-Ebing, for example, assumed that women's natural sexuality was passive, that no normal woman would feel or express active sexual desire.

Faderman also notes how congruent these assumptions were with how women for whom love of women was a central dimension of their lives spoke of their own experience. What they emphasized was the importance of the emotional intimacy, the ease and joy of sharing daily life, rather than genital acts. She believes this represents more than simply the internalization of male views about women, that it says something about a scale of values that may truly be the women's own. Almost nostalgically, she relates how unselfconscious women could be about their passionate love for one another, about their intense commitment to one another, in these earlier periods when there was no label to apply to their bond. She also shows how contaminated such bonds often were by the introduction of the label, by the naming that condemned such love as an abnormal condition, a sickness—which made of it a sexual identity, which forced women to choose between their love of women and normality.

Havelock Ellis's understanding of "female homosexuality" (like Krafft-Ebing's description of the female invert) made distinctions within the group of women committed to one another. From the perspective of these sexologists only the "dyke," the "butch," the masculine partner, was a *real* homosexual. She, however, was not a real *woman*, but a member of a "third sex." Her "condition," though no longer viewed as a sin or crime, as it might have been in some earlier periods, was now understood to be "constitutional," an inherited given. The painful consequences of the internalization of this view of same-sex love by women is clearly evident in Radclyffe Hall's novel *The Well of Loneliness*. In her own life, too, Hall seems to have found that the only way to escape being forced into heterosexual patterns was to appropriate Ellis's interpretation and put herself forward as "really" a man trapped in a woman's body. That a woman might *choose* to love women rather than men seems never to have occurred to the sexologists.

At least not consciously. As Faderman suggests, it is unlikely to be only coincidence that "female homosexuality" becomes visible and castigated at just the time when economically women could afford to reject financial dependence on males, could afford to make their bond to another woman the visibly central relationship of their lives. As she shows, the sexologists' view of female-female bonding could be used to show that a woman's desire for independence meant she was not really a woman. Feminism made lesbian love a threat to the established order; sexology made lesbian love evidence of "inversion," of pathology. Thus the label also served to *divide* women from one another; it could be used as a scare term to keep women within the socially sanctioned feminine role and suspicious of close bonds with one another.

The inclusion of women's love of women and men's love of men in the same category denies the enormous difference in the sociocultural conditions that shape female and male experience. By failing to take into account the power imbalance between the sexes, this lumping together obscures the fact that female bonding arises in the context of the oppressed social position of women. Thus feminists have insisted that lesbian identity can only be understood in the context of the construction of female gender identity, which is radically different from the construction of male identity, whether heterosexual or homosexual. Women may turn to women as a way of rejecting their powerlessness in heterosexually defined contexts. That powerlessness stems not from their sexual orientation but from their gender.

The sexologists missed this radical difference between male and female "homosexuality" because of their tendency to focus on *behaviors* rather than on what the behaviors *mean* to the actors—as well as by their assumption that the most salient behaviors are *sexual* behaviors. Their term homosexuality implies that what matters most is the desire for a particular "sexual aim" or "sexual object"; furthermore, by equating sex with genitality and orgasm they radically disassociate sexual from sensual contact.

The views from within are more complex. Some lesbians seem to regard their rejection of a heterosexual male-dominated environment as more central to their self-identification than sexual attraction to women per se. They celebrate the intimacy, the emotional closeness and mutuality, possible among women, at least as much as the particular joys associated with lesbian sexuality. Others would want to affirm the power of their desire for other women as a self-validating reality. They turn to women because of the sexual and emotional fulfillment they find women giving one another—not because they are turning away from men. From this perspective, to minimize the importance of the sexual dimension of lesbianism is to deny its most vital dimension. Lesbianism is a way of claiming one's sexuality (and thus one's female life) as fully one's own.

GAY IDENTIFICATION

Although I appreciate the insights gained from viewing lesbianism within a feminist context, I nonetheless regret the disassociation from gay men that is often the correlate of this perspective. I understand the historical background—how women often became second-class participants in the gay liberation movement in the late 1960s and early 1970s, as they also had in the earlier civil rights and antiwar movements. I understand the resentments that underlie lesbian criticisms of the promiscuity and privilege they see as having been so characteristic of the male homosexual world. But I see in that now almost defunct "promiscuity" not only irresponsibility but also a beautiful reaching toward a real celebration of our embodiment—as I have seen among the gay men I know well a serious and honest rejection of the power and privilege accorded males by heterosexist polity. And as I watch gay men suffer from AIDS and from the fear of AIDS, I know—as I have known all along—these men are my brothers.

There are differences between what pulls women to women and what pulls men to men—but there are also some powerful similarities. It seems just as mistaken to assume there are no commonalities or continuities as to assume that same-sex loving means exactly the same thing to women as to men. (Or indeed to all women or all men—for, as Mary Daly notes, not all "female homosexuals" are feminists nor, as we'll see, are all "male homosexuals" gay.) Certainly as long as the same label is applied to all of us, we will suffer some of the same oppression. My hope is that as we explore the various histories, the various stories, the various myths that have been told about and by women who love women and about and by men who love men, we may see more clearly where each of us would want to insist on differences, where each would be ready to affirm similarities.

It may be part of my particular perversity to discover in male homosexuality some of the lineaments more often associated only with lesbian love— that is, to reverse the more familiar approach, which interprets female experience on the basis of a male model. Yet I find some warrant for this in the protestations of those men who insist that the term *homosexual* radically distorts what their love of men means to them. Their attempts to articulate what their love means to them clearly echo the testimony of their lesbian sisters and in some instances, at least, have been directly inspired by that testimony. As though once again "Diotima" is helping men to name how Eros enters into their lives.

More than fifty years ago some men, seeking to reject the "homosexual" label, decided to describe themselves as "homophiles"; more recently the self-chosen designation has been "gay." Both terms deliberately repudiate the emphasis on sexuality in the term *homosexual*—an emphasis that "gay" spokespersons regard as a manifestation of the phallocentrism of the male heterosexual perspective. Gay identity, so its proponents affirm, focuses more on a critique of the dehumanizing effects of hetero*sexism*, of patriarchy, than on a rejection of hetero*sexuality.*

Although Judy Grahn relates "gay" to the primordial earth goddess of ancient Greece, Gaia,[11] scholarly etymology seems to take us back only as far as the French troubadors who were associated with a sensually affirmative deviant eroticism. In Restoration England the term *gay* was applied to persons associated with the theater and to prostitutes; toward the end of the nineteenth century it became a kind of in-group self-designation of those the sexologists labeled "homosexual."

In discussing what "gay" means today, both Don Clark and John Boswell emphasize the importance of its being principally a self-assigned category. Gay persons, writes Boswell, are those conscious of erotic preference for their own gender. Being a gay male is not defined by whether one has or has not slept with a man or by how often one has done so. It avoids the presumption that sexuality figures more centrally in the lives of gay people than of others. It leaves open "the relative importance of love," affection, devotion, romance, eroticism or overt sexuality in the lives of persons so designated."[12]

Thus both lesbians and gay men reject the myth of homosexuality. Yet it is important that we recognize that it *is* a myth—not just in the sense of being a falsehood but also in the sense of representing a cultural vision that has tremendous effective power, which is part of a whole "cosmology," a comprehensive view of gender, sex, human selfhood. To move beyond this myth, we need to bring it into relation to alternative myths—especially, I believe, to the myths about same-sex love told in ancient Greece, a culture where such love was seen as normal rather than pathological.

But first we may need a more in-depth understanding of this myth than the somewhat critical and reductive one offered thus far. For I have been attacking the simplistic secondhand versions of this myth, the form of the myth that has entered popular culture. But depth psychology's myth about homosexuality is actually "deeper," more complex and more profound, more illuminating and more challenging, than has thus far been admitted. Fully to explore this myth means turning to the writings of Freud and Jung with a willingness to read slowly, extensively, carefully, free of the prejudice that we already know what they have to say.

·2·

FREUD:
THE PERSONAL DIMENSION

As I have looked anew at all the relevant texts, I have been surprised to discover what a central role homosexuality plays in Sigmund Freud's work—and how different what he says about it is from what he is generally taken to have said. I have also been struck by how when Freud writes of the importance of homoerotic impulses in human life, he writes of *us* not *them*.

Whenever I read Freud I am impressed by how deeply and naturally he assumes the universality, the archetypal nature, of his own experience. If *he* is Oedipus, then all of us are; if the encounter with the unconscious is initially bewildering and disconcerting for him, then it will be so for each of us. During the period when he was discovering psychoanalysis—the period during which he came to recognize the universal importance of unconscious factors, first glimpsed how each of us relives Oedipus's story, and felt forced to acknowledge the active sexuality of children—he found himself to be his own most difficult and most fruitful patient. He found confirmed in his own case what he had suspected in others; from reflection on his self-analysis he learned what to look for elsewhere. Remembering this, perhaps we should have expected that Freud's awareness of a "feminine," intuitive, receptive dimension to his own creativity and his acknowledgment of his own pull to intensely intimate relationships with men would have led him to posit that, consciously or unconsciously, all of us are homosexual *and* heterosexual, all of us are "really" bisexual.

THE BIRTH-GIVING FANTASY

In exploring the personal dimensions of Freud's relationship to bisexuality and homoeroticism, it seems appropriate to begin by looking at his ambivalent relationship to what he sometimes spoke of as his own "femininity."

What Freud means by the "feminine" is, of course, an enormously com-

13

plicated issue in its own right, since he himself challenges the equation of psychical femininity with the possession of anatomical female characteristics and furthermore acknowledges that the conventional identification of femininity as passivity ignores the *activity* inherent in such prototypically female behaviors as birth giving and breast feeding (*SE* 22:115).[1] Yet (as Freud also saw) we live within a culture, think within a language, that insists on viewing femininity and masculinity as simple antitheses—or more accurately, within a culture, a language, that defines the masculine as the norm, the feminine as the not-masculine, that looks upon the male as subject, the female as object, and that therefore regards the masculine as by definition the active, the feminine as the passive.

Though Freud has brilliantly described how these associations enter into our consciousness, he also lives *within* the patriarchal culture they imply. Thus, though he may explicitly or implicitly put "feminine" in quotes, he will nevertheless continue to use the term in its conventional sense as signifying passivity. Though he may recognize that coming to terms with one's own "femininity" is the most challenging task of human life for men and women alike (*SE* 23:250–53), he may nevertheless fail to overcome his own ambivalence. He told the imagist poet H.D. when she was in analysis with him in 1934: "I do *not* like to be the mother in transference—it always surprises and shocks me a little. I feel so very masculine." Yet he acknowedged, wistfully and ironically, that it often happened.[2]

Of course, for Freud "passivity" connotes those other words drawn from the Latin root, *patio, passus sum,* and its Greek antecedent, *pathos:* passion, compassion, patient, pathos, pathology. This family of words encompasses suffering and endurance, vulnerability and dependence, all that happens to us without our willing it. It is thus easily connected with that in us that is unconscious, and with our contingency and finitude—with our inaccessible beginnings and unavoidable end, with birth and death, womb and tomb.[3] As we pursue the associations, the reasons for the male ambivalence about femininity become more apparent. For the associations lead to the unsettling realization that male being is dependent on female being, on the mother—and that this dependence issues in a longing for a return to the life-giving source and an equally powerful fear of being swallowed by it (*SE* 11:195–96). The associations lead to the recognition that the prototype of all creative activity, birth giving, is a female prerogative—a recognition so provocative of envy that it must be denied—by way of "infantile sexual theories" that maintain that birth giving is not an exclusively female capacity (*SE* 9:220), by way of an androcentric culture's assertion that not the womb but the penis is the only "real" sexual organ, by way of an emphasis on cultural creativity as superior to biological procreativity. Perhaps Freud understood these dynamics so well precisely because of his own participation in them.

In any case, Freud felt it appropriate to speak of a side of himself, a side involved in his intimate relationships with men and in his creative work, as "feminine." Nor does it seem accidental that the period of most intense homoerotic involvement, the period of Freud's life in which Wilhelm Fliess played such an important role, should coincide with the period of greatest intellectual fertility. The exploration of his own psychic depths, which underlay his creative effort, was initially inspired by the death of his father and entailed the acknowledgment of powerful negative feelings toward him. The friendship with Fliess provided a safe context in which Freud could be dependent, vulnerable, intuitive—"feminine." As he told Fliess directly: "No one can replace the intercourse with a friend that a particular—perhaps feminine—side of me requires" (5/7/1900).[4]

Freud's letters to Fliess are filled with analogies between his own creative activity and birth giving: "After the frightful labor pains of the last few weeks, I gave birth to a new piece of knowledge," he writes in reference to his discovery of how repression explains our amnesia concerning childhood sexuality (1/14/1897). When reading the proofs of the dream book (which he had earlier described as a "dream-child" to which Fliess has stood as godfather [3/23/1900]), Freud refers to "the painful feeling of parting with something which has been one's very own" (10/4/1899).

In a convincing reinterpretation of the "Irma dream" (which Freud in *The Interpretation of Dreams* calls the "specimen" dream of psychoanalysis), Erik Erikson suggests that the analogy between biological and intellectual conception, between parturition and the publication of his book, may first have presented itself to Freud in this dream.[5]

The manifest dream involved a close family friend of the Freuds' (she was godmother to his daughter Anna) who came to Freud as a patient for a few sessions after the death of her husband. Yet, although Freud himself never acknowledges this in his published associations to the dream, the "Irma" of the dream must have immediately reminded him of another patient, Emma Eckstein, who had been a cause of great concern to him in the months immediately preceding the dream. Freud had sent her to Fliess for a nasal operation that Fliess claimed would cure her dysmenorrhea; unwittingly Fliess had left some gauze in the cavity created by the surgery that nearly caused her to bleed to death a few days later. Thus Emma Eckstein was a patient whose relation to Freud is closely echoed by that of "Irma" in the dream: her nose and throat had often been exposed to Freud's scrutiny; she had nearly died because of a physician's error.[6]

As Erikson shows, the original German account of the dream suggests an unusual degree of intimacy between Freud and his patient (they address each other as *du*) and includes many terms whose sexual connotation is concealed in the English translation—though it is true that Freud does not explicitly analyze these connotations in his avowedly incomplete published interpretation. Erikson is still more interested in how the translation tends to obscure the centrality of the theme of "conception" evident in the German version. He notes how Freud's associations lead him to understand the dream as picturing a *birthday* reception, how closely the word for "reception" is linked to the word meaning "conception," indeed how complex are the associations between biological and intellectual conception throughout the dream analysis. The connections were clearly facilitated by the fact that Freud had just learned that his wife was pregnant with their sixth child at a time when he was already worried and guilty about his difficulty in providing financially for his growing family while immersed in the creative work on his dream book. (We might also note that years later Freud will speak of this dream as marking the birthday of his understanding of the secret of dreams [6/12/1900].)

Erikson highlights the passage in Freud's interpretation where he acknowledges that for a moment within the dream (as his two colleagues come over to examine the patient) he had felt Irma's pain as though it were his own, felt it inscribed on his own body. Here the dreamer, the doctor, the man, fuses with the image of the female patient. As he looks into the gaping cavity, the dreamer abandons male initiative and yields to a diffusion of roles; it becomes unclear whether he is doctor or patient, benefactor or culprit.

The letters to Fliess inform us that in waking life Freud had had a very similar experience as he watched the doctor who had been called in to deal with Emma's postoperative hemorrhage pull out that half meter of gauze—Freud felt sick and had to leave the room, overwhelmed he says not by the blood but by the effects the scene provoked: the recognition that Emma had been done an injustice by their suspicions that her bleeding was hysterical. She was normal and they, Fliess and he, were guilty (3/8/1895).

In the dream, as Erikson notes, "For a fleeting moment [he becomes] the feminine object for the superior males' inspection." The allusion to Freud's double role in the investigation of dreams—where, as his own most important patient, he is both observer and observed—is clear. Erikson speaks of Freud's self-analysis as requiring "an unfathomable division within the observer's self, a division of vague 'feminine yielding' and persistent masculine precision. . . . The 'mouth which opens wide,' then, is not only the oral cavity of a patient and not only a symbol of a woman's procreative inside which arouses horror and envy because it can produce new 'formations.'" It may also represent the dreamer's unconscious, his own birth-giving capacity.[7]

In his climactic paragraph Erikson makes explicit how closely he connects Freud's sense of his own generativity to the value Freud attached to Fliess's friendship and inspiration:

> That a man may incorporate another man's spirit, that a man may conceive from another man, and that a man may be reborn from another, these ideas are the content of many fantasies and rituals which mark significant moments of male initiation, conversion, and inspiration; and every act of creation, at one stage, implies the unconscious fantasy of inspiration by a fertilizing agent of a more or less deified, more or less personified, mind or spirit. This 'feminine' aspect of creation causes tumultuous confusion not only because of man's intrinsic abhorrence of femininity but also because of the conflict (in really gifted individuals) of this feminine fantasy with an equally strong 'masculine' endowment which is to give new and original form to that which has been conceived and carried to fruition. . . . At the height of consummation (the creative individual may) identify with father, mother, and newborn child all in one.[8]

Freud recognized this "feminine" aspect of himself—and was made uncomfortable by it.

UNRULY HOMOSEXUAL FEELING

"The Fliess Period" is spoken of by Ernest Jones in his biography of Freud as "the only really extraordinary experience in Freud's life." Although Jones's public account of this experience strives to be respectful and sympathetic, an exchange of letters between him and James Strachey in 1954 suggests that an important guiding principle in the 1954 much-abridged edition of Freud's letters to Fliess had been the wish to minimize the erotic dimensions of the friendship, which the psychoanalytical "establishment" evidently found embarrassing. Strachey wrote Jones:

> I was very much interested by your account of the suppressed passages in the Fliess letters. It is really a complete instance of *folie à deux*, with Freud in the unexpected role of hysterical partner to a paranoiac. I do hope that if they ever come out in English the censorship may be lifted a bit. Unless Anna proposes to burn the originals, they're bound to come out in the end, and surely it is better that they should while people are alive who can correct their effect.

In Jones's reply, he says: "I don't quite agree with what you say about Freud gradually reconciling himself to bisexuality. I think myself he was over-reconciled to it, if you see what I mean. He never really emancipated himself from Fliess."⁹ It remains amazing how Freud's biographers, who, of course, must honor the central role this relationship occupies in his life, continue to evade dealing directly with its homosexual dimension—which Freud himself so readily admitted. Although there are no grounds for suggesting that this emotional bond was ever physically consummated, on Freud's own terms it was nonetheless a homosexual relationship. (By 1893 Freud was already persuaded that "sexuality" is not to be equated with literal genitality [5/30/1893].)

The friendship began in 1887 when Wilhelm Fliess, a Berlin physician two years Freud's junior, introduced himself after attending several of Freud's lectures. Clearly impressed by Fliess's magnetism, brilliance, and voluble self-confidence, Freud wrote him soon afterward: "I must confess to begin with that I have hopes of continuing the intercourse with you, and that you have left a deep impression on me which could easily tempt me to say outright in what category of men I would place you" (11/24/1887).¹⁰

Although in the years that followed they met at least twice yearly in cities or resorts where they would be free from professional or familial interruptions, the letters they exchanged seem to have been as important to the development of their relationship as the face-to-face meetings. By 1892 Freud was addressing Fliess by his first name and as *du*, calling him his "most cherished friend," his "dear magician," and signing his letters "dein Sigm. Freud." Between 1894 and 1900 Freud wrote Fliess twenty, thirty, sometimes as many as forty letters a year. Looking back at their years of friendship in 1898, Freud writes, "I rejoice once again that eleven years ago I already realized that it was necessary for me to love you in order to enrich my life."

The published correspondence makes evident how deeply stirred Freud was by his meetings with this beloved friend. He writes that he looks forward to their "congresses . . . as to the slaking of hunger and thirst" (9/30/1886). The relatively rare meetings provide "an infusion of vital strength" (5/30/1896) that undergirds his creativity afterward. "Since [our congress] I have been in a continual euphoria and have been working like a young man" (5/2/1897). "After each of our congresses I was strengthened anew for weeks, ideas kept crowding in thereafter, the pleasure in hard work was reestablished, and the flickering hope that the way through the under-brush will be found burned quietly and radiantly for a while" (4/3/1898).

The letters reveal Freud's dependence on Fliess: "You are the only other, the *alter*" (5/21/1884). "How much I owe you: solace, understanding, stimulation in my loneliness, meaning to my life that I gained through you, and finally even health that no one else could have given back to me" (1/1/1896). Freud fantasizes about projects the two might work on together and in doing so expresses the fusion longing that sometimes characterized his side of the relationship: he hopes they might "blend our contributions to the point where our individual property is no longer recognizable" (12/17/1896). After sending his "only other" a draft of *The Interpretation of Dreams,* Freud assures him: "I shall change whatever you want and gratefully accept contributions. I am so immensely glad that you are giving me the gift of the Other, a critic and reader—and one of your quality at that. I cannot write entirely without an audience, but do not at all mind writing only for you" (5/18/1898). (As promised, although not without regret, Freud even lets Fliess persuade him to omit the one fully analyzed dream he had intended to include in the book on dreams.) Even when the relationship has become very strained, when it is to all effects over, Freud laments, "I am sorry to lose my 'only audience.' . . . For whom do I still write?" (9/19/1901).

It is easy to discern in Freud's feeling for Fliess the overestimation of the beloved that Freud himself has taught us to look for as a correlate of erotic attraction. How he exaggerated Fliess's intellectual gifts; how often he speaks of Fliess as the "the Kepler of biology"! In the very midst of all the turmoil associated with the botched operation on Emma Eckstein's nose (for which Fliess might well have been convicted of malpractice), Freud writes: "For me you remain the healer, the prototype of the man into whose hands one confidently entrusts one's life and that of one's family" (4/20/1895).

Eventually Freud came to recognize that there was also an undercurrent of latent hostility in his feelings toward Fliess. The ambivalence is, of course, overdetermined. On the one hand, Freud has unacknowledged doubts about Fliess's medical competence, about his obsession with periodicity as the clue to all human events; on the other, he seems to have half known all along that the relationship was more important to him than to Fliess and to have resented his own dependency.

At one point while profoundly despondent about the progress of his self-analysis and his failures with his other patients, he wrote: "Something from the deepest depths of my own neurosis set itself against any advance in the understanding of the neuroses, and you have somehow been involved in it" (7/7/1897). Two months later he shares with Fliess "the great secret that has been slowly dawning on me for the last few months": his discovery that it is not literal incest but fantasy that lies behind hysteria (9/21/1897). Somehow the block is now removed; the discovery of the negative, unconscious aspects of his relation to Fliess has been profoundly liberating. During the next few weeks Freud is flooded with dreams that revive childhood memories and that lead him to his understanding of the gripping power of the Oedipus legend. "All of what I experienced with my patients . . . I find again here. . . . I live only for the 'inner work' " (10/27/1897).

It is at this point in the course of his self-analysis that Freud also recovers the childhood memory that helps him to understand his attachment to Fliess. A dream reminds him of the murderous jealousy he had felt toward a one-year-younger brother who died when only a few months old and also of his close friendship with a nephew only a year older than himself, "the companion of my misdeeds." "This nephew and this younger brother have determined what is neurotic but also what is intense, in all my friendships" (10/3/1897). Fliess is in some way a *revenant* of that youthful companion—whereas Jung, as we shall see, more often stirs up feelings associated with the brother.

Freud's loneliness and isolation during these years was, he believed, due in large measure to his insistence on the role played by sexuality in the etiology of neurosis, and particularly to his explicit questioning of his female patients about their early sexual experience. Part of what brought the two together was that Fliess, too, was engaged in scientific research outside of the conventionally accepted channels and that he, too, was a risk-taking scientist, "an even greater fantasist" (10/31/1895) than Freud himself.

Both Freud and Fliess were fascinated by sexuality, the topic from which Freud's earlier older intimate and mentor, Josef Breuer, had shied away. Freud valued Fliess in part because he expected him to contribute the organic physiological complement to his own psychological discoveries. But Fliess's interest in sexuality was highly idiosyncratic, issuing in a theory about parallels between nose and genitals, and increasingly focusing on a theory of periodicity involving male cycles of twenty-three days that complement female cycles of twenty-eight days in all of us—male and female. He believed that all somatic and psychological disturbances could be plotted and predicted on the basis of these cycles. Freud tried hard to keep track of his own ups and downs and those of his family and to relate them to the putative cycles but had poor luck in confirming Fliess's theory.

Yet it was Fliess's obsession with these cycles that introduced into their interchanges the theme of bisexuality, which intrigued both. In a long letter about neurosis and sexuality (12/6/1896), Freud for the first time speaks of the importance of beginning with the assumption "of the bisexuality of all human beings." A year later, immediately after one of their congresses, he writes of their shared fascination with the subject: "Back home and in harness again, with the delicious aftertaste of our days in Breslau. Bi-bi [bisexuality-bilaterality] is ringing in my ears" (12/29/1897).

How aware either was that the topic of bisexuality provided them with an indirect way of talking about their own relationship is unclear. Yet we can see that Freud almost immediately applied the idea to himself. A week after the meeting in Breslau, explaining his continued reservations about "bilaterality" (that is, Fliess's association of left-handedness with homosexuality), Freud states: "I embraced your stress on bisexuality and consider this idea of yours to be the most significant one for my subject since that of 'defense'" (1/4/1898). Later in the same letter he adds: "I had the impression, furthermore, that you considered me to be partially left-handed; if so, you would tell me, since there is nothing in this bit of self-knowledge that would hurt me." And on January 22, 1898, he writes that after observing the way he unbuttons his clothes, he has concluded that Fliess is right. Though he still doubts the bilateral theory, he seems not at all hesitant to admit his own latent left-handedness or the latent homosexuality Fliess would associate with it.

In March Freud reaffirms his conviction of the importance of the bisexual hypothesis: "I do not in the least underestimate bisexuality either; I expect it to provide all further enlightenment, especially since that moment in the Breslau marketplace when we found both of us saying the same thing." Yet they weren't saying quite the same thing after all. For Fliess bisexuality continued to be associated with the periodic theory, which Freud continued to have difficulty understanding and so, as Freud sadly recognizes, they seem to be "becoming estranged from one another through what is most [their] own" (2/1/1900).[11]

Nonetheless, for Freud bisexuality remains bound up with the relationship to Fliess. After composing his case history *Dora*, he confides: "Bisexuality is mentioned and specifically recognized once and for all, and the ground is prepared for a detailed treatment of it on another occasion" (1/30/1901). A half a year later he writes with great excitement:

As far as I can see, my next work will be called "Human Bisexuality." It will go to the root of the problem and say the last word it may be granted to me to say—the last and the most profound. For the time being I have only one thing for it: the chief insight which for a long time now has built itself upon the idea that repression, my core problem, is possible only through reaction between two sexual currents. I shall need about six months to put the material together and hope to find that it is now possible to carry out the work. But then I must have a long and serious discussion with you. The idea itself is yours. You remember my telling you years ago, when you were still a nose specialist and surgeon, that the solution lay in sexuality. Several years later you corrected me, saying that it lay in bisexuality—and I see that you are right. So perhaps I must borrow even more from you; perhaps my sense of honesty will force me to ask you to coauthor the work with me, thereby the anatomical-biological part would gain in scope, the part which, if I did it alone, would be meager. I would concentrate on the psychic aspect of bisexuality and the explanation of the neurotic. That, then, is the next project for the immediate future, which I hope will quite properly unite us again in scientific matters as well. (8/7/1901)

Yet it is in his very next letter that Freud for the first time explicitly acknowledges how much their relationship has changed. The dream of going to Rome with Fliess, which had for so many years been his fondest hope, has been given up: Freud has finally gone to Rome—alone. Fliess has in the meanwhile evidently communicated his objections to Freud's taking over what Fliess believes is *his* idea of bisexuality and also confessed his belief that therapeutic insight represents only the therapist's projections. Freud is deeply hurt, is now convinced that Fliess in actuality does not accept his method of working any more than do all the others (9/19/1901). This loss is so wounding that Freud decides to withdraw *Dora* from publication, because "I had lost my last audience in you" (3/11/1902).

Soon thereafter the letters stop—until 1904, when Fliess writes Freud to accuse him of having facilitated the plagiarism of his ideas about bisexuality in a work of Otto Weininger's. In the meanwhile Fliess has come to believe that Freud himself had vehemently resisted the idea of bisexuality when they first spoke of it in Breslau. Freud tries to suggest that the theme of bisexuality has been around for some time and is no one's privileged intellectual property. Freud also makes clear that the controversy has led him to want to shy away from the topic as much as he can: "At present I am finishing 'Three Essays on the Theory of Sexuality' in which I avoid the topic of bisexuality as far as possible" (7/12/1904). A week later he sends Fliess the proofs of the book, asking him to change the remarks on bisexuality to his satisfaction. (We will have occasion to examine these essays in the next chapter and to see what a central place—despite the disclaimer—bisexuality plays in the sexual theory they articulate.)

We cannot know how soon either became conscious that in talking about bisexuality they were talking about their own relationship. It is evident, however, that Freud felt more comfortable about admitting this than Fliess. Because we do not have Fliess's side of the correspondence available to us, it is impossible to know if the relationship was ever as central, as intense, as intimate on his side. But clearly it was important for a long while—and then it became uncomfortable and eventually intolerable. Although it is often suggested that Freud may have needed Fliess less once the self-analysis was complete and the dream book done, nevertheless it was clearly Fliess who withdrew from the relationship—and Freud who was hurt and wanted to deny what was happening. "Everything is different once you do not need me" (5/17/1899).

According to Marie Bonaparte, Martha Freud accepted that Fliess could "give her husband something beyond what she could,"[12] but Fliess's wife, Ida, was jealous of the friendship and evidently sought to disrupt it from early on—perhaps because Breuer (who had had some experience of Freud's proclivity for intense friendship) had told her that she was lucky Freud did not live in Berlin and so could not interfere with her marriage. Indeed, Freud comes to blame the increasing distance between himself and Fliess at least in part on Ida. In a letter of August 7, 1901, Freud notes that Ida Fliess is reportedly obsessed with the suspicion of Freud's love that Breuer had planted years ago—and complains that now Fliess himself seems to look with distaste upon the homoerotic dimension of their friendship. Freud proudly affirms his own acknowledgment of that dimension: "I do not share your contempt for friendship between men, probably because I am to a high degree party to it. In my life, as you know, woman has never replaced the comrade, the friend."

But although the friendship between them was by then outwardly at an end, it took Freud a long while really to get over it. Several years later he wrote Ferenczi (who had voiced some curiosity about Fliess, concerning whom Freud was always so reticent): "You not only noticed, but also understood, that I no longer have any need to uncover my personality completely, and you correctly traced this back to the traumatic reason for it. Since Fliess's case, with the overcoming of which you recently saw me occupied, that need has been extinguished. A part of homosexual cathexis has been withdrawn and made use of to enlarge my own ego." A few weeks later, he wrote Ferenczi again: "You probably imagine that I have secrets quite other than those I have reserved for myself, or you believe that my secrets are connected with a special sorrow, whereas I feel capable of handling everything and am pleased with the greater independence that results from my having overcome my homosexuality."[13]

Yet full "overcoming" still eludes him. In late 1909 he confides in Jung that he is still trying to interpret his own swings of mood in relation to Fliess's periodic schema—and still failing (160F).[14] A year later he tells Jung that his work on the Schreber case had once again stirred up his "Fliess complex" (225F) and writes Ferenczi that his dreams have been *entirely* concerned "with the Fliess affair."

In 1912, during a discussion with Jung and some other colleagues, Freud fainted in a Munich hotel. Later he wrote Jones that this was a repetition of a fainting spell years earlier when he had been with Fliess in the same room of the same hotel (perhaps on the occasion of their final quarrel). "This town seems to have acquired a strong connection with my relation to that man. There is some piece of unruly homosexual feeling at the root of the matter."[15]

As Jones observed in the 1954 letter to Strachey quoted from earlier, Freud may never have fully emancipated himself from "that man."

AN INDIAN SUMMER OF EROTICISM

Freud's relationship with Carl Jung was at its most intense between 1907 and 1912, and though Freud acknowledged that it, too, had homoerotic overtones, it was clearly never as passionate as the one with Fliess. Because Jung was considerably younger than Freud, there was all along another vector, that of father-son, which both used to defuse the homoerotic dimension of their attraction to each other. (As we have already observed, whereas the relations to Fliess may in some ways have been a recapitulation of his positive relation to that one-year-older brotherlike nephew who was Freud's childhood playmate, the relation to Jung may have stirred up some of the murderous feelings Freud remembered having felt toward his short-lived next-*younger* brother. Certainly, as we shall see, the *negative* dimensions of the relationship were more consciously recognized with Jung than they had been with Fliess.) Also, because Jung made it clear from early on that he feared the homosexual element of their relationship and Freud's intensity in general, Freud soon learned to inhibit the expression of his feeling.

Yet in some ways the relationship was more mutual—or at least, since both sides of the correspondence are available to us, we have more intimate access to its mutuality. Again the relationship was primarily an epistolary one. Again the letters give evidence of an interfusion of professional and personal concerns; they include the sharing of theoretical explorations, concerns about patients, gossip about colleagues, family news, confidences about personal depressions and anxieties. But whereas Fliess's wife had sought to undermine the relationship, Jung's supported it and intervened to try to prevent its foundering.

Freud and Jung first met face to face in March 1907, about a year after their initial exchange of letters. Reflecting on this meeting, Jung writes Freud that "the complexes aroused in Vienna" are still in an uproar several weeks later. Though he does not specify what this might mean at a personal level, in the next paragraph he expresses his continued reservations about Freud's "broadened conception of sexuality," his wish for a less offensive collective term (17J). On the other hand, this first visit leads Freud to address Jung as "Lieber" for the first time and to tell him that he already regards him as his own successor in the exciting, far-reaching, beautiful work of psycho-analysis. As he had done with Fliess years before, Freud finds himself imagining their freely collaborating: "I must say that I regard a kind of intellectual communism, in which neither party takes anxious note of what he has given and what received, as a highly estimable arrangement" (18F). (Though a year later, when talking about a patient both have worked with, Freud sees it differently: "The difficulty would have been that the dividing line between our respective property rights in creative ideas would inevitably have been effaced; we would never have been able to disentangle them with a clear conscience" [94F]. Freud is still subject to fusion longings but now also more suspicious of them.)

How quickly Freud moves to investing in Jung the same power to relieve him of his loneliness once attributed to Fliess! He tells Jung that their relationship has at last brought to an end the many years of solitary isolation; he writes that finally he hears a voice from the unknown answering his own (42F).

But the naive enthusiasm of the early years of the relationship with Fliess is unrecoverable. The possibility of failure, loss, betrayal, is this time ineluctable. Almost from the beginning the theme of death intrudes on this friendship. Freud is in his fifties and often conscious of his own mortality; he often also accuses Jung of harboring death wishes against him.

Freud is prepared for Jung's ambivalence toward him, and yet hopes somehow to deflect it. When Jung with some embarrassment admits to a long-suppressed wish to have a photograph of Freud, Freud replies: "But please, don't make too much of me. I am too human to deserve it" (45F). Confirmation of Freud's fears comes about a month later when Jung writes to confess: "My veneration for you has something of the character of a 'religious' crush. Though it does not really bother me, I still feel it is disgusting and ridiculous because of its undeniable erotic undertone. . . . I think I owe you this explanation. I would rather not have said it" (49J). A few days later, having had no reply from Freud in the interval, he writes again:

I am suffering all the agonies of a patient in analysis, riddling myself with every conceivable fear about the possible consequences of my confession. There is one consequence I must tell you right now, as it might interest you. You will remember my telling you a short dream I had while I was in Vienna. At the time I was unable to solve it. You sought the solution in a rivalry complex. (I dreamt that I saw you walking beside me as a *very, very frail old man.*) Ever since then the dream has been preying on my mind but to no purpose. The solution came (as usual) only after I had confessed my worries to you. *The dream sets my mind at rest about your + + + dangerousness!* This idea couldn't have occurred to me at the time, obviously not! (I hope to goodness the subterranean gods will now desist from their chicaneries and leave me in peace. (50J) [+ + + was a symbol Freud and Jung used to refer to the sexual.]

Four months later, as Freud is sharing with Jung his emerging theory about the connection between paranoia and homosexuality, he ends his letter with a reference, his first, to Fliess: "My one-time friend Fliess developed a dreadful case of paranoia after throwing off his affection for me, which was undoubtedly considerable. I owe this idea to him, i.e., to his behaviour. One must try to learn something from every experience" (70F).

Though he says he is ready to accept "the Fliess case" as an example of the correlation between autoerotism and paranoia, the mention of Fliess frightens Jung, who writes back:

The undeserved gift of your friendship is one of the high points in my life which I cannot celebrate with big words. The reference to Fliess—surely not accidental—and your relationship with him impels me to ask you to let me enjoy your friendship not as one between equals but as that of father and son. This distance appears to me fitting and natural. Moreover it alone, it seems to me, strikes a note that would prevent misunderstandings and enable two hard-headed people to exist alongside one another in an easy and unrestrained relationship. (72J)

Again we see Jung ready to admit his fear of the homoerotic feelings stirred up by their relationship.

A year after the "confession" Freud feels confident in addressing Jung as "my friend and heir" (110F), and in response Jung is for the first time able to address him as "Lieber" instead of as "Hochverehter." Jung now seems willing to ask for Freud's help as he wrestles with what he calls his "polygamous instincts" and how they have complicated his relationship to his former patient Sabine Spielrein (133J). When Freud admits that their "dwindling correspondence" had stirred up memories of the end of the Fliess relationship, Jung reassures him: "You may rest assured, not only now but for the future, that nothing Fliess-like is going to happen. . . . Except for moments of infatuation my affection is lasting and reliable" (135J). Overtly "nothing Fliess-like" refers to the bitter ending of Freud's relation to Fliess, an ending that Jung promises will not recur. But surely Jung is also trying to ward off any possibility that the present relationship might assume the emotional power and intensity of the earlier one.

Nevertheless two weeks later, in March 1909, as Jung was visiting Freud in Vienna, there was some "spookery"—while talking about parapsychology they heard a loud noise emanating from a bookcase, which Jung rightly predicted would soon be repeated—that somehow provoked the idea of a "Fliess analogy." Afterward Jung wrote Freud that the experience had had the happy consequence of freeing him inwardly from the oppressive sense of Freud's paternal authority (138J). Since Freud had seen the same evening as the occasion during which he had happily "anointed" Jung as his adopted son and successor, Jung's response seems deliberately hurtful. Jung waited a month before writing again and then completely ignored Freud's sadness, his sense of having been rejected.

Less than half a year later, in August and September 1909, Freud and Jung went together to a conference at Clark University in Massachusetts. During the voyage across the Atlantic they agreed to analyze each other's dreams, but Jung was offended by Freud's "hiding behind his 'authority' " and not being willing to disclose relevant associations to one of his dreams, and disappointed by Freud's insisting on interpreting one of Jung's dreams at a "personal level" as expressing a death wish directed at Freud rather than at the "collective level" as symbolizing an exploration of the archetypal depths of the unconscious.[16]

The trip clearly aggravated the growing distance between the two men, but there are no explicit retrospective references to it in their correspondence, except for a few regretful words from Freud: "My Indian summer of eroticism that we spoke of on our trip has withered. . . . I am resigned to being old" (177F). A few simple words—but they express much of what the relation to Jung meant in Freud's life. For to any Austrian of Freud's generation the word *Nachsommer* (here translated as "Indian summer") inevitably conjured up associations with Adalbert Stifter's 1857 novel *Nachsommer.* In the novel an older man initiates a younger into his spiritual world and thus, long after having resigned himself to a life of renunciation, experiences an unexpected flowering of love. Freud's hopes and his disappointment are encapsulated in this unremarked allusion.[17]

By 1912 Jung acknowledges that he is the colder of the two (292J). He clearly wants to assert his own viewpoint, wants more approbation and agreement from Freud than he believes he gets—and more independence. Freud responds: "If . . . you want greater freedom from me, what can I do but give up my feeling of urgency about our relationship, occupy my unemployed libido elsewhere, and bide my time until you discover that you can tolerate greater intimacy?" (304F). Eight months later he adds: "Believe me, it was not easy for me to moderate my demands on you; but once I had succeeded in doing so, the swing in the other direction was not too severe, and for me our relationship will always retain an echo of our past intimacy" (329F).

In November 1912 Freud and Jung met for a business discussion in Munich. Ernest Jones, who was also present, remembers that when Freud's persistent protests at having his name omitted from Jung's and Bleuler's writings about psychoanalysis were dismissed as paranoid, he fell to the floor in a faint. Jones believed that Freud had understood the omission as an expression of Jung's parricidal wishes.[18] He also later learned, as we noted above, that for Freud the occasion had stirred memories of his last meeting with Fliess. Jung's account of what precipitated the fainting fit is different. He recalls that they had been talking about Ikhnaton. Freud had commented on the negative attitude that had led to this Egyptian pharaoh's erasing his father's name from the steles. Jung had responded by rejecting the personalistic interpretation and praising Ikhnaton's creativity and spirituality. Yet in Jung's version, too, the faint was Freud's response to what he took to be Jung's death wishes.[19]

For Jung this fainting spell made it evident that their relationship had all along been based on fantasy. As he wrote Freud immediately after his return from Munich: "I am glad we were able to meet in Munich, as this was the first time I have really understood you. I realized how different I am from you. . . . I am most distressed that I did not gain this insight much earlier. It could have spared you so many disappointments" (328J). In retrospect, as we shall see, Jung will come to view these years of closeness to Freud as time spent in "cloud-cuckoo land."

Freud's last personal letter to Jung ends:

> I propose that we abandon our personal relations entirely. I shall lose nothing by it, for my only emotional tie with you has long been a thin thread—the lingering effect of past disappontments—and you have everything to gain, in view of the remark you recently made in Munich, to the effect that an intimate relationship with a man inhibited your scientific freedom. I therefore say, take your full freedom and spare me your supposed "tokens of friendship". (342F)

Despite their painful endings, Freud gained much from these two intense intimate relationships with men—including the theoretical understanding of the role of same-sex love in human life that we will explore in the next chapter.

·3·

FREUD: THE THEORY

Freud accords homosexuality a more central role in his "anthropology," his theory, than is often recognized—and views it more sympathetically. His vision of homosexuality is illuminating in unexpected ways—and also at unforeseen points challenging and discomforting both to homosexuals and heterosexuals.

Given Freud's awareness of the role that homoeroticism and bisexuality play in his own history, it is not surprising that when he began to write about these topics in more general terms his focus would fall on *male* homosexuality. Yet, as we shall see, he has some interesting things to say about lesbian experience as well and particularly in his later work is well aware of the asymmetry between male and female homosexuality.

FREUD'S POETICS OF SEXUALITY

In order to make sense of what Freud has to say about *homo*sexuality, it is important to begin by recalling some of his more general observations about human *sexuality*. First, we must remember that in Freud's view all human sexuality in civilization (and there is no *human* sexuality outside civilization) is a *wounded* sexuality—male sexuality is as distorted by castration anxiety as female sexuality is by penis envy, "normal" sexuality is as restricted as that of the "pervert." Adult human sexuality is inescapably characterized by repression and denial, by limitation and constriction. (From Freud's perspective this would be true not only of so-called "Victorian" sexuality but also of the "liberated" performance-principle sexuality of the 1960s—though *what* is repressed may be quite different.) Forgetting this leads to misunderstanding what he has to say about the homosexual's woundedness as a moral judgment rather than as compassionate embrace.

Freud's starting point was pathology. Ernest Jones says that Freud taught us that the secrets of the human soul were to be apprehended only in connection with suffering, through being able to suffer oneself and thus enter into the suffering of others.[1] Freud began his psychological explorations by attending to hysterical symptoms in which the psyche uses the language of the body to express itself. He learned to read symptoms as symbols, to see them as emblematic of the element in the psyche most foreign to the ego. In *The Introductory Lectures* he says that symptoms are like mythological figures, "all powerful guests from an alien world, immortal beings intruding into the turmoil of mortal life" (*SE* 16:278). His starting point remains pathology, *pathos-logos*, the speech in us of that in us which seems to happen to us—our passivity, our feeling, our suffering, our vulnerability. He believes that the pathological in us has its own voice and wishes, that it longs to be heard and understood. Freud is deeply persuaded that we all suffer, are all conflicted, that there is no radical difference between the normal and the neurotic, the analyzed and the unanalyzed.

Many of those who were close to Freud—Jung, Jones, Lou Salome, the poet H.D.—have testified that Freud responded to sex (and death) as numinous realities long before he began speaking of Eros and Death as sacred forces. (We will return to those late reflections when at the end of this book we focus explicitly on the interrelation between the themes of sexuality and death in depth psychology, mythology, philosophy.) In *The Interpretation of Dreams* he spoke of his awe before the energies that inhabit the unconscious; he referred to them as "indestructible forces which the ancients recognized as being due their homage." Already, then, he sensed that what is unconscious in us, what is most repressed, is connected to the embodiment we long to transcend, to our sexuality and our mortality—and that the denial itself enhances the mythical power of these indestructible forces.

Freud's understanding of sexuality was always transliteral, always encompassed much more than genitality. From very early on he connected our sexuality to our imaginative capacity, to our human gift for symbolization, for mythmaking. Freud saw us as having defined sexuality too narrowly—*and* as having asked too much of it. He sees it as the vehicle through which we express our deepest human longings—our longing to give all of ourselves, our longing to be fully accepted, our longing to have another direct all their love to us alone, our longing to *be* ourselves and our longing to *lose* ourselves. He sees our individual ways of living our sexuality as symbolic of our way of being in the world, as representing how we see ourselves and how we interact with others.

Thus, we must keep in mind that we radically misunderstand the psychoanalytical apprehension of human sexuality if we identify sexuality with genitality. Accepting psychoanalysis, Freud says, requires accepting the expansion of the idea of sexual function; it entails a move toward a *trans-*

literal understanding of sexuality. Our tendency to think in terms of manifest, conscious, adult sexuality, *literal* sexuality, must yield to a willingness to recognize latent, unconscious, infantile sexuality, *metaphorical* sexuality. When Freud speaks of sexuality he means to include all sensual and affectional currents, all the ways in which we experience bodily pleasure, all our intense emotional attachments. Even our characteristic ways of being in the world are described in sexual terms—if active we are "masculine," if passive "feminine," if narcissistic "oral," if compulsive "anal." The vital ambiguity of his discourse is provided by the ever-shifting relationship between the literal and the metaphoric, the manifest and the latent.

(Many of the most critical differences among the various readings of Freud stem from the fact that careful, good readers will disagree about what to understand literally, what metaphorically—usually on the basis of their own epistemological convictions or of whether they are looking for a teacher or for someone who can serve as a stand-in for a position against which they define their own. Obviously, as my reading betrays, I value poetic and mythological "truth" and would rather read Freud as someone who sees more deeply and complexly than I, someone who challenges me to think and learn, than as someone against whom I must defend myself. I *do* learn, though I do *not* always agree.)

Freud (as I read him) is reaching for a way of talking about human selfhood that takes seriously that we are embodied souls, ensouled bodies, a way of speaking that reminds us of the inescapable biological constraints on human existence. He hopes his language might help us see connections more conventional language obscures. As Auden wrote:

> Our bodies cannot love:
> But, without one,
> What works of love could we do?[2]

But Freud does not take the body literally (as his rejection of medical training as appropriate preparation for psychoanalytical practice makes clear). His own favorite literary trope is synedoche, taking a part for the whole—the penis for the man, the body for the self.

The use of this trope may be misleading—if we take it literally, causally. The penis does not make the man, anatomy is not destiny—at least not in a simple way, at least only as mediated through the psyche. For Freud recognizes that the genitals do not necessarily define gender—which is a constructed rather than a given reality and remains an insecure one. Our gender identity, our identification as male or female, arises, he asserts, in response to our discovery of the value accorded the penis. (Lacan suggests we substitute "phallus" for "penis" as a reminder that what is in question is a value-laden symbol not a simple physical object.[3] Yet Freud deliberately used "penis" lest we fall into the trap of thinking "it's *only* a symbol.")

The discovery of this value-endowed physical organ is concomitant with the discovery that we do not have it (females) or are threatened with losing it (males). For Freud the discovery of being male and of being under threat (or of being female and of being deprived) *occur together.* I am not first self-consciously female and then later come to view this as a mutilation, or first an already existent male now suddenly in danger. I become "me," I assume an identity, in response to others' perception of me (what Lacan calls "mirroring"). That gender identity is defined in relation to the penis has nothing to do with whether biologically womb and penis are equally important; it has to do with how as psychological beings we come to know ourselves. What Freud asserts is that we become subjects only within the division into two sexes on the basis of the presence or absence of penis/phallus—a division that is both arbitrary and alienating, essential and precarious. The emphasis falls not on what each sex has, but on what makes them different. From Freud's position boys and girls *become* different only through this discovery. There is no pregiven difference; sexual identity is always an adoption.

Furthermore, for Freud it is not the boy's delight in his own penis, not his confusion or dismay at seeing the penisless body of his sister, that is decisive. The child's own body is almost irrelevant; it becomes meaningful only retrospectively. What counts is not the perception but the discovery of the already assigned meaning. What signifies is the father (or, as Lacan puts it, so as to make clear that "father" is a role, a symbolic event, not necessarily literally enacted by the literal father—the "Law of the Father"), who says "no" to the child's desire for the mother, who forbids, and in forbidding gives significance to *his* penis. Penis is what *he,* the possessor of the mother, the forbidder, has. By breaking the mother-child dyad the father initiates self-consciousness. Thus it is event, history, not biology that creates the difference between the sexes.

The anatomical difference comes to *figure* sexual difference; it becomes the sole representative of what that difference is allowed to be. It covers over the complexity of the child's early sexual life with a crude opposition in which that very complexity is refused or repressed. It thus indicates the reduction of difference to an instance of visible perception, a *seeming* value. But the unconscious refuses the reduction; as a feminist reader of Freud and Lacan, Juliet Mitchell, expresses it:

[The unconscious] reveals the fictional nature of the sexual category to which every human subject is nonetheless assigned . . . the unconscious reveal[s] a fragmented subject of shifting and uncertain sexual identity. To be human is to be subjected to a law which decentres and divides: sexuality is created in a division, the subject is split; but an ideological world conceals this from the conscious self who is supposed to feel whole and certain of sexual identity.[4]

The division also "creates" heterosexuality, which from this perspective is no more a pregiven natural orientation than is gender. When the categories "male" and "female" are seen as representing an absolute and complementary division, the opposite sex becomes "the Other," comes to stand, mythically and exclusively, for that which brings satisfaction and completion. The notion of sexual complementarity is a construction.

This analysis of how sexual identity enters consciousness rests, of course, on another analysis that we may discover as an undertext in Freud but never as a fully elaborated one: that is, an analysis of how the penis/phallus came to play its determinative role, how it is that sexual *difference* came to be so crucial. As I mentioned briefly in the last chapter, Freud does on occasion recognize that the valorization of the penis arises initially as a reaction formation, as a protest against fusion and contingency, as envy of female generativity, as an emphatic affirmation that to be different and separate is gain not loss, superiority not inferiority. The emphasis on the penis *means* an emphasis on difference, means thinking in antithetical, oppositional modes—male *or* female, homosexual *or* heterosexual. Freud's analysis is not intended to suggest we cannot think otherwise, but to show us how we come to think as we do.

The central point I have been making here is that for Freud human sexuality is psychological not biological; he writes of the sexual "drive" not the sexual "instinct," of need become wish, and admits that "the theory of the drives is our *mythology.*" He is interested in the drives and their vicissitudes, in the complexity of psychological transformational processes. He offers us a *poetics* of sexuality, a description of the mechanisms—displacement, condensation, reversal—whereby our sexual impulses become expressed in myriad ways. Polymorphousness, malleability, divertibility, are the central features of human sexuality. The nonperiodic character of human sexual arousal means that we have to choose when and where, with whom and what. It implies the necessity of delay, substitution, sublimation, symbolization. The drive can be diverted to an expression we would still easily recognize as sexual—this woman rather than that one, him instead of her, cunnilingus instead of intercourse—or it can lead toward a more metaphorical expression, into overwork or poetry or hysterical symptom.

It is an aspect of Freud's own affinity with mythic thinking that he sees in how things were in the beginning, in *illo tempore*, a clue to how they always really are. Thus in his reflections on sexuality Freud is particularly interested in *infantile* sexuality—or rather in the adult's reconstruction of childhood experience, a reconstruction that is inevitably a fusion of literal remembrance with fantasy, a fusion of what happened with what was longed for and feared. Freud sees how the child's sexuality begins as response to loss, to the recognition of its own insufficiency; he regards our sexuality as from the beginning mediated through intersubjectivity. The image we carry into adulthood of an earlier time of complete fulfillment is an illusion, for that earlier time is preconscious, enters consciousness only as a fantasy about an inaccessible "before."

Although he speaks of stages of sexual development in a way that suggests a linear, progressive, biologically grounded unfolding, Freud at the same time undermines this simple view. He emphasizes how multiple are the currents, physical and emotional, which must be woven together to eventuate in what the culture defines as normal mature sexuality—how mysterious this process is, how rarely achieved, how precarious. (How usual it is, for example, that in men sensual pleasure and emotional intimacy are so detached from one another that they cannot be directed toward the same other.) He acknowledges the importance of social factors, of our relations with the world of others, in shaping this "unfolding," particularly with respect to "latency," the hiatus between infantile and pubertal sexuality that makes our sexuality diphasic in a way peculiar to our species. Latency issues in amnesia with respect to the first, the infantile, sexual phase—and thus in repression, in the creation of an *unconscious* sexuality. Here is where Freud most radically critiques the linear model of sexual development. He believes that nothing that was once conscious ever really disappears; it only goes "underground," becomes unconscious. The early memories and wishes are still alive and powerful. The teleological vector is challenged by an "archaeological" one.[5]

It helps to remember that Freud's interpretations are retrodictive, not predictive. He may use the language of causality, but he uses it strangely. A student of Brentano (who affirmed that psychological "explanations" focus on intentionality, purpose, motive) and of Gomperz (who was noted for his work on Aristotle), Freud, I believe, knew exactly what he was doing when he spoke of wishes as causes (Aristotle's final cause) and when he spoke of the connections only apparent retrospectively between childhood and adult experience as causal (Aristotle's formal cause). In any case, because of the complexity of those transformational processes to which we alluded above, it is never possible to say that a particular childhood will issue in a particular adult life—though looking back we can say, "Yes, it is the same life," can discern a pattern in the mosaic of the child's experience. Literary critics call this retrospective mode of interpretation "typological"—a term borrowed from biblical exegesis, where it referred to the Christian conviction that Old Testament prophecy can only be rightly understood from the perspective of New Testament fulfillment, that Adam and Moses are given their true meaning only when recognized as prefigurations of Christ. We will need to bear this in mind when we come to consider the "etiologies" Freud proffers for homosexuality.

What may interest Freud most about the sexuality of early childhood is that it begins as the search for sensual pleasure. Although itself initially a derivative of nonsexual hunger, body pleasure—the enjoyment of sucking and cuddling—becomes an intrinsic aim. He concludes from this that pleasure for its own sake is the first and primary, the "real," meaning of human sexuality. Reproduction as an aim enters only later, at puberty.

We should also recall how deeply persuaded Freud is of the ambivalent character of all primary relationships. We hate where we also love, desire where we are repulsed, long for that which we dread. This implies that an emphatic denial is always suspicious—as is an emphatic affirmation. But so is the absence of affect: disinterest, impotence, frigidity. The insistence on the latent meaning, on the unconscious, hidden, often unwelcome other side is, of course, central to psychoanalysis—and likely to be unsettling both to those who consciously identify themselves as heterosexual and to their consciously homosexual sisters and brothers.

For Freud sexuality is the meeting place not only of body and soul but also of self and other. Our sexuality takes us out of ourselves, reveals the inadequacy of a purely intrapsychic psychology. It directs us toward the world and particularly toward human others. Yet for Freud our longing for connection with an other is interfused with dread. The fear of real connection encourages us to escape the other as other through the twin illusions of narcissistic self-fulfillment or of separation-effacing fusion. We either disavow any need for an other or seek to erase the otherness of the other. But *life* for Freud requires the courage of being willing to love, to love again even after we have learned how inevitably love and loss are conjoined. For Freud, as we shall explore more fully in the Epilogue, our sexuality brings us into touch with our finitude and mortality and with all in us that longs to transcend limitation. Freud's repeated references to the sadness that seizes us after intercourse as we feel how once again our impossible longing for complete satisfaction has been denied remind us that the starting point and end point of his anthropology are pathology, woundedness, suffering.

THE UNIVERSALITY OF HOMOSEXUAL DESIRE

As noted earlier, Freud's own writings reveal a rather different understanding of homosexuality than that usually attributed to psychoanalysis.[6] Freud believes that all of us have homosexual impulses and that it remains a mystery why in some they are the source of the predominant form of conscious manifest sexuality. In his view homosexuality is not degenerate and is a "perversion" only in a conventional sense. Rather than establishing a single etiology, he recognizes a great variety of patterns of early emotional and physical experience characteristic of adults who consider themselves homosexual. In confirmation of his belief that the repression of homosexuality is a central element in all neurosis, homosexuality (as we shall discover in the next chapter) appears as a central issue in every one of Freud's case histories. He finds the denial of homosexuality to be a primary source of resistance to therapy and regards homophobia as an expression of latent homosexuality. He insists on the pointlessness of all attempts to "cure" homosexuality. Only gradually does Freud come to recognize the significant differences between male and female homosexuality. Because his emphasis fell on male experience, we shall have to go beyond the texts to extrapolate a "Freudian" interpretation of lesbianism.

Freud's conviction that all of us have homosexual impulses is most clearly stated in "Sexual Aberrations," the first of the essays in *The Three Essays On Sexuality.* To begin a general study of sexuality with a discussion of sexual aberrations, as Freud does here, is obviously provocative; it seems designed to force on us a recognition of the polymorphousness and malleability of all human sexuality. Steven Marcus calls *The Three Essays* Freud's "most truly Darwinian work" because of his focus on the "variations" in form and structure characteristic of human sexuality.[7] Freud says he intends to investigate the relation between the great variety of deviations with respect to both sexual aim and sexual object and "what is assumed to be normal." As the chapter unfolds it becomes clear that Freud wants to help us to recognize that all these so-called perversions are really part of the sexual repertoire or fantasy life of everyone. Although he discusses oral and anal sex, bestiality, fetishism, voyeurism, sadism, and masochism, the "aberration" that is considered first and that receives by far the most attention is "inversion." (This term, taken over from Krafft-Ebing and Ellis is used consistently in the first edition of the *Three Essays*, whereas in the 1915 edition Freud speaks of "homosexuality" and in a 1920 footnote adopts Ferenczi's proposed alternative, "homoerotism" (*SE* 7:147). By then he has, in *Beyond the Pleasure Principle*, begun to focus on the role of Eros in human life and to interpret sexuality within a different context.)

As we attend to what Freud has to say about homosexuality in *The Three Essays*, we might bear in mind that in 1905, when the first edition appeared, Freud had never had a homosexual as an analytical patient. What he writes is based on the work of earlier sexologists, on his speculative reflections—and on his self-analysis.

He begins his discussion with an allusion to the tale told by Aristophanes in Plato's *Symposium* (though Freud gives no specific reference)—a tale that we will have occasion to consider at greater length later in our study. But Freud's use of the tale is odd. This is what he says: "The popular view of the sexual instinct is beautifully reflected in the poetic fable which tells how the original human beings were cut into two halves—man and woman—and how these are always striving to unite again in love. It comes as a great surprise therefore to learn that there are men whose sexual object is a man and not a woman and women whose sexual object is a woman and not a man" (*SE* 7:136). Yet in the original context Aristophanes tells the story to explain *same-sex* love as originating in the same event as the one that gives rise to love between men and women. In the Platonic dialogue (which Freud recalls accurately in *Beyond the Pleasure Principle*) some of the original human beings when cut in half become two men who thereafter yearn for reunion, some two women, and only some become a man and a woman destined to search for each other. Misrememberings, as Freud has taught us, are always interesting. Freud's version of the story does not serve him well here, where he could have used a story that challenged the view that inversion is a pathology (but it does seem relevant to his consideration of "bisexuality" a few pages further on, where he does not refer to it).

For one of the first points Freud makes is that his predecessors had regarded inversion as a degeneracy primarily because physicians only saw those inverts suffering, or appearing to suffer, from neurosis. Freud, in contrast, firmly rejects the attribution of pathology to inversion per se because, as he insists, "inversion is found in people who exhibit no other serious deviations from the normal." Indeed, he goes on to assert, inversion is found in persons "distinguished by specially high intellectual development and ethical culture."

He reminds us that inversion "was a frequent phenomenon . . . an institution charged with important functions—among the peoples of antiquity at the height of their civilization" (*SE* 7:139). Oedipus, Narcissus, Thanatos, now the public validation of homosexuality—how often Freud finds in classical civilization clues to the full truth of human experience evaded in the consciously avowed ideologies of his own culture. So often in Freud's writing (and Jung's, too) about homosexuality there are references to its role in ancient Greece—as though fully to understand what same-sex love means in *our* psychology, to our souls, entails taking into account what it meant *there*. (My own agreement with this is, of course, reflected in the ordering of this book, where consideration of what depth psychology has to tell us about homosexuality leads inevitably to an exploration of the testimony of Greek mythology.)

In his essay Freud goes on to distinguish between different forms of inversion: between absolute and contingent inversion, between episodic and permanent inversion, between inverts who are comfortable with their sexual orientation and those who are not, between those who feel their inversion to be innate and those who see it as having developed during the life span.

Freud is particularly interested in this last distinction and ends up rejecting the either/or (as he had done in *The Interpretation of Dreams* with the previously accepted view that dreams must be nonsensical *or* meaningful, about the past *or* about the future, caused by some transcendent agency *or* by our own minds). In this instance Freud reminds us how many inverts are not exclusively inverts, but what he calls "amphigenic inverts," that is, persons attracted to members of their own sex only when members of the other are inaccessible, or "psychosexual hermaphrodites," what we today would call "bisexuals." This, he suggests, challenges the notion that inversion is necessarily innate. On the other hand, many persons are subjected to exactly the same early sexual influences adduced as the determinative events by defenders of the view that inversion is "acquired" without becoming inverts. Having rejected the adequacy of both views, Freud introduces what he calls the "bisexual hypothesis," the notion that both heterosexual and homosexual impulses are innate in each of us. What is somehow acquired is that one set of impulses ends up being repressed.

In developing this hypothesis, Freud is careful to distinguish psychical bisexuality from anatomical hermaphroditism. Athough the hermaphrodite may serve as a *figure* for the bisexual, hermaphroditism and bisexuality are not causally linked and are indeed on the whole independent of each other. Furthermore, Freud here explicitly rejects the notion held by Krafft-Ebing and others that inverts have the mental qualities, instincts, and character traits usually marking the opposite sex. It is at this point that Freud introduces that distinction between sexual *object* and sexual *aim* I referred to earlier. No single aim, he reminds us, is characteristic of all inverts; it is not the case that all want to adopt the sexual aim deemed characteristic of the opposite sex. Not all male inverts feel they are women in search of men, not all want to take on a passive sexual role. What makes one an invert is that one's preferred sexual *object* is a member of one's own gender. Freud is particularly struck by how very *masculine* many male inverts are and how often what they seem to look for in their male partners are in fact *feminine* mental and physical traits. Thus, although in 1905 Freud is still using the term *invert*, he already rejects its presuppositions.

In the 1915 edition of *The Three Essays* Freud appends to these reflections the suggestion that an attraction toward someone who combines the characters of both sexes, who is a male and yet in some sense feminine, is "a kind of reflection of the subject's own bisexual nature." He then also adds this signally important footnote:

> Psycho-analytic research is most decidedly opposed to any attempt at separating off homosexuals from the rest of mankind as a group of a special character. By studying sexual excitations other than those that are manifestly displayed, it has found that all human beings are capable of making a homosexual object-choice and have in fact made one in their unconscious. Indeed, libidinal attachments to persons of the same sex play not less a part as factors in normal mental life, and a greater part as a motive force for illness, than do similar attachments to the opposite sex. On the contrary, psycho-analysis considers that a choice of an object independently of its sex—freedom to range equally over male and female objects—as it is found in childhood, in primitive states of society and early periods of history, is the original basis from which, as a result of restriction in one direction or another, both the normal and the inverted types develop. Thus from the point of view of psycho-analysis the exclusive sexual interest felt by men for women is also a problem that needs elucidating and is not a self-evident fact based upon an attraction that is ultimately of a chemical nature. (*SE* 7:145–46)

As Juliet Mitchell asserts, there is nothing in *The Three Essays* compatible with any notion of natural heterosexual attraction; the *Essays* erode any idea of normative sexuality and "by deduction, if no heterosexual attraction is ordained in nature, there can be no genderized sex—there cannot at the outset be a male or female person in a psychological sense."[8] For Freud psychical bisexuality is rooted in the processes of personal identification, not in duplications of anatomy.

The "bisexual hypothesis" introduced in the first edition of *The Three Essays* comes to play an increasingly important role in Freud's attempts to understand the complexities of sexual identification. Freud's early understanding of bisexuality was compatible with the idea of the Oedipal complex (which is not mentioned in *The Three Essays*) and indeed serves to rescue it from the crudity of gender determinism. That is, in its original formulation, bisexuality means that all of us as children are drawn to both same-sex and contrasexual others. But by 1915, when he adds the crucial footnotes about the problematics of defining masculinity and femininity, his view of bisexuality has deepened and it comes to represent the uncertainty of sexual division itself. It is at this point also that the castration complex is given its focal significance in Freud's psychosexual theory. The "bisexual hypothesis" no longer means that each of us has as part of our given psychical makeup a bit of the opposite sex but rather that to begin with we are not defined sexually. What comes to be left out of our conscious sexuality becomes unconscious—we *become* bisexual. Our bisexuality refers not only to the fact that we are really subject to both homosexual and heterosexual impulses but that our sexuality comes to have both a conscious and an unconscious component. Freud sees us as beginning with an undifferentiated sexual nature. We are then forced (by culture, by language) to line up on one side or other of the sexual division—but anyone "can cross over and inscribe themselves on the opposite side from that to which they are anatomically destined." Bisexuality has come to mean "the availability of all subjects to both positions in relation to the difference."9

Thus the discussion of inversion leads Freud not to an easy distinction between homosexuality and normal sexuality but rather to the *mystery* of sexual identification. Heterosexuality turns out to be as problematical as homosexuality.

THE MYSTERY OF SEXUAL IDENTIFICATION

That in some of us the homosexual impulses come to be the predominant form of conscious manifest sexuality, whereas in others the heterosexual ones do, remains for Freud a mystery—as also at very end of life in *An Outline of Psychoanalysis* he says it remains a mystery why some are overtly, problematically neurotic and others in response to apparently identical outward situations are "normal." With respect to both issues, he again and again concludes, this happens "in a manner that is not yet understood." In *The Three Essays* (1905) he challenged the notion that inversion was innate; in *Leonardo* (1910) he wonders if "constitutional factors" may not be determinative after all. Usually he seems to regard sexual identification as the result of a complex combination of constitutional and accidental factors, including the relative strength of one's sexual drive. Thus in a 1908 essay (" 'Civilized' Sexual Morality and Modern Nervous Illness") he suggests that "perverts" with weak sexual drives can often suppress the inclinations that, if acted on, might bring them into conflict with society, but that they then are likely to have no energy left for any other cultural activity. On the other hand, if one's drive is strong, one will either suppress it and develop a neurosis or express it and live with the social consequences. Freud acknowledges he cannot explain why in some persons homosexual impulse is expressed manifestly as a "perversion" and in others repressed and expressed only as a neurosis; often, he says, these alternative choices may be made by different members of the same family.

The quotation marks around perversion in the last sentence are not my interpolation. Freud *implies* them often, as he makes clear that "what are called normal channels" of sexuality (*SE* 11:45) are the socially approved or conventionally defined ones. He employs them *explicitly* in the *Introductory Lectures*, where he writes that "these 'perverse' people" whom we call homosexuals are "men and women who are often, though not always, irreproachably fashioned in other respects, of high intellectual and ethical development, the victims only of this one fatal deviation" (*SE* 16:304). In *An Autobiographical Study* (1925), after a few sentences about sexual perversity in general, he says:

> The most important of these perversions, homosexuality, scarcely deserves the name. It can be traced back to the constitutional bisexuality of all human beings and to the after-effects of phallic primacy. Psycho-analysis enables us to point to some trace or other of a homosexual object-choice in everyone. If I have described children as 'polymorphously perverse', I was only using a terminology that was generally current; no moral judgment was implied by the phrase. Psycho-analysis has no concern whatever with such judgments of value. (*SE* 20:38)

Already in *The Three Essays* Freud had explicitly said that "many people are abnormal in their sexual life who in every other respect approximate to the average." Psychological "normality" is defined not by one's sexual orientation but by one's capacity to love and to work, pathology by diminished capacity for enjoyment and effectiveness. On several occasions Freud remarks that, rather than being "degenerate," homosexuals often seem to have a special aptitude for cultural sublimation, to be "characterized by a special development of their social instinctual impulses and by their devotion to the interests of the community" (*SE* 18:232).

Since he did not regard homosexuality as a pathology or illness, it is not surprising that Freud regarded as pointless attempts to "cure" it. As he wrote in 1935 to an anonymous American woman:

> I gather from your letter that your son is a homosexual. I am most impressed by the fact that you do not mention this term yourself in your information about him. May I question you why you avoid it? Homosexuality is assuredly no advantage, but it is nothing to be ashamed of, no vice, no degradation; it cannot be classified as an illness; we consider it to be a variation of the sexual function, produced by a certain arrest of sexual development. Many highly respectable individuals of ancient and modern times have been homosexuals, several of the greatest men among them. (Plato, Michelangelo, Leonardo da Vinci, etc.) It is a great injustice to persecute homosexuality as a crime—and a cruelty, too. If you do not believe me, read the books of Havelock Ellis.
>
> By asking me if I can help, you mean, I suppose, if I can abolish homosexuality and make normal heterosexuality take its place. The answer is, in a general way, we cannot promise to achieve it. In a certain number of cases we succeed in developing the blighted germs of heterosexual tendencies, which are present in every homosexual; in the majority of cases, it is no more possible. . . .
>
> What analysis can do for your son runs in a different line. If he is unhappy, neurotic, torn by conflicts, inhibited in his social life, analysis may bring him harmony, peace of mind, full efficiency, whether he remains homosexual or gets changed.[10]

Fifteen years earlier he had noted that "to undertake to convert a fully developed homosexual into a heterosexual does not offer much more prospect of success than the reverse, except that for good practical reasons the latter is never attempted" (*SE* 18:151).

As Freud suggests in this letter, homosexuality is not itself an illness, but homosexual men may suffer from the same disturbances of their sexuality that heterosexual men do, particularly a divergence between affection and sensuality: "A normal sexual life is only assured by an exact convergence of the affectionate current and the sensual current, both being directed toward the [same] sexual object and. . . . It is like the completion of a tunnel which has been driven through a hill from both directions" (*SE* 7:207). Though he is speaking primarily of heterosexuals, there are, of course, also homosexual men who have endless sexual relationships but cannot love (*SE* 11:168), or who feel compelled to debase the objects of their love (*SE* 11:188), or who have difficulty maintaining their love in the "passionless intervals" (*SE* 18:111).

In the *Introductory Lectures* (1914) Freud asserts that though, practically speaking, the difference between manifest and latent homosexuality remains significant, it has little theoretical import (*SE* 16:308). "Those who call themselves homosexuals are only the conscious and manifest inverts, whose number is nothing compared to that of the *latent* homosexuals." Indeed, as we shall see, Freud seems to be more interested in *repressed* than in consciously *expressed* homosexuality—as he is so often more fascinated by the latent than by the manifest.

He recognizes that in emphasizing the psychical genesis of homosexuality and the parallels between heterosexual and homosexual development, he is challenging the claims of contemporary homosexual men to represent a "distinct sexual species," a "third sex" (*SE* 11:98), but holds fast to his convictions about the given bisexuality of all.

Freud is also convinced that there is no way of knowing ahead of time whether the homosexual or the heterosexual current will come to predominate in adult life. "It takes a certain time before the decision in regard to the sex object is finally made. Homosexual enthusiasms, exaggeratedly strong friendships tinged with sensuality, are common enough in both sexes during the first years after puberty." Psychoanalysis can help us *understand* the final outcome; it cannot *predict* it:

> So long as we trace the development from its final outcome backwards, the chain of events appears continuous, and we feel we have gained an insight which is completely satisfactory or even exhaustive. But if we proceed the reverse way, if we start from the premises inferred from the analysis and try to follow these up to the final result, then we no longer get the impression of an inevitable sequence of events which could not have been otherwise determined. We notice at once that there might have been another result, and that we might have been just as well able to understand and explain the latter. (*SE* 18: 167)

Accordingly, Freud believes that most neurotic symptoms and many dream images are sexually "overdetermined," that they call for both heterosexual and homosexual interpretations (*SE* 5:396). For example, the same symbol may easily mean both anus and vagina, buttocks or breasts; left-handedness might represent homosexuality or incest (358). And many dreams in which there is some clear "reversal" of a logical relation or a known fact are to be interpreted as though what is manifestly female is really male and vice versa (359); Freud suggests that such reversals frequently appear in dreams arising from repressed homosexual impulses (*SE* 4:327).

In Freud's understanding, as we noted earlier, homosexuality may arise either because of the direction of one's sexual aim or because of the character of one's choice of object. He believes preferences with respect to aim are likely to be determined earlier than those based on object-choice, for they do not depend on the recognition of sexual difference. The distinction between active and passive sexual aims, between in the most exaggerated cases sadism and masochism, precedes the distinction between male and female objects (*SE* 11:44). Often Freud, following what he asserts to be common usage, will speak of the active aim as masculine and the passive one as feminine—but he is also careful to say explicitly that that does not mean that men will in this sense be masculine or women feminine, that biological males will necessarily be active in their sexual aim or biological females passive—for he does not "assume that a person's sex is to be determined by the formation of his genitals" (*SE* 17:201). Because "masculinity" and "femininity" are determined independently of and prior to object-choice, the possible outcomes are myriad. A man may adopt a masculine attitude toward men or toward women, or a feminine attitude toward men, or toward women. The same range of possibilities is available to women. Among the cases of which he gives us detailed written accounts, Freud found examples of all of these possible outcomes.

Freud believes that the passive attitude is encouraged by anal erotism. If the pleasures associated with this erotogenic zone, the undifferentiated cloaca of early childhood, have been experienced as particularly satisfying, the child may be reluctant to relinquish them. This may encourage a predisposition to homosexuality in men. When the next stage of psychosexual development in which the genitals are given primacy is reached, it sometimes happens that the last stage is erected upon the preceding one and the sexual aim becomes having another's penis stimulate or penetrate one's anus (*SE* 12:322). But as we shall see, Freud also recognizes that homosexuality cannot by any means be identified with anal-stage fixation; there are homosexualities where oral longings and memories seem to be the most powerful, and others clearly associated with genital-phase orientations.

In trying to understand homosexual object-choice, Freud begins with his assumption that there are two kinds of object-choice open to all of us: one, which he calls (or, rather, his translators call) "anaclitic," is based on attachment to those who responded to our needs in infancy; the other, named "narcissistic," is based on self-love. "We say that the human being has originally two sexual objects: himself and the woman who tends him" (*SE* 14:88). All later object choices, for all of us, heterosexual and homosexual, are modeled on these infantile prototypes.

Freud sometimes writes as though there were a single developmental pattern characteristic of those who become manifest homosexuals in

adulthood. For instance, in a 1910 footnote to *The Three Essays* he writes
that

> in *all* the cases we have examined we have *established* [emphasis mine] the fact
> that the future inverts in the earliest years of their childhood pass through a
> phase of a very intense but shortlived fixation to a woman (usually their
> mother), and that, after leaving this behind, they identify themselves with a
> woman and take *themselves* as their sexual object. That is to say, they proceed
> from a narcissistic basis, and look for a young man who resembles themselves
> and whom *they* may love as their mothers loved *them*. (*SE* 7:145)

This is, of course, the etiology also put forward in almost identical terms in
Leonardo da Vinci in the same year (*SE* 11:100), and in "On Narcissism" in
1914 (*SE* 14:88). In all these passages Freud is associating homosexual
object-choice with that form of narcissism in which one loves not one's
present or ideal self but one's past self. He is also suggesting that such
homosexuality is to be understood as a *repression of heterosexual impulse*. As
he writes in *Leonardo:* "A man who has become a homosexual in this way
remains unconsciously fixated to the mnemic image of his mother. By
repressing his love for his mother he preserves it in his unconscious and from
now on remains faithful to her. While he seems to pursue boys and to be
their lover, he is in reality running away from the other women, who might
cause him to be unfaithful" (*SE* 11:100). As he puts it in *The Three Essays*,
"Their compulsive longing for men has turned out to be determined by their
ceaseless flight from women."

The understanding of homosexuality that Freud had moved toward by the
time of the 1910 edition of *The Three Essays* and that receives its fullest
articulation in the 1914 essay "On Narcissism" emphasizes a stage of psychosexual development intermediate between autoerotism and object-love in
which the individual takes himself, his own body, as his love-object. Freud
believes that many people "linger" in this stage for a long while and carry
some of its features into later stages. Those who become manifest homosexuals in adulthood may at this stage have chosen the genitals as that aspect of
themselves taken as love-object; then in later life they may require that the
external object of their love has genitals like their own (*SE* 12:61).

Despite his "always" and his "in all cases," Freud actually recognizes that
there are several different etiologies for manifest homosexuality. (Such emphatic overstatements, followed by modifications and demurrals, are a reg-
ular feature of Freud's rhetorical style. I tend to see the device as
characteristic of the skillful storyteller. Others regard its appearance as

indicating those points in his argument where Freud is least secure. Of course, the two explanations are not incompatible.)

Immediately following the passage from *The Three Essays* cited above, Freud continues: "It must, however, be borne in mind that hitherto only a single type of invert has been submitted to psycho-analysis. . . . The problem of inversion is a highly complex one and includes very various types of sexual activity and development." In *Leonardo*, too, he admits how limited the psychoanalytic evidence is and then acknowledges: "What is for practical reasons called homosexuality may arise from a whole variety of psychosexual inhibitory processes; the particular process we have singled out is perhaps only one among many, and is perhaps related to only one type of homosexuality" (*SE* 11:101).

Indeed, Freud himself suggests other etiologies, other types of homosexuality. Even those texts that emphasize the relation to the mother suggest some not insignificant variations. Sometimes, as in the passages already cited, it is the excessive tenderness, the overprotectiveness of the mother, that is focused upon. At other times it is her overwhelming "phallic" power. In his 1908 essay "The Sexual Theories of Children" Freud describes how the small boy's fantasy of the phallic mother, his early inability to imagine a penisless person, may become so fixated that as an adult he will be "unable to do without a penis in his sexual object." The later discovery that his mother has no penis only aggravates the situation by arousing consequent anxiety about the possibility of losing his own. "The woman's genitalia, when seen later on, are regarded as a mutilated organ and recall this threat, and they therefore arouse horror instead of pleasure" (*SE* 9:216). Thus here it is depreciation and indeed aversion to women rather than idealization that is given central place. Though, of course, we must remember how compatible from the psychoanalytic perspective overvaluation and repudiation may be. The homosexual male may identify with the mother in her role as passive sexual object (as the Wolf Man does) or in her role as active nurturer (as does Leonardo).

Often, however, it is the relation to the *father* that Freud looks on as most significant. In *Leonardo* Freud concludes the very paragraph in which he had spoken of the role played by the overly affectionate mother thus: "I was more strongly impressed by cases in which the father was absent from the beginning or left the scene at an early date, so that the boy found himself left entirely under feminine influence. Indeed, it almost seems as though the presence of a strong father would ensure that the son made the correct decision in his choice of object, namely someone of the opposite sex" (*SE*

9:99). Here, it is the *absence* of the male parent that is seen as decisive; in some of Freud's case histories, as we shall see, it is the *presence* of a strong father that seems to be the most salient factor. "Regard for the father or fear of him" may be a powerful motive for homosexual object-choice, "for the renunciation of women means that all rivalry with him (or with all men who may take his place) is avoided" (*SE* 18:231).

In a 1922 essay, "Some Neurotic Mechanisms in Jealousy, Paranoia and Homosexuality," Freud mentions another factor that must be reckoned with: "the effect of seduction, which is responsible for a premature fixation of the libido." The context does not make clear whether Freud has in mind maternal or paternal seduction or both, but given all the accusations (cf., for example, Jeffrey Masson's *Assault on Truth*) that in repudiating his "seduction theory" in 1896 Freud also denied the reality of the psychological effects of seduction, this reiteration is noteworthy (*SE* 18:231).

Freud also introduces yet another possible scenario, one that does not focus on either parent but rather on *brothers*. He is speaking here of situations in which originally intense jealous feelings against older brothers are repressed and transformed. In response to their continued powerlessness and the influence of upbringing, younger brothers come to look on the rivals of an earlier period as homosexual love-objects. Here Freud is interpreting homosexual love as a reaction formation against repressed aggressive impulses (*SE* 18:231–32). This etiology was first explicitly proposed in *Group Psychology and the Analysis of the Ego* (1921)—though in a footnote Freud suggests that it was already implicit in the myth of the primal parricide included in *Totem and Taboo*, where it was the sons' advancement "from identification with one another to homosexual object-love" through which they "won freedom to kill their father" (*SE* 18:124). Freud believes that homosexuality originating in the relationship between brothers usually becomes manifest at an earlier stage and leads to "homosexual attitudes which [do] not exclude heterosexuality and [do] not involve a *horror feminae*" (*SE* 18:232). He also associates such homosexuality with the likelihood of a special development of social impulse and devotion to communal interests.

Though it is introduced late into the theoretical literature, this last-named etiology seems to be the one Freud's analysis of his own relationship to Fliess had found most illuminating. One recalls what he wrote then about the formative influence of his ambivalently charged relationship with his brotherlike nephew (Though one must acknowledge also Freud's frequent allusions to the love lavished upon him, her firstborn son, by his adoring mother, and recall how unworked through this relationship seems to have been in Freud's self-analysis.)

It is also imperative to remember, as Freud always does, that these "explanations" of homosexuality are not really explanations at all: "Attachment to the mother, narcissism, fear of castration, [sibling rivalry] . . . have nothing specific about them" (*SE* 18:231). "Probably no male human being is spared the fright of castration at the sight of a female genital. Why some people become homosexual as a consequence of that impression, while others fend it off by creating a fetish, and the great majority surmount it, we are frankly not able to explain" (*SE* 21:154). Indeed, Freud believes that in most cases the "decision in favour of homosexuality" takes place not at the time of the infantile influences, but only at puberty (*SE* 11:121). Psychoanalysis can, in specific cases, *describe* the operative mechanisms; it cannot *explain*. The *mystery* remains.

For Freud we are all in some sense homosexuals. Among those who are manifest heterosexuals, "the homosexual tendencies are not, as might be supposed, done away with or brought to a stop; they are merely deflected from their sexual aim and applied to fresh uses" (*SE* 12:61). It makes an enormous difference, however, whether these deflected homosexual aims are *repressed* or *sublimated*.

That Freud looks on the repression of homosexuality as a central element in all neuroses (*SE* 16:308) we will see confirmed as we give detailed consideration to his case histories in the next chapter. He is convinced, for instance, that paranoia represents an attempt to fend off exceptionally strong homosexual impulses by transforming the excessively loved other into a hated and feared other (*SE* 19:43). The paranoid transforms the unacceptable proposition "I, a man, love him, a man" into "I do not love him—I hate him, because he persecutes me." Similarly, in pathological jealousy the repudiated statement is transformed into "It is not I who love the man—*she* loves him (*SE* 17:225). Freud is also persuaded that the fear of one's denied passive homosexual longings constitutes one of the most powerful elements in resistance to analysis.

Homophobia, too, is seen as an expression of repressed homosexuality. Freud regards it as the individual's attempt to reject admission of his own unconscious homosexual desires with "vigorous counter-attitudes" (*SE* 11:99). What is feared and denied is not only the pull toward genital relationships with same-sex others but the pull toward disavowed contrasexual character attributes—in a man the pull to be vulnerable, passive, feminine.

Freud attributes to sublimated homosexuality the erotic factor in friendship and the love of humanity in general. One wonders if he is half consciously thinking of himself when he writes: "It is precisely manifest homosexuals, and among them again precisely those that set themselves against an indulgence in sensual acts, who are distinguished by taking a particularly active share in the general interests of humanity" (*SE* 12:61).

In an 1899 letter to Fliess, Freud had asked, "What would you say if male homosexuality were the primitive form of sexual longing?" (10/17/1899). The context does not tell us what he meant by the question, but in his later writings he often returns to the notion that for children sexual difference is not a primary fact and that its discovery entails anxiety and conflict. Thus Freud suggests that our "primitive," infantile sexuality may be *homo*sexual precisely because for the infant there is only *one* sex. Perhaps in all of us that early longing, innocent of sexual difference, persists as our deepest longing.

But once sexual difference is introduced, our sexuality is divided into two currents—homosexual and heterosexual. In one of his very last writings, the 1938 essay "Analysis Terminable and Interminable," Freud reflects on the conflict this division engenders. Why, he asks, if homosexual and heterosexual impulses are both always present—why don't we simply divide our libidinal energy between them? Why do we impose on ourselves this painful inner conflict? *That* is the mystery. Part of the answer Freud tentatively provides has to do with the power in our psychical life of what he calls the death drive (which will receive careful and appreciative consideration in the Epilogue of this book) and of all that leads us to direct this drive against ourselves. But he also takes account of what he calls the "repudiation of femininity" by both men and women. Why, he asks, is the adoption of the feminine attitude toward other males (much more than toward women) so terrifying to men? Without diminishing the fear, Freud seeks to help his readers recognize how essential overcoming it is in regard to some of the most important realms of human life—in analysis, for example, and in accepting the inevitability of our death (*SE* 22:250).

Freud's deepest reflections about homosexuality, about the role played by homosexual longing and by fear of our own homosexuality in the lives of all humans, concern so much more than sexuality in any simple sense. Coming to terms with these longings and fears is a central life task—and part of our preparation for death.

To see what is involved in undertaking this task—and how easily it is shipwrecked—we must look at the individual life stories Freud presents in his major case histories.

·4·

FREUD:
THE CLASSIC CASES

Homosexuality, manifest or latent, expressed or sublimated, figures prominently in every one of Freud's case studies, both those devoted to actual analysands and those focused on figures he knew only indirectly, like Schreber, Leonardo, and Dostoevski. Most of these cases come from a particular period in Freud's life, between 1907 and 1914, when we know from his correspondence with Jung and Ferenczi that in his own analysis he was once again engaged in working through his continued obsession with Fliess.

Freud's case histories were not written only to exemplify psychoanalytical technique or to illustrate his theory of neurosis. He saw them as relevant to the self-understanding of all of us, for like myths they present the universally human in exaggerated form. As we read these accounts, Freud's own countertransferential identifications with his subjects is inescapable. It is part of what gives these cases their power, part of what makes them still, seventy-five years later, *the* classic cases of psychoanalysis. He recognized himself in these figures (or recreated them in his own image); he wrote of them in a way that allows us to recognize ourselves.

These cases testify to the central role Freud believed same-sex love plays in the inner life of all of us. They reveal the deep soul longings, often hidden or denied—to be completely taken care of, to be utterly self-sufficient, to be seen as who we really are, to become just like the one we admire most, to be a birth giver, to just *be* with no expectations or responsibilities—that homosexual desire may express, and the profound cost of the denial of such desire. Freud tells the story of "Little Hans" to demonstrate the universality of childhood homosexuality and to disclose the power of the longing to be able to bear children. He offers us Leonardo as a paragon of creative, sublimated homosexuality. The case of the "Rat Man" shows the cost of not being able to choose between one's heterosexual and one's homosexual impulses; that of the "Wolf Man" the far greater costs of being totally incapacitated as an adult because all one's life energy has been drawn into resistance against denied homosexual longing.

Most of these cases involve the homosexuality of those who are not overtly or consciously homosexual. Most show the woundedness correlative with their repudiation of homosexual feeling; some suggest how those rejected energies might be given creative expression. One might wonder how relevant such stories can be to the self-understanding of those whose *conscious* sexual identity is homosexual. Freud's answer would be that the same complex psychological processes involving one's relation to mother, father, and siblings, to the stages of psychosexual development, to the values communicated by the social environment, shape manifest homosexuality as shape latent homosexuality. His tales serve to remind the male heterosexual of his secret brotherhood with the homosexual—and to apprise the homosexual of his brotherhood with heterosexual men.

LITTLE HANS

The earliest of these accounts, that recorded in *Analysis of a Phobia in a Five-Year-Old Boy* (1909), involves a child with whom Freud met only once; the "analysis" was conducted through the boy's father, a member of Freud's Wednesday night group. Little Hans was important to Freud because his case seemed to confirm the conjectures about infantile sexuality developed on the basis of Freud's work with adults. Hans, Freud tells us, "was a homosexual (as all children may very well be), quite consistently with the fact, which must always be kept in mind, that *he was acquainted with only one kind of genital organ*—a genital organ like his own" (*SE* 10:110). After describing how much pleasure the boy took in hugging his male cousin and the son of his landlord and telling them how much he loves them, Freud adds with evident delight in the child: "This is the first trace of homosexuality that we have come across in him, but it will not be the last. Little Hans seems to be a positive paragon of all the vices" (15).

What particularly strikes Freud in this case is the understanding of sexuality consequent upon Hans's fascination with his own genital organ, his penis, and his ignorance of the vagina. Freud shows how naturally, how inevitably, this issues in a penis-focused sexuality. The case history emphasizes Hans's preoccupation with "widdlers" and his early delight with his own. But Hans, who has assumed that his "big" mother has a big penis, becomes very distressed when his father tells him that his mother has no penis at all. This information leads him to become concerned about the inviolability of his own.

He seems equally distressed to learn from his father that only women can have children. He vehemently denies both "truths"—continues to insist that his mother and sister have "widdlers" and begins to fantasize about his own capacity to bear children. When reminded, "You know quite well that boys can't have children," he replies: "Well yes. But I believe they can, all the same" (*SE* 10:95). Hans assumes that birth resembles shitting, and his preoccupation shifts from his penis to his feces, which he speaks of as his children. Because he has no notion of the role played by the male organ, he imagines conception as a parthenogenetic event, involving only a single parent. When his father asks, "But who do you think you'd got the children from?" he replies: "Why, from me" (94). In his fantasies Hans is a mother who gives his children the same love his mother had given him—but which he must now share with his sister.

Freud added a postscript to this case in 1922, which simply reaffirms the not-so-hidden thesis of the original essay: that neither Hans's phobia, his childhood "neurosis," nor his "homosexuality" had in any way interfered with his later emotional development. Hans's fantasies and longings testify to the universality of infantile homosexuality; they are equally compatible with adult homosexuality or heterosexuality.

Freud tells us of Little Hans to help us recall the hidden moments of our own childhood, our own forgotten attachments and fantasies, fears and longings, to help us remember how we learned the "truths" about our own sexuality, to remind us of the anxiety engendered by the discovery of sexual difference and of the envy little boys feel when they learn they are precluded from being birth givers. Freud had no children as patients. His wife refused to let him "psychoanalyze" their children. Hans becomes *the* child, a surrogate for Freud's own childhood self, and for ours.

THE RAT MAN

The other case study published in 1909, *Notes upon a Case of Obsessional Neurosis*, involves a patient, almost thirty when he began his analysis, who is known as the "Rat Man" because of the experience that was the immediate occasion of his coming to Freud. While on maneuvers a few months previously, a rather sadistically inclined captain had told him of a horrible Oriental punishment in which a pot full of rats is turned upside down on the buttocks of a tied up criminal; the rats then proceed to bore their way into the man's anus. Freud reports that while the patient with much reluctance and confusion was telling his story, his face took on a look "of horror at pleasure of which he himself was unaware." During the course of the analysis, the reasons for the patient's intense and ambivalent response to the captain's tale came into view.

The Rat Man went on to tell Freud that his immediate response to the captain's tale had been the idea "This is happening to a person who is very dear to me." Soon it becomes clear that actually he had imagined it as happening to *both* of those most dear to him, his fiancée and his long dead father. This "both" becomes the clue to the Rat Man's neurosis, for he seems to be paralyzed by the struggle between his drive toward men, his homosexual love for his father, and his drive toward women, his heterosexual attachment to his lady—and, as Freud reported to the Vienna Psycho-Analytical Society within a month of the beginning of treatment, "the drive toward man" seems to be the stronger of the two.[1]

Thus the topic of the conflict between homosexual and heterosexual interests appears as focal at the very beginning of the treatment, and, indeed, the patient's wrestling with his bisexuality will be for Freud the central issue underlying his obsessional neurosis. Still, it is only fair to say that my reading of the text will highlight this theme more than Freud's own reconstruction of the treatment in the published case history does. Freud himself gave this theme greater prominence in his process notes than in his published account.[2] For instance, these notes refer to several early homosexual experiences reported by his patient that are not mentioned in the 1909 text. For example, from them we learn that as a child "in the course of homosexual games with his brother" the Rat Man "was horrified" when "while they were romping together in bed, his brother's penis came into contact with his anus"; and that at fourteen he and a friend had "homosexual relations" (that is, looking at each other's penis; *SE* 10:273). This was followed by "a homosexual period with male friends, but there was never mutual contact but only looking" (309).

The notes also include many specific references to the infantile anal eroticism that the monograph describes in very general terms as stirred up by the account of the rat punishment. A fascination with buttocks and excrement seems to permeate all of the Rat Man's sexuality. As a child he found the "behinds" of his female cousin and governess particularly exciting; as an adult he was aroused by his mistress's buttocks (*SE* 10:277).[3]

Anal obsessions were manifest also in the patient's dreams. During the treatment he dreamt of lying on his back on top of Freud's daughter and copulating with her "by means of the stool hanging from his anus" (*SE* 10:287), and on another occasion of having Freud's wife "lick his arse" (293). In still another dream he saw a herring stretched between the anuses of Freud's wife and mother.

These dreams suggest the homosexual vector of the transference in this analysis. While telling them to Freud, the patient would get up from the couch and walk agitatedly around the consulting room; he admitted to Freud that this was out of fear of being beaten by him. Patrick Mahony suggests that these dreams represent the Rat Man's "identification with the female members of Freud's family circle."[4] Freud does deal with the transference elements during the treatment, but he uses them primarily as clues to the patient's infantile relationship to his father—and evades dealing directly with what is presently going on between the patient and himself. As so often Freud says almost nothing of the countertransferential dimensions of his relationship to the Rat Man. Yet I think almost any reader of the interchange between Freud and the Rat Man during the first reporting of the rat torture would catch the homosexual overtones, would see Freud's encouraging probes as a "boring in" analogous to the rat's own gnawing and would also see how the Rat Man succeeds in enticing Freud into filling in the holes of his narrative.[5]

The differences between Freud's response to the Rat Man and to Dora (his first published case, which we will discuss in the next chapter) are striking: with the young women he had been dogmatic, critical, combative; with this young man he is encouraging and empathic, patient in the pace of his interpretations, genial in his didactic instruction. He sends the Rat Man a postcard, lends him a novel, feeds him one day when he arrives hungry. There seem to be good grounds for Mahony's contention that Freud, who recognized himself as an obsessional type, identified with this patient.[6]

The abusive dreams became decisive in the analytical work; for they provide compelling evidence of the negative dimensions of the Rat Man's feelings toward his father. Freud believed that the core of the Rat Man's neurosis lay in his relationship to his father. At one point he names as decisive the patient's repression of his infantile hatred of his father; at another he points to his denial of the reality of his father's death. Obviously the two are connected: the Rat Man denies the death because he sees it as the consequence of his (repressed) parricidal wishes.

Freud went looking for evidence of infantile masturbation followed by punishment and perhaps castration threat, but the Rat Man could reconstruct no specific infantile event like the one Freud suspected. He did, however, remember early experiences of conflict between his love of his father and his heterosexual interests. As a child he had a belief that if his wish to see girls naked was fulfilled, his father might die (*SE* 10:162). Later on, after his first experience of intercourse, he found himself thinking, "How glorious! One might murder one's father for this!" (201). Later still, after his engagement, he realized that if his father died, he would become rich enough to marry. Then his father did die, and of course the Rat Man was obsessed with guilt—guilt for all those murderous wishes, as well as for having been asleep at the moment of his father's death. Indeed, the guilt was so intense that it led him to deny the reality of the death. The Rat Man told Freud that long after his father had died, he would study until late at night and then at midnight go to the door as though to welcome his father's ghost. Upon returning to his room, he would then go to stand naked before a mirror, looking at his penis. Freud's interpretation of this ritual accesses its meaning by reversing the order of events; he sees it as signifying the youth's fear that his father will come to punish his sexuality.

The Rat Man is caught between love of his father and love of women—and the father, though dead, has won: he still interferes with his son's sensual drive. Though now free to marry his lady, the Rat Man acknowledges he no longer feels any sexual longing for her. He also still feels himself paralyzed by the challenge to choose between his father and her. The precipitating event of the patient's adult neurosis was his mother's sharing with him, after his father's death, the family expectation that he should follow in his father's footsteps and marry a wealthy cousin rather than his relatively impoverished fiancée. (The Rat Man recreates this situation in the context of the transference by imagining that Freud wants him to marry *his* daughter rather than Gisela, the fiancée). The Rat Man falls ill, becomes unable to establish himself in the world so as to be in a position to marry—in order to avoid having to choose between the two women, between his father's choice and his own. Even though his father is dead, he still finds himself thinking, if I marry my lady, something dreadful will happen to my father.

Freud beautifully demonstrates the connections between the Rat Man's compulsions, his doubts, and his bisexuality. The Rat Man wants to stay in doubt *(Zweifel)* between the two *(zwei)* possibilities. Because he is incapable of making a decision, everything is postponed. The more uncertain he is, the more doubtful he is about the efficacy of his protective measures and thus the more compulsive. Not only is he torn between his father and his lady, but he discovers that his attachment to each is profoundly ambivalent.

Although Freud suggests that in a sense the Rat Man is confronted with the question put to every child, "Who do you love most, Daddy or Mummy?" as one reads this case history one cannot help but notice how little attention Freud pays to the patient's relationship to his mother, and how he fails to explore possible connections between the relationship to her and to Gisela. Freud is clearly more interested in the relationship to the father, in the homosexual vector of the Rat Man's eroticism. What Freud does emphasize about the Rat Man's widowed mother are the many ways in which she has become a *father* surrogate! He notes that the mother is paying for her son's treatment and that she has taken over the father's role in interfering with his marriage plans, in that it is she who has communicated to him the expectation that he marry the rich cousin. There are, however, implications that the Rat Man's attraction to women is somehow damaged. We learn that he finds his mother physically repugnant; she is unclean and has a foul genital odor. We also discover that the Rat Man's heterosexuality is divided in its sensual and affectional currents: he is potent with his dress-maker mistress but has no sensual feeling for his fiancée. He is all along much more comfortable about acknowledging the negative side of his feel-ings for Gisela than of those for his father; his fiancée is clearly experienced as exerting a less total claim than his father.

Thus in this case Freud presents us with a case of a man whose heterosex-uality represents a flight from his homosexuality. The attachment to Gisela seems to exist only as an expression of the negative vector of his ambivalent feelings toward a father who remains the most important figure in his erotic life. The Rat Man is really impaled by his bisexuality. He understands the two currents of sexual feeling—heterosexual and homosexual—as represent-ing an either/or between which he *must* choose, but *can't*. The consequence is paralysis.

The analysis may have helped. Not all readers of the case are as sanguine about this as Freud. The young man's death in World War I came so shortly after the treatment was ended that those Freud scholars who have researched the biography of Ernst Lanzer (the Rat Man's real name) can offer little as evidence either way.

LEONARDO

Freud completed his work on the Rat Man's case history just before sailing with Jung to America; shortly after his return he found himself preoccupied with his "most illustrious analysand," Leonardo da Vinci; early the next summer he was ready to publish the "half-fictional" results, *Leonardo da Vinci and a Memory of His Childhood*—a study that Freud years later still spoke of as "the only beautiful thing I have ever written."

Like Oedipus and Narcissus, Jacob, Joseph, and Moses, Leonardo was one of the figures with whom Freud felt deep identification. He does not exempt himself from his observation that most biographers are "fixated on their subjects in a quite special way. . . . They have chosen their hero . . .

because—for reasons of their personal emotional life—they have felt a special affection for him from the very first" (*SE* 11:130). That Leonardo, like Goethe, was both artist and scientist is clearly one of the reasons for Freud's sense of affinity, since Freud, too, sought to honor both callings. There is more to it than that, however; Freud is also drawn to Leonardo as a model of an "ideal" sublimated homosexuality.

It is Leonardo's apparent *asexuality* that Freud sees as the clue to the enigma of his life. Freud notes that the artist's writings reveal a disgust with physical sexuality and that there is no evidence of his ever having had an intimate friendship with a woman. Although Leonardo surrounded himself with young male pupils chosen for their beauty rather than their talent, Freud is persuaded that his affectionate relationships with them were not (in the conventional sense) sexual. Indeed, Freud (as is consistent with his understanding about the origins of Leonardo's homosexuality) describes Leonardo's relation to his students as *maternal:* "When they were ill [he] nursed them himself, just as a mother nurses her children, and just as his own mother might have tended him" (*SE* 11:102).

Leonardo, an illegitimate child, was for the first years of his life raised without a father; later he was adopted by his father and his father's legitimate wife. But during those earliest years, Freud believes, his abandoned mother gave him her undiluted love. Consequently, as Freud understands it, the adult Leonardo, unwilling to be faithless to his first love, turned away from women.

Freud devotes the central part of his study to an analysis of a childhood fantasy of Leonardo's in which a bird came to him as he lay in his cradle and struck his lips many times with its tail. He interprets this as a fellatio fantasy; the childhood experience of sucking at its mother's breast has been transformed into a passive homosexual fantasy. Much of Freud's detailed analysis depends on a mistake: the German rendition of the dream had "vulture" where it should have had "kite" and Freud makes much of Egyptian mythological traditions about the vulture goddess, Mut, whose name suggests the German *Mutter,* and of the Egyptian belief that all vultures were wind-impregnated females. This leads Freud to posit that Leonardo (who in his earliest years had a mother but apparently no father) thought of himself as such a vulture-child, and that his sexual orientation was shaped by his early attachment to a female whom he imagined as endowed with a penis (what psychoanalysts call the "phallic mother")—symbolized by the vulture and its tail.

What may be most interesting about all this is that, although the mistake was pointed out in 1923, Freud never acknowledged it—though he could have done so without much loss to his primary theses. One wonders if he associated Leonardo's childhood fantasy with that dream from his own childhood in which he had seen his "beloved mother, with a peculiarly peaceful, sleeping expression on her features, being carried into the room by two (or three) people with birds' beaks and laid upon the bed" (*SE* 5:583). In *Interpretation* Freud connects these bird-beaked creatures to Egyptian deities; his interpretation then moves from the obvious fear that his mother might be dying to a more "obscure and evidently sexual craving." When later on in his study of Leonardo, Freud introduces the "two mother" theme—the influence on Leonardo's psychosexual development of his dual relation to his natural mother and to his father's legitimate wife—we again cannot help but note that Freud's accounts of his own childhood also include this theme. Many of his recollections of his early years reveal the complex interplay between his relation to his mother and the Catholic peasant who served as his nurse. Indirectly, as Freud analyzes the psychological factors correlated with Leonardo's sublimated homosexuality, Freud seems to be also offering an analysis of his own.

Freud sees Leonardo not as someone devoid of passion but as one who has "converted his passion into the thirst for knowledge"; and though he clearly admires the artistic and scientific results of this sublimation, he is also sensitive to the human cost: "A conversion of psychical instinctual force into various forms of activity can no more be achieved without loss than a conversion of physical forces" (*SE* 11:75). "The almost total repression of a real sexual life does not provide the most favorable conditions for the exercise of sublimated sexual trends" (133). He sees this cost made manifest in Leonardo's middle years, in his increasing dedication to scientific investigation rather than artistic creation, in his indecisiveness and procrastination, in his tendency to leave his works unfinished.

But then, "at the summit of his life, when he was in his early fifties"—as Freud himself was at the time of this writing—"a new transformation came over him":

Still deeper layers of the contents of his mind became active once more; but this further regression was to the benefit of his art, which was in the process of becoming stunted. He met the woman who awakened his memory of his mother's happy smile of sensual rapture; and, influenced by this revived memory, he recovered the stimulus that guided him at the beginning of his artistic endeavors. . . . He painted the Mona Lisa, the St. Anne with Two Others and the series of mysterious pictures which are characterized by the enigmatic smile. With the help of the oldest of all his erotic impulses he enjoyed the triumph of once more conquering the inhibition of his art. (*SE* 11:134)

This image of a truly creative sublimation seems to serve Freud as an articulation of his hopes for his own mature work. It seems not irrelevant that in *Leonardo* Freud for the first time introduces two figures who will become focal in his writings during his last years, two figures whom we will consider more fully at the very end of our study: Eros, the preserver of all living things (70), and Ananke, the ancient goddess who embodies the inexorable laws of nature (125).

SCHREBER

A few months after the publication of *Leonardo*, Freud found himself once again engaged in analysis at a distance. This time his attention was drawn[7] to the *Memoirs of a Nerve Patient* by Judge Daniel Paul Schreber, an autobiographical account that Freud described as the case history of a paranoid composed by the patient himself. Freud's *Psycho-Analytical Notes on an Autobiographical Account of a Case of Paranoia* (1911) is based entirely on these *Memoirs*, which he saw as providing unique access to the rich complexities of paranoid constructions.

Schreber's *Memoirs*, which fully describes his delusions, reflects his belief that he has been assigned the mission of redeeming the world—but can only do so by becoming a woman. Freud is concerned to understand the formation of this belief-structure. He takes as the first symptom of Schreber's illness his waking one morning with the thought "that after all it really must be very nice to be a woman submitting to the act of copulation" (*SE* 12:13). Soon afterward, in the clinic he began to complain that he felt himself to be "dead and decomposing," that "his body [was] being handled in all kinds of revolting ways." Then he began accusing his former physician of persecuting him and subjecting him to sexual abuse.

Schreber's immediate response to his "feminine fantasies" was indignant repudiation—and repression. He accused his former doctor of "soul murder" and of organizing a conspiracy to transform his body into that of a woman and subject it to sexual abuse (*SE* 12:44). "The person he longed for now become his persecutor, and the content of his wishful phantasy became the content of his persecution" (47). Freud does not pretend to know why Schreber, now fifty-one, who had for many years been an apparently successful and well-adapted jurist,[8] fell ill at just this point in his life, nor why what had earlier been feelings of affectionate dependence on his doctor should suddenly be "intensified to the pitch of erotic desire" (42). He wonders again, as he had with Leonardo, if there might not be a male equivalent to menopause that makes men especially susceptible to such redirecting of their instinctual energies.

What interests Freud most is the next step, the replacement of the doctor by God and all that it entails. For this step represented the turning point of Schreber's illness and made possible the solution of Schreber's conflict:

> It was impossible for Schreber to become reconciled to playing the part of a female wanton toward his doctor; but the task of providing God Himself with the voluptous sensations that He required called up no such resistance on the part of his ego. Emasculation was now no longer a disgrace; it became 'consonant with the Order of Things,' it took its place in a great cosmic chain of events, and was instrumental in the recreation of humanity after its extinction. (*SE* 12:48)

According to Schreber's new belief system, he has been called to redeem the world and restore the lost state of bliss. To accomplish this he must be transformed into a woman. It is not that he *wishes* for such a transformation; it is a *must* based on the Order of Things (17). Schreber comes to believe that he is God's wife and that God has impregnated him. On two distinct occasions, he asserts, he had possessed female genitals. He confides that pressure on his breasts and buttocks "evoked a sensation of voluptousness such as women experience" during intercourse. He was persuaded that cultivation of "voluptousness" and of "femaleness" had now become a religious duty (32).

Freud emphasizes the signal importance of this elaborate belief system: "The delusional formation, which we take to be the pathological product, is in reality an attempt at recovery, a process of reconstruction" (*SE* 12:71). Schreber's struggle ceases; his illness recedes, and as his sense of external reality becomes stronger, the shape of his vision changes: his transformation into a woman is postponed to the remote future. Schreber is allowed to return from the asylum to the world because he has learned to temper his fantasies. He has, however, not surrendered them. He carries back with him a version of the idea of being transformed into a woman *now*—rather than only in the future. When alone, he confesses, he sometimes undresses his upper body, puts on "sundry feminine adornments," and poses in front of the mirror (21). Transvestism provides some relief of the pressure to become female. What made it possible for Schreber's illness to terminate in "something approximating to a recovery" (78) seems to have been his *reconciling* himself to his homosexual fantasy.

Although Freud believed that the exciting cause of Schreber's illness was the homosexual attraction to his former physician, he, of course, suspected that this was at least in part a transference phenomenon. Freud became convinced that the persecuting doctor was a *revenant* of Schreber's brother and that God was the reappearance of a still more important early love, his father. What Freud says about Schreber's relationship to his father has little specific about it. It is simply the by now familiar picture of a father who interfered with his son's sensual satisfaction and threatened him with castration.[9] This threat, Freud suggests, provided the material for Schreber's fantasy of being transformed into a woman. Schreber's God ends up requiring the very voluptuousness the father had forbidden (*SE* 12:56). Freud's belief that Schreber had found a way of living with his passive homosexual longings without literally living them out—by channeling them into fantasy activity, by allowing himself the indulgence of solitary cross-dressing—was wrong. Schreber fell ill again (after his wife suffered a debilitating stroke) and died in an asylum. Yet his account of Schreber remains illuminating—as an account of a man who late in life became overwhelmed by homosexual longings that he had until then successfully repressed, as an account of a valiant though unavailing struggle against those longings, as an account of a complex religious fantasy system created as a substitute for literal sexual expression.

THE WOLF MAN

The last of Freud's major case histories, *From the History of an Infantile Neurosis* (1918), involves a patient known as the Wolf Man. The analysis was a lengthy one. Freud's treatment initially lasted from 1910 until the outbreak of World War I and was resumed for a short while afterward. At later periods the patient was treated by several other analysts. Despite all this therapeutic attention, the Wolf Man never fully recovered, never really managed a self-sufficient existence. Many who have studied the case believe the Wolf Man was unanalyzable, more severely disturbed than Freud recognized.[10] Certainly the Wolf Man's own account of his life, written long after his work with Freud, communicates little self-understanding—only his happy acceptance of his role as the paradigmatic analytic patient.[11]

What progress the Wolf Man apparently made in the analysis may have simply been due to how well he played his favorite role—passive compliance. Although Freud recognized some of the transference dimensions of the analysis, he does not seem to have brought them into clear focus and so not to have recognized the degree to which the analysis was a *replay* of the Wolf Man's most treasured fantasy—to be the object, the recipient, of his father's love. Because the Wolf Man did not contest Freud's interpretations as Dora and the Rat Man had, Freud was not pushed to discover the degree to which his reconstructions of the Wolf Man's childhood were *his* constructions, at least as derivative of his own childhood as of the Wolf Man's.

Central to the Wolf Man's story, as we shall see, is Freud's reconstruction of what he calls the "primal scene"—a putative occasion during which the patient as a very young child had observed his parents making love and then interrupted them by defecating. The aristocratic surroundings of the Wolf Man's childhood make such an event suspiciously unlikely. But we know that Freud as a child shared his parents' bedroom until he was three and in *Interpretation* he recalls urinating in their room and being told by his father, "The boy will come to nothing" (*SE* 4:216). In the end, and especially in his footnotes (where Freud's most important conclusions so often hide), and only after much vacillation, Freud seems to explain the Wolf Man's childhood dream that had led him to posit the primal scene as based on a "primal fantasy" (imaginal events that play a powerful role in the psychical life of all of us irrespective of literal experience)—but he devotes much more of his monograph to the possibility of an actual witnessing. We come away with the sense that it is very important to Freud that *something* "really" happened, though his theory about the power of infantile fantasy makes such a claim essentially irrelevant. The "really," I propose, refers to Freud's childhood rather than that of his patient.[12]

The Wolf Man offered some challenge to Freud's interpretation but soon desisted. He trusted Freud more than himself. Mahony offers a striking image of their interaction: "The reclining patient let himself be penetrated, *more ferarum* ['from behind,' as in the reconstructed primal scene], by the fantasies coming from behind," that is, from where Freud sat behind the couch.[13] Freud himself glimpses—and evades—the homosexual dimension of the interaction between his patient and himself. He acknowledges how painfully slowly the work proceeded, how long the patient remained "unassailably entrenched behind an attitude of obliging apathy" (*SE* 17:11). In a paper on analytical technique written during the time he was working with the Wolf Man, Freud notes that such passive resistance to analysis is often characteristic of men "with over-strong repressed homosexuality"—who fear (and long for) subjection by the analyst (*SE* 12:138).

Yet Freud saw in the difficulties of this case, in the slowness with which it unfolded, a gain—for in the long run this permitted access to "the deepest and most primitive strata" of the soul (*SE* 17:10). What he found most fascinating was that in the Wolf Man, to an unusual degree, no erotic attitude that had once been established was ever fully replaced by a later one:

> His mental life impressed one in much the same way as the religion of Ancient Egypt, which is so unintelligible to us because it preserves the earlier stages of its development side by side with the end-products, retains the most ancient gods and their attributes along with the most modern ones, and thus, as it were, spreads out upon a two-dimensional surface what other instances of evolution show us in the solid. (119)

Once again Freud uses a dream as the organizing center of his presentation, though in this case his real focus is on the "primal scene," whose importance and character is arrived at through the dream's interpretation. As the adult patient recounted it to Freud, as a child he had once dreamt that he was lying in his bed on a winter night looking toward the window beyond its foot:

> Suddenly the window opened of its own accord, and I was terrified to see that some white wolves were sitting on the big walnut tree in front of the window. There were six or seven of them. The wolves were quite white, and looked more like foxes or sheep-dogs, for they had big tails like foxes and they had their ears pricked like dogs when they pay attention to something. In great terror, evidently of being eaten up by the wolves, I screamed and woke up. (*SE* 17:29)

Associations to oft-heard fairy tales in which wolves eat children were, not surprisingly, easily accessible, as were some relevant recollections of the period preceding the dream. The Wolf Man remembered being told by his Nanya (nanny) that he was his father's child (which he evidently at first understood very literally), as his somewhat older sister was his mother's. He also recalled his sister's attempt to seduce him into letting her play with his penis. Though he rejected *her* (even in later life the girls with whom he was sexually involved were all servants, as though he still needed to debase his female initiator), for the rest of his life he retained the passive sexual *aim* of being touched on the genitals (*SE* 17:22). When he in turn tried to seduce his Nanya into playing with him, as his sister had done, she warned him that children who "did that" got a "wound" (24). Soon thereafter he gave up masturbating and, as Freud explains it, "his sexual life, which was beginning to come under the sway of the genital zone, gave way" and "was thrown back . . . into an earlier phase of pregenital organization" (25), the sadistic-anal phase (108). The child became naughty and cruel, a tormentor of humans and animals—and at the same time subject to masochistic fantasies of being beaten, especially on the penis (26).[14]

Freud believes that the child had turned to his father—with whom he had earlier *identified* on a narcissistic ("I want to grow up to be like you") model—as the *object* of his passive sexual aim (after having rejected his sister and having been rejected by his Nanya; *SE* 17:27). The child's fits of rage served this aim; they were attempts to seduce his father into punishing him and satisfying his masochistic longings. The Wolf Man had replaced identification with object-choice—and at the same time his *active* attitude had been transformed into a *passive* one. In one way the new orientation was an advance, in another a regression.

All this, as Freud slowly concluded from the analysis, had preceded the dream. The dream in a sense sums up, serves as an "objective correlative," to use T. S. Eliot's term, of the whole complex process. It was important primarily as a turning point—its images brought to consciousness the real character of the child's longing and its imagined cost—and therefore led to the immediate repression of the wish and to the forgetting of the dream. What fascinates Freud most in this case is what it reveals about the complexity of the ways in which our psyches appropriate and integrate experience.

The longing Freud saw as most operative in the dream's formation was the boy's wish for sexual satisfaction from his father. "The strength of this wish made it possible to revive a long-forgotten trace in his memory of a scene which was able to show him what sexual satisfaction from his father was like; and the result was terror, horror of the fulfillment of the wish, and repression" (*SE* 17:36). I will not retrace here how Freud proceeds, detail by detail, from the dream to the reconstructed "primal scene"—from (for example) the window's opening to the boy's waking up in his parents' bedroom, from the stillness of the wolves to the parents' violent intercourse, from the fear of being eaten by the wolves to the fear/wish "to be copulated with by his father"—but only rehearse his central point: the memory that the dream reactivated was evidence to the boy of the wound of which his Nanya had warned him. Whether he had ever really seen his parents make love or had somehow fantasized this on the basis of watching his father's sheep copulate, he now *knew* a truth he had sought to ignore, the "truth" of castration (57). That is, he had now understood that his mother had no penis and concluded from this that the "necessary condition of intercourse with his father" was to lose his own (46).

The condition asked too much. It threatened what Freud calls his narcissistic attachment to his penis. On the other side of this dream and the anxiety it aroused, the boy repudiated his wish and repressed his sexual aim, the passive attitude toward his father. What predominated now was fear of his father—manifested initially as a wolf phobia and then as a more generalized animal phobia.

As Freud understands it, by impressing upon the child the difference between male and female, the dream could have brought him back to the genital phase—as it became clear that the passive longings directed toward his father could be satisfied by adopting a feminine attitude toward him, by homosexuality, rather than by masochistically welcomed beatings. But because this feminine aim was unacceptable, it was repressed. The Wolf Man had identified with his mother in the dream—and now rejected that feminine identification (*SE* 17:47).[15] Freud highlights what he calls the Wolf Man's "disavowal" of the "truth" about sexual difference, which the dream had impressed upon him—he both *accepts* and *repudiates* the "fact" of castration. The two views coexist and complicate his relationship to both parents.

The Wolf Man paid an inexorable price for the repression of his overpowering homosexuality. For the repression kept his homosexual impulse in the unconscious "withdrawn from the possibility of sublimation and tied to its original sexual aim" (*SE* 17:118). Although Freud celebrates the "liberations" of his "shackled homosexuality" that the analytical treatment helped the Wolf Man achieve, what we know of his later life suggests that most of it remained bound.

Even the heterosexuality of his adult life was shaped by the dominance of that repressed homosexuality: he chose only women whom he could look down on as inferior; he felt large buttocks to be the most attractive features in women; he could only enjoy copulating from behind (the position in the reconstructed "primal scene"; *SE* 17:41). From the time of his dream onward he turned to women as his conscious sexual object, "but he did not enjoy their possession, for a powerful, and now entirely unconscious, inclination toward men, in which were united all the forces of the earlier phases of his development, was constantly drawing him away from his female objects" (118). Too few of his psychical trends were available for heterosexual object-choice.

The result of the dream, as Freud reconstructs the process, was not the triumph of the Wolf Man's masculinity but rather a reaction against his femininity. Although Freud emphasizes the importance of the Wolf Man's relation to his *father*—he also tells the story in a different way, in a way that puts the stress on the Wolf Man's ambivalent relationship to his own *femininity*. By 1938 Freud will have come to believe that the "repudiation of femininity" poses the most intractable psychological problem—confirmation of that view is already available in this case. Freud was well aware of his own ambivalence toward his "feminine" side (as we noted in Chapter 3). The Greeks, who lauded the active role in male homosexuality, also had strong prejudices about males who enjoyed the passive "feminine" role (as we shall see in Chapter 10). Male homosexuality brings this issue to the fore, to consciousness—which is why it is so often repressed and castigated. Male homosexuals may not *resolve* the issue in their own lives—they may insist on playing the active role, on looking for hyper-"masculine" partners, on exaggerating their own masculinity in other aspects if they do take on the passive role, on parodying their "femininity" in hyperbolic self-demeaning mannerisms or dress—but they *address* it consciously. Conscious confrontation with what Freud called our "bisexuality" is to him a signally important part of a conscious, relatively whole life. The Wolf Man, even more than Freud's other cases, shows the cost of trying to evade this feminine side of oneself—and in the very attempt being overwhelmed by it.

The cases of men wrestling with the homosexual component of their sexuality that we have considered in this chapter were written before Freud became aware of the important role in the psychological development of men played by the "pre-Oedipal mother." His own emphasis on the role of the father in male development, his consequent highlighting of the importance of infantile homosexuality, the phallocentrism of his early sexual theory—all may in part be expressions of his own ambivalent relation to the feminine, to his own mother, to the maternal as such. That is, I am suggesting that there is a *homosexual cast to Freud's theory*—not just an important homosexual vector in his personal life, not just a focusing on the issue of homosexuality in his major cases.

Making male psychology paradigmatic of human psychology as such, as though there were "really" only men, only *one* sex, yields what is essentially a homosexual psychological theory. But Freud in the last years of his life began to move toward a recognition that female psychology could not be understood on the basis of male psychology—moved toward a recognition *in his theory* that there really are *two* sexes!

·5·

FREUD:
FEMALE HOMOSEXUALITY

Freud acknowledges that most of what he has to say about same-sex love applies to male experience. Indeed, despite the preponderance of women among his patients, especially in the early years, Freud from the beginning to the end of his career admitted how baffled he was by female sexuality. In 1899 he wrote Fliess: "I do not yet have the slightest idea what to do with the + + + [as noted earlier, + + + is a symbol Freud used for sexuality] of the female aspect and that makes me distrust the whole [sexual theory]" (11/5/1899); in the 1905 edition of *The Three Essays* he acknowledged that the sexual life of women is "still veiled in impenetrable obscurity" (*SE* 7:151). He reiterated this view in 1924: when it comes to the sexual development of little girls "our material—for some incomprehensible reason—becomes far more obscure and full of gaps. . . . Our insight into [them] is unsatisfactory, incomplete and vague" (*SE* 19:177, 179); and two years later added: "The sexual life of adult women is a 'dark continent" for psychology" (*SE* 20:212). (On the other hand, Freud recognized that women may have valid access to male psychology and male sexuality—for they have been "masculine" not only in the consciousness of their pregenital years, but in their clitoral sexuality [*SE* 7:220].)

Although Freud seems all along to have recognized the important role played by bisexuality in female psychology, one senses that he has difficulty in taking his own insights quite seriously, in really crediting the possibility of a sexuality in which the penis plays no part. His early discussions of women's sexuality are also flawed by his assumption that female psychology can be understood simply by inference from male psychology: "Things happen in just the same way with little girls, with the necessary changes" (*SE* 16:333); the male and female processes are "precisely analogous" (*SE* 19:32). It is only as he comes to discover the lack of symmetry between male and female development, the primary importance for women of their original attachment to a same-sex other, the mother, that he fully appreciates the

68

significant differences between male and female homosexuality. Thus, in order to understand what Freud has to say about lesbians, we must first consider what he has to say about women as such and particularly about their sexuality.

Here, again, I will be presenting "my" Freud, a Freud who cannot be reduced to a univocal system of ideas, a Freud who himself recognizes that the various contributions to his sexual theory do "not admit of being merged into an entirely uncontradictory whole" (*SE* 19:141). My reading of Freud is close to that of those European feminists who discover in his texts a Freud with audacious insights into the complex fluidity of female sexuality—in tension with another Freud who fearfully retreats from some of his own insights into more biologistic and more conventional perspectives. Thus I credit Freud with seeing (*and* "disavowing")[1] what some American feminists claim are unconscious "undertexts" in his writing.[2]

FREUD'S PSYCHOLOGY OF WOMEN

Catherinine Clement, one of the French feminist readers of Freud referred to above, notes: "Theory, when it is able to state its own roots, when it is able to trace its genealogy even as it is being written, will appear as what it never fails to be: self-projection."[3] Put another way, as Karen Horney once observed, what has been put forward as the "psychology of women" is in truth but "the deposit of the desires and disappointments of men."[4]

In Freud's case his own failure fully to work through his ambivalent feelings toward his mother seems to affect his readiness to follow through on his most perceptive intuitions about female psychology. Yet our very proclivity to assume a possible relationship between infantile experience and adult theory building is something we have learned from him. And though Freud may shrink from conscious exploration of all the ramifications of the lifelong impact of our primal pre-Oedipal relationship to our mother, it is nevertheless he who *named* her, who recognized how different that all-powerful mother of our earliest years is from the more human figure to whom we find ourselves relating a few years later. (Though his naming her the *phallic* mother is obviously a strange naming.)

In his letters to Fliess and in *The Interpretation of Dreams* Freud communicates the powerful hold his own mother had over his inner life. He recalls how clearly he knew himself to be the adored favorite of a beautiful young mother. Though he acknowledges the intensity of his own feelings of sibling rivalry, he never admits that her love for him was ever diluted or compromised. Perhaps, as Coppelia Kahn suggests, Freud managed to continue to idealize her, to see in her only the "good mother," by identifying the nursemaid of his earliest years as the "bad mother."[5]

Throughout his life the figure of the mother is associated with unconsciousness and death. The analysis of the dream of his dead mother carried to her bed by the three bird-beaked persons, which we have already discussed, reveals the sexual fantasies that were part of Freud's childhood feelings toward her—and the denied death wishes. The other dream in *Interpretation* whose analysis evokes associations to his mother, the dream of "The Three Fates," shows her as engaged in persuading Freud to accept the inevitability of his own death, teaching him that he, like all of us, is made of earth and must return to earth (*SE* 4:204–5). At several points in *Interpretation* Freud speaks of the "navel" of the dream—the unanalyzable element that connects us directly to the unplumbable depths of the unconscious. He ends the lovely 1913 essay "The Theme of the Three Caskets" thus:

> What is represented here are the three inevitable relations that a man has with a woman—the woman who bears him, the woman who is his mate and the woman who destroys him; or that they are the three forms taken by the figure of the mother in the course of a man's life—the mother herself, the beloved who is chosen after her pattern, and lastly the Mother Earth who receives him once more. But it is in vain that an old man yearns for the love of woman as he had it first from his mother; the third of the Fates alone, the silent Goddess of Death, will take him into her arms. (*SE* 12:301)

In 1930 he begins *Civilization and Its Discontents* with a recognition of the relationship between mystical fusion with the divine and the earliest bonds with the mother, but concludes that the "oceanic feeling" is not really to be associated with the origin of religion—for religion proceeds not from the experience of primal bliss but from the terrors of infantile helplessness and the longing for the father's protection (*SE* 21:64–73).

Freud's theory about women is, not surprisingly, shaped by his fear (and longing) for fusion, his association of the feminine with the loss of self and with death. We cannot help but hear the personal echoes when he writes about a *theoretical* problem for psychoanalysis: "Everything connected with the first mother-attachment as in analysis seemed to me so elusive, lost in a past so dim and shadowy, so hard to resuscitate, that it seemed as if it had undergone some specially inexorable repression" (*SE* 19:226).

What Freud writes about women (and especially about women who love women) will be shaped by his "personal complex"—which is, of course, not all that personal, not all that idiosyncratic, but rather in many respects typical of the male perspective. I also believe that though Freud evaded full acknowledgment of what he saw, he saw much that others had not seen. It was the psychology of women, of his early hysterical patients, that first drew him to *depth* psychology; it was again the psychology of women that evoked some of his most creative thinking during the last decade of his life.

Women originally entered depth psychology as patients, as objects not subjects—as in science generally the knower has been male and the known has been conceived in female terms.[6] Thus Freud, in a letter to Fliess, writes that trying to understand dreams is like coming to know a mysterious woman, and later explicitly speaks of the assumption of the role of subject as a male characteristic, whereas "femaleness takes over [the factors of] object and passivity" (*SE* 19:145).

Yet from the beginning of his analytical work Freud also sought to move beyond this perspective, to move to a subject-subject rather than subject-object relationship. He sought to attend to the *psyche-logos*, the speech of the soul, of the female hysterics who were his first patients. Unlike his predecessors, who had seen hysterics as morally and intellectually inferior women, as weak, deceitful, and infantile, Freud viewed them as women of exceptional intelligence, imaginative capacity, and energy, who as girls had been tomboys and as women were unreconciled to the limited lives sanctioned by their culture. He listened to them and was able to hear in their symptoms an unconsciously voiced protest against the cultural limitations imposed on them by virtue of their gender. He saw them as, like the maenads of Dionysian religion,[7] full of instinctual, sexual energy for which there was no approved outlet. Because, consciously, they accepted their world's morality, this sexuality had been repressed; its only outlet was their symptomology. These women became Freud's *teachers* as well as his patients; they forced upon him the recognition of a structure of consciousness different from the one acknowledged by Victorian culture, that is, of what could in the terms of the culture only be called the *un*conscious.

Nevertheless, Freud was in a sense extorting their confessions, as well as clearly interpreting their experience from his own male perspective. We might even say that Freud's psychology of women is really about male fantasies about women, male fear of women, and male fear of becoming women. What interests him about women is the ways in which they are *different* from men. Thus his psychology of women proceeds from a commitment to antithetical thinking, which easily moves into an assumption that women are *opposite* to men and that one can deduce what they are like from knowledge of what men are like.

Yes, as we noted earlier, Freud himself is aware that one's genitals do not determine one's sex, aware of what we today would describe as the difference between biological sex and gender. The primary way he wrestles with this is in trying to distinguish the terms *masculine* and *feminine* from being identified with biological men and women. By masculine he intends to mean "active," by feminine, "passive." As he puts it in *Civilization and Its Discontents:*

> For psychology the contrast between the sexes fades away into one between activity and passivity, in which we far too readily identify activity with maleness and passivity with femaleness. . . . If we assume it as a fact that each individual seeks to satisfy both male and female wishes in his sexual life, we are prepared for the possibility that those demands are not fulfilled by the same object, and that they interfere with each other unless they can be kept apart and each impulse guided into a particular channel that is suited to it. (*SE* 21:105, n. 3)

Freud both rejects this language and makes use of it; he speaks of all libido, in both men and women, as "masculine" and then adds, "properly speaking the libido does not derive from any gender" (*SE* 20:131).

Our bisexuality means to Freud that all of us are both "masculine" and "feminine" in this sense, but that society seeks to persuade men to adopt a masculine conscious attitude and women to adopt a passive, or feminine, conscious one. The cost of this for women he had already begun to see when he wrote *Studies on Hysteria;* the cost of this for men was made evident in the case studies considered in Chapter 4. Sometimes the cost is evidently felt to be so great that it leads to refusal to make the socially sanctioned choice.

From very early on in his career Freud wrestled with the inadequacy of a purely passive view of female sexuality. I understand his move away from the seduction theory, the notion that neurosis originates in actual infantile incest, as not primarily a denial of the reality of sexual abuse—indeed, Freud (as we noted in our reading of the Wolf Man case) throughout his career keeps returning to the idea that something really happened or was really witnessed—but rather as a recognition that memory inextricably interweaves history and fantasy, and that children, male and female, even when still very young have *active* longings for affection and sensual pleasure. Unfortunately, from my perspective, Freud continues to speak of the girl's active sexuality as her "masculinity" and to suggest, as Peter Gay phrases it, "that femininity is essentially acquired by the successive renunciation of masculine traits."[8]

At first Freud seems to have assumed that the stages of female development would parallel those of the male; that for women as for men the first love-object would be contrasexual. Her love would initially be directed toward the parent of the opposite sex, the father, and for the young girl as for her male counterpart the resolution of the Oedipal complex, the acceptance of her father's unavailability, would be the central event. Indeed, in the 1924 essay "The Dissolution of the Oedipus Complex," Freud stated that this process was "much simpler" in the girl's case than in the boys (*SE* 19:178). Yet in this very essay he had discussed how bisexuality implies that the Oedipus complex will have a "double orientation," that it offers the child both active and passive possibilities of satisfaction, identification with both parents, rivalry with both, desire for both (176). Thus Freud has come to recognize that the difference between the sexes is more elusive than it at first appears, and yet he has not fully integrated all the consequences of this discovery.

Males and females are even alike, Freud asserts, in the high value both place on the penis. He is persuaded that for males a pivotal event is the young boy's discovery that not all humans have a penis, as the child had earlier assumed. Women become defined for him (for the boy, but *in a sense for Freud as well*) as "without a penis." Because they are now seen as deprived of an attribute they were earlier seen as having, to the boy they are "castrated" and their castration arouses fears that the same might happen to him. The discovery of difference stirs up fear. What is most amazing is how, when Freud turns to women, he so readily speaks of "the fact of castration," as though the little girl too, to begin with, has assumed that she had a penis, had regarded her clitoris as a penis analogue. He writes as though she, too, took male being as the norm. (In *The Three Essays* he had initially postulated the infantile theory that all humans are born with penises only of males, but in a 1920 footnote he added that little girls, too, come to believe that originally they had a subsequently lost penis [*SE* 7:195].) Thus women are defined in negative terms—by a not-having, a negation; they are regarded as representing a deviation from the male norm, as deficient, castrated males; as wounded, mutilated.

The emphasis on the importance of "penis envy" persists even when in the 1925 essay "Some Psychical Consequences of the Anatomical Distinction between the Sexes" Freud for the first time really considers the psychical significance of the "self-evident" fact that the earliest attachment of the female child is a homosexual one, her attachment to the mother who gives her birth and nurses her. In this essay his interest is directed to "how it happens that girls abandon [this object] and instead take their father as an object" (*SE* 19:251). Although he has an answer on hand—that the loosening of the relation to the mother is occasioned by the girl blaming her for her "narcissistic wound," her lack of a penis—hints of a very different (*not phallocentric*) theory have now been introduced.

For the first time Freud is really considering the theoretical importance of the pre-Oedipal period. It becomes clear that what lay in the way of earlier recognition was that for the boy the pre-Oedipal and Oedipal love objects are the same, whereas for females there is a shift from a same-sex to a contra-sex object. Admitting the importance of a pre-Oedipal period in female history entails the discovery of its importance for males as well—and *that* is painful. Indeed, it is so painful that Freud both sees it and hides from seeing it—as he had accused the Wolf Man, for instance, of both seeing that his mother had no penis *and* denying it. Indeed, much of the controversy about Freud among feminists is over this point: did Freud himself really see it or just see enough to enable us to see what he didn't?

What is problematical about recognizing the importance to male psychology of the pre-Oedipal mother is that she is different from the Oedipal mother. To recognize her is to recognize the fearfulness of our utter dependence on her in the earliest period; it is to be confronted with our own vulnerability and contingency. Without her, I would not be. To be reminded of that dependency is also to be reminded that to begin with all children, male and female, are "feminine"—that is, passive. It is also to be reminded of our earliest losses, the loss of the womb and the breast, the discovery of otherness. It is to be brought back in touch with the profound anger associated with these losses and the inadequacy of all later substitute loves to measure up to the satisfactions of that primal connection. It is to be exposed to the dissatisfactions inherent in all sexual experience.

This heightens the degree to which, as Freud had long ago recognized, male psychology is a psychology based on anxiety, on castration fear (which he acknowledged to be more powerful than penis envy)—which, like all fear, hides a wish. The fear and wish are about losing one's distinctive identity as a male; about "femininity," passivity, death. Women are fearful to men—for men come from women and might be swallowed up by them. Flaccidity after intercourse is seen as a little death. Male personhood is associated with the biological mark of difference, the penis. Male identity comes to depend on *difference*, on not being female. To lose the penis is to die. The fear issues in an emphasis on separateness, difference, autonomy, and thus on character attributes and activities that lead to external domination of women, to "thralldom," and to the equation of masculinity with activity—an equation whose importance we have already noted. Then males project: women want to be like us, are deficient versions of us. The original sexuality of girls is called "masculine." Their later receptivity is deemed "passive."

The results are manifold. This way of viewing sexual difference may most often issue in outward conscious depreciation of women; but it may also lead to their overestimation—or to male identification with femininity, as in some forms of male homosexuality. What all responses have in common is a (usually hidden) envy of female generativity. For the denied knowledge that women aren't castrated males after all—that actually men are humans who have no wombs—persists. It is interesting in this connection to note that it is in just this essay that Freud corrects a statement made at the time he was working with Little Hans. Then he announced that the sexual interest of children is first aroused by the mystery of where babies come from; now he asserts that primary interest falls on the question of sexual difference (*SE* 19:252, n. 2). The second question seems to yield a phallocentric answer: the visible difference is the presence or absence of a penis. The first yields a gynocentric answer: only women give birth. Thus we see Freud defensively putting more theoretical emphasis on the penis just when he is acknowledging the prior importance of the mother.

It is the activity of females, not their passivity, that terrifies. In a discussion of Medusa's head, Freud says explicitly that it is the *mother's* genitals, not just female genitals as such, that terrify (*SE* 19:144, n. 3); which I take to imply that it is the confrontation with the place of our origin, not with the absence of a penis, that is most salient. This gives a somewhat different cast to those infantile male sexual theories that fantasize that birth giving is not a female prerogative, theories that seek to ignore or deny the existence of the vagina or womb. Freud often speaks of women's longing for a penis and their coming to accept as a substitute having a male lover or, better, a male child, a masculine being who begins as part of their own body. But there are hints in Freud that it is really the other way around: that the male is drawn to heterosexual coitus so that he may possess a womb by entering it sexually. Perhaps the male's emphasis on his penis is a substitute for not being able to bear a child. Perhaps the emphasis on sublimated sexuality, on cultural creativity, is a substitute for procreative capacity. (Again, let me be clear: there are hints of this in Freud—in his footnotes, his qualifications, the implicit connections between different texts—but nowhere does he spell it out as explicitly as I have done here.)

The anxiety about being inferior leads to an assertion of superiority; it makes impossible the acceptance of male and female as two different but equally necessary and significant realities. Freud also helps us to see how—because by virtue of their fearful response to the mother, men do come to have dominant social power—many of their viewpoints become "true." The move into the Oedipal phase means a move into a male-defined world in which many women envy men, are self-deprecating, and invest their libido in their children.[9]

Although Freud began to move beyond the simple deduction of female psychology from male psychology by 1925, there is another perhaps even more evident shift in his attitude toward women after the death of his mother in 1930 (when Freud himself is already seventy-four). The death of his father, which at the time had seemed to him to be the most important event in a man's life, had allowed Freud to explore the ambivalence of his feelings toward his male parent. But somehow, as long as his mother lived, Freud seemed to be inhibited from really confronting and owning up to his ambivalence toward her. As Peter Gay observes, there is no evidence that in his self-analysis Freud ever explored "this weightiest of attachments." Consequently, it is not surprising that he "exiled mothers to the margins of his case histories"[10] and that there is something clearly "off" in his theoretical reflections about women—an overt appreciation, a not so hidden denigration, an unwillingness to explore the fear of fusion. He acknowledged to several friends the unexpected liberation he felt at this mother's death; for one thing, he (who had suffered so painfully from his own cancer for the preceding seven years) now felt free to die, as he had not while she lived (perhaps remembering how unbearable it had been for him to have a daughter and a grandson die out of the generational order). He also spoke of a "shifting" at the deepest layers—as though some of his resistance to his own femininity were released at last.

I believe we can see some of the effects of this shifting in the two important essays about women published after his mother's death, the 1931 "Female Sexuality" and the 1933 essay on "Femininity" in the *New Introductory Lectures*. Yet it is also true, as Sarah Kofman notes, that

> the more he abandons parallelism and symmetry between girls and boys, the more he shores up the initial "identity" and proclaims the primacy of the phallus. . . . The privileging of the male model continues to impose itself upon Freud at a time when, after the revolutionary discovery of the wholly other, he ought to have been proceeding with a methodological revolution. . . . [Instead] he continues to give his account of sexuality the "benefit" of lengthy discussions of male sexuality, which remains the referent and standard for what is said to lack any common standard.[11]

Freud seems to be blocked from integrating the full implications of his own insights because of his participation in the modes of thinking encouraged by the male separation experience—antithetical, normative, hierarchical—and because of his failure fully to acknowledge the ambivalence inherent in the male's relation to the mother.

He remarks in the first of these late essays that he had long ago given up any expectation of a neat parallelism between the psychology of men and of women. The discovery of the signal importance of the phase in a girl's life before she forms an attachment to her father, the pre-Oedipal phase in which the mother dominates, he sees as comparable in its significance to the discovery of the Minoan-Mycenaean period of Greek history when the most important divine figures were mother goddesses. (Yet by calling it "pre-Oedipal" he is, of course, *still* acting as though the Oedipal period were the truly focal one, still writing as though male experience represents the norm.) He speaks of how dim and elusive this stage is, but wonders if that is because he is a male analyst, wonders whether it would emerge more clearly with a woman analyst, who would be more likely to inspire a transference to the "prehistorical" mother. His representation of this primal mother highlights her fearsomeness: she may devour *or* abandon; and she is the source of the first resented restrictions.

Because of this early same-sex bond, women, Freud suggests, may be more clearly bisexual than men (as in *The Three Essays* he had suggested that the "polymorphous perversity" of infancy may be more easily reaccessed by women than by men [*SE* 7:19]). He reminds us that anything that once was will forever be, that the mother will always remain a primary love-object (that even a woman's husband may be loved more as a mother- than a father-surrogate), that the clitoris will always remain a privileged erotogenous zone. The bisexual strain in women may also make them more predisposed to neurosis in a culture that does not accept it. All men and women seem to be called upon to repress some of their initial bisexuality so that masculinity or femininity may be established, but this may be more difficult for females (especially because in being asked to give up their culturally privileged "masculine" side, they are given double messages).

Culture will call upon the girl to relinquish her "masculinity" and her mother; to turn from an active to a passive sexuality; from the clitoris, which gave her autoerotic pleasure, to the vagina, which represents her dependence on penetration for sexual satisfaction; from mother to father. The girl will respond to these calls in one of three ways. Freud admits that he cannot explain why a particular one gets chosen. Anatomy is *not* destiny. The girl may resign her own active sexuality and "masculine proclivities in other fields" and be defined by inhibition or neurosis. She may rebel and cling to her "masculinity," take on an active life and perhaps become a homosexual. Or she may adopt the "normal," conventionally ascribed "feminine attitude" established at the Oedipal period, marked by a dependence first on father and later on other men, and lavish love on her male children as a substitute for her own relinquished masculinity. (Spoken like a son!) The norm of "femininity" is motherhood—*but* this is seen as the fulfillment of the woman's *masculine* desires.[12]

In the essay on "Narcissism" Freud had suggested that a woman's love of her child is object-love on the masculine model, but there he had seen motherly devotion as a transformation of narcissism. Her child (originally part of her own body) was understood to represent the woman's *self*, not a penis. Even a woman's heterosexuality was viewed as a kind of *self*-love: in loving men women are really loving their own childish "masculine" selves (*SE* 14:89, 90).

One cannot help but notice how in continuing to use the "masculine"/ "feminine" language, Freud takes away at the same moment he gives, denies what he affirms.

Originally, as Freud describes it, the girl's aims toward the mother are both active and passive. She receives the first stimulation of her genitals from her mother's diapering attentions; like her brothers she longs to be able to give her mother a baby (*SE* 21:238–39). A female's earliest erotic fantasies are, he suggests, probably directed at the mother; but she is probably also the one to prohibit her daughter's masturbation. Since the mother both excites and forbids the young girl's sexuality, it is not surprising that the girl's feelings toward her are marked by the ambivalence characteristic of all primary attachments. The girl's transition to love of the father is encouraged by the hostility engendered by the mother's failure to completely satisfy the child's longing for nurturance and affection, by her forbidding autoerotic sexual satisfaction and—Freud still insists—by her not giving her a penis and thus making her an inferior kind of being.

Freud also insists on speaking of this all-powerful mother of infancy as phallic; he writes as though he were himself still in thrall to the male child's fantasies about sexuality, as though they were in some sense "fact." How difficult it seems to be to credit that the mother is loved as a *mother*, as a female, as the birth giver. Freud's view implies that the little girl, in loving the mother as a presumed bearer of a penis, actually continues to be fixated on a single object, when, after discovering her mother's "castration," she turns from her to the father. (As Kofman suggests, it might be true that the girl wants from the father what she first sought from the mother, but that it wasn't the penis either time, but rather something better represented by the breast.)[13] How strange it is for Freud to make the all-power of the mother be "really" male power. It is as though he wants to refute, to refuse, the very insight he's proposing.

Two years later, in his *New Introductory Lectures*, Freud returns to the topic of female sexuality. The real psychological question, he asserts, is "How does a woman develop out of a child with a bisexual disposition?" Clearly, one isn't born but *becomes* a woman. Why do girls turn away from their mothers, and with such hostility, while boys do not (*SE* 22:588)? How does the initial sameness *become* a difference? The insatiability of longing for the mother's love and the consequent ambivalence toward her are there for both girls and boys. Although perhaps the girl's love is originally more intense because of her awareness of her likeness to her mother, and so bound to perish, bound to be more ambivalent. Perhaps also, since she is less likely to perceive her father as a rival with the intensity that boys do, he is less available to her than to her brothers as an object on which to focus her hostile feelings (*SE* 22:234–35). Freud's answer by 1933 is slightly different: girls blame their mothers for their own lack of a penis—or rather, for loving their sons more than they love their daughters.

Again Freud mentions the three possible outcomes of female psychosexual development and says that constitutional factors seem to determine which is chosen. He suggests also that the establishment of "normal femininity" is always tentative, that most women seem to alternate all through their lives between two currents, the feminine and the masculine one. Thus "normal femininity" seem to mean staying in touch with one's given bisexuality, remaining fluid in one's sexual definition.

Freud's own ambivalence about the pre-Oedipal mother also informs what he writes about the differences between the adult psychologies of men and women. He acknowledges that the formation of the male superego is based on the fear of punishment, on the threat of castration. He sees that female psychology is not fear-based, and that consequently the female superego is "never so inexorable, so impersonal, so independent of its emotional origins as we require it to be in men." It follows that women "show less sense of justice than men, that they are less ready to submit to the great exigencies of life, that they are more influenced in their judgments by feelings of affection or hostility" (*SE* 19:257–58). Women, he says in one place, are weaker in their social interests and have less capacity for sublimation (*SE* 22:134). Yet elsewhere he notes that women are more open than men to "aim-inhibited sexuality," to focusing on affectional rather than genital expression (*SE* 19:179). This suggests that there may be different modes of sublimation, that women may be drawn to forms of sublimation where the relation to the personal, the concrete and embodied, the emotional, is more palpable, and may be less drawn to more abstract, more "spiritual" forms of sublimation. In *Civilization* Freud acknowledges that in the beginning women "laid the foundations of civilization by their claims of love," but later become a retarding influence because they hold on to the priority of family and sexual life (*SE* 21:103). Freud judges the female attitude to be inferior, yet it is not difficult to accept much of the description and reverse the evaluation. (This is, in a sense, what Carol Gilligan has done in *In a Different Voice*. Similarly, in *Freud, Women and Morality* Eli Sagan emphasizes the central importance for human life of "the moral virtues that we learn from the pre-oedipal mother: nurturance, pity, compassion, love, conscience.")[14]

The difficulty Freud has in admitting that daughter-mother love may *really* be the female-female love it appears to be is paralleled by the contortions visible in his attempts to explain the etiology of female homosexuality. Although he recognizes the importance of that first same-sex attachment, he still suggests that female homosexuality arises not as a direct continuation of it but only via disappointment in the father. Forced to relinquish her object-love for him, she identifies with him and thus "returns to her masculinity complex" (*SE* 19:256). When Freud suggests that the relationship between two women lovers may be modeled more on the mother-child relation than on the husband-wife relation, we wonder: is he really imagining a girl loving a "phallic" mother in a "masculine" mode? Is he reinterpreting *female homosexuality* as "really" *male homosexuality*? Luce Irigaray believes this to be the case: "Nothing of the special nature of desire *between women* has been unveiled or stated. That a woman might desire a woman 'like' herself, someone of the 'same' sex . . . is simply incomprehensible to Freud, and indeed inadmissable."[15] Perhaps. But perhaps Freud glimpses a little more than he admits.

Freud is struggling. Relinquishing the privileged position the male accords the penis is difficult. Yet in his last major writing, the posthumously published *Outline of Psychoanalysis*, Freud recognizes that "the mother is the prototype of all later love relationships for both sexes" (*SE* 23:188). In "Femininity" he *does* recognize that the homosexual current is likely to be stronger in women than in men because it is connected to the earliest experiences of nurturance and sensual satisfaction. He sees also that there is something askew at the very heart of heterosexuality—that the husband looks to his wife for a mothering that she gives her son. In *Civilization and Its Discontents* Freud spoke of men as more dependent on women than women are on men; women love men in order to have a child—that is, they *use* men (*SE* 21:99).

Much earlier, in his essay on narcissism, Freud had suggested that women are more self-sufficient than men, that object-love seems less necessary to them, that they are more likely to love on the narcissistic than the "anaclitic" model. Freud concludes from this that they aim more at *being* loved than at loving; but perhaps that conclusion is a projection, expressing the male hope that women do need men despite their acknowledged self-sufficiency. Perhaps what Freud calls women's "narcissism" simply means that a woman is more apt to love another like herself than a member of the other sex.

When Freud reflects on the mystery of sexual identification, on the problem of explaining why some of us become heterosexual in our conscious sexuality and others homosexual, he recognizes the important role played by social expectations and pressures in encouraging us to become heterosexual. He also notes the enormous pull toward heterosexuality in males exerted by the fact that their first experience of love relates them to a heterosexual other, their mother (*SE* 6:229). For women, as Freud himself has so clearly shown, the pull throughout our lives of that first love will direct us to same-sex others.

LESBIAN LIVES

When we turn to those of Freud's case histories that involve women, we will find the same perplexing amalgam. On the one hand he demonstrates profound insight into the central place in women's lives of their infantile attachment to the mother and of their homoerotic relationships later on, while on the other hand he attempts to minimize or hide this dimension of his female patients' lives. It is stunning to discover how often what is said to be most important in a particular case appears only in footnotes or postscripts. (Again: Freud has taught us how to understand such "displacements.")

In Freud's earliest case studies, those included in *Studies on Hysteria*, the theme of homosexuality does not appear. The recognition of the role played by repressed sexuality in the formation of hysterical symptoms was innovation enough in a culture that had sought to repress acknowledgment of the very existence of active female sexual desire. It is not surprising that it did not immediately occur to Freud that this sexuality might be "perverse," or "polymorphous," or "bisexual." Indeed, at the times when *Studies* appeared, he and Fliess had not yet begun to take up the topic of "bisexuality" in their letters or face-to-face meetings, nor had Freud yet become explicitly aware of the homosexual current in his own affectional life.

However, by the time he began to work with the eighteen-year-old female patient whom he wrote of as "Dora," at the end of 1900, bisexuality was very much part of his thinking. His first public theoretical discussion (in *The Three Essays*) appeared almost simultaneously with the publication of this case, *Fragment of an Analysis of a Case of Hysteria,* which he describes as the first *psychoanalytic* case. The hesitations and misdatings connected with this publication, the half-conscious choice of a maidservant's name as the nom-de-plume of his patient, Freud's insistence within the treatment that he knows the truth of Dora's life better than she—all betray the intensity and ambivalence of Freud's investment in this case, what we have learned to call his "countertransference."

Freud himself had come to believe that it was his mishandling of Dora's transference that led to her prematurely breaking off their relationship. Most of the written account focuses on Dora's relationship to her father, who had brought her to Freud, and to Herr K., the husband of her father's mistress, who had made sexual overtures to her that she had passionately rejected. Freud's inability to accept the truth of that rejection betrays his own identification with Herr K. Freud acknowledges the truth in Dora's conviction that her father is ready to hand her over to her suitor so as to assure the continuance of his own affair, but insists—when she tells him how disgusted she had been at fourteen by the close embrace and unsolicited kiss forced on her by a man whom *he,* Freud, found "still quite young and of prepossessing appearance"—that her repugnance was "entirely and completely hysterical" (*SE* 7:38, 29, n. 3). When Freud hears how, two years later, Dora had responded to a lakeside "proposal" from Herr K. with a resounding slap, Freud asserts, "Her behavior must have seemed as incomprehensible to the man after she had left him *as to us*" (46; italics mine). (Indeed, Freud's continued hurt at how Dora later rejected and left *him* is easily discerned between the lines of his retelling.) Freud interprets an appendicitis attack Dora suffers nine months after the scene by the lake as evidence that in her unconscious Dora fantasized that something had really happened, that her unacknowledged wish to be impregnated by Herr K. had been fulfilled.

Although Freud admits that Dora's own associations throughout treatment were always connected with her father (*SE* 7:32), Freud continues to insist that the revival of her love for her father is designed to hide the deeper truth: that she still loves and longs for Herr K. (58, 70, 88). Yet he also recognizes that her hysterical symptoms and suicide note are designed to punish her father for what, despite his protestations to the contrary, she knows full well is his sexual involvement with Frau K. Freud sees that Dora is in love with her father, that she acts "like a jealous wife," and identifies with both her mother and her father's mistress (56). Freud tells Dora that the associations to the first dream worked on in analysis signify that she is ready to give her father the sexual favors her mother withholds. Despite Freud's emphasis on the more recently established relation, the material seems clearly to show that Dora's primary positive heterosexual attachment is directed toward her father.

But then at the very end of the introductory "Clinical Picture" Freud introduces another note—a complication that, he says, he would omit if he were a writer of fiction, an element that will "obscure and efface the outlines of the fine poetic conflict" thus far ascribed to Dora (*SE* 7:59f.): "Behind Dora's supervalent train of thought which was concerned with her father's relations with Frau K. there lay concealed a feeling of jealousy which had that lady as its *object*—a feeling, that is, which could only be based upon an affection on Dora's part for one of her own sex" (60).

He recalls Dora's closeness to a governess and to a female cousin, intimacies that had been broken off as soon as Dora learned these women had befriended her not for her own sake but for her father's. He learned that Dora and Frau K. had long been close, that on visits to the K.'s she had shared Frau K.'s bedroom, that she had been Frau K.'s "confidante and adviser in all the difficulties of married life" (*SE* 7:60), and that she had for many years "given every possible assistance to her father's relations with Frau K." (36). Freud notes how rapturously Dora would speak of Frau K.'s "adorable white body." But when Dora's accusations against Herr K. threatened Frau K.'s affair with Dora's father, the woman had turned against her and "sacrificed her without a moment's hesitation." Freud comes to believe that this betrayal—the betrayal by the *woman* she loved—is for Dora the most wounding of all. In Freud's view Dora's homosexual love for Frau K. was "in a deeper sense [more] unconscious" than her love for her father or Herr K.; she had used her protestations of love for her father to conceal from herself the pain inflicted on her by "the woman she loved" (62–63). (Typically, Freud speaks of this current of Dora's sexual feeling as "masculine, or more properly speaking, *gynaecophilic.*" Here, as still in 1932, the *active* dimension of *female* sexuality is described as somehow *masculine.*)

This homoerotic current of Dora's feelings is almost completely ignored for the next fifty pages of the case history, pages that are devoted to an analysis of two dreams in which it is again Dora's feelings toward Herr K. and her father that are explored. Toward the end of this section, in a footnote, Freud surmises that Dora's extensive knowledgeability of sexual matters may have had an *oral* source: Frau K. This is intriguing because Dora had earlier let Freud know that though she knew her father was impotent, she also knew "that there was more than one way of obtaining gratification" (*SE* 7:47). Freud writes as though he takes it for granted that she is thinking of fellatio. But one wonders, as one reads the footnote, which so unnecessarily underlines *oral*, whether he may not now himself recognize that

Dora might have been thinking of cunnilingus, of "another way" in which a *woman* might obtain gratification—from a man or from another woman. (Recognition of the female-female aspect appears less directly, less consciously, in his suggestion that in fellatio the sucked penis is a substitute for the long ago relinquished nipple.) For Freud concludes two sentences later: "Behind the almost limitless displacements which were thus brought to light, it was possible to divine the operation of a single simple factor—Dora's deep-rooted homosexual love for Frau K." (105). In yet another footnote a few pages later he returns to the theme, to the "mostly deeply buried thoughts—those relating to her love for Frau K.," as he reflects on the significance of Dora's having identified with a male dream figure.

A "Postscript" follows and in it yet another footnote: "The longer the interval of time that separates me from the end of this analysis, the more probable it seems to me that the fault lay in this omission: I failed to discover in time and to inform the patient that her homosexual (gynaecophilic) love for Frau K. was the strongest undercurrent in her unconscious life" (*SE* 7:120). The relegation of these discussions of "the most important factor" to footnotes is stunning. It is surely connected to Freud's own discomfort with his discovery. Although he missed working with it, he is clearly comfortable about acknowledging Dora's transference of her heterosexual feelings for Herr K. and her father on to him. Freud also barely conceals how easily he identifies with these two men and how much countertransference is involved in his attempts to find the "key" to Dora's secrets, to penetrate her unconscious. He even recognizes the homosexual dimension of the way in which Dora's father hands over his daughter first to Herr K. and then to Freud— and includes a completely gratuitous appreciation of the important social functions accorded male homosexuality "by a people so far our superiors in cultivation as were the Greeks" while defending his discussion of sexual matters with his female patient. How strongly, however, he resists his *identification* with Dora,[16] the possibility that she might have also transferred onto him her feelings for Frau K.[17] and any exploration of her feelings for her mother.

What is most striking in Freud's account is his failure to give any consideration to the possibility that the truly "strongest undercurrent" in Dora's feelings might have involved not Frau K. but rather her mother. This woman is pushed to the far margins of Freud's account. He describes her as foolish, frigid, and obsessed with household tasks. According to Dora, she and her mother had for long been on unfriendly terms; she describes her mother in mercilessly disparaging tones, and Freud never questions her about the more hidden dimensions of her feelings. When he learns that it was to her mother that Dora first confided about Herr K.'s proposal, Freud asks no questions.

Nevertheless he has, in large part by way of his footnotes and digressions, succeeded in rendering an illuminating account of the fluidity of sexual identification: the "normal Oedipal plot" of the main text is disrupted by Dora's bisexuality. She wants to be and have everyone, to love both men and women and to be loved by both.

Almost twenty years intervened between the time of Freud's work with Dora and his writing another case study devoted to a female patient. All the case histories involving men that we reviewed in Chapter 4 were composed during this interval. In 1915 he did publish a ten-page account of a case involving a woman with whom he met only twice, "A Case of Paranoia Running Counter to the Psycho-Analytical Theory of the Disease" (*SE* 14:263–72). He became interested in the case because, as the title suggests, the woman's paranoia involved fantasies about a *male* persecutor and so seemed to challenge Freud's theory about the homosexual etiology of paranoia. Not too surprisingly, Freud soon learned that in actuality the "persecutor" was the patient's close-binding mother, and that she had sought unsuccessfully to escape from this homosexual attachment by forming a relationship with a man (though Freud acknowledges that the transposition of gender is unusual in the development of paranoid delusions). In a rather dilute sense the case involves female homosexuality, but it adds little to our understanding of lesbian love or of Freud's views of it.

In 1920 Freud wrote his last major case history, "The Psychogenesis of a Case of Homosexuality in a Woman." Though twenty years have intervened since "Dora," Freud has not yet come to the explicit recognition of the importance of the pre-Oedipal attachment to the mother, which we discussed in the first section of this chapter. There are many parallels between Dora and the young woman of the later account. Once again we have an eighteen-year-old girl brought to Freud by her father and a treatment interrupted long before Freud believes the analysis complete. But there is a difference: in this instance homosexuality is the presenting problem—at least in the eyes of the father. In the eyes of the daughter there is no problem.

Freud begins by noting that homosexuality in women, no less common than in men though "much less glaring," has been ignored by law and neglected by psychoanalysis. He makes clear that he had communicated to the parents how unlikely it was that analysis would lead the young woman to change her sexual orientation. The most, he tells them, that analysis can sometimes achieve is the restoration of full bisexual function. In the present instance the analysis lasted only long enough for Freud to construct some hypotheses concerning the genesis of the daughter's homosexuality but not for her to get actively enough involved in the work to confirm or correct his inferences.

Freud says explicitly: "The girl was not in any way ill (she did not suffer from anything in herself, nor did she complain of her condition)" (*SE* 18:150). Her parents were distressed by the passionate and public way in which she was pursuing a "society lady" about ten years her senior who was known to be involved in a lesbian relationship with a married woman. They saw their daughter's infatuation as but a more intense continuation of earlier attachments to members of her own sex. The mother, who, as the girl saw it, was much more involved with her three sons than with their older sister, was, so it seemed, much less upset than the father. "There was something about his daughter's homosexuality that aroused the deepest bitterness in him, and he was determined to combat it with all his power" (149).

Freud soon learned that, although the girl's feelings were passionately homoerotic and she felt "she could not conceive of any other way of being in love" (*SE* 18:153), she had had but little homo*sexual* experience in the literal physical sense: some kisses, some embraces, but no genital contact. Indeed, the current object of her love had allowed her no more than a kiss on the hand. Freud also makes a point of noting that the girl was beautiful and feminine in her physical appearance; though, he says, some might describe her mental acuity and objectivity as "masculine." He himself speaks of her active "masculine" attitude toward her female beloved.

As Freud uncovers her history, he discovers that until she was sixteen the young woman had been close to her father and that in early adolescence she had taken a motherly interest in a neighbor's three-year-old son. But she turned away from the boy and began her attachments to a series of young mothers of small children—at just the time her mother gave birth to a third son. This time Freud is clear—or at least seems to be—about the central role played by the *mother*. "The analysis revealed beyond all shadow of doubt that the lady-love was a substitute for—her mother" (*SE* 18:156). Freud is impressed by how closely his patient's erotic behavior corresponded to that of "a special type of choice of object made by men" on the basis of an unworked-through mother attachment. She courted women of bad reputation and unavailable women and had "rejected without any question the willing advances made by a homosexual friend of her own age" (161). In this case of a woman whose conscious sexual orientation had from early on been homosexual, Freud affirms that her homosexuality is "probably a direct and unchanged continuation of an infantile fixation on the mother" (168).

But Freud is also quick to note that her latest love's slender, severe beauty also reminded the girl of her favorite brother and thus "combined satisfaction of the homosexual tendency with that of the heterosexual one"—and then goes on to say that her turn to women was really motivated by anger at her *father*, for letting her "unconsciously hated rival, her mother," bear him the child that she herself had longed to give him. Furious at this betrayal, she had turned from him and from men in general. Freud believes that the girl's repudiation of her father reappeared in the analytic transference; in resisting treatment the patient "transferred to me the sweeping repudiation of men which had dominated her ever since the disappointment she had suffered from her father" (*SE* 18:164). Freud says that he had recommended that if she were to continue treatment it should be with a woman.

Thus it once again appears that for Freud the relation to the father is the decisive one. It seems as though for Freud the *repressed heterosexuality* is what requires uncovering in a case of *manifest homosexuality*. This is, of course, consistent with his general emphasis on the latent, the unconscious; yet one feels there is more to it than that. It seems to be important to Freud to establish that female love is "really" heterosexual, that the father be the most important figure in this woman's psychology, as Freud had asserted him to be in the male cases considered in Chapter 4. The same concerns that lead Freud to insist on the importance of homosexuality in male psychology lead him to emphasize the importance of *female heterosexuality*.

But perhaps there is another factor at work here as well. Perhaps Freud was sensitized to the influence of fathers on their daughters' sexual orientation by observation of the effects of his own close bond with his youngest daughter. Anna—the daughter whom he identified with Cordelia, Lear's youngest and most devoted daughter, and with Antigone, the daughter who accompanied blind Oedipus through his years of exiled wandering—clearly found it easier to form relationships with women than with men. I am not suggesting that Anna Freud was a lesbian in the explicitly physical sense but only taking account of Freud's awareness that her primary attachments (other than her attachment to him) were to women. He sensed that her repudiation of other men was connected to her closeness to him.

When Anna is only nineteen Freud tells her that, unlike her sisters, she has "more intellectual interests and will not be quite so satisfied with some purely feminine activity." That same year he writes Ernest Jones: "She does not claim to be treated as a woman, being still far away from sexual longings." As Peter Gay notes: "Freud's denial of his daughter's sexuality is transparently out of character; it reads like the surfacing of a wish that his little girl remain a little girl—*his* little girl."[18] From 1918 to 1921, and again in 1924, Anna undertook analysis with Freud as her analyst; from the time of his first cancer operation in 1923 onward she became his nurse at home and his voice in the outside world.

By 1921 Freud had become concerned about her emotional isolation. He wrote his friend Lou Andreas-Salomé (the intimate of Nietzsche and Rilke who had entered the psychoanalytical circle a decade earlier), "Inhibited on the male side, she has so far had a good deal of bad luck with women friends," and told another friend, "Anna has a comprehensible thirst for friendships with women."[19] In response to Freud's urging, Lou Salomé and Anna developed a close association, "one of the few intimate friendships of Anna's life."[20] Salomé gave Anna support and encouragement in her early analytical practice and writing and served the younger woman as a model of how a woman might combine intellectual power and emotional warmth. But Anna Freud was only twenty-five, Lou Salomé already over sixty, when they first met; Salomé could not satisfy Anna's longing for an intimate *peer.*

Freud's concern was not assuaged. In 1924 he wrote Salomé: "The child gives me enough worries: how will she bear the lonely life [after my death]?" He doubts "whether I can drive her libido from the hiding place into which it has crawled." A little later he writes again: "I am afraid that her suppressed genitality may some day play her a mean trick. I cannot free her from me, and nobody is helping me with it."[21]

In 1925 a divorced American heiress, Dorothy Burlingham, came to Vienna to do analysis with Freud. Her children were among Anna Freud's first patients and the two women soon became intimate friends. Burlingham moved into the apartment above the Freuds at 19 Bergasse in 1928 and lived there until she and the Freuds emigrated to London in 1938. In 1930 she and Anna bought a weekend cottage outside Vienna together, and after Freud's death Burlingham lived with Anna Freud in Maresfield Gardens until her own death in 1979. The two women directed the Hampstead Child Therapy Course and Clinic and the Hampstead Nurseries together and published joint writings.[22]

Freud seems to have been pleased that his daughter had found a friend with whom she could share so much of her life. One wonders whether he ever saw any parallels between Anna Freud's attachment to Burlingham and his own to Fliess. One wonders also at the silence surrounding this relationship within the psychoanalytic community.[23] Intimacy between women seems to be invisible—or so taboo as to be unmentionable.

Before the digression about Anna Freud, we were discussing the young homosexual woman who was the subject of Freud's last case history. We have already noted that Freud wrote no case histories during the period subsequent to his discovery of the "Minoan-Mycenaean" mother-dominated period, which precedes the Oedipal period in infantile development. In 1933 and 1934, however, the Imagist poet H.D. came to work with Freud and left us her report of their sessions—a case history from a patient's viewpoint.

For H.D., Freud was an old hermit living on the edge of the great forest of the unknown; an old owl sitting quietly in a tree listening; the blameless physician, Asclepius; a lonely old man who complains, "You do not think it worth your while to love me"; Cerberus, guardian of the gates of the underworld; a thief who nonchalantly unlocks vaults and takes down barriers that generations have carefully built; an old Janus; midwife to the soul; Faust, the alchemist.

H.D. had many important relationships with men—with Ezra Pound, Richard Aldington, D. H. Lawrence—but during the 1920s, 1930s, and early 1940s she lived with a woman, Winifred Ellerman. With Ellerman (usually referred to by her pen name, Bryher), she formed an enduring and intense relationship that became the permanent anchor of her life. H.D. never called herself a lesbian (and her daughter, Perdita, says that she believes H.D. and Bryher were "platonic lesbians"),[24] but her poetry and fiction reveal the strong erotic emotions she directed toward Bryher and earlier toward a girlhood friend, Frances Gregg.

Bryher's historical and autobiographical fiction provides powerful images of women rebelling against male-dominated society. H.D.'s writing communicates a more vulnerable image of a woman who felt fragmented and insecure in relationships with men and whole and affirmed in her relationships with women. During the 1920s she wrote several semi-autobiographical novels (*Paint It Today, Asphodel,* and *Her*) in which she explores her passionate feelings for Gregg (and less explicitly for Bryher). None was published in her lifetime, perhaps because of the furor aroused by the appearance of Radclyffe Hall's *Well of Loneliness* in 1928.

In *HERmione*, the most moving of these accounts, H.D.'s persona, Hermione, is nicknamed "Her"—a name that communicates her sense of being an "object" to the young male poet who hopes to marry her. She feels that with him she is playing a role, "Hermione out of Shakespeare," that his kisses "smudge her out," that he wants to make her *his* poem rather than a poet in her own right. But then in Fayne Rabb (the fictional version of Gregg) Her finds a "twin", a "sister" who matches her own hidden and almost lost self, "straight and brave like the maiden Artemis." "Her" becomes a name that signifies her identification with a sisterly alter ego. They are like two huntresses, free in the forest, stirred by mutually felt erotic longing. With this woman Her's ambivalence toward sexuality disappears and brings her to her first confident assertion of her own identity. "I know her. Her. I am Her. She is Her. Knowing her, I know Her. She is some amplification of myself like an amoeba giving birth by breaking off, to amoeba. I am a sort of mother, a sort of sister to Her."[25] This sense of recognition, of sameness, of shared desire, does not threaten Her's poetic creativity but inspires it. Her discovers herself as woman and as poet through her love of this sisterly other.[26]

But outside her fiction H.D. seems to have been more confused by her sexual identity, by the relation between her intense but ambivalent pull to men and her equally passionate attachments to women. Evidently her analysis with Freud helped her to a healing acceptance of her bisexuality. In a poem about Freud she wrote:

> I had two loves separate,
> God who loves all mountains,
> alone knew why
> and understood
> and told the old man
> to explain
>
> the impossible
>
> which he did.[27]

It was Bryher who encouraged H.D. to work with Freud, and he clearly understood and blessed the relationship between the two women. In her account of the analysis H.D. writes: "The Professor had said in the very beginning that I had come to Vienna hoping to find my mother." The images that emerge during her treatment reveal how deep in H.D. lies a longing for fusion, for reunion with the pre-Oedipal mother. Images associated with the sea appear frequently and are often interfused with images of immortality. Her love of mythology and of Greece not only expresses her longing for connection to a lost timeless world but is explicitly connected to her mother. "The shrine of Helios (Hellas, Helen) has really been my main objective. . . and my mother's name was Helen." Much of the analysis focuses on the interpretation of a visionary experience H.D. had had years earlier in Corfu, when she and Bryher had gone to Greece together at the very beginning of their relationship. Freud understood the mystical dimensions of that vision—which both fascinated and terrified H.D.—as "a desire for union with the mother." The longing lies close to consciousness. "*If* one could stay near her always, there would be no break in consciousness. . . . One can never get near enough."[28]

In her analysis H.D. came to a kind of reconciliation with that mother longing—and to a renewal of her own creative impulse. Freud helped her reenter "the chasms or gulfs where the ancient dragon lives." Mother and Freud become strangely interfused. "Vienna? Venice? My mother came here on her honeymoon."

> The Professor's surroundings and interests seem to derive from my mother rather than from my father, and yet to say the 'transference' is to Freud as mother does not altogether satisfy me. He had said, 'And—I must be frank with you (you were frank with me and I will be frank with you), I do *not* like to be the mother in transference—it always surprises and shocks me a little. I feel so very masculine.' I asked him if others had what he called this mother-transference on him. He said ironically and I thought a little wistfully, 'O, *very* many.'[29]

Thus in these last years, after his mother's death, Freud knows to look for the mother, and is able (though a little regretfully) to accept a mother transference. The Freud whom H.D. came to know, who helped her change her inner relation to her long-dead mother, to the complexities of her own sexual impulse, and to the feminine source of her poetic creativity, was able to help her find access to regions he himself could only dimly glimpse.

·6·

JUNG:
THE PERSONAL DIMENSION

Freud makes us aware of how wounded we all are in our sexuality; how compelled we are by our longings for love, safety, and autonomy; how ambivalently bound we are to our mothers and fathers. He brings us in touch with how all-demanding, how insatiable, how contradictory are the hungers that most stir our bodies and souls. He reminds us how *alike* we all really are—how superficial, how almost accidental, the overt differences among us are when we regard them from a *depth* psychological perspective. In his view homosexuality and heterosexuality are equally valid—and flawed—paths.

Carl Jung makes us aware of how we use and misuse sex to express our deepest longings, which are really soul longings; how we ask of sexuality what it cannot give. He tries to wean us from our identification with our bodies and from our dependence on others and to help us discover the universal, the mythic, the archetypal significance of our embodied existence. He is more optimistic than Freud about the possibility of transcending our woundedness, more persuaded that homosexuality is a corrigible misunderstanding. Jung recognizes that homosexuality is an archetype—as its persistence and universal prevalence, the sense of its being a *given* (biologically based "inborn") destiny, and its *compelling* (that is, numinous) character confirm.[1] But to his mind the archetype is misunderstood when taken to imply literal homosexuality, for its real meaning is not sexual but spiritual; it signifies the longing to be a complete, whole self.

We must also admit from the beginning that homosexuality plays a much less salient role in the psychology of Jung than in that of Freud. This is true both of his personal psychology and of his psychological theory. In part this is simply because sexuality as such figures so much less centrally in his understanding of the psyche. Where Freud sees sexuality as the hidden meaning of many manifest images and activities, Jung sees manifest sexual images and desires as symbolic of spiritual longings. "One can say that a church spire is a phallic symbol, but what is it when you dream of a penis?"[2] "The phallus is not just a sign that indicates the penis," he says. "It is a 'symbol' because it has so many other meanings" (*CW* 10:337, n. 3). Thus what interests Jung in homosexuality is its archetypal meaning: from his perspective literal homosexuality is a misdirected attempt at initiation into adulthood; symbolically, homosexuality is connected to age-old images of human wholeness. Jung offers us an exploration of the *psychical* significance of same-sex love. He sees it as a symbolic expression of profoundly important human longings.

With Jung as with Freud, I believe the characteristic themes of his psychological theory can be illumined by his personal history. Theory is always to a degree autobiography. Therefore I propose to begin exploring Jung's understanding of homosexuality by seeking the childhood roots of his theoretical emphasis on the mother archetype, his assumption that mature sexuality will be contrasexual, and his seeing psychic androgyny as a privileged model of inner wholeness.

Admittedly, this means beginning our consideration of Jung by looking through Freudian lenses; but Jung himself agreed that we must often confront the personal unconscious, the subjective dimension of experience, before proceeding to consider what interests him most: the archetypal dimension.

THE UNDERGROUND PHALLUS

As we turn to look at experiences in Jung's life that might be relevant to his theoretical understanding of sexuality, and particularly of homosexuality, these lines to Freud from a letter written about seven months after their first meeting provide an obvious starting point:

> My veneration for you has something of the character of a "religious" crush. Though it does not really bother me, I still feel it is disgusting and ridiculous because of its undeniable erotic undertone. This abominable feeling comes from the fact that as a boy I was the victim of a sexual assault by a man I once worshipped. . . .
> This feeling, which I still have not quite got rid of, hampers me considerably. Another manifestation of it is that I find psychological insight makes relations with colleagues who have a strong transference to me downright disgusting. *I therefore fear your confidence.* (49J; emphasis in original)

As far as I know, none of Jung's biographers has sought to investigate the historical basis of this childhood memory. Indeed, most have ignored it.[3]

Nor does his autobiography, *Memories, Dreams, Reflections,* provide clues as to who the man might have been or when the assault might have occurred. But there are other childhood remembrances that suggest that as a young man Jung found male sexuality both fearful and numinously attractive.

In writing his autobiography at eighty-three, Jung confesses that he has "never fully unwound the tangle" of his earliest memories: "They are like individual shoots of a single underground rhizome, like stations on a road of unconscious development" (*MDR,* 27). Without pretending to be able to map out all the connections, it seems worthwhile to look at some of these individual shoots.

Jung himself believed that our relation to the a priori images of our parents that live in our psyches irrespective of the nuances of individual experience— what he calls the mother and father archetypes—shapes us more profoundly than do the idiosyncratic features of our childhood history. He also affirms that his early awareness of the evident fallibility of his father, his early (though temporary) abandonment by his mother, may have protected him from being caught, as he believes Freud was, in a literalization of the Oedipus complex, that is, from confusing the father and mother of his deepest fantasies with those inadequate stand-ins, his natural parents.

Still, it is interesting that Jung's earliest recollections of physical affection involve his father rather than his mother. He remembers a very early scene in which as a sick and restless child he was carried in his father's arms and sung to in the stillness of the night (*MDR,* 8). He also recalls that a few years later his father came into his room one night and woke him. Again carrying his son in his arms, he brought him outside so that they might together watch the magical panorama of a shimmering sky turned green by a distant volcanic eruption. All the memories of his earliest years show that as a child Jung felt more intimate and safe with his father than with his mother, whom he felt to be unpredictable and mysterious—perhaps because of her disappearance when he was three. (She had some kind of breakdown and was hospitalized for several months.) Jung writes that the relation between his parents when he was a child was so tense that the atmosphere of the house was often "unbreathable."

Despite their early closeness, before he reached adolescence Jung had come to despise his pastor father as weak and powerless, as drained of all vital energy by an inner uncertainty of his own religious faith, which he was unwilling to risk acknowledging even to himself. Eugene Monick believes that his wife's sexual rejection may have helped to undermine the self-confidence of the elder Jung.[4] Monick also suggests that a father like Jung's "who has lost the power and raw energy of chthonic phallos would in turn deny it to the son," thus relating Jung's later emphasis on the mother to his father's impotence. "By default when the father abrogates masculine authority it goes to the mother and the son is left by himself to fend in a hostile maternal environment."[5]

I cannot help wondering whether it was simply a question of the father's weakness, or whether the homosexual assault mentioned in Jung's letter to Freud may not also have played a part in turning Jung from his father—and in leaving him somewhat wounded in his capacity to relate to men in later life.[6] Part of what later attracts Jung to Freud is that he finds him embodying the imago of the powerful father as his own father could not; but part of what makes him resistant to Freud is his fear of the homosexual current of his own feelings that are stirred up in their relationship.

Although so much of his later theory will be mother-focused, Jung tells us in his autobiography that all his life he has been preoccupied with an image first introduced in a childhood dream—the image of a phallus. The dream (which he says is the earliest one he remembers, dreamt between the ages of three and four) began with his discovering a dark rectangular hole in the middle of a meadow. Peering in, he saw a stone staircase, which he fearfully began to descend. At the bottom was a green-curtained arch. Pushing the curtain aside, he found himself in a dimly lit stone chamber with a red carpet running from the entrance to a low platform on which sat a magnificent gold throne. Standing on the throne was a mysterious object that he at first took to be a tree trunk—twelve to fifteen feet high, about two feet thick, made of skin and naked flesh. On top there was something like a rounded head with no face but only a single eye gazing motionlessly upward. Above the head was an aura of brightness. "The thing did not move, yet I had the feeling that it might at any moment crawl off the throne like a worm and crawl toward me. I was paralyzed with terror. At that moment I heard from outside and above me my mother's voice. She called out, 'Yes, just look at him. That is the man-eater'" (*MDR*, 11–15).

Jung says that this dream haunted him for years. "Only much later did I realize that what I had seen was a phallus, and it was decades before I understood that it was a ritual phallus." In the interpretation of this dream offered by the octogenarian Jung he says that "the abstract significance of the phallus is shown by the fact that it was enthroned by itself, 'ithyphallically'" (upright) and that the underground chamber was a temple. The phallus was a "subterranean God 'not to be named'"—an underground counterpart to the Jesus worshiped in his father's church. "Through this childhood dream I was initiated into the secrets of the earth," into a chthonic spirituality. Jung believes that the dream introduced him to the creative and generative power that can be found *within*, in the depths of the unconscious.

Without denying the validity of Jung's understanding of the dream, we may reflect that the phallus is also a penis. The overtly sexual significance was ignored not just by Jung but by most of his followers. For instance, Marie Louise von Franz tells us that "a volume could be written about this mysterious dream symbol, so laden with meanings." She reminds us that to the Romans the phallus symbolized a man's "genius," his creative power and joy in life. She associates the phallus with Eros, god of love, and Telesphorus, a god of inner transformation, with Osiris, as a god of resurrection, and with Hermes, as a psychopomp—but not with male sexuality.[7] Jung himself writes that he does "not know where the anatomically correct phallus can have come from," but as Monick suggests, he may well at some point have seen his father's penis "and found it huge"; Jung may also have understood his mother's cry, "That is the man-eater," as related to her fear of her husband's sexuality. The dream may at least at one level have been about Jung's anxiety about his own sexuality, his concern about the tensions between his parents and his own relation to them.[8]

But I am also struck that it communicates Jung's awe before masculine, phallic power. The mythological interpretation Jung offers is not just evasion but also recognition: it honors the full mysterious significance of what led Freud to his emphasis on "castration anxiety," how the erect male organ carries the psychological significance of the male's Self. It sees the penis as a ritual phallus "transforming the male emblem of gender identification into inner symbol," "a primal symbolic presence able to stand on its own." As Monick puts it:

> Physical phallos has become a religious and psychological symbol because it decides on its own, independent of its owner's ego decision, when and with whom it wants to spring into action. It is thus the appropriate metaphor for the unconscious itself, and specifically the masculine mode of the unconscious. . . . Unless phallos is lodged independently in the depths of the unconscious, there is no masculine source to which a man can resort and depend upon as he moves beyond [identification with] the ego.[9]

Freud, too, was persuaded that sex is always more than just sex, but Jung highlights the *more* (perhaps at the cost of remembering that it is also "just sex"). Freud communicated, albeit indirectly, his recognition of the numinous power of sexuality; Jung made that power focal.

In *Memories* Jung recounts another early memory that seems revelatory of his ambivalent relation to male sexuality. He tells us of carving a little manikin that he hid in a pencil case along with an oblong black stone and secreted behind an attic roof beam. Reflecting on the importance of this secret in the light of years devoted to the study of myth and symbol, he speaks of the stone as an image of the life force hidden in a *kista*—an allusion to the basket carried in Dionysian processions whose mysterious hidden content was probably a snake representing the phallus. (Nor Hall proposes a further association, that *kista* implies a punning relation to *kustos*, cunt.)[10] Jung calls the manikin a *kabir* and thus connects it to the Cabiri of Greek ritual tradition, male deities associated with the Great Mother, who were symbolized by the male organ of generativity and worshiped as embodying the power of underworld fertility.

Thus, as the amplifications attest, this memory, too, refers to the powerful hold phallic imagery had over the young Jung's imaginal life. Again, the phallicism is secret, mysterious, hidden. As Daniel Noel says: "In one sense, of course, Jung's orientation to this psychic energy was necessarily masculine. But if the creative power thrusting up out of the eternally uncreated . . . was for Jung clearly phallic, it seems never to have been entirely unveiled. That is, we can see the phallic self-image of C. G. Jung as *essentially* 'hermetic,' as a secret, undisclosed."[11]

Aniela Jaffe notes how at the end of the dream of the underground phallus the mother calls on the boy to stay in her realm and avoid contact with the phallic father, who could be creative for masculine growth. Jaffe warns: "If he were to yield to this maternal temptation, a perilous venture would not be undertaken, a destiny would go unfulfilled." The danger the mother represents is as great as that posed by the phallus. Jaffe sees Jung in this childhood dream as suspended between opposites, between the pull to creativity represented by the phallus and the pull to inertia represented by the mother. She reminds us how, a few years later, Jung (as he tells us in *Memories*) was rescued from a childhood neurosis by the voice of his father, worrying over the future of a young boy apparently lost in passivity. Although Jaffe sees the danger of Jung's choosing the mother over the phallus, she clearly believes Jung overcame it. Not perhaps in childhood, but later, in the period of sustained exploration of his inner depths that he came to call his "confrontation with the unconscious."[12]

But Monick, like Noel, is less sure. He notes how often in Jung phallus remains hidden, remains in the underground chamber, and believes that the initiation associated with it does not take place. He wonders whether Jung kept the phallus hidden, disguised, because it aroused fears about homosexuality. "For all his stated lifelong preoccupation with his childhood dream, Jung did not write much about phallos per se. He subsumed it in his investigation of the phallic gods . . . particularly Hermes-Mercurius . . . a god-image filled with spirit, *logos spermatikos,* the seminal word that enlivens psyche." The difficulty, as Monick sees it, is that Jung so identifies the unconscious with the mother "that at the primordial level there is no father." Jung recognizes no primal ground for an archetypal phallus in the psyche.

Noting again that "Jung's avoidance of focused attention upon male sexuality is [not] congruent with the importance he attached to the ritual phallos of his early dream," Monick suggests: "It may be that Jung could afford to examine phallos only from the distance afforded him by his interest in symbolic referents." Monick here is approaching what, I too, see as a limitation in Jung's theory and one that seems determined at least in part by his childhood experience. Jung's differentiation between the physical and archetypal dimensions of sexuality is an important contribution; his tendency wholly to divorce them is, however, to my mind, a regrettable denial of their fluid interplay. Jung seems to identify genital phallic masculinity with the body and to see all that is body as subordinate to the mother. "True masculine identity can be established only by denial of physical phallos . . . only by translating [it] into symbol."[13]

Jung says he never spoke of the phallus dream to anyone until he was sixty-five. "A strict taboo hung over all these matters. . . . My entire youth can be understood in terms of this secret" (*MDR,* 41). Yet though Jung talks about childhood secrets, his account gives little sense that his childhood is hidden from himself. There are no discussions of screen memories, of obscuring revisions or omissions, no hints of memories accessed only through interpretation or reconstruction. We have no indication that he saw anything problematical in the almost lifelong secrecy that surrounded this dream image.

We can, however, discern signs of his lifelong preoccupation with the phallus dream. A letter to Freud reveals that Knight's *Essay on the Worship of Priapus* inspired the investigations culminating in *The Psychology of the Unconscious,* in which Jung first articulates his own approach to depth psychology. In many of his writings he relates the single experience that most convinced him that archetypes reappear spontaneously (without benefit of cultural transmission): a psychotic patient's fantasy about the solar phallus duplicated precisely a phallic image contained in an ancient Mithras ritual. During Jung's later alchemical period the phallic images of the philosopher's tree and the ithyphallic chthonic psychopomp, Hermes-Mercurius, continued to play a central role.

Von Franz says that Jung and Freud were both gripped by the same mythical theme, the phallic god, but that when it came to interpretation of that central power in the unconscious, they had to take different paths (which led to very different understandings of sexuality and homosexuality).[14] Or, as Jaffe puts it, each in the end had to follow his own daimon.[15]

IN CLOUD-CUCKOO-LAND

It is not surprising that the relationship between Jung and Freud should be charged with archetypal energy. Jung told Freud how powerfully his "complexes" were aroused at their first face-to-face meeting. The feelings associated with his childhood dream and the memory of the childhood abuse were both stirred up in the relationship that played such an important role in Jung's life during his early thirties. In finding Freud (a man almost twenty years his senior), he for a time felt he had discovered a true father. Perhaps it was almost fated that in time this father would be rejected for the sake of Jung's unmediated exploration of what both he and Freud, each deeply influenced by Goethe's *Faust*, called "the realm of the Mothers"—that is, the Unconscious. Once again the mother called—and Jung left Freud to write his book on the hero's engagement with the mother and to undertake his exploration of his own inner world.

Perhaps at least in part to counterbalance the feelings stirred by Freud, this was also a time when Jung's *hetero*sexuality became troublesomely activated. In several of his letters to Freud, including the one immediately preceding his admission of the homoerotic dimension of his relationship with Freud, he asks what he should do about women for whom treatment gives "voluptuous pleasure" and leads to indulgence in "sexual fantasies" (48J). In succeeding letters Jung writes Freud about several analytical relationships in which erotic transferences have become problematical. These include the relationship with Sabine Spielrein, in which Jung seems clearly to have encouraged emotional intimacy and erotic fantasies whether or not there was a literal affair,[16] and the beginnings of the lifelong extramarital relationship with his former analysand Toni Wolff.[17] Jung writes that Spielrein has "kicked up a vile scandal solely because I denied myself the pleasure of giving her a child" and admits that through their relationship he has come to a more adequate idea of his own "polygamous components" (133J). He accuses her of having systematically planned to seduce him and seems to take no responsibility for her infatuation. Indeed, Jung comes close to blaming it all on Freud, on the feelings stirred in him by his meeting with Freud. "My first visit to Vienna had a *very* long unconscious aftermath, first the compulsive infatuation in Abbazia, then [Spielrein]" (144J).

Early in his relationship with Toni Wolff Jung writes Freud: "The prerequisite for a good marriage, it seems to me, is the license to be unfaithful"—though this time he doesn't explain to Freud what has aroused Emma Jung's jealousy (175J). In his next letter he indulges in what he later admits was "another of those rampages of fantasy" (180J). He tells Freud that "religion can be replaced only by religion." The real task of psychoanalysis is to "revivify among intellectuals a feeling for symbol and myth, ever so gently to transform Christ back into the soothsaying god of the vine" and again make "the cult and the sacred myth what they once were—a drunken feast of joy where man regained the ethos and holiness of an animal. . . . what infinite rapture and wantonness lie dormant in our religion" (178J). To which Freud not surprisingly replies: "I am not thinking of a substitute for religion; this need must be sublimated" (179F).

By then, of course, the tie to Freud had already begun to loosen. Years later, looking back on the time of his infatuation, Jung sees it all as mistake: "That accursed correspondence [is] for me folly that filled the days of my youth. The journey from cloud-cuckoo-land back to reality lasted a long time."[18] It is almost as though he were proposing that this manifestation of phallus in his life, too, should be hidden, ignored. Yet there is also a nostalgic aspect to the disavowal. Cloud-cuckoo-land, *Schlaraffenland*, may be a fool's paradise but it is a paradise, a land of milk and honey, a land where all one's desires are fulfilled.[19]

As we turn again to the correspondence, looking this time for the clues it provides concerning Jung rather than Freud, we discover that in his very first letter (October 5, 1906) Jung had already indicated his reservations about Freud's emphasis on sexuality (2J); although the reference is obviously to the role sexuality plays in Freud's theory, Jung's words seems to forewarn that he may also want to avoid the sexual dimension between them. One might object that at this point Jung would have had no basis for expecting any kind of intimate connection with Freud. But Vincent Brome suggests that Jung may already have been alluding to an awareness of his homosexual impulses in a letter of December 29, 1906, when the correspondence had newly begun, long before their first meeting. Freud had asked why in a published interpretation of one of Jung's own dreams about an impetuously galloping horse Jung had not interpreted the log the horse was dragging as a penis. Jung responded that the rationalistic interpretation was merely a screen to hide "an illegitimate sexual wish that had better not see the light of day."[20]

In any case, as we have already seen, for a time the relationship between them seems to have been vital and intense on both sides, and from early on to have aroused some fear on Jung's part of being taken over by Freud, a fear that was sexually tinged. He admits that directly in the letter in which he confesses to the sexual assault of his childhood. In the letter that directly follows the "confession" he mentions with evident relief his dreaming of Freud as a very frail old man who therefore poses no sexual danger (50J). Soon after, he communicates being frightened by Freud's analogies between his present relation to Jung and his earlier one to Fliess (72J).

Eventually the relationship becomes intolerable for Jung. His turning away from Freud seems to have become inevitable during the August 1909 trip to Clark University. The eve of their departure was marked by the ominous intrusion of the theme of death wishes. Jung's fascination with local Bremen traditions about some prehistoric mummies upset Freud. He fainted and said he understood all this conversation about corpses as betraying Jung's death wishes toward him (*MDR*, 156). Once on the boat they analyzed each other's dreams, and it was Jung's turn to become upset. First he was furious at Freud's unwillingness to share the personal details that would have allowed full interpretation of a dream of Freud's. Then he was disappointed in Freud's insistence on interpreting at a purely personal level a dream of Jung's that Jung felt referred to a deeper, more collective aspect of the psyche—the aspect he would later call the archetypal unconscious.

In this dream Jung finds himself in the upper story of "his" house, in rooms beautifully furnished in the rococo style. Curious about the lower story, he descended to a darker fifteenth-century series of rooms. Then he opened a heavy door and took the stone staircase down to the cellar, a vaulted room dating back to Roman times. Below that he found a low rock-hewn cave with pottery remnants, scattered bones, and two human skulls lying on the dusty floor.

Jung says that when Freud asked him for his personal associations, he answered with a lie: "It would have been impossible for me to afford him any insight into my mental world" (*MDR*, 160). As C. Jess Groesbeck notes, the language Jung uses in describing this interchange with Freud—"I *resisted* his interpretation," "I *submitted* to his intention," "I *want* his thoughts"—all suggest homosexual wishes or fears. Jung invites and then resists "penetration" by Freud.[21] Jung wants to deny that the dream might include the death wishes toward Freud that Freud understands the skulls to signify, even though very soon afterward he has another dream in which Freud appears as a stooped and vexed old customs official, "one of those who couldn't die properly" (*MDR*, 163).

Jung seems to be uncomfortable admitting that the dream might have personal *and* archetypal significance. He chooses the archetypal meaning as the true one—though in that very choosing he makes the dream signify the imminent end of the relationship. After their return from America Jung begins the immersion in mythology and anthropology that will issue in his *Psychology of the Unconscious*, the book that makes public how very different his interpretation of incest and sexuality is from Freud's. Though Jung may evade full acknowledgment of the personal dimension of his dream, the dream nevertheless leads him to the important new insights articulated in that book. The dream seems also to presage the journey into his own depths that the symbolic "death" of Freud (that is, the death of the relationship) plummets him into. As Jung now begins to venture to "tackle the mother" (300J), it is, of course, impossible to sort through what is cause and what effect—the separation from Freud, the involvement with the Mothers, the turn to a spiritual interpretation of sexuality.

The separation is difficult for Jung. He is at first very unsure of the worth of his own work and uncomfortable about rivalry with Freud. After their return from America, he avoids contact, postpones writing. When he does write, he acknowledges that his delay in writing is a resistance due to a father complex and to his fear that his own work is "garbage." A paragraph devoted to some psychoanalytical organizational business follows and then, with no explicit recognition that this might have anything to do with *his* resistance, Jung writes that he has come to see that "homosexuality is one of the richest sources of resistance in men" (180J).[22] Somewhat later Jung writes Freud about his discomfort with what he takes to be a homosexual dimension in the feelings that Bleuler, the chief of the Burgholzli clinic where he works, has toward him. He speaks of Bleuler asking for help in analyzing a dream of himself nursing his child:

> So now he's becoming a woman. . . . At last he holds *me*, his child, to his breast again. He is dying to be analysed and torments himself with delusional ideas: I haven't the time, reject his love, etc. He does not feel in the least homosexual. Consequently, from love of me, he is turning himself into a woman and wants to behave exactly like a woman, to go along with our Society only *passively*, to be scientifically *fecundated* since he cannot expressly himself *creatively*, he is afraid of being violated. So, for the time being, he won't join chiefly because of homosexual resistance. (220J)

Nothing in the letter suggests that Jung sees any parallels between Bleuler's alleged feelings toward him and his own toward Freud.

As the separation becomes more pronounced, Jung's anger and long-suppressed rage become evident. He writes Freud:

You go around sniffing out all the symptomatic actions in your vicinity, thus reducing everyone to the level of sons and daughters who blushingly admit the existence of their faults. Meanwhile you remain on top as the father, sitting pretty. . . . You see, my dear Professor, so long as you hand out this stuff I don't give a damn for my symptomatic actions; they shrink to nothing in comparison with the formidable beam in my brother Freud's eye. I am not in the least neurotic—touch wood! I have submitted *lege artis et tout humblement* to analysis and am much the better for it. You know, of course, how far a patient gets with self-analysis: *not* out of his neurosis—just like you. (338J)

Freud responds:

It is a convention among us analysts that none of us need feel ashamed of his own bit of neurosis. But one who while behaving abnormally keeps shouting that he is normal gives ground for the suspicion that he lacks insight into his illness. Accordingly, I propose that we abandon our personal relations entirely . . . [by which] you have everything to gain, in view of the remark you recently made in Munich, to the effect that an intimate relationship with a man inhibited your scientific freedom. I therefore say, take your full freedom and spare me your supposed "tokens of friendship." (342F)

The end of the relationship plunges Jung into the long period of psychic disintegration and discovery that he describes as his "Confrontation with the Unconscious" in his autobiography. He was forced to realize that though he had spoken of the living power of myths in *The Psychology of the Unconscious*, he had not yet discovered what myths shaped his own life. During this time he finds himself flooded with dreams, with fantasies that something dead is somehow also still alive.

In one dream as he walked past a whole row of mummified men lying in their graves, each from a century earlier than the preceding, each in turn moved his hands to indicate that he was still living after all. This dream suggested to Jung that he should try to get back in touch with his own dead childhood, that doing so might help him get back in touch with his own inner perspective, so long under submission to Freud's. He began playing in the sand again as he had done as a child and built a village out of rocks and stones. It included a church, of course, which needed an altar. The climax came when Jung found the perfect stone and placed it under the dome of his church. Suddenly he recalled the underground phallus of his childhood dream.

Through this ritualistic playing Jung felt he was beginning to discover his own myth. The journey was actually a long and difficult one; for almost six years Jung devoted himself primarily to inner exploration. At times the psychical material that began to surface almost overwhelmed and destroyed him, but he learned how to work with it. He knew he had to go back underground. One day, he says, he let himself drop. At the end of his fall he found himself entering an underground cave. At its center on a projecting rock was a glowing red crystal, which he lifted. Below it he saw a swiftly flowing stream with the corpse of a blond young man floating past, followed by a black scarab and then a red newborn sun. As he tried to replace the crystal, a jet of blood began to spurt forth. A few days later Jung had a dream in which he kills a blond youth whom he identified as Siegfried and as the heroic ego attitude in himself. As the dreams continued Jung met a young woman named Salome (in some sense a dream image of Toni Wolff, who was such an important support to him during these years), whom he describes as an anima figure, as a personification of his own inner feminine aspect, his soul. Later he met two male dream figures, Elijah and Philemon, inner figures who to a degree take the place of Freud and perhaps of the underground phallus as well.

Jung knew this material was very like that which appears in psychosis and that it was imperative to find ways of bringing it into the world of others. As he did. This stream of lava ends up being the *prima materia* for his life work. When he emerged from this period in the underworld he brought back with him his own theory of the psyche and his own way of practicing psychotherapy.

Attempting to sum up what he learned from Freud, Jung in his autobiography says that throughout his later career he continued to pursue the two questions that had been important to Freud: "archaic vestiges" and sexuality. "My main concern has been to investigate, over and above its personal significance and biological function, [sexuality's] spiritual aspect and its numinous meaning, and thus to explain what Freud was so fascinated by but was unable to grasp" (*MDR*, 168). For Freud, he says, "'sexual libido' took over the role of a *deus absconditus*, a hidden or concealed god. . . . The name alone had changed . . . the lost god had now to be sought below, not above." Although sexuality was undoubtedly a *numinosum* for Freud, Jung believes that he couldn't acknowledge its spiritual dimension. Thus Jung sees Freud as in flight from his own mystical side (*MDR*, 151–52).

·7·

JUNG: THE THEORY

As epigraph to a 1935 essay Jung chose these lines from Virgil's *Aeneid:* "The way downward is easy. Black Dis's door stands open night and day. But to retrace your steps to heaven's air, there is the trouble, there the toil" (*CW* 12:29). The contrast with the Virgilian lines Freud put at the beginning of *Interpretation*, "If I can move no heavenly hearts, I'll rouse the world below," captures the essential difference in their understandings of their life tasks.[1]

SEX AND SYMBOL

In order to contextualize what Jung has to say about homosexuality in his theoretical writing, we must again look first at the role sexuality as such plays in his psychological theory. As we noted in discussing the Freud-Jung correspondence, Jung had from the very beginning of their relationship believed that Freud overemphasized the importance of sexuality and misinterpreted as sexual much that is not, such as a child nursing at the breast or its affectional feelings for its parents. During the time that they were intimate this difference in perspective not only seemed tolerable to both but may have been part of what contributed vitalizing energy to their interchanges. Later, this same disagreement became focal and was understood by both as at the center of the theoretical chasm that had opened between them.

In the *History of the Psychoanalytical Movement*, written to clarify his differences from Adler and Jung, Freud announced that acceptance of the psychoanalytic expansion of the meaning of sexuality was the shibboleth that distinguished its adherents from its detractors. In his 1912 lectures at Fordham, although still giving lip service to the importance of Freud's work, Jung asserted that it was time for psychoanalysis to abandon the sexual definition of libido and, returning to Schopenhauer's equation of libido with the Will, redefine it as generalized psychic energy. Then, in place of polymorphous perversity, we could speak of the polyvalence of the libido. In these lectures there were already clues that Jung would sever body and spirit more than

Freud (for whom "drive" means their inevitable conjunction in human life); that for him our bodies are more animal, our instincts (he uses that term rather than "drive") less malleable. From Jung's perspective libido directed toward spiritual interests is in no sense sexual. Where Freud sees *sublimation*, a redirection of that which is still essentially (because originally) sexual, Jung sees *enantiadromia*, a complete transformation of the instinctual into the spiritual.

The irreconcilable differences in their understanding of libido became publicly visible in Jung's 1912 book *The Psychology of the Unconscious*,[2] in which he introduced an understanding of incest radically different from Freud's. Not only had psychoanalysis begun with Freud's recognition of the shaping power of infantile incestual longing, his discovery of what we have come to call the Oedipus complex, but Jung's quite different depth psychology was given its first articulation as a *reinterpretation* of incest. His letters to Freud make clear that it was upsetting to Jung that Freud should just then have embarked on a project so similar to his own—exploration of the role of the incest taboo in prehistory, which issued in his *Totem and Taboo*. Jung both wanted to have a view of his own and dreaded the break it would make inevitable.

Jung's book uses the fantasies of a young prepsychotic former patient of Theodore Flournoy, "Miss Miller," to provide an organizing structure for his book. He regards these fantasies as the "Ariadne's thread" that will prevent his getting lost in the overwhelming mass of mythological material, which he has assembled in order to show how such age-old images and motifs reappear spontaneously in the modern psyche. The almost casual allusion to Ariadne suggests Jung's identification with Theseus, the hero who dared enter the labyrinth, the realm of the Mother, and at its center found the Minotaur, symbol of Self. I am persuaded that Jung also remembered that in *Oedipus at Colonus* Theseus is the only one allowed to accompany Oedipus to his death, and that it is to Theseus that Oedipus hands on his blessing. For Jung's book opens with a beautiful evocation of his first enthralled reading of *Interpretation of Dreams*. What had most moved him, he tells us, was Freud's retelling of the Oedipus legend in a way that communicated to Jung for the first time the still-living power of myth.

Since then Jung had come to believe that Freud had "succumbed to the numinous effect" of this one image and so had dogmatically reduced all others to it. That is, he sees Freud as recognizing only one archetype—Oedipus—and hopes his book will make us more aware of the polyphony of archetypes.[3]

Jung hopes to show how the images of "the forgotten and long buried primitive mind" can constellate a *collective* unconscious, a heritage potentially present in each of us. He is interested in helping us learn how to think symbolically again. It is the atrophy of this capacity, not sexual repression, that he identifies as the real neurosis of the modern psyche. Myths are pertinent to psychological understanding because they are symbolic discourse about psychic processes—and because symbols are the psyche's native language about itself. To uncover the archetypal significance, the still relevant symbolic meaning, of ancient mythological material is thus healing, transformative, as sexual interpretation cannot be.

Initially Jung had introduced his approach as a *supplement* to Freud's; in the original version of his book he wrote that there are always two vectors of meaning: lower and higher, sexual and spiritual, personal and transpersonal, causal and teleological. But his own focus was already on the religious significance of incest longing. What, in his view, love of the mother *really* signifies is the longing for rebirth—not sexual penetration of the literal mother's vagina but symbolic return to the symbolic womb from which we come, the transpersonal unconscious. We return to this source in order to emerge no longer wedded to literal thinking, to ego consciousness or cultural pieties, but now open to a new mode of consciousness, symbolic thinking. Thus, what may look like regression is really a creative process. The fantasied return to the maternal womb is not a turn to the personal unconscious, to repressed personal history, but to deeper more universal strata—what Freud had called the storehouse of racial memories, our phylogenetic heritage, collective mind. (As we saw at the end of Chapter 6, Jung was well aware of Freud's own profound interest in "archaic vestiges," but he believed that Freud had shrunk from full exploration of this transpersonal aspect of the unconscious. He also recognized that their emphases were different: Jung was most interested in the reactivation of a neglected mode of apprehension, Freud in the recovery of lost memories.) In this book, which marks his theoretical break from Freud, Jung sees the incest taboo as signifying not primarily the need to repress a strong sexual desire but the possibility of spiritual transformation.

Psychic growth, Jung believes, depends on regression back to the psychological past where the decisive factors *seem* to be our parents. But Jung believes that our relationship to our literal parents is too conscious, too familiar, for them to be the source of the most numinous, most sacredly powerful images in our psyche. He posits rather that there exist a priori psychic images, what he calls *archetypes*, which direct all fantasy activity and which shape our experience of our literal parents (as contrasted with the Freudian view that our experience of our own parents is the basis for projections like that of the father god or the mother goddess). Regression will appear as incest longing because of our adult overestimation of sexuality, but the point of regression is introversion, turning inward to discover our relation to the collective unconscious rather than to recover our childhood relation to our parents. Pursued, introversion leads us beyond memories of our individual infancy to archetypal images.[4]

The incest taboo channels the libido into the mother analogies thrown up by the unconscious, and thus the libido becomes progressive again. The pull toward the mother and the taboo that says, "Not the literal mother; not literal sex," move us toward spiritual transformation, to the discovery that literal gratification is not the appropriate aim.

Whereas Freud finds sexual meaning in many different images and activities—though he means by sexuality so much more than genitality—Jung finds spiritual meaning in manifestly sexual images and behaviors. His vector of interpretation is teleological rather than "archaeological"—what something "really means" is what it aims at, what it becomes.

Jung's conception of libido as undifferentiated psychic energy rather than as sexuality and its vicissitudes also implies a very different hermeneutics. Freud makes a clear distinction between manifest and latent, vehicle and tenor, image and meaning. His interest is in latent rather than manifest sexuality; he sees many different vehicles or images as really "meaning" sexuality. Hence what some have called the "monotony" of psychoanalytical interpretations. Jung dissolves the distinction. By symbol he means the manifest image that stands for an otherwise inexpressible meaning (whereas Freud means by symbol the hidden referent). From Jung's perspective, if we know what a symbol means it is no longer functioning as a living symbol (whereas Freud believes we resort to the symbolic expression because we are not willing to "know" what we really mean). Instead of a fixed one-directional relationship between vehicle and tenor, Jung posits a system of cross-referential analogies between symbols, none of which is ultimate. The focus is on the manifest and its many meanings rather than on a particular latent meaning. Thus, properly speaking, Jung does not practice "interpretation" but what he calls "amplification." Freudian symbolism and the notion of repression, of unconscious meaning, go together. As Jung moves toward an understanding of the relation between conscious and unconscious, which does not emphasize repression, which does not posit a "censor," the point becomes to weave as rich a tapestry of allusions, associations, and analogies as possible.

Jung challenges Freud's conviction that the primary aspects of embodied existence—our relation to our parents, to our children, and to our own bodies—are the bedrock of symbolic expression. For Jung birth and death and sexuality are themselves symbolic of inner psychological processes: renewal, transformation, integration. He sees that there are certain features of the natural world—the cycles of the sun and moon and of vegetal growth, the relation between earth and sky—that universally provoke symbolic thinking because they offer such obvious analogies to human psychic processes. Because such associations are not dependent on cultural transmission, these archetypes reappear spontaneously in the psyches of humans in all periods, in all places. The capacity for symbolic thinking is as native to us humans as the patterns of discursive thought defined by Kant—though this capacity may often persist only in atrophied form in a culture like ours, where it is devalued or ignored. To recover this capacity, and to recognize the archetypal dimensions of one's own images, is to be liberated from a restrictive obsession with the problems and pains of one's personal existence—or from narcissistic inflation of one's own achievements or gifts.

Implicit in the above is Jung's very different sense of the relation between consciousness and the unconscious. Freud discovered the unconscious at midlife—as a radically unknown and terrifying aspect of himself. Jung suggests that from early childhood on he had moved easily back and forth between the unconscious—by which he means the inner world of feeling-toned images—and consciousness, orientation in the outer social world. Thus his view puts much less emphasis on the radical inaccessibility of the unconscious, on repression, than does Freud's. For Jung the unconscious is what has been neglected, undervalued, left unrealized—but it is accessible if we but open ourselves to it. Jung is also much less interested in what he calls the *personal unconscious* (those aspects of our personal history not integrated into our conscious acknowledged ego-selves) than in the *collective* or archetypal unconscious, where we gain access to the universally human—which he sees as an unfathomable source of creative energy. The aim of analysis, as Jung understands it, is to recover our connection to universally human patterns of association and meaning, to awaken our ability to respond to the world wakingly with the capacity for symbol making that we exhibit nightly in our dreams. We might then be able to see the symbolic meaning (rather than just the pragmatic or rational significance) of our actions and our relationships, our thoughts, fantasies, and feelings.

Though I have been describing how Jung differs from Freud, it is important not to oversimplify. I am persuaded that Jung deliberately emphasizes the *psychical* dimension of psychology in order to *balance* what he takes to be Freud's overemphasis on the body. Although some of Jung's followers seem to make analytical psychology into a *spiritual* psychology, it is my belief that what Jung meant to articulate was a psychology with *soul*, a psychology devoted to the *psyche*.[5] "Spirit" (the Greek *pneuma*) finds meaning by flying upward, by leaving the earth and the body behind; it esteems abstraction and transcendence. "Soul" finds meaning *in* the embodied, the concrete, the particular. Jung's Christian upbringing may have made him susceptible to sometimes confusing soul and spirit, but from early childhood on the distinction (not expressed in these sophisticated terms, of course) was important to him. His dream of the underground phallus, of a sacred reality within the earth to complement that which resides in the heavens, his adolescent vision of God shitting on the cathedral, his pull to alchemy and its heretical claim that the material realm is to be redeemed rather than fled, his insistence that the divine is better represented by a quaternity that includes the feminine, the chthonic, than by the orthodox trinity—all are expressive of Jung's orientation to soul (wholeness) rather than spirit (transcendence).

Thus for Jung our sexual feelings are to be understood as really meaning our longing for inner wholeness and integration—as being about our embodied souls, not only our bodies. When we come to consider more explicitly what he has to say about homosexuality, it will be important to remember this—to recognize that if Jung says homosexuality really means a longing for a particular kind of inner fulfillment, he would say the same of heterosexuality. Almost.

I say "almost" because of the degree to which *contrasexuality* is a central, never seriously questioned assumption in Jung's theory. Jung takes it for granted that the primary psychological task for men is establishing a conscious relation to their hidden inner feminine capacities, what he calls their anima. Psychological wholeness (or "individuation") can thus be represented by the androgyne or the hermaphrodite, the integration within oneself of masculine and feminine ways of being. For most men, he believes, the way toward a creative relationship with the inner anima initially proceeds by way of a relation to anima in projected form—that is, by way of a relationship to a woman.

It is important to be clear that Jung's "contrasexuality" is not the same as Freud's "bisexuality." Freud, as we noted earlier, was talking primarily about the domain of our interpersonal relationships to others. He believes all of us want intimate relations with both same-sex and contrasexual others, and that all of us at times want to take on a "masculine" (active) role and at other times want to adopt the "feminine" (passive or receptive) role in our relationships and in our very way of being in the world. We may live these longings only in fantasy; they may persist only unconsciously. Nonetheless they are directed toward *others*, toward "objects" (or, in narcissism, toward our own self as an object). Jung's "contrasexuality" is primarily intrapsychic. He believes that socialization forces upon us an ego identification with the psychological attributes assigned by our culture (though he rarely acknowledges that cultures may differ with respect to such assignment) to members of our biological gender *and* a deep longing for connection to the psychological attributes assigned to the other gender, which are unconscious—that is, unrealized—potentialities within ourselves. To look for such connection through relationships with members of the other sex is an immature and ultimately unsatisfying substitute for what we really want, which is not relationship but inner wholeness.

HOMOSEXUAL ILLUSIONS

Now, finally, what does Jung have to contribute to our understanding of homosexuality? First, that in a theoretical sense it doesn't exist! That is—although Jung's works do yield one incidental acknowledgment of the possibility of "constitutional" homosexuality (*CW* 9i:199)—when he is seeking to articulate a *psychological* understanding of homosexuality, he seems to assume the transformability, the mutability, of sexual impulse, and thus suggests that the same energy can be directed either toward same-sex or toward contrasexual others. He is not assuming, as Freud does, that there are *two* sexual currents active in each of us, but that there is *one* that may flow in a variety of directions: "If we regard sexuality as consisting of a fixed heterosexual and a fixed homosexual component we shall never explain this case [involving a young man who had been homosexual in adolescence, heterosexual in early adulthood, and later again homosexual], since the assumption of fixed components precludes any kind of transformation. . . . We must assume a great mobility of the sexual components" (*CW* 4:109). It follows that Jung will be more likely to credit the possibility of "curing" homosexuality than Freud, and will also tend to see "cure" as desirable. Because Jung believes that mature sexuality will be contrasexual, he sees redirecting homosexually oriented sexuality into a heterosexual path as a matter of education, of helping the psyche move forward in its natural direction.

As was true of Freud, most of what Jung writes about homosexuality refers to male homosexuality. Indeed, in Jung's psychological theory the assumption that male experience is the norm of human experience remains essentially unquestioned. Accordingly, Jung is much less sensitive to the differences between male and female homosexuality than was Freud. (We will reserve consideration of what he has to say about lesbian experience until the end of this chapter.)

In his 1912 Fordham lectures (that is, at a time contemporaneous with the studies of Leonardo and Schreber in which Freud acknowledges his awareness of the variety of possible etiologies for homosexuality), Jung asserts that homosexuality is invariably due to "a disturbance in relation to women" and is at a deeper level really an expression of the "infantile state of the man's character" (*CW* 4:110). This early conviction that homosexuality is evidence of a disturbance in a man's relationship to women and especially to the mother is reiterated twenty-five years later in "Psychological Aspects of the Mother Complex": "In homosexuality the son's entire heterosexuality is tied to the mother in an unconscious form. . . . In the son [a mother-complex] injures the masculine instinct through an unnatural sexualization (*CW* 9i:85, 86).

In his 1925 essay "Marriage as a Psychological Relationship," Jung writes in a way that much more clearly lays the blame for a son's homosexuality on his mother—as though what is in question is not how the child internalizes his experience of his mother in a way that may amalgamate fact and fantasy but rather what the mother actively and literally, albeit half consciously, *does* to "force" a son into homosexuality: "A mother who deliberately keeps herself unconscious so as not to disturb the pretence of a 'satisfactory' marriage unconsciously binds her son to her, more or less as a substitute for a husband" (*CW* 17:191).

In the long 1950 monograph *Aion: Researches into the Phenomenology of the Self*, Jung explores at greater length the impact on a son of an overly devoted mother. The son's "Eros is passive like a child's; he hopes to be caught, sucked in, enveloped, and devoured." He lives regressively, "seeking his childhood and his mother, fleeing from a cold cruel world which denies him understanding." His fitful attempts at autonomy are "crippled by the secret memory that the world and happiness may be had as a gift—from the mother." To escape, "he would need a faithless Eros," but his mother, "foreseeing this danger, has carefully inculcated into him the virtues of faithfulness, devotion, loyalty. . . . He has learnt these lessons only too well, and remains true to his mother (*CW* 9ii:11, 12). Here Jung sees the guilt as equally divided between the two: "This naturally causes [the mother] the deepest anxiety when (to her greater glory he turns out to be a homosexual, for example) and at the same time affords her an unconscious satisfaction that is *positively mythological*" (*CW* 9ii:12; italics mine). For in their relationship the "immemorial and most sacred archetype of the marriage of mother and son" is consummated.

This passage is important for in it Jung is trying to move beyond a causality that focuses on the historical accidents of a particular mother-son bond and asks us instead to look at the archetype that is here being re-enacted. The son is lost, not in a relationship to his literal mother, but in an illusion, a projection, that can only be dissolved when the young man recognizes it as such—and freeing himself from an enmeshment with the real mother fostered by the illusion that she could be an adequate embodiment of the archetypal woman, moves instead into relationship with his own inner femininity, his anima (*CW* 9ii:11–13).

As Jung understands it, however, what often happens in the case of a homosexual is that he is likely to *identify* with the anima rather than *relate* to her (*CW* 9i:71). That is, whereas heterosexual men identify with their persona, their socially perceived and anatomically defined self, the homosexual man will instead identify with his contrasexual inner self. Such a man feels that his inner processes constitute his real character. Then it is the persona (the socially expected role) that is unconscious and that gets projected—onto a same-sex other. This deviation from the usual process provides the foundation for open or latent homosexuality. Note that the premise of contrasexuality has not been abandoned here; all that is different is that the inner psychic identification is not congruent with one's socially assigned gender.

Jung says that in such cases there is always a "defective adaptation to external reality and a lack of relatedness," because of the predominant orientation to inner processes (*CW* 6:471). Yet, although convinced that mature sexuality will be heterosexual, Jung does not regard homosexuality as a perversion:

> In view of the recognized frequency of this phenomenon [homosexuality], its interpretation as a pathological perversion is very dubious. The psychological findings show that it is rather a matter of incomplete detachment from the hermaphroditic archetype, coupled with a distinct resistance to identify with the role of a one-sided sexual being. Such a disposition should not be adjudged negative in all circumstances, in so far as it preserves the archetype of the Original Man, which a one-sided sexual being has, up to a point, lost. (*CW* 9i:71)

Indeed, Jung recognizes that a homosexual son's mother-complex may often have important positive consequences:

Since a "mother-complex" is a concept borrowed from psychopathology, it is always associated with the idea of injury and illness. But if we take the concept out of its narrow psychopathological setting and give it a wider connotation, we can see that it has positive effects as well. Thus a man with a mother-complex may have a finely differentiated Eros instead of, or in addition to, homosexuality. (Something of this sort is suggested by Plato in his *Symposium*.) This gives him a great capacity for friendship, which often creates ties of astonishing tenderness between men and may even rescue friendship between the sexes from the limbo of the impossible. He may have good taste and an aesthetic sense which are fostered by the presence of a feminine streak. Then he may be supremely gifted as a teacher because of his almost feminine insight and tact. He is likely to have a feeling for history, and to be conservative in the best sense and cherish the values of the past. Often he is endowed with a wealth of religious feelings, which help to bring the *ecclesia spiritualis* into reality; and a spiritual receptivity which makes him responsive to revelation. (CW 9i:86–87)

Jung also believed that homosexuality may sometimes be an entirely appropriate orientation during adolescence. For, as he writes in his 1936 essay "Concerning the Archetypes, with Special Reference to the Anima Concept," the establishment of an inner relationship to the anima is a task for the second half of life. Earlier the important thing is "for a man to be a man . . . [to] be able to free himself from the anima fascination of his mother" (CW 9i:71). It may well happen that escaping from the mother's thrall will involve an initiation into manhood by way of an intense, intimate relationship with a man.

In a 1922 lecture to Zurich University students Jung observed that homosexual experiences are common during puberty. He says he is speaking of "normal youngsters who [during this period of their lives] enjoy such a rapturous friendship [with members of their own sex] that they also express their feelings in sexual form" (CW 10:105). Yet he notes that in contrast with classical times homosexuality has today "lost its glamour as a social and educative institution, and now ekes out a miserable terror-stricken existence as a so-called perversion and punishable offence" (99). Thus it is less likely in our world that homosexual relationships will actually serve this ideal initiatory function. Yet even now, he suggests, homosexual relations between students and teachers may serve a valuable function: "When such a friendship exists between an older man and a younger its educational significance is undeniable. . . . [It] can be of advantage to both sides and have lasting value. An indispensable condition for the value of such a relation is the steadfastness of the friendship and their loyalty to it" (107). Still, Jung seems to doubt that such "ideal homosexuality" is very often realized:

> But only too often this condition is lacking. The more homosexual a man is, the more prone he is to disloyalty and to the seduction of boys. Even when loyalty and true friendship prevail the results may be undesirable for the development of personality. A friendship of this kind naturally involves a special cult of feeling, of the feminine element in a man. He becomes gushing, soulful, aesthetic, over-sensitive, etc.—in a word, effeminate, and this woman-ish behavior is detrimental to his character. (107)

THE HERMAPHRODITE

If one looks up "homosexuality" in the Index to Jung's *Collected Works*, one finds relatively few entries; most of those few come from the period when Jung was still weaning himself from Freud's influence or from the 1920s and 30s, before Jung had begun fully to immerse himself in alchemy. In the late alchemical period there are no such references; there are, however, many to "hermaphrodite." Fully to understand Jung's view of homosexuality we must pay some attention to these, for Jung believes that homosexuality is really a misguided attempt to actualize psychical androgyny[6]—misguided because the homosexual lives at a literal, object-oriented, body level what is really a symbolic, inner, spiritual possibility. That is, the real meaning of homosexuality is the longing to integrate the feminine and masculine in oneself, to escape from the narrow gender definition that cuts us off from half of our psychic potentiality.

Jung suggests that the creators of the alchemical image of the hermaphrodite may have been individuals unusually aware of the contrasexual side of their own psyche who then projected their inner experience of being psychically both masculine and feminine onto a physical reality. In Jung's alchemical works the image of the hermaphrodite appears over and over again as a privileged symbol of what he calls the Anthropos, the Original Man. Jung sees this image as playing a central role in a complex interplay of analogies. Because the image points forward to a creative union of opposites, not back to an undifferentiated unity, it encompasses all other conjunctions: soul and body, base and sublime, spirit and flesh, divine and human. The hermaphrodite is thus a symbol of the Self—of the union of our archaic past and our present reality, of unconscious and conscious, of the archetypal and the unique. It serves as an image of our unconscious potential wholeness, the goal of individuation.[7]

Very rarely in alchemy there are allusions to a union of "like with like" rather than "like with other" imagined on the model of same-sex relationships, father and son or brother and brother—but this stage, Jung asserts, is always represented as a *preliminary* stage, preceding the stage represented by the image of brother-sister incest (CW 16:170n, 218n). In *Mysterium Coniunctionis*, Jung's exploration of "psychic opposites in alchemy," he includes a discussion of a series of pictures from an illustrated alchemical manuscript showing two male figures conjoined, each of whom has only one foot. The inscription under the first picture, which shows a king in a yellow robe and a priest dressed in white, reads "They make but one." In the next picture, described as "The Revelation of the Hidden," the king has a blue robe and black foot, the priest a black robe and blue foot. It is followed by one showing the two figures separated, each with two feet, one wearing a robe whose right half is blue and the left black, the other a robe whose left half is blue and the right black. The next picture shows them dressed in the same complementary fashion but rejoined, and each now has but one blue foot. The sequence concludes with the king of the series standing with a green-clad crowned woman; their arms are joined but they stand apart; he still has but one foot, blue tipped with black.

Jung interprets the sequence involving the two male figures as representing the relation between the spiritual and the earthly, corporeal aspects of the masculine—which initially are radically differentiated from each other and yet inextricably mutually dependent; then their complementarity is discovered, which makes possible a separation in which each stands alone but in relation to the other, and then a new union on the basis of the recognized complementarity. Thus Jung's interpretation sees homosexual union serving here to symbolize an important inner realignment in which the profound interconnections between our spirituality and our instincts are recognized. But he also sees this process as preliminary to a union that can only be represented through heterosexual images, through the image of the sacred marriage or the hermaphrodite (CW 14:505–9, plates 4–7).[8]

Jung is well aware that at a literal level the hermaphrodite represents a "monstrosity," "a hideous abortion and perversion of nature"—yet as a symbol it signifies the overcoming and healing of inner conflict. Biologically, hermaphrodites are sterile and yet they symbolize the "capacity for spontaneous and autochthonous reproduction" (CW 14:177).

Jung also acknowledges that the alchemists themselves seem often to have believed they were aiming at physical rather than psychic transformations (CW 16:313). In a sense, Jung is saying, the alchemists, Freud, and homosexuals all make the same mistake. They understand symbolic expressions too literally. The alchemists thought they were talking about an anatomical fusion of male and female genitalia; Freud thought we literally long for intercourse with our parents; the homosexual believes he can identify with his anima, with his feminine side, and then achieve wholeness through relationship with a man. From Jung's perspective what they all misunderstand is that the point is not the crude reality but the psychic processes.

The image of the hermaphrodite points us to the process whereby we can integrate the masculine and feminine sides of *our own being*. Yet Jung recognizes that even when we achieve this psychic hermaphroditic wholeness, we are not complete as humans. "The unrelated human being lacks wholeness, for he can achieve wholeness only through the soul, and the soul cannot exist without its other side, which is always found in a "You." "If no bond of love exists, there is no soul." Thus there will inevitably be sexual longings, relationship longings. "Even the hermaphrodite needs the human other" (*CW* 16:243–45).

Jung never explicitly says that this hermaphrodite/hermaphrodite relationship, this I/You bond between two individuated persons, must necessarily bring together a man and a woman, never explicitly excludes the possibility that it might involve two men or two women. But the emphatic contrasexual bias I find in all his work suggests to me that he imagines this possibility only in its heterosexual form.

·8·

JUNG: THE CASES— MALE AND FEMALE

That Jung means by homosexuality manifest homosexuality and is plainly impatient with Freud's whole conception of latent homosexuality is made evident in a passage from *The Vision Seminars* of 1930–34:

> I will tell you a case. A man came to me and told me among other things that he was a homosexual. He didn't look so and I get rather suspicious when people assure me that they have sexual peculiarities, so I asked him whether he had had a Freudian analysis, and found that he had—for some months. Then I said to him, "Now tell me, have you had any love affairs with boys?" "Oh, no," he said, quite upset, "it is not as bad as that." "But of what does your homosexuality consist? Do you have phantasies about boys, do you like them better than girls?" "Oh, no, I have always been in love with girls. When the analysts told me I was homosexual I was shocked, I didn't know it." "But how did the analyst know since you did not know?" "It came as a great surprise; I once dreamed that I was sleeping with someone who I thought was a woman and it turned out to be a boy. I woke up terribly shocked."
>
> Now of course, one can dream anything, one can dream that one is sleeping with an animal, but that does not prove that one is a sexual pervert, it is simply a symbol. But those people take it quite literally, and are convinced that it is sexual which just isn't true. That symbolism does not come from a repression.[1]

Jung says the dream is just a symbol and not to be taken literally as "those people" do, though he doesn't in this instance try to explore what it might symbolize.

In the published notes of Jung's 1928–30 English Seminar more details and more analysis are provided regarding another patient whose dreams include apparently homosexual themes. Jung retells one of this man's dreams:

> I am in a bedroom with my wife, and I see a door which leads into another room slowly open. I immediately go to the door, push it open, and in the other

room I find a little boy completely naked. I carry him into the bedroom and I am convinced in the dream that he is not a natural boy. In order to prevent his getting away (he is struggling in my arms) I press him against me, and he gives me the most remarkable feeling (not at all a sexual feeling) of satisfaction as if this true thing were satisfactory to the longings of my feelings. Then my wife brings in a variety of food for the child. I see black bread and white bread. The child does not want to eat the black bread but eats the white. Then suddenly he flies out of the window and beckons to us from the air.[2]

The dreamer told Jung he associated the naked baby boy with Eros, and Jung goes on to interpret the dream as meaning that Eros, intimate feeling, was lacking between the dreamer and his wife. Jung draws special attention to the dreamer finding it odd that the deep satisfaction he got from hugging the child was not sexual. "That is one of the foolish ideas which men have. They think that Eros is sex, but not at all. Eros is relatedness" (170).

Later the same patient reported a dream of being led to a temple by an old Buddhist monk who, once inside, changed into a beautiful little boy with a hooded face. The dreamer fell down and worshiped the boy as if he were a divine being. This dream image suggests to Jung associations with the Cabiri and Telesphorus, the little god from the Asclepian tradition whom Jung identified with completions and initiations (431)—the same associations, we may recall, Jung also made to the little manikin and stone hidden away in the pencil box of his own childhood. Later Jung notes that the dreamer had wondered whether there was "something homosexual" in his adoration of the boy; Jung himself is, however, confident that "it was merely symbolical, a certain immaturity. . . . This simply means that the man in certain respects is not mature, and his immaturity may express itself in different ways—that he is not up to women, or not up to life, or not up to spiritual things. . . . His sex is perfectly normal but it is unrelated sex, a sort of auto-eroticism. There is no relation to the object." Again Jung concludes, "Eros is un-developed, not his sexuality" (490).

With respect to this patient, Jung once more protests against the imputa-tion of unconscious or latent homosexuality. He reports that when he asked the man, " 'Did you get into trouble with a boy,' he exclaims indignantly that he would not touch a boy. 'Men, then?' 'No.' 'Then why the devil do you call yourself a homosexual?' " (490).

The insistence that by "homosexuality" we should mean overt, expressed, "clinical" homosexuality is not new; Jung had voiced it emphatically much earlier in a 1909 letter to Ferenczi.[3] The date suggests to me that part of the reason for Jung's passionate rejection of the idea that latent, unconscious homosexuality nevertheless *is* homosexuality may be how important it is to him to deny the reality of his own homosexual impulses.

Freud may frustrate by his unwillingness to recognize any theoretical difference between manifest and latent homosexuality. Jung, on the other hand, will insist on the difference, but then end up by telling us that even manifest homosexuality is not really homosexuality—only a stage, a defense, or a misunderstanding of a spiritual longing. Such reinterpretations are as evident in his discussions of particular cases as in his more theoretical formulations.

As any reader of Jung soon discovers, Jung's writings include very little case material. Though he often urged Freud to make public accounts of the course of actual treatments to show other analysts how it was really done (and, indeed, most of Freud's cases were written during the years he was close to Jung), Jung himself never wrote a single fully articulated case history.[4] We do find in his writings a few extended dream analyses, but even then Jung typically provides little in the way of case context. This is largely because in his writings Jung was more interested in elucidating the archetypal, mythological dimension of fantasy material—which is often not what is most appropriate to work on in therapy, especially in its initial stages. "The Archetypes are of course always at work everywhere. But practical treatment, especially in the case of young people, does not always require the patient to come to close quarters with them" (*CW* 7: 107). Thus Jung's *Psychology of the Unconscious* (as we noted earlier) explores the fantasies of an American woman whom Jung never met; the 1936 monograph "Individual Dream Symbolism in Relation to Alchemy" elucidates the archetypal meaning of a series of dreams dreamt by another analyst's patient, and Jung evidences no interest in seeing how the dream images might relate to his individual history, to day-residues, or to the course of the treatment.

AN UNPOETICAL AFFAIR

Yet among the very few accounts in all Jung's published work of a series of dreams, we do have *one* devoted to a young male homosexual.[5] We should note that Jung introduces the case *not* in order to present his understanding of male homosexuality, but simply to give an example of a case where dreams serve as clues to the resolution of a problem rather than, as in the case he had just finished discussing, as evidence of how deep and intractable the problem is.

The case involved a young man in his early twenties whom Jung describes as boyish, indeed girlish, in his looks and manner of expression, intelligent, and very interested in the arts. His feelings, we are told, were tender and soft, and somewhat effeminate. "Undoubtedly he is too young for his age, a clear case of retarded development. It is quite in keeping with this that he should have come to me on account of his homosexuality" (CW 7:104). (Note that here the patient comes for treatment in order to be cured of homosexuality; in this case homosexuality is the *conscious* issue.)

Jung begins by discussing a dream the youth had had the night before the first session: "I am in a lofty cathedral filled with mysterious twilight. They tell me that it is the cathedral at Lourdes. In the centre there is a deep, dark well into which I have to descend" (CW 7:101). Jung observes: "One might almost suppose that the dreamer came to the doctor in a highly poetic mood and was entering upon the treatment as though it were a sacred religious act to be performed in the mystical half-light of some awe-inspiring sanctuary. But that does not fit the facts at all. The patient merely came to the doctor to be treated for that unpleasant matter, his homosexuality, which is anything but poetic" (101). In the rest of the paragraph Jung continues to contrast the poetical tone of the dream with "that highly unpoetical affair" that had brought the young man to treatment. Perhaps, he suggests, the one compensates the other.

The patient's associations led straight to the mother: "As in nearly all cases of this kind, he had a particularly close tie with his mother . . . [not necessarily] a particularly good or intense *conscious* relationship, but something in the nature of a secret, subterranean tie which expresses itself consciously, perhaps only in the retarded development of character, i.e., in a relative infantilism" (CW 7:102).

Although he communicated nothing of this to the patient during their first session, Jung felt the dream gave him a good understanding of what the young man's homosexuality really meant: that it was a spiritual yearning misunderstood as a sexual orientation. It seemed clear to Jung that the church in the dream signifies a longed-for higher spiritual substitute for the youth's natural carnal tie to the literal mother. The Catholic church comes into the dream as a symbol of a contemporary institution able to offer that same possibility of an initiatory detachment from a young man's "original animal-like condition" (CW 7:103), which in primitive cultures is provided by pubertal rites of passage. Jung reminds us how in such rites the youths of the tribe are violently separated from the matriarchal family of childhood, taken to the "men's house," and there initiated into the religious mysteries. Through participation in the ritual the young men are ushered into a new world with new and changed personalities. Because such age-old rebirth rituals are "engraved in the unconscious as primordial images," echoes of them may appear in the dream of a modern youth who has no conscious relation to them (104).

The dream, Jung believes, shows how the boy had longed for the kind of male spiritual mentor provided in such traditional cultures, but in his case none had been available. So "the longing for a man's leadership continued to grow in the boy, taking the form of homosexual leanings—a faulty development that might never have come about had there been a man there to educate his childish fantasies" (104).

"Viewed in this light, the homosexuality of adolescence is only a misunderstanding of the otherwise very appropriate need for masculine guidance" (104). Jung sees the fear of women often felt by such immature youths as being well founded; at this stage to avoid being swallowed by the mother they need the support of a male. Thus the dream means that "what the initiation into treatment signifies for the patient is the fulfillment of the true meaning of his homosexuality, i.e., his entry into the world of the adult man" (104).

Though Jung had communicated none of the above to his patient, the young man brought a second dream to their next meeting: "I am in a great Gothic cathedral. At the altar stands a priest. I stand before him with my friend, holding in my hand a little Japanese ivory figure, with the feeling that it is going to be baptized. Suddenly an elderly woman appears, takes the fraternity ring from my friend's finger, and puts it on her own. My friend is afraid that this may bind him in some way. But at the same moment there is a sound of wonderful organ music" (105).

Jung understands this dream to mean that at some level the longed-for initiation has now really occurred: "The homosexual tie has been cut and a heterosexual relationship substituted for it, a platonic friendship with a motherly type of woman" (106). He believes that the appearance of a priest in the second dream, a male spiritual guide of the kind Jung had found so evidently absent from the first, signifies that "the unconscious meaning of the youth's homosexuality has been fulfilled and that a further development can be started" (105). The ceremony about to take place in the cathedral represents the passage from adolescent homosexuality into the sexuality appropriate to an adult male: heterosexuality. The ritual the dreamer expects involves the baptism of a little manikin, which reminded him of a penis. Thus the ceremony promised to provide some kind of blessing of his homosexual relationship with the friend in his dream (who is his sexual partner in waking life). But then the elderly woman appears and a very different ritual occurs: something resembling a heterosexual marriage. This signifies, Jung says, that "the homosexual relationship seems to have passed over into a heterosexual one" (106).

Jung admits that the woman is elderly, a friend of the patient's mother. "In fact," the patient says, "she is like a mother to me." But Jung insists that the dream's meaning is progressive, not regressive. The woman is *not* his mother; the relationship to her "signifies a step beyond the mother toward masculinity" (106). As warrant of his optimistic interpretation he offers the beautiful organ music at the end of the dream.

Nevertheless Jung does acknowledge that the transformation represented in the dream had no correlate in the dreamer's conscious attitude. The dream offered promises, guidance, encouragement—but consciously the patient was "full of hesitation and resistance; moreover, as the treatment progressed, he constantly showed himself antagonistic and difficult, ever ready to slip back into his previous infantilism" (107).

Jung does not tell us how the treatment ended or what happened to the young man. His interest is with the dreams that show how "the images of the collective unconscious [may] play an entirely positive role" when a patient "has no really dangerous tendency to fall back on a fantasy-substitute for reality" (107). Whether the youth ever consciously came to accept that his homosexuality was but a stage, was a mistaken sexualization of his longing for an adult male mentor, a misguided literalization of his spiritual longing for an intiation into his own masculinity, is not revealed.

FEMALE HOMOSEXUALITY

Jung writes relatively little about same-sex love among women. There are a few epigrammatic references scattered through his works. He acknowledges that lesbianism may serve a social function in binding women together for political (one presumes feminist) activity (*CW* 10:99); he suggests that intimate same-sex friendships among women are more likely to involve the "exchange of tender feelings" and "intimate thoughts" than genital desire (108); he believes that women inclined toward lesbianism are "high-spirited, intellectual and rather masculine," intent on maintaining their superiority vis-à-vis men (108).

In the 1924 series of lectures *Analytical Psychology and Education* Jung writes of an intelligent and rebellious thirteen-year-old girl who had gone through puberty early and was frightened by her own sexuality. Her pent-up emotions were directed into homosexual fantasies rather than real relationships. She spoke of longing for caresses from a certain teacher and fantasized finding herself undressed in this teacher's presence—and of dreaming of her mother's death. Jung sees the homosexual fantasies as evidence that the girl's need for maternal love is not satisfied. He believes her brilliant, ambitious, "masculine" mother had used the child to flatter her own vanity but had failed to give her any real love or understanding. Therefore the girl "craves love from her teachers, but of the wrong sort. If tender feelings are thrown out the door, then sex in violent form comes in through the window." Here Jung is laying the responsibility on the mother, who, he says, is the one who *should* be in treatment, and sees the girl's "homosexuality" as simply a plea for her mother's tender affections (CW 17:126–28).

A more extended discussion of a case of female homosexuality immediately precedes the account of the case of the young man with the cathedral dreams considered above. Again, as the context makes clear, from Jung's perspective it is almost incidental that the case involves homosexuality. It is introduced to illustrate that point in a treatment where one moves from a focus on the analysis of the personal unconscious to the consideration of collective or archetypal material.

In this instance the patient was a middle-aged woman, involved in a "sentimental attachment, bordering on the homosexual, that has lasted for years." Jung believes that the relationship between the two women is "too intimate and excludes too many of the other possibilities of life." Their mutual irritability and quarrels suggest that the unconscious is trying "to put distance between them, but they refuse to listen":

> The quarrel usually begins because one of them finds that she is still not sufficiently understood, and urges that they should speak more plainly to one another; whereupon both make enthusiastic efforts to unbosom themselves. Naturally a misunderstanding comes about in next to no time, and a worse scene than ever ensues. *Faute de mieux*, this quarrelling had long been for both of them a pleasure substitute which they were unwilling to relinquish. (CW 7:81)

According to Jung, although the patient knew that the relationship was "moribund," she also admitted to being still caught in the fantasy that something might yet be made of it. She was also well aware that her relation to her mother had been similarly based on fantasy, and that after her mother's death she had simply transferred this pattern onto the new friendship. The patient played "the masculine role with her friend and had corresponding sexual fantasies." Although her homosexual desires were not "agreeable to her," the patient at this stage of the treatment had long since come to terms with them (CW 7:92).

Jung's account centers on a dream: "She is about to cross a wide river. There is no bridge, but she finds a ford where she can cross. She is on the point of doing so, when a large crab that lay hidden in the water seizes her by the foot and will not let her go" (CW 7:80). The dreamer told Jung that she had woken from the dream terrified. She saw the river as representing her difficulty in making the necessary transition in her relationship and the ford as signifying the possibility offered by the treatment of finding a way. The crab reminded her of cancer, of incurable disease, of being pulled backward.

The dreamer herself saw that the dream expressed her ambivalence about the relationship: her wish to move beyond it *and* her infantile longing to return to the maternal embrace the friendship recalls. That even to the dreamer *this* meaning is by now all too familiar suggests to Jung that it is time to look more deeply, to move to the "subjective" level where the crab is not mother or friend but some aspect of the dreamer herself, to use the dream to help her see that the obstacle to moving forward is in herself not in her friend.

As Jung viewed the dream, the crab represents something "animal" or subhuman in the patient that threatens to drag down her whole personality, that is like some incurable disease. He believes this to be her violent, overpowering infantile craving for love—an untamed, undifferentiated, compulsive, instinctual longing. When the patient says that she associates the crab with cancer, she immediately begins to reminisce about a former friend who had died of cancer, a woman who had had a series of intense heterosexual affairs. To Jung this means that the dreamer is really afraid of those instinctual cravings in herself that are directed toward men. Thus she clings to her lesbian friendship "so as not to fall victim to this other tendency, which seems to her much more dangerous. Accordingly, she remains at the infantile, homosexual level because it serves her as a defence" (CW 7:85).

Jung sees in this feared heterosexual longing the germ of a more healthy personality that might not shrink from the hazards of life; but to the patient it portends death. The crab, Jung believes, is a symbol for the unconscious contents, for the collective unconscious, for the realm of archetype and myth that can move us beyond obsession with our personal difficulties. *But,* as Jung reminds us, "in the dream the collective unconscious appears under a very negative aspect, as something dangerous and harmful." He attributes this to the danger that more fantasy, more mythology, would pose for this woman. The dream had begun to move the treatment to a new phase, one in which a transference onto Jung had been stirred up that brought with it the activation of a host of archetypal figures that Jung felt she was ill equipped to deal with because she was already too involved in her rich fantasy life. "Her powers of fantasy are a symptom of illness, in that she revels in them far too much, but allows real life to slip by. Any more mythology would be exceedingly dangerous for her" (CW 7:98). He saw this patient as having too little hold on life to risk the complete reversal going forward would entail. "The dream as it stands leaves the dreamer no alternative at present, but to withdraw her foot carefully; for to go on would be fatal. She cannot yet leave the neurotic situation, because the dream gives her no positive indication of any help from the unconscious" (CW 7:100).

Again, we do not know what happened to the woman. But at the end of Jung's account she is left in her relationship with her female friend—unwilling to consummate it or to leave it, uncomfortable with it and yet even more terrified of the heterosexual longings from which it protects her.

Obviously here, as in the case of the young man, Jung assumes that the deeper pull is heterosexual. Homosexuality is a sign of her neurosis, as it was a sign of his immaturity. Unlike Freud, Jung never considers the possibility that for women the homosexual pull, the pull to the same-sex other, which recapitulates the primary attachment to the mother, might be the stronger pull. Indeed, it is striking that in his essay "Psychological Aspects of the Mother Complex," in which he discusses four different forms a daughter's mother complex might take, he does not even refer to female homosexuality (CW 9i:87–100). For Jung, even more than for Freud, male experience is the norm for human experience; female experience can be known through deduction from the male pattern. It was Jung who proposed to Freud that if men have an Oedipus complex, then women will have an Electra complex (an idea whose inadequacy Freud soon recognized); and Jung who later assumed that if men have an anima, it logically follows that women have an animus.

THE ARCHETYPAL MEANING OF HOMOSEXUALITY

Contrasexuality as the deepest truth of our inner and outer lives seems self-evident to Jung. This means that we cannot expect to receive from him an understanding of homosexuality that will see it as a valid form of adult sexuality. His emphasis on the psyche, on inner experience, also means that for Jung literal sexual expression, not only among homosexuals, is in a sense always a misdirection of a soul longing—rather than an appropriate expression of it.

Yet Jung's emphasis on trying to explore the psychical longings that we use sexuality to try to fulfill, his attempt to discover the symbolic meaning of our sexual fantasies and behaviors, may immeasurably deepen our experience of our own sexuality, whether we are homosexual or heterosexual, women or men. He reminds us to ask what age-old image of transformation or fulfillment is being reenacted here. We may regret that he never considers that to love another like oneself may represent not narcisssism or immaturity, but a love directed toward the Self; that he never looks on same-sex love as signifying a longing for a love that is clearly not directed toward reproduction but toward psychical relationship, a desire to be free of being defined by cultural gender definitions. Nevertheless, the notion that homosexuality might express such meanings emerges from a way of looking taught us by Jung.

Von Franz said that both Freud and Jung were gripped by the same mythological theme: the phallic god. Freud sees the cost of repressing the sexual power represented by the phallus, Jung the cost of denying its spiritual significance. Both help us to see the relevance of homosexuality to the self-understanding of all of us. Freud says that we all have those desires and fears. Jung says that what the homosexual really wants is what we all want—to be whole, to be free of the inner split between feminine and masculine, to love and be loved, to reaffirm the connection between body and soul.

That archetypal psychology need not perpetuate a contrasexual bias (which may at least in part be rooted in Jung's personal psychology as well as in the essentialist thinking about male and female natures characteristic of his culture) has been suggested by several recent writers on Jungian theory. (Like Jung, most of them still shy away from accepting the possibility that literal, lived homo*sexuality*, might be congruent with psychological maturity.)

In an essay called "Some Archetypal Themes in Male Homosexuality," Melvin Kettner recognizes that homosexuality may have many different psychological meanings, but asserts that the interrelated themes and symbols associated with homoeroticism are "grouped around a predominant central archetypal symbol—the phallus. Unlike Jung, he says he has no direct experience of feminine-identified (or anima-identified) male homosexuals; those he has met in his practice are dominated by their intolerable (and largely unconscious) sense of being inadequate as males—and so look to other men for the maleness they fail to find within. Yet he also acknowledges the relevance of the homosexual's "quest for the secret of the masculine principle" to a culture like ours where the inherited canon of the masculine ideal has come to seem outmoded. He sees homosexuality as a kind of male mystery cult that may be part of our culture's so necessary return to a reaffirmation of the feminine and a consequent redefinition of the masculine, which would recognize it as complementary to, rather than suppressive of, the feminine. Thus he recognizes a possible *progressive* rather than neces- sarily *regressive* aspect of male homosexuality: "The homosexual movement may also be a compensatory phenomenon in the collective psyche which could lead to a reshuffling of the cultural standards for the ideal man and thus could achieve a better harmony or balance with the feminine side."[6]

But though Kettner has a more approbative view of homosexuality, his very affirmation is still shaped by contrasexual assumptions not all that different from Jung's. For to Kettner the "obsession with the phallus" he finds characteristic of homosexuals, "unbeknownst to the participants, takes place in the lap of the Great Mother," the castrating and devouring goddess. He regards homosexuals as men who have not been initiated into their masculinity by their fathers (more likely by default than by intention) and so are still caught by the overwhelming power of the maternal principle. Longing for phallus, for male potency, they "mistake the penis for this trancending symbol and get caught in a compulsive pattern which does not lead anywhere."

James Hillman sees Jung's and Kettner's tendency to posit a close associa- tion between homosexuality and a mother-complex as an example of a "bewitchment by the fantasy of opposites" characteristic of much in Jungian theory.[7] Challenging the association, he suggests that it may be depth psychology that is motherbound rather than the homosexual.[8] To under- stand homosexuality only in relation to the mother is to perpetuate a view of homosexuality as incomplete development, as *puer* religion. But there are archetypes other than the *puer* equally relevant to the homosexual—father, son, brother.

Although Hillman doubts that we can imagine beyond the "fantasy of opposites," he insists that "within it, however, our possibilities are lim- itless," that we will discover that there are "ceaseless pairings and couplings" of anima, animus, ego and shadow, persona and Self once we free ourselves of being "locked into the contrasexual definition of anima and animus. . . . Every archetype always implies another," but not always the *same* other. "Alchemy excels in exemplifying this interlocking of terms, where each term shifts its valence according to the constellation. Thus anima can have all sorts of names and valences and images depending upon the tandem she is in."[9]

There are many different couplings, many different stories. The anima may appear in the imagery of a woman's unconscious; the animus may be found working in men. Hillman is here suggesting the possibility of what we might call an *inner homosexuality*, the possibility of a vital psychical relationship between a man's masculine ego and an inner masculine figure, between a woman's female-identified ego and an inner feminine soul image. Hillman has elsewhere explored the inner meaning of images of male-male bonds, particularly the bond between older and younger male. In place of the image of the androgyne, he proposes the inner reconciliation of *senex* and *puer* as a model of male wholeness.[10] Though as far as I know he never says so explicitly, this implies that outer same-sex relationships might be given archetypal validation. They may be congruent with powerful inner reality rather than with misunderstandings.

Mitch Walker has introduced yet another archetype relevant to the understanding of same-sex love among men—the archetype of the Double. The Double is a soul figure with the erotic and spiritual significance ordinarily associated with the anima, but of the same sex. It is not the same as Jung's "shadow," the negatively viewed repressed personal unconscious—though if rejected it may function as a shadow. "Double-love is distinguished from Anima-love by uncanny feelings of unity, strength and reinforcement of personal identity." The double is one's deeper support, a partner, helper, guide, a friend who is profoundly equal, deeply familiar, with whom "a mysterious, joyful sharing of feelings and needs, a dynamic intuitive understanding" is possible. The archetype contains the images of father, son, brother, lover. The Double is an inner soul guide; when the archetype of the Double enters into outward relationships, these are dedicated to a mutual encouragement of psychic growth. Walker says, "The double motif may include a tendency to homosexuality, but it is not necessarily a homosexual archetype. Rather, the double embodies the *spirit* of love between those of the same sex." Thus Achilles and Patrocles exemplify the Double relationship, whether or not one veiws them as sexually involved.[11]

In his book on Hermes, Rafael Lopez-Pedrazo notes how rarely depth psychology has explored Eros among men. He comments sadly on how little we have inherited from Freud and Jung and their man-to-man relationship. As we read their letters "we have a picture of two men trying to gain power over each other. . . . Their friendship shows few traces of having much relationship to each other's psyche. . . . If eros among men does not appear in relationships between psychologists, then how can it be expected to appear in psychotherapy?"[12]

Lopez-Pedrazo believes that the conceptual frame of depth psychology "has placed homosexuality within a sterile causalism that tries to understand it in terms of the father and the mother." Hillman has described the limitations of the emphasis on the natural mother. Thomas Moon shows how the focus on the literal father is equally beside the point: "The fathers of gays are no more 'absent' than the fathers of straights—rather, gay men are 'absent' from the world of their fathers." The alienation is from the collective father, not the personal one. What is represented mythologically by the "Slaying of the Father" is the battle with patriarchy, not with one's own father.[13]

Our real loss, Lopez-Pedrazo argues, is that Western culture has "lost contact with the archetypes which are behind eros among men. Thus an archetypal view of homo-erotica has been falsified."[14] We have lost access to the gods (and goddesses), the archetypal patterns, that underlie these relationships. A truly *depth* psychological approach to same-sex love (among women as well as among men)[15] requires us to turn to the differentiated representations of Greek mythology in search of the lost archetypes. Jung once wrote that the ancient gods have become our diseases, our pathologies, our perversities (CW 13:75). In order to free homosexuality from being viewed through the lens of pathology and perversity, we may need to return it to the gods.

MYTHOLOGY'S MYSTERIES

·9·

DEMYTHOLOGIZING GREEK HOMOSEXUALITY

Toward the beginning of Mary Renault's novel *The Charioteer*, the older of two youths, Ralph Lanyon, who has just been expelled from their preparatory school, gives the younger, Laurie, his copy of Plato's *Phaedrus* as a farewell gift. "It doesn't exist anywhere in real life, so don't let it give you illusions. It's just a myth really," he tells him. Years later, when they meet again, Ralph repeats, much more bitterly, "A lot of bull is talked about Greece by people who would just have been a dirty laugh there."[1]

Before turning to look at ancient Greece's mythological representations of same-sex love, it may be helpful to look at some of *our* myths about homosexuality in classical Greece. It is striking how often in their discussions of homosexual love both Freud and Jung refer back to Greece as a culture where same-sex love was not only accepted but given important educational and social functions. Many of us, too, may imagine that world as one where our dreams of a truly healthy and fully affirmed homosexuality were realized. Yet while it is true that the Greeks believed that sexual desire for members of one's own sex was something that almost everyone would feel at some time, and also true that there were culturally sanctioned ways of living that desire, those accepted ways are not necessarily congruent with our contemporary fantasies about how same-sex love might most fulfillingly be lived. Indeed, some scholars believe that the ancient Greek presuppositions surrounding the accepted forms of male love of males are so radically different from the modern concept of homosexuality as to make their perspectives irrelevant to our lives.[2] My own aim, like Michel Foucault's, is "to examine both the difference that keeps us at a remove from a way of thinking in which we recognize the origin of our own, and the proximity that remains in spite of the distance which we never cease to explore."[3] Therefore I begin by looking at the language through which the Greeks articulated their views, and as far as possible try to avoid interpreting *their* experience through *our* linguistic categories.

133

Ralph's sense of the gap between the "real life" attitudes and behaviors of the Greeks and our myths about them is given scholarly confirmation in K. J. Dover's, *Greek Homosexuality.*[4] Because in classical Greece there were no religious or medical institutions that defined what constituted permissible or normal sexuality, what Dover seeks to discover are the attitudes toward same-sex eroticism ordinary Athenians in the fifth and sixth century B.C.E. would have deemed it appropriate to express publicly (although he recognizes and also discusses the gulf between their idealized conventions and their actual practice). The interest in popular attitudes leads Dover to base his study primarily on court proceedings and vase paintings and to give less weight than previous scholars have to literary testimony. Confrontation with the realities Dover exposes can be a disturbing experience, yet it makes possible a more complex understanding of the Greek mythological representations. We will be able to see what in their myths is projection of their own daily experience, what derives from their memories or imaginings about earlier periods, what expresses dreams and fears that they may not consciously have acknowledged.

APHRODISIA

As was also true when we looked at Freud and Jung, in order to understand the Greek attitude toward homosexuality we need to relate it to their more general understanding of sexuality, which was radically different from ours. The Greeks associated sexual desire closely with other human appetites—the desire for food, drink, and sleep—and saw all these appetites as entailing the *same* moral problem, the problem of avoiding excess. Their term *aphrodisia* (literally, "the things of Aphrodite") encompasses all actions and desires pertaining to a certain kind of pleasure. Aphrodisia refers to outward actions and consciously recognized desires, not to hidden inner drives—not, David Halperin explains, "to some mute force within us that makes itself in all sorts of indirect and devious ways other than the performance of sexual acts."[5] As Foucault puts it: "When philosophers are laughed at for claiming to love only the beautiful souls of boys, they are not suspected of harboring murky feelings of which they may not be conscious, but simply of waiting for the [opportunity] to slip their hands under the tunic of their heart's desire."[6] The "things of Aphrodite" are never seen as bad in themselves but as potentially morally problematic because they refer to an inherently inferior mode of pleasure, which is animal rather than distinctively human, and with which we might become obsessed. Therefore the moral aim with respect to sexuality is not to be a slave to one's desires, to be free. The Greek sexual ethic emphasized not *what* one did but *how* one did it; it involved not an index of particular forbidden acts but an inculcation to act with moderation. Virtue in the sexual realm involves achieving mastery over self, what Foucault calls "an esthetics of being."

Another salient aspect of the Greek view of sexuality was its emphasis on roles. From their perspective the most important question was the distinction between subject and object, between the active and the passive participant. Sex was not conceived as a mutual dyadic engagement but as what one person does to another. As constituted by the "public masculine discourse," sexual activity was defined as phallic penetration. "Phallus," not "penis," is the right word here because the point is not so much the physical organ as the cultural meaning attributed to it, "which enables its possessor to play an 'active' sexual role."[7] Even when there was no physical penetration, the question was "Who has the phallus?" "Whose pleasure is being promoted?" "Who has put him/herself at the service of another's pleasure?"

Absolutely critical to our understanding of Greek sexual morality is a recognition of the central role played by the phallus. As Wilamowitz-Moellendorff noted a century ago: "We must accept that for the Hellenes the phallus symbolized the full force of manliness not just procreative power. This would apply to gods as well as to mortals."[8] More recently, in her *The Reign of the Phallus*, Eva Keuls has stressed anew the pervasive presence of this emblem of male power in ancient Athens, where it functioned not as symbol of union with the female or mutual pleasure but as a "scepter of sovereignty."[9] (Keuls is also sensitive to how the insistence on phallic supremacy betrays an obsessive fear of women, a theme to which we will return.) She describes the omnipresence of phallic images: the herms (stone pillars dedicated to Hermes topped with sculpted heads from which, about midway, protruded testicles and an erect penis) standing at the entry to every private home and marking the boundary of public and sacred precincts, and the enormous phalli carried in the ritual processions honoring Dionysus. Because of the symbolic significance attributed to the phallus, the mutilation, or as she says "castration," of herms all over the city during a summer night in 415 B.C.E. was regarded as a serious challenge to the established social and political order. (We shall return to this event in our consideration of Plato's *Symposium*.)

In Greece the sexual relationship was assumed to be a power relationship, where one participant is dominant and the other inferior. On one side stands the free adult male; on the other, women, slaves, and boys. Sexual roles are isomorphic with social roles; indeed, sexual behavior is seen as a reflection of social relationships not as itself the dominant theme.[10] Thus it is important for us to remember that for the Greeks it was one's role, not one's gender, that was salient. "Sexual objects come in two different kinds—not male and female but active and passive."[11]

As Foucault notes, Greek sexual ethics was an ethics for men in which women figured only as objects, not as moral agents themselves (even though it was an ethics that put severe constraints on their sexual freedom). The conjugal bond was not seen as primarily "erotic." Aristotle subsumed it under the rubric of "politics," since the relation of men to women was the relation of ruler to ruled. To exercise power over another responsibly, without exploitation, was further evidence of the self-mastery also expected of men in exercising restraint over their own instinctual impulses. Foucault describes the marital relation under the rubric of "economics," since the legal term for wife makes clear that she is the man's property. Her role is to run the household and to produce male children. Because within marriage sexuality is defined in terms of its reproductive function, the debates about conjugal sexuality revolve around how to assure the birth of healthy progeny. What are the best ages for men and women to marry? How often and in what seasons should intercourse ideally occur? Women are expected to be monogamous so that the legitimacy of the couple's children may be guaranteed.

Because of the emphasis on the phallus as *the* sexual organ, women were imagined as more lustful than men, "as obsessed with an insatiable lust to fill up their vaginal void with penises."[12] Since moderation is defined as an *act* of self-mastery, immoderation is seen as deriving "from a passivity that relates it to femininity. To be immoderate is to be in a state of submission to the forces of pleasure."[13]

All this does not mean that sexual passion was excluded from the marital relationship, only that it was not part of its definition. The testimony in Xenophon's *Symposium* to the interplay between Eros and Anteros, love and responding love, in the relation between Niceratus and his wife is evidence that erotic intensity and mutual affection were not considered incompatible with marriage.[14] Thus, radically to separate marriage from Eros misrepresents the case; nevertheless, Eros was not seen as constitutive in matrimony, whereas it was in the relationships between men and boys, where both are free agents.

PAIDERASTIA

Dover reminds us that the Greeks had no word for a "homosexual." They assumed that at one time or another almost everyone would respond to both heterosexual and homosexual stimuli. There were homosexual behaviors but not homosexual persons. Yet to describe the Greek attitude in these terms is to impose our categories, our mode of drawing distinctions. For the Greeks there were not two competing currents of sexuality but one: "a single, undifferentiated phallic sexuality of penetration and domination."[15] They recognized that there were variations—some men might be more strongly pulled toward females, others toward males—but this was a matter of taste, like the preference for red wine rather than white. (Plato, for example—who was a bachelor and thus had evaded the civic obligations involving marriage and paternity—seems to have been at the far end of the spectrum, someone who evinced no erotic interest in women.)

The Greeks combined an easy acceptance of same-sex attachments with a strong bias against effeminacy in men. "The dividing line between a virile man and an effeminate man did not coincide with our opposition between hetero- and homosexuality; nor was it confined to the opposition between active and passive homosexuality."[16] Male femininity was seen as manifesting itself in immoderate promiscuity directed toward males or females—in yielding to desire rather than being master of it—or in taking pleasure in assuming a passive role in sexual intercourse.

The model of socially validated homosexuality was *paiderastia* (following Thorkil Vanggaard I will use this form to avoid identifying the Greek practice with the associations "pederasty" has in our world),[17] the love of an older man for a youth. (By older man here we mean mostly men in their twenties, while the youths were adolescents.) The context was the *gymnasium*, where the youths went to exercise (and display) their physical gifts, and the older men went to watch, appreciate, and select. The arena was an upper-class one; paiderastia was essentially an aspect of the *paideia*, the training for citizenship of aristocratic youths. (That same-sex love tended to be mocked in comedy, an art form that attracted the masses, may indicate it played a less focal role in their lives.)

Beauty was an all-important criterion and was usually associated with unambiguously masculine bodily features—suntanned skin, muscular development, heavy thighs, and small penis—although in the fourth century a more "feminine" model became more acceptable. (We can perceive the shifts in the ideal by attending to alterations in the sculptural representations of Eros and Dionysus.) Yet as Socrates says in the *Republic:*[18]

> It does not become a lover to forget that all adolescents in some sort sting and stir the amorous lover of youth and appear to him deserving of his attention and desirable. Is that not your reaction to the fair? One, because his nose is uptilted, you will praise as piquant, the beak of another you pronounce right royal, the intermediate type you say strikes the harmonious mean, the swarthy

are of manly aspect, the white are children of the gods divinely fair, and as for honey-hued, do you suppose the word is anything but the euphemistic invention of some lover who can feel no distaste for sallowness when it accompanies the blooming time of youth? And, in short, there is no pretext you do not allege and there is nothing you shrink from saying to justify you in not rejecting any who are in the bloom of their prime. (474de)

Pausanias, according to the *Symposium*, insisted that despite the emphasis on physical attributes, beauty of mind and soul were also recognized as important: "Being in love openly is said to be more creditable than being in love secretly, and especially being in love with the noblest and the best, even if they are not as good-looking as others."[19]

Although the Greeks believed that the same desire attracted one to whatever was desirable, they nonetheless thought this desire entailed particular problems when it arose in a relationship between two males of distinct age cohorts, one of whom had not yet achieved the status of adult citizen. The disparity was what gave the relationship its value—and what made it morally problematical. An elaborate ritualization of appropriate conduct on the part of both participants was designed to give such relationships a "beautiful" form, one that would honor the youth's ambiguous status. As not yet a free adult male, he was an appropriate *object* of masculine desire; as already potentially a free citizen, his future *subject*ivity must be honored. The active role can only be played by the older partner, but the younger partner must be treated as *free* to accept or reject his suitor. Thus the Greeks believed that the relationship should be designed so as to provide an opportunity for the younger to begin to learn the self-mastery that would be expected of him as an adult. The older man's desire was seen as unproblematic; what was difficult was how to live that desire in such a way that its object might in turn become a subject.[20]

Dover asserts that reciprocal desire between partners of the same age was almost unknown and that the distinction between the man, who takes on the active penetrating role (the *erastes*) and the youth, who accepts the passive role (the *pais* or *eremenos* or *paidika*), was a rigid one. "Virtually no male both penetrates other males and submits to penetration at the same stage of his life."[21] (Although a youth engaged in a passive relationship with a man might at the same time be taking on the active role vis-à-vis females.) An illustration of how distinct these roles were assumed to be can be found in the fable Plato attributed to Aristophanes in the *Symposium*, which describes the sexuality of those descended from the original all-male being (that is, males attracted to other males):

They show their masculinity throughout their boyhood by the way they make friends with men, and the delight they take in lying beside them and being taken in their arms. . . . When they themselves have come to manhood, their love in turn is lavished upon men. They have no natural inclination to marry and beget children. Indeed, they do so only in deference to the usage of society, for they would just as soon renounce marriage altogether and spend their lives with one another. In a word, such persons are devoted to lovers in boyhood and themselves lovers of boys in manhood. (*Symp.* 192)

Furthermore, it is only the desire to play the active role that is regarded as "natural." The younger male yields to the older's importunities out of admiration, compassion, or gratitude but is expected to feel neither desire nor enjoyment. As evidence Dover quotes Xenophon: "The boy does not share in the man's pleasure in intercourse, as a woman does; cold sober, he looks upon the other drunk with sexual desire." The sexual desire felt by the active partner is called *eros;* the younger's friendly affection, *philia.* Because it is important that the younger not identify with the object role, that he not be seen as effeminized by the relationship, much emphasis is placed on his reluctance to accede and his lack of enjoyment. (Foucault questions Xenophon's emphasis on the youth's "coldness" and reminds us that he was expected to yield out of affection and gratitude: "He was supposed to feel pleased at giving pleasure.")[22] A man who *enjoys* playing the receptive partner is derogated as a prostitute and as having forfeited his right as a citizen to hold office. The assumption is that a man who would willingly make himself available would do *anything!* Only slaves, women, and foreigners would willingly choose to be treated as objects.

Though youths were taught to resist, they were also taught that it was acceptable to yield to the worthy eremenos. They could take it for granted that their taking on the roles of erastes and later eremenos would be acceptable to their fathers and uncles—as long as they followed the rules for playing those roles, played their assigned role within the highly stylized pursuit-and-flight pattern.

The relationship between erastes and eremenos was seen as having an educational and moral function, to be part of the youth's initiation into full manhood. Therefore it was a disgrace not to be wooed—although also shameful to yield too easily. The lover became responsible for the youth's development and honor. Because the more mature partner was assumed to be motivated by true regard for his beloved's well-being, and because what he wanted was love and consent not simply sexual satisfaction, rape, fraud, or intimidation were disallowed (indeed proof of coercion was grounds for banishment). The two shared fame and shame.

Some students of Greek paiderastia have tried to assimilate it to Cretan rituals of male initiation as those were described by Strabo. According to this Hellenistic historian and geographer, in ancient Crete when a boy reached puberty an older male would abduct him (after having actually received permission for the ritual kidnapping from the youth's father) and carry him into the countryside, where he would teach him the adult skills of the warrior and hunter, have sexual intercourse with him, and after two months send him home laden with ritually specified gifts. Upon completion of this initiation, the youth would have attained adult male status. The inclusion of sexual intercourse in the ritual signified the transfer of manliness from the adult male to the youth. Classicists disagree as to whether the belief (found in some cultures that include homosexual intercourse as part of their pubertal rites) that the older man's semen was endowed with magical potency—serving as a carrier of such male virtues as strength, courage, endurance, fidelity, trustworthiness—was part of the Cretan tradition.

Many scholars regard the application of the Cretan model to classical Athens as questionable. Although paiderastia did serve a social function there, its motives were clearly erotic and sexual. Participation in such relationships was not based on a binding social obligation but on individual attraction. As Vanggaard says, "The love of boys remained in Athens a more personal, erotic, and esthetic phenomenon."[23] We radically misunderstand the Greeks if we overemphasize the educational function and deny the erotic component. David Halperin believes that to impose on the Greeks a "pederasty-without-homoeroticism" is as much of a misunderstanding as to assume that the same behaviors invariably have the same meaning no matter what their historical context.[24]

The relationship between an erastes and an eremenos was expected to come to an end as soon as the youth was old enough to grow a beard—that is, as soon as he, too, was a fully mature male—for its purpose was precisely the transfer of manliness, of phallic potency, from the older to the younger. The expectation was that the eremenos would now graduate from pupil to friend. This conversion of the inherently transient and unequal relation into a lasting and fully mutual one depends on the cultivation of friendship having begun during the earlier phase. Indeed, in his *Symposium*, Xenophon views such friendship, its reciprocal kindnesses and shared feelings, not so much as a substitute for Eros as its *telos*, its real goal. "It is by conducting themselves thus that men continue to love their mutual affection and enjoy it down to old age."[25]

The evidence of vase painting suggests that the most accepted form of physical contact between males is not anal intercourse, fellatio, or mutual masturbation (though all are often represented in depicted scenes of hetero-sexual contact), but face-to-face "intercrural" copulation. The respectable eremenos refuses payment, postpones bodily contact until the erastes has proved worthy, and expects no physical gratification. When he finally ac-cepts his suitor, he insists on upright posture, avoids eye contact, and refuses penetration. The vases represent both partners standing. The youth, with no erection, stares straight ahead. The erastes rests his head on the eremenos's shoulder; his knees are bent, his penis thrust between the other's thighs just below the scrotum. (By contrast, vases depicting two heterosexual partners making love face to face show them looking at each other with affection.) "An honorable eremenos does not seek or expect sensual pleasure from contact with an erastes, begrudges any contact until the erastes has proved himself worthy of concession, never permits penetration of any orifice of his body and never assimilates himself to a woman by playing a subordinate role in a position of contact."[26]

The refusal of penetration is central because it is construed as a demeaning act that effeminizes the receptive partner. (The vases suggest that anal inter-course was often engaged in with *hetairae*, female prostitutes, precisely because it was objectifying and because the Greeks believed it yielded little or no pleasure to the passive partner. Thus they saw greed as a more likely explanation for a youth's accepting the passive role than the expectation of pleasure or the prompting of desire.) The rituals of courtship and persua-sion, the suitor's gifts, the avoidance of humiliating contact—all were an important part of honoring the youth's anomalous position as present object and future subject.

Of course, that this was the socially validated form of homosexuality does not mean it was the only one practiced. There were also male prostitutes available in brothels, where the moral conventions applicable to paiderastia did not apply, where the point was simply sexual pleasure—though here, too, the roles were clearly defined. The citizen played the active role.

> Often enough the inmates of such houses may have been young people who had been taken as prisoners of war and afterwards sold. The best-known example of this is Phaedo of Elis, with whom Socrates held the famous dialogue on the immortality of the soul. Phaedo belonged to a distinguished family and at the time of the war between Elis and Sparta and while still very young, had fallen into the hands of the enemy who had sold him to Athens, where he was purchased by the possessor of a "public house." There Socrates made his acquaintance, and induced one of his well-to-do adherents to buy him off. It is surely a remarkable fact, that the much-admired dialogue *Phaedo* . . . is named after a young man, and is carried out for the most part with one

who . . . only a short time before was at the disposal in a brothel of anyone who cared to pay for him.[27]

It is important to qualify even the idealized description of the relationshps between freeborn males, which we have so carefully delineated, with Dover's admission that it represents what it was prudent to profess in public, with his acknowledgment of the gulf between reality and the convention. It would be a serious misunderstanding to believe that there was no anal intercourse, no love between men of the same age cohort, no lifelong sexual relationships (or no greedy youths, no exploitative adults).

Dover says that "homosexual anal copulation, by contrast with the inter-crural mode, is portrayed by vase-painters only when it involves people of the same age group" and admits that in Greek comedy and Hellenistic poetry anal intercourse is assumed to be the only mode of lovemaking practiced by men with same-sex partners (whereas fellatio, at least as far as vase paintings go, is a mode of sexual activity peculiar to satyrs). He speaks of the "comic poets' invariably unfriendly treatment of males who submit to the homosexual desires of others" (a common abusive term is "having a wide arse") but finds in Greek comedy no ridicule of "men for aiming at homo-sexual copulation with beautiful young males or preferring them to women."

Relations between young boys were seen as completely natural and as not being subject to the constraints imposed on the paiderastic relationship. Dover describes one vase painting "in which a boy with a small but no doubt imperious erection lolls seductively on a chair while another boy mounts the chair to oblige him (perhaps they will change places afterwards)."[28]

Keuls believes that because "a mutual sex relationship between two adult men of approximately the same age and social standing negates the use of sex as the underpinning of a power structure"—not because "it is 'unnatural' or breaks the link between sex and procreation"—it was viewed as constituting "a rebellion against the social order."[29] But Dover points to some literary and some vase-painting indications of homosexual relationships between coevals "perhaps conventionally disguised by the acceptance, on the part of one partner, of the designation *pais*." He reminds us that one of the partici-pants in Plato's *Symposium*, Agathon, had continued as the eremenos of another, Pausanias, well into adult life. Agathon, his contemporaries agreed, was an unusually beautiful fair-skinned man; as an adult he was teased for trimming his beard closely so as to retain the appearance of a beardless youth. "Whether he declined an active heterosexual role or whether he wore feminine clothing, we do not know." His unwillingness to grow out of the eremenos stage into sexual dominance leads Aristophanes in his *Thes-*

mophoriazusae to mock him as "fucked," but in the *Symposium* the abiding love relationship between him and Pausanias evokes neither humor nor censure.[30]

Dover has little to say about female homosexuality—because of "the virtual silence of male artists and writers" and the paucity of women writers or artists. (The *only* classical literary reference is in the myth attributed to Aristophanes in the *Symposium*.) The male assumption that sexuality requires a phallus made love between women—except in situations where one woman's overdeveloped clitoris served as an inferior penis or use was made of a dildo—virtually unimaginable to Greek men. Dover also notes that what we call lesbianism (in the ancient world the term denoted fellatio, not female homosexuality) seems to have been a taboo subject even for comedy, which respected few taboos. This suggest that the very topic may have been avoided because it inspired male anxiety. Because what we do know of Eros among women in the ancient world is mostly based on Sappho, we will postpone our more extended discussion until we turn to her. Dover does say that what evidence there is suggests that in female-female relationships there was a much greater emphasis on mutual Eros and that the dominance/submission pattern so central to male-male love was absent.

In trying to understand how same-sex erotic bonds came to play such an important role in classical Athens, Dover reminds us how little intimacy or affection, how little opportunity for sharing intellectual or cultural interests, there was within Greek marriages. "Erastes and eremenos clearly found in each other something which they did not find elsewhere," something that satisfied their longings for intimacy, intensity, and emotional depth in a personal relationship.[31]

In *The Glory of Hera* Philip Slater offers a more elaborated psychoanalytically based account of the circular relationship between the patterns of Greek familial life and the validation of paiderastia. A woman was typically exluded from political and intellectual life, virtually uneducated, married soon after puberty to a man often twenty years her senior, and thereafter sequestered in his home, while he spent most of his time outside it with other men. This meant that male children grew up in a mother-dominated environment and inevitably came to see mature women as dangerous, omnipotent, and devouring. So, when it came time for them to marry, they—like their fathers—would be more comfortable with young, virginal brides. The father's absence from the home means he has no emotional tie to his own son. The mother's feelings toward her sons are, Slater suggests, profoundly ambivalent. The sons become the object of some of the sexual feelings the woman's husband fails to satisfy and the scapegoat for the anger and resentment she dare not express to their father. Naturally the son will then go in search of a more neutral, nondevouring protector.

Thus, says Slater, are produced fathers with an idealized son image and sons with an idealized father image. The nurturant erastes made up for the actual father's neglect, and later when the youth became an erastes, "he loved his own childhood image in a new youth as compensation for his own deprivations. . . . Thus pederasty was far from being a trivial by-product of Greek society; it became an almost vital institution, diluting the mother-son pathology, counteracting rivalry between father and son, and providing a substitute father-son bond. . . . By substituting a young boy for a woman the Greek male could . . . still play a phallic male role but avoid the dangerous female."[32]

George Devereux, too, sees the paiderastic relationship as replacing not the marital bond but that between fathers and sons: "The Greek father usually failed to counsel his son; instead, he counseled another man's son in whom he was erotically interested. As for the boy, who needed an effective father to model himself upon, he had to rely on his *erastes*, who also served as a father surrogate."[33] Keuls agrees. "If the primary impulse had been to replace a heterosexual relationship, corroded by alienation and hostility, with a nobler one, where sex could be mingled with friendship and intellectual stimulation, the ideal partnership would have been that between two men of comparable age, status, and educational level."[34] But that is not the primary model offered us by ancient Athens.

We may envy the acceptance that a particular expression of homosexuality had in Greece and yet be saddened by the limitations of the model, by the hierarchical character of the relationships, the denigration of enjoyment on the part of the receptive partner, the repudiation of anal intercourse.

Somehow, however, the confrontation with the reality and its limitations does not exhaust the significance Greek homosexuality has for us. Homosexuality in Greece was not just socially condoned, it was endowed with religious significance. Delphic Apollo was invoked to bless homosexual unions. Homosexuality was regarded as a sacred institution, practiced by the gods themselves and by the ancient heroes.

Even when *our myths* about Greek homosexuality are scuttled, the *Greek myths* about homosexuality remain as testimony to the deeper, archetypal significance of same-sex bonding. Their myths, as we will see, express the cultural view—*and* go far beyond it. Thus they give us models, images, for facets of our experience ignored or denied by the conventions surrounding paiderastia. Attention to these myths helps us to confirm and articulate our own sense that homosexuality signifies something more than sexual preference, though it is not separable from it. Our understanding of homosexualities may be expanded by becoming aware of the full range of the Greek mythic representations—while we may also become more appreciative of elements of our own experience that the Greeks ignored or devalued.

The myths bring into view the "deeper mysteries of love."

·10·

SAME-SEX LOVE
AMONG THE GODS

Not too surprisingly, we discover that much of what Dover and other scholars have found to be true among mortals who engaged in sex with members of their own gender is true of the gods as well. None of the Greek gods or goddesses is a homosexual, but most are seen as attracted to members of their own sex *and* to members of the other.

That the love directed to same-sex mortals by the gods was a *sexual* love is not explicit in the epics, in Homer or Hesiod; but in the Athens of the tragedians and of Socrates and Plato the sexual aspect was taken for granted. The most forthright representation of divine homosexuality in classical literature is in the lyric poetry of the same period, especially in Pindar. Scholars disagree as to the meaning of Homer's silence, in part because they also disagree about the date when paiderastia became an accepted practice among the Greeks.

That their deities were represented as involved in homosexual experience is a powerful testimony to the Greek recognition of same-sex love as a given permanent aspect of life—for *theos*, the divine, simply signifies that which is immortal, that which persists and endures, that which is not subject to death as we mortals are. In Greek mythology more than in most, the divinities were viewed primarily in humanlike form, anthropomorphically. They were removed from any direct relation to the landscape or to animal life; in Homer and in later literature the gods no longer were rivers or volcanos or heavenly bodies, though they might rule over them; they no longer were wolves or eagles or geese, though Zeus might be spoken of as having an eagle's majesty and Aphrodite depicted riding a goose. Rather than being seen primarily in relation to the natural world, these divine beings were seen as representing the ever-reappearing, eternal aspects of human experience— not only the desirable or valued aspects but also those that are painful and ugly. The Greek gods and goddesses illumine our lives; they help us discover the connections between the joyful and dark aspects of our own experience. They also help us recognize the polymorphousness of aspects of human life we tend to see univocally. Just as each of the goddesses—Demeter, Hera, Aphrodite, Artemis, for example—mother in distinctively different ways,[1] so each god and goddess loves in a way peculiar to his or her particular character. Each brings into view a different sexuality, a different homosexuality.

Just as the validated same-sex relationships between mortal men are always (or almost always) between an older erastes and a younger eremenos, so in Greek mythology when a male god is represented as loving a member of his own sex, it is always a human who serves as the object of his desire. (And as among humans, the physical beauty of the youth is what marks him as desirable. The mortal youth beloved by a god is invariably described as the most beautiful of mortal men.) I know of no myth that tells of a god loving another god. The hierarchical pattern so important in everyday life informs the myths as well.

Not surprisingly, it is also almost always the god who is the active partner, the one who takes the initiative and who obtains sexual gratification. The mortal partner is assigned the receptive, feminine role, which gives him no direct sexual pleasure but here, too, serves as a kind of initiation.

The one (or perhaps two) exceptions—instances in which the god takes on the part of the eremenos—are, obviously, of great significance and interest.

As we will discover, Greek mythology offers us two patterns of same-sex relationships between males. The most prominent is one that emphasizes the initiatory function of such relations. Another, which recognizes the peculiar beauty of more mutual and more permanent bonds, appears in some myths about love between mortal men. This alternative pattern will not be considered until Chapter 11, which deals with same-sex love among mortal heroes, for all myths about the homosexual loves of the gods follow the initiatory model.

In his *Homosexuality in Greek Myth*, Bernard Sergent provides a carefully detailed account of the initiatory pattern. He understands the myths as the narrative correlates of a sacred rite marking the passage from youth to adulthood, a rite similar to the Cretan tradition referred to in Chapter 9. Sergent's central argument—that the Cretan practice and, indeed, all of Greek paiderastia derive from Indo-European rites and myths brought to Greece by early Hellenes around 2000 B.C.E.—leaves me unpersuaded. I find his delineation of the typical structure of the myths about divine homosexuality enormously helpful, however. I agree that the myths represent a more profound appreciation of the sacred transformative power of paiderastia than existed in Athens during the classical period. They refer back to an older, more genuinely religious, understanding.[2]

As Sergent shows, ritualized homosexuality honors the intrinsic significance of male-male relationships. It has nothing to do with a dearth of women or a denigration of women. It simply refers to something that a male can only receive from another male. Prior to participation in the ritual the youth is a nonmale, a member of the same category to which women are assigned. To be excluded from participation would mean to be deprived of a mentor and to be prevented from making the essential passage into adulthood. Thus not to be chosen is truly disastrous.

The rite as practiced in Crete began with an abduction (to which the youth's father had given his consent) and a liminal period during which the youth and his suitor were alone in the wilderness. The boy was taught the skills of hunting and other manly arts and initiated sexually. Sergent believes that in receiving the older man's sperm, the youth was thought to incorporate the seeds of manhood into his own body. Upon return to the ordinary world, the youth received some ritually prescribed gifts—including a warrior's gear, an ox, and a goblet. Sergent understands the ox, a castrated bull, to signify an emphasis on male creative rather than procreative power; the boy is no longer simply biologically but now also socially, culturally, a man. The goblet refers to the paradigmatic mythic eremenos, Ganymede, the cupbearer of the gods, whom we will discuss below. The gift of the cup signifies that the youth now has the right to participate in adult male rituals—for in Greece wine drinking was reserved for men. Younger males might attend the symposia at which wine was drunk, but only as cupbearers.[3]

Completion of the ritual marked the end—the death—of the initiate's youth and his rebirth as an adult male. On the human plane this "death" was followed by the youth's entry into the adult world, by his readiness for marriage and for taking on the erastes role.

In myth the "death" is represented in a variety of ways, mostly symbolic, not only by the youth's dying but also by his metamorphosis into a new life form (for example, from the blood of the dying youth, a plant may begin to grow) or his deification (the youth may be welcomed into the world of the gods).[4]

ZEUS AND GANYMEDE

The prototypical story of a god involved with a mortal youth naturally involves Zeus, the dominant figure in the Greek pantheon. This seducer of so many goddesses, nymphs, and mortal maidens is also celebrated as the lover of Ganymede, "who was the loveliest born of the race of mortals."[5]

The youth's very name (it means "happy genitals") presents him as the paradigmatic eremenos. (The Latin form of his name yields our word *catamite*, a term referring to the passive partner in anal intercourse.)

The iconic representations of Zeus and Ganymede tend to emphasize the disparity between them. In vase paintings the youth is often shown playing with a hoop and stick, as though to underline his childish innocence. The famous terra-cotta group at Olympia shows Ganymede as a tiny boy clasped by Zeus in an almost fatherly embrace. In the earlier literary accounts Zeus is represented as coming to carry off the youth in his humanlike form; in Ovid and in Hellenistic art he comes disguised as an eagle and swoops the youth up in his wings. Ganymede is also given a place in the sky; as the constellation Aquarius, he appears, appropriately, immediately adjacent to Aquila, the eagle constellation.

In the *Laws* Plato asserts that the myth about Zeus and Ganymede is of Cretan origin: "We all blame the Cretans for having made up the myth of Ganymede; they were convinced, we say, that their legislation came from Zeus, so they went on to tell this story against him that they might, if you please, plead his example for their indulgence in this pleasure too" (*Leg.* 1.636d). The Cretan provenance is not established—in the most familiar versions of the myth Ganymede is associated with Troy—but the myth does in many of its aspects conform to what we have been describing as the Cretan pattern (and according to some versions of the tale, Minos, king of Crete, not Zeus, was Ganymede's lover).

According to Homer, Ganymede was the youngest of the three sons of Tros, the eponymous king of the Trojans, himself a great-grandson of Zeus. Because of Ganymede's unmatched beauty the gods "caught him away to themselves, to be Zeus' wine-pourer . . . so he might be among the immortals" (*Il.* 20.234–35). In the Homeric "Hymn to Aphrodite" it is Zeus himself who abducts the beautiful youth:

> It was for his beauty that wise Zeus
> grabbed the blond Ganymede, so that
> he might live among the gods and serve them
> wine in the house of Zeus. He's a wonder
> to behold, and honored by all the gods
> as he pours red nectar out of a golden bowl.[6]

Neither account makes the sexual relationship explicit, but in the "Hymn to Aphrodite" the context certainly implies it. Aphrodite has just revealed herself to Anchises, after having tricked the solitary shepherd for whom she felt irresistible and "terrifying desire" into making love with her. Although he admits that he has half known all along who his beautiful seductress really is, he is terrified by the explicit disclosure and begs the goddess to let him die: "Pity me. For a man who sleeps with immortal goddesses loses his potency." But she makes light of his concern, reminding him of two earlier members of his family who had been just as intimately involved with divinity: Ganymede and Tithonus—the latter, like Anchises himself, a grandnephew of the divine cupbearer—whom Dawn had snatched away to be her lover and to whom Zeus had granted immortality but not, alas, eternal youth. Since Aphrodite's encounter with Anchises is overtly sexual, the goddess's reference to the two antecedents clearly implies that they are also.

Other, less reticent accounts make explicit Zeus's sexual infatuation with the youth. (Indeed, Dover refers to four lost comic treatments of Ganymede that clearly presented his relation to Zeus in coarse physical terms.)[7] In the *Phaedrus* Plato speaks of the "flood of passion" that seizes hold of Zeus as the lover of Ganymede (*Phdr.* 255c). Ovid includes the story of Ganymede among those tales that Orpheus tells as he mourns his failure to bring Eurydice back from the underworld. As Orpheus himself now turns from women to become a lover of men—whether because no other woman could replace his bride or because he now regards all women as faithless—he sings of "boys whom the gods have loved and of girls seized with unlawful passion." In his version Zeus is "fired with love," and Ganymede's attentions to him on Olympus provoke Hera's jealous annoyance.[8]

Among the sites named as the scene of this theophany is Harpagion, a place-name derived from *harpage*, a technical term for homosexual abduction also used in the myth about Laius and Chrysippus.[9] Clearly, as Dover observes, when the suitor is a god the eremenos forfeits that freedom to accept or reject his advances so important to the Athenian conception of acceptable relations between a human erastes and the youth he desires.[10] Nevertheless, Keuls notes, the inside of a cup by the Penthesilea painter depicting Ganymede's flight from Zeus shows the god with thunderbolt and scepter dropped, gently restraining the youth's attempt to reach for the scepter. "Lover and beloved look deeply into each other's eyes, signifying that, despite Ganymede's flight, an emotional tie is already developing."[11] (And as Monick observes, at the center of Jung's city, Zurich, a statue of Ganymede shows the youth fondling an eagle at his feet "as if it were his favorite dog.")[12]

The myth about Zeus and Ganymede is not a myth about some casual amorous dalliance. Their relationship is an ongoing one, not just an affair of a moment. The Homeric hymn tells us of Ganymede's father's concern at his son's disappearance:

And a pitiless grief seized the mind of Tros,
not knowing where the divine storm had snatched
away his dear son. And he mourned for him
every single day.

Zeus may not have secured the father's permission beforehand, but he does give the older man gifts that compensate his loss, that serve as the equivalent of a bride price:

And Zeus pitied him,
and gave him as payment for his son
the same fast-footed horses that carry
the gods! He gave them to him as a gift!
And Hermes the guide, by order of Zeus,
told him all the details, that he would be
immortal, and like the gods, never
grow old. And when he heard the message of Zeus,
he didn't mourn anymore, he rejoiced
in his heart![13]

As Plato (in a passage in the *Phaedrus* that we will return to later) describes the kind of love he sees Zeus and Ganymede as modeling, he says that the lover finds he cannot contain all the flowing stream of love that pours in upon him, and so some of it, like a breath of wind or an echo, returns to its place of origin. It reenters the eyes of the beloved and thence "reaches his soul and gives it fresh vigor, watering the roots of the wings and quickening them to growth, whereby the soul of the beloved in its turn, is filled with love. . . . He feels a desire—like the lover's, yet not so strong—to behold, to touch, to kiss him, to share his couch, and now ere long the desire, as one might guess, leads to the act" (*Phdr.* 255cde). Thus for Plato Ganymede serves as an image of a beloved who is himself stirred to love by being loved.

Ganymede is taken to Olympus and made a god, the now immortal eremenos of Zeus. He serves as cupbearer of the gods, as their wine pourer. This, remember, was a service performed by young males before they have completed the initiation ritual and attained full adult status. Thus Ganymede remains eternally fixed in the middle of the initiation ritual—forever Zeus's beloved.

In becoming the divine cupbearer, Ganymede replaces Hebe, the daughter of Zeus and Hera, a goddess who is his female counterpart—for, as goddess of marriage, Hebe represents the female passage from youth to adulthood, the moment when the maiden becomes wife. In one variant tradition, Ganymede is also the husband of Hebe (who more often is said to be the heavenly bride of Heracles) and thus represented as transformed by his involvment with Zeus into an adult ready for marriage.[14]

A passage in Apollonius's *Voyage of the Argo* presents a very childish Ganymede playing draughts with an equally youthful Eros. Greedy Eros laughingly beats a furiously despairing Ganymede. Eros's indulgent mother, Aphrodite, chides him: "Why this triumphant smile, you rascal. I do believe you won the game unfairly by cheating a beginner."[15] Ganymede is *still* Eros's innocent victim.

The mythological traditions about Ganymede beautifully evoke the numinous dimension of same-sex love. The myth persuades that to love a youth with the passion, tenderness, and fidelity exhibited by Zeus is divine. It also expresses the sense in which the beloved is eternally young and beautiful, how what is literally true at the beginning of a relationship may for the soul, the psyche, remain true "forever." Of course, a darker truth may also be discovered in the tale. It can be seen as representing the obsession with youth and beauty that may lead a lover to turn from one beloved to another, wanting to stay "forever" at the beginning stage of love. It can also be seen as depicting a love stuck in its beginning phase, with no opportunity for Ganymede (or Zeus) to move beyond the roles assumed in their initial encounter. How quickly our perspective shifts; at one moment Ganymede is seen as the fortunate recipient of an idealized love, at the next as an innocent victim of another's overweening passion. Both are true, and therein lies the power of myth to illuminate experience.

Ganymede is *the* eremenos of Zeus, as none of his female conquests is *the* mistress. There is, however, one other account of Zeus being attracted to a beautiful youth. According to Hyginus, Prometheus fashioned Phaenon out of clay but neglected to submit this especially handsome figure to Zeus for the usual approval. When Eros reported this oversight to the king of the gods, he sent Hermes to bring him the boy. Hermes succeeded in persuading Phaenon of the advantages of immortality and carried him off to the heavens, where he became the planet now called Jupiter. Since Jupiter is the Roman equivalent of Zeus, one might wonder in what sense Phaenon *is* Zeus, is Zeus as himself in some sense a desirable youth. Since as the supreme god Zeus was imagined as uniting in himself all attributes, he might be the beloved as well as the lover. Perhaps this tale expresses some of the narcissism, the self-projection, that is so often an element in same-sex love.

We must also note that although Zeus is never represented as taking on the passive role in sexual intercourse, he nevertheless is represented as having some "feminine" experience. After hearing that his divine mistress Metis was fated to give birth to a son stronger than his father after bearing the daughter she was already carrying in her womb, Zeus determined to avert the fulfillment of the prophecy. Metis fled from him, taking various shapes; when he finally caught up with her, she changed herself into a fly, which he, alas, easily swallowed. Months later Zeus found himself experiencing a headache of divine proportions. Recognizing his pain as birth pangs, he persuaded Hephaestus to split open his head with an ax. Out of the wound sprang the goddess Athene, full grown.

Nor is Athene the only child to be born of Zeus. Jealous of Zeus's affair with Semele, Hera in disguise persuades the Theban princess to invite Zeus to come to her with the same divine energy that his divine mistresses experience. Though Zeus tries to dissuade her, Semele insists and, of course, when Zeus makes love to her as a lightning bolt the mortal mistress is consumed by fire. Zeus snatches from the flames the unborn child lying in her womb. Because the fetus is not yet viable he has it sown into his own thigh and there carries the child as though in a male womb until it can safely be brought into the world. (Keuls suggests that the choice of thigh instead of abdomen to represent the womb may be connected to the practice of intercrural copulation; as we noted in the last chapter, the preferred mode of homosexual intercourse in the classical world was ejaculation between the thighs.)[16]

We might recall here that Zeus's father, Kronos, had also engaged in this practice of taking unborn or newborn children into his own body and then giving birth. Kronos had desexed, castrated, *his* father, Uranus, in response to his mother, Gaia's, appeal for help against her husband's refusal to allow her to give birth to the strange creatures stirring in her womb. Upon assuming power, Kronos feared that someday a son might do the same to him; to avoid this calamity, he swallowed each of his children as soon as they were born. As substitute for the sixth child, his wife tricked him into swallowing a stone. That child was Zeus, who when grown tricked his father into swallowing an emetic (in a sense a labor-inducing drug), which forced him to disgorge Zeus's sisters and brothers. How vividly this myth represents the fear felt by males of the (sexual) potency of both their fathers and their sons—the homosexual rivalry that is the other side of homosexual identification and desire. The myth also expresses the male longing (discussed in our chapters on Freud) to be the only sex, to usurp the birth-giving prerogative nature has assigned to women.

Thus Zeus's "femininity" can be read in two ways: as an acceptance of the mutual complementation and interdependence of masculine and feminine attributes and capacities, or as an arrogation to himself (and to males) of all powers, those conventionally deemed feminine as well as those traditionally recognized as masculine.

APOLLO, THE IMMORTAL ERASTES

As Ganymede embodies all our fantasies about the beloved, the dark ones that see him as victim of his lover's desires, the more attractive ones that see him as forever loved, forever desirable—so Apollo is in Greek mythology represented as the paradigmatic lover.

To him are attributed more love affairs with beautiful youths than to any other of the gods. For Ganymede to be *the* beloved it is appropriate that he essentially be his lover's only love; but a lover fulfills *his* role by fulfilling it many times. Unlike Zeus, Apollo is not a father god, but forever the just-grown son, the eternally young *kouros*, the accomplished initiate who becomes the model initiator. (Of course, Apollo is also a father—but not *essentially*. His most well-known sons are Orpheus and Asclepius, with whom he has no personal relations—one simply inherits his musical gifts, the other his mastery of the healing arts.)

As Callimachus describes Apollo, he is "always fair, always young! Never do traces of down touch his blooming cheeks."[17] Kerenyi says: "The reason why boys were numbered among the god's reputed lovers was that he himself was the god of just that age at which boys used to leave their mother's tutelage and live together. . . . They attached themselves to individual older men. . . . This was the age of fugitive bloom."[18] Burkert says that the god of the culture which saw in the *kouros* its ideal was Apollo.

Apollo is "the patron of young people entering their manhood, the leader in the stages of adult life. . . . At his most important festivals it was mainly boys and youths who made their appearance. To him the boy attaining manhood dedicated his long hair."[19] Hesiod says that he develops boys into men. Apollo, the god most often represented nude, is the patron of the festival of the naked boys, Gymnopaidia, from which unmarried men were barred, and of the *appelai*, the annual gatherings that served as initiation festivals for youths newly come of age. The god "with unshorn hair," Apollo is the "epitome of that turning-point in the flower of youth, *telos hebes*, which the *ephebos* has attained and which he also leaves behind with the festival which gains him admittance to the society of men." According to Burkert, the festivals of Apollo mark not only the one-time event of transition *from* youth, but also "youthfully pure renewal."[20]

Because of the reiterated association of Apollo with the point of transition into adulthood, I find persuasive Sergent's suggestion (which he acknowledges will scandalize many Hellenists) that the erastes par excellence may himself have undergone initiation.[21]

The relevant tale is a familiar one, its interpretation less so. It concerns Apollo's relation to Admetus, but fully to understand the myth and its possible meaning we have to begin earlier. When he was only four days old Apollo came to Delphi and there killed the she-dragon (called Python in later tradition but originally known as Delphyne, a name connected to the word for womb) who served as guardian of the oracle, which was at that time dedicated to the earth goddess Gaia. In punishment Apollo was banished for eight years to northern Thessaly, an exile that Wilamowitz-Moellendorff understood as a period spent in the underworld. (There is indeed a version of the story according to which Apollo—like Jason when he contends with the dragon guarding the golden fleece—was slain by the dragon and buried under the omphalos.)[22]

Somewhat later Apollo joined Poseidon, Hera, and Athene in an unsuccessful plot against Zeus; in punishment he and Poseidon were sent to serve the Trojan King Laomedon for a year. The king set them to build a wall around his city and upon its completion, refused to pay them their wages and threatened to sell them into slavery. Although Apollo retaliated by sending a plague upon Troy, during his stay in the city he had clearly been the servant, Laomedon the imperious royal master.

Sergent sees both these exiles as the equivalent of initiation ordeals—the young god must conquer the mother and then serve an apprenticeship to an older male before he attains the status of adult divinity. Sergent regards the temporary exile of the criminal god as not just representing the expiation of a crime but as part of an initiation complex: the period of withdrawal from society is followed by the god's return in a new status.

That this god stands forever just on the other side of the passage suggests that an account of the passage might well be an integral part of his story. The definitive story, which brings together motifs separated in the other tales, involves the year Apollo spent working for the Thessalian king Admetus. This servitude was undergone as punishment for Apollo's killing the Cyclopes, whose thunderbolts Zeus had used to kill Apollo's son, Asclepius (whom Zeus sent to Hades for having used his gifts as a healer to restore the dead to life).

All accounts agree with Callimachus 'that during the year he spent at the Thessalian court, Apollo "was burning with love for unmarried Admetus" and that this king, unlike Laomedon, treated him with respect and kindness.

Their year together was marked by fruitfulness: among the king's herds and flocks "all bore young, and not single offspring, but twins." Later, when Admetus wished to marry Alcestis, Apollo in gratitude for the king's favors came to his assistance. He provided the chariot drawn by two wild beasts that enabled the king to succeed at the trial set by Alcestis's father; he instructed the king how to propitiate Artemis (who in anger at having been ignored during the wedding sacrifices had filled the bridal chamber with snakes). Then when Admetus (while still in the prime of life) fell mortally ill, Apollo persuaded the Fates that if the king could find another to die in his place, his own death might be postponed. Thus we see that while their intimacy was confined to the year Apollo spent in Thessaly, their bond persisted throughout Admetus's life. Upon the completion of that initiatory phase, Apollo helps Admetus succeed at a superhuman trial and win his bride—as befits a worthy erastes.

Yet, as Sergent suggests, it is not that simple. Aspects of the tale suggest that in this instance the god may have played the role of eremenos rather than that of erastes. In this story the god was the mortal's servant; perhaps he also served him sexually. Perhaps the mortal master, no adolescent but already a ruling king, took on the active erastes role. Perhaps it is Apollo not Admetus who is "the novice undergoing initiation and who, if there is a pederastic ritual, is in the female position." The "perhaps" is mine; Sergent is more definite. He admits there are *no* texts that explicitly affirm this; it is a deduction from the parallels between the structure of the myth and the typical structure of homosexual initiation. Two descendants of Admetus, Hyacinthus and Hymenaeus, were later loved by Apollo—which suggests that Admetus might have been regarded in Thessalian legend as the mythical founder of initiatory homosexuality.[23]

Sergent also recalls the nineteenth-century German mythographers who identified Admetus (whose name means the "untameable") with Hades, thereby suggesting that the royal hero might himself be a chthonic deity, not just an ordinary mortal. This leads Sergent to conclude: "It is not impossible (nor, admittedly, is it certain) that in archaic times men ascribed to the god who took a wife . . . by kidnapping her [the reference is to Hades' abduction of Persephone] the task of educating Leto's son, the young god and new Olympian, in the usual protohistorical fashion"—that is, through homosexual initiation.[24] Here Sergent is proposing that a lost archaic tradition presented Hades as Apollo's erastes.

How difficult these periods of servitude, this image of a god subordinating himself to a man (or even to another god), are to reconcile with Walter Otto's vision of Apollo as one who "cannot be imagined as making any appearance without demonstrating his superiority," without reminding us of "the per-ishability of all beings earthly, even the greatest, before the presence of deity." After all, the motto of Apollo's oracle at Delphi, "Know thyself," meant "Know that you are human and no god." Otto emphasizes Apollo's purity and holiness, his calmness and unapproachability—though he admits that in Homer we still catch glimpses of a more original character, that of "a terrible death-dealing god." Otto sees Apollo as rejecting "whatever is too near—entanglement in things, the melting gaze, and, equally, soulful merg-ing."[25]

Yet Otto's view of Apollo seems incompatible not only with our interpre-tation of the relation to Admetus but with all the many love stories told of the god—"the greater number and most famous of which," as Kerenyi tells us, "ended tragically, whether the object of the god's love was a boy or a girl. . . . The tales represent Apollon's [sic] love, for a person of either sex, as having been very dangerous."[26] Perhaps the explanation for the discordancy is that Otto shows us an Apollo immune to passion, whereas the love stories show us an Apollo in whom passion is so divorced from his acknowledged character that he cannot be the lucid, clearheaded Apollo when in love—and so his love is dangerous not only to its objects but to himself.

Nevertheless, Apollo without these stories is not Apollo. Most of his love affairs, as Kerenyi indicates, end with the death of those whom the god loves. Kerenyi sees these endings as tragic; Sergent interprets them as sig-nifying the beloved's death as an eremenos, his rebirth as an adult male. Perhaps it is too simple to choose between these alternatives. Perhaps the myths are what Freud called "overdetermined," susceptible of more than one interpretation.

Because it issues in an influential cult, the most important myth about Apollo in the role of erastes involves the son of a Spartan king (and perhaps of the muse Clio), Hyacinthus. Loved by a man and three gods—by the mortal musician Thamyris (who comes to be known as the first human male to have loved a member of his own sex, to have aspired to the role of erastes), by Apollo, and by both Zephyrus, the west wind, and Boreas, the wind of the north[27]—Hyacinthus comes to be seen as the paradigmatic *mortal* eremenos, as Ganymede is the paradigmatic *deified* beloved.

Like the human eremenoi of later times, Hyacinthus is given the freedom to choose among his suitors, and chooses Apollo. Ovid lets Orpheus tell us how utterly absorbed Apollo was by his infatuation for the beautiful youth: "My father, Phoebus, loved Hyacinthus beyond all other mortals, and Delphi, the centre of the earth, lost its presiding deity, while the god haunted Eurotas and Sparta's unwalled city, neglecting his harp and his arrows.

Heedless of his old habits, Apollo was willing to carry hunting nets, or direct a pair of hounds, as he accompanied Hyacinthus over the rough mountain ridges, and by constant companionship, added fuel to the fire of his love" (*Met.* 10.162–219). During their sojourn in the wild Apollo instructed the youth in the arts of the hunter and sportsman, the musician and the diviner. But then one fatal midday "the god and the boy stripped off their garments, rubbed their bodies, till they gleamed with rich olive oil, and began to compete with one another in throwing the broad discus." After Apollo took his turn, Hyacinthus eagerly ran forward to pick up the discus, which bounced off the hard ground and hit him full in the face. All Apollo's medicinal art was of no avail; the youth died in his arms. (Some say that jealous Zephyrus caused the discus's unexpected rebound, but most accounts see Apollo as responsible for having accidentally killed the boy.) Apollo may wish that he could give his life in exchange for that of Hyacinthus, but that cannot be, for he is a god, he is immortal. But he vows to give the youth such immortality as is available to mortals—he will never forget him, his songs will celebrate his memory, and from his blood a plant with stunningly beautiful lily-shaped purple flowers will grow, a plant that will bear his name and remind all who look upon it of the youth's beauty and the god's grief.

Central to this story is the emphasis on the youth's humanness and thus his mortality. Zeus carries Ganymede in his arms up to Olympus, Apollo watches Hyacinthus die in his arms. The point seems to be the conjunction of an immortal lover and a mortal beloved. In Apollo's realm the divide between god and human is inescapable. There is no avoiding the death of the beloved.

But like the heroes at Troy who choose glory over homecoming, the immortality granted by cult and poetry over old age, Hyacinthus in a sense becomes an immortal mortal precisely by dying. (According to Pliny, the hyacinth plant, which is not *our* hyacinth, could delay puberty; that is, it signifies the perpetuation of Hyacinthus's adolescence.)[28] Only by dying young could Hyacinthus remain forever an eremenos, forever the beloved. It is not surprising, then, that a cult should arise at his tomb, where offerings are made to Hyacinthus as a hero, before sacrifices are offered to Apollo as the god. (Ovid even has Apollo institute the Hyacinthian festival at the very moment of his beloved's death.)

Sergent rightly to my mind rejects understanding this cult in agrarian terms, as though the story of Hyacinthus was "really" a story about vegetal fertility. Rather, he interprets the death as representing the "passage from the condition of beardless, adolescent eremenos to that of bearded adult and therefore, implicitly erastes." In substantiation he points to an altar frieze that shows a bearded (that is, adult) Hyacinthus being carried to heaven and to a hymn sung at the Hyacinthia that speaks of Apollo bringing his beloved back to life. "Hyacinthus's death is mystical and temporary—a first stage in his transformation," says Sergent. "His resurrection brings him back to life in a different state, a superior mode of existence."[29]

But I find Sergent's interpretation almost as inadequate as the one he contests. The many stories of gods loving mortal men do not all have the same reiterative meaning. Part of the difficulty seems to lie in Sergent's complete identification of vegetal and chthonic cults—which prevents him from seeing the way this myth is about mortality and death, about the inescapable connection in human lives between love and transcience, about how much in us resists that conjunction and about how the only transcendence of death available to us is through acceptance of it. To my mind the festival celebrates the recognition that Hyacinthus is dead and still lives, *as* a dead hero—whereas the god lives eternally. Thus the festival is not just about initiation but (as Burkert affirms) about universal renewal, and therefore one in which all men and not just youths participated.

The god lives—to love again. Among those other loves is the one directed to Cyparissus. Kerenyi sees him as clearly a double of Apollo himself. For just as Apollo had accidentally killed Hyacinthus, so Cyparissus unintentionally kills a creature he loves, a beautiful, tame, golden-antlered stag.[30] One day when he is out hunting, the youth, mistaking his pet for an ordinary stag, throws his spear at it and kills it. Like Apollo he wishes he might join his beloved in death; unlike Apollo, as a mortal he can. Apollo allows the youth to kill himself and then turns him into an ever-sorrowing, ever-green cypress, a tree that symbolizes the triumph of life over death. But here what is given immortality is loss, regret, grief. In this instance we know nothing of the courtship, nothing specific about Apollo's love.

This by no means exhausts the list of mortals whom Apollo loved. He is also reputed to have been involved with Helenus (one of Priam's sons, twin brother to the seer Cassandra), with the seer Carnus (identified as the patron of the initiation rituals associated with an important Apollo festival, the Karneia, and sometimes spoken of as Apollo's adopted son), and with the warrior hero Phorbas. But the connections are tenuous, the sexual dimension unclear; these reputed affairs add little to our understanding of the god's homosexuality—or of our own.

FEMININE DIONYSUS

In the traditions associated with Apollo, the model erastes, the notion of initiation is a subtle one; it may be hinted at (as the necessary prelude to his taking on the initiator role), but it may not be made focal (for danger of compromising his integrity as the epitome of the masculine ideal). With Dionysus it is far otherwise—for what this god means is the transgression of boundaries. Dionysus is the god not of the mean but the extreme, the god of wine and ecstasy, madness and confusion. Among the many antitheses he confounds is that between masculinity and femininity.

This "gender confusion" is not an incidental aspect of the god but a central element in his myth. Dionysus, you may remember, is in a sense born of a male mother. For while still a fetus he had been snatched from the holocaust that destroyed his mother and sewn into Zeus's thigh; there he was kept safe until, when the child was ready to be born, Zeus untied the stitches. The meaning, as so often in the myths surrounding Dionysus, is ambiguous. On the one hand, it may be understood to signify that Zeus has male *and* female capabilities; on the other hand, we must acknowledge that the cut into Zeus's thigh is a wound, is castration.[31] (There are other versions of Dionysus's birth. The Orphics taught that Dionysus was originally a child of Zeus and Persephone whom the Titans, at jealous Hera's instigation, abducted, tore to bits, and ate. Athene somehow managed to retrieve the infant heart and brought it to Zeus, who cut it up and fed it to Semele, thus reconceiving the child.)

After Dionysus's "second birth," the birth from Zeus's body, Hermes secretly took the child to Semele's sister, Ino, who agreed to rear him as a girl in the hope of protecting him from Hera's still unappeased wrath. Hera eventually uncovered the deceit and punished Ino and her husband by driving them mad. Ultimately Hera's vengeance found the youth, too, and drove him mad as well. He ran away from his nurse (or perhaps was kidnapped) and wandered distractedly through Egypt and other Eastern lands. (While there he adopted the Oriental costume, the flowing feminine garment, that distinguishes him and his followers.) Eventually he came to Cybele's shrine in Phrygia and there was purified of his madness.

Among the many boundary obliterations associated with Dionysus is that between human and divine. The stories suggest that he was born a mortal; at some point he becomes a god. Greek mythology is full of tales (like the one retold in Euripides' *Bacchae*) of those who resist his claim to be a god. That the unsettling energy Dionysus embodies, the unrestrained instinctual passion, should be accepted as *divine* arouses violent opposition whenever he appears. Although a god, Dionysus represents not the steady presence of some permanent aspect of the world but the unexpected appearings and disappearings of an energy incapable of being tamed. As Otto describes him, he is the "always coming" god. Dionysus represents a force that is *always new*, that is always coming from "elsewhere." Myth may represent him as a newly arriving, recently introduced god, but the myths that do so are as old as any others.

Dionysus represents the discovery that being passive, being taken over by the god *(en theō)*, losing one's everyday identity, can be blessing and not only curse. The festivals in honor of Dionysus all seem to provide a time of license, of the suspension of the rules that constrain everyday life; the rituals sanction intoxication, ritual transvestism, the inversion of sex roles, ritual dismemberment, phallic processions. There is joyous revelry—and mourning and lamentation. Dionysus's gifts bring joy—and danger.

One of the stories associated with Dionysus may refer to the moment of transition between his mortal childhood and his adult divinity. It is also a tale of a homosexual initiation, which in Dionysus's case may be plainly admitted. When Dionysus grows up he determines to rescue his mother, Semele, from Hades and bring her to Olympus. To deify his mother would be to assure his own godliness, for the sons of Zeus by his divine mistresses are by definition gods. Greek mythology makes plain that for the psyches of the dead to find their way to Hades is easy, but the gates through which a still living embodied person might make entrance are difficult to find. Clement of Alexander tells of Dionysus's search:

> Dionysus wanted desperately to go down to Hades, but he did not know the way. Someone named Prosymnus promised to tell him how to go, but in exchange for pay, pay that was not pretty, though it was pretty for Dionysus; the favor asked was erotic, the requested pay was Dionysus himself. The god willingly heard the request, promised to respond if he returned from the underworld, and confirmed his promise with an oath. Informed of the path, he set off. When he came back Prosymnus, who had died, was nowhere to be found. To pay his sacred debt to his lover, Dionysus went to his tomb and underwent intercourse. He cut the branch of a fig tree that happened to grow there, carved it to resemble the male member, sat on it and thus fulfilled his promise to the dead man. In the various cities phalli are dedicated to Dionysus as a mystic memorial of this event.[32]

Prosymnus (whose name means "the much sung of") teaches Dionysus the way to Hades, to his mother, to his own change of status. I like Kerenyi's suggestion that the original "pathfinder" is the cult object itself, the carved phallus—that which leads Dionysus to his particular mode of divinity is his relation to this phallus.

Here, again, my interpretation differs somewhat from Sergent's, who credits the tale with initiatory significance but sees it as marking Dionysus's transition to active male status. As Sergent sees it, the assumption of the passive role with the wooden dildo is simply the ritual on the other side of which Dionysus emerges in his new role—as a god. The descent to Hades is the death that precedes the rebirth, the mature epiphany. Prosymnus serves as erastes, as master and educator as well as initiator; as the wooden phallus he even achieves a kind of immortality (since he remains present even after death).[33]

But this interpretation ignores what is distinctive in the Dionysian tradition. For this god's relation to the phallus is typically ambiguous, an ambiguity that cannot so simply be resolved into "before" and "after" but instead requires a more simultaneous "both/and" interpretation. Dionysus both has and has not a phallus. He may be represented with an enormous phallus of his own, or be shown carrying a detached phallus. His epithets include *phales*, "the phallic one"; *orthos*, "the erect"; *enorches*, "the betesticled"—but also *pseudanor*, "the man without true virility"; *gymnis*, "the womanish"; and *thelymorphos*, "having a woman's appearance." He is called *dyalos*, "the hybrid" and *arsenthelys*, "the man-womanly."[34]

The gate through which Dionysus entered Hades was near Lerna. The mysteries of Dionysus at Lerna were celebrated in commemoration of his descent. Pausanias, the second-century C.E. Greek geographer and traveler, who visited Lerna, says that he is not permitted publicly to reveal the mysteries' nightly rites; we are no doubt right to assume that they would have involved some homoerotic sexuality. Burkert agrees that the Dionysian rites included actual homosexual intercourse.[35]

That in the *Bacchae* Dionysus seduces the young adult king Pentheus into dressing up like a woman suggests that possibly one of the points of the Dionysian ritual may have been initiating *adults* into the eremenos role—as though some complete human fulfillment requires adding to one's prized masculinity a femininity, becoming complete like the bisexual god himself. (One might in this connection also recall that in the Greek theaters, which were dedicated to Dionysus, men played the women's roles.) Presumably also, as in the mysteries associated with Demeter and Persephone at Eleusis, this Dionysian cult involved some coming to terms with death, some acceptance of the passivity that the Greeks associated with femininity and yet which they knew—and dreaded—lay ahead as their own inescapable fate. In this connection homosexual submission might have been understood to represent a very deep mystery indeed, a ritual anticipation of death.

The Orphic transmutation of Dionysian worship seems to recognize this, for though its religion was puritanical where the earlier religion of Dionysus had been sensually affirmative, it nevertheless retained as a central element in its ritual artifacts the winnowing basket from which a large, erect phallus emerges. In the new context the phallus signifies neither procreative power nor sexual pleasure, but Dionysus's power to give his followers access to a joyous afterlife.[36]

Another confusion of boundaries associated with Dionysus is the merging of god and devotee that characterizes surrender to this god, a fusion otherwise uncharacteristic of Greek piety. Both the god and his worshiper are called *Bacchus;* they become one. This god is directly available—through the drinking of wine, through sexual ecstasy—without the priestly intermediaries associated with the worship of the other divinities. And whereas the other Greek deities have attendants of their own sex, Dionysus is attended by women as well as men.

As Otto suggests, the feminine aspect of Dionysus is also revealed in his relation to his female votaries.[37] For Dionysus opens them to their own female sexuality, to a sexuality in which the phallus plays no part! On vase paintings the female devotees of the god are represented as emphatically rejecting male advances. In their rituals all men are excluded, except for the god himself. These women are called maenads because of their *mania,* their possession by ecstasy, by the god himself. Yet as the *Bacchae* makes clear, the maenads were not mad in any ordinary sense—that happens only to those who try to repress what the god represents and then find themselves taken over by it against their will. Ritually sanctioned "raving" protected against true insanity. The maenads were *Bacchae,* fully identified with the god who signified the pleasure that "feminine" sexuality provides. Indeed, it was primarily because of his relation to women that Hera so adamantly opposed Dionysus, who called them from their identification as wives and mothers, who invited them (at least temporarily) to throw off the bonds imposed by patriarchy and discover their own power, their own sexuality, their sensual bonds with one another and their connection to the natural, instinctual world. Their celebrations occurred not in the confines of a temple but on the mountaintops at night. Originally these rites were reserved for women, but toward the end of the classical period men were allowed to participate— provided, as Evans puts it, that they were willing "to lay aside all signs of male privilege and adopt a *feminine* persona" (italics mine).[38]

In Dionysian processionals, on the other hand, the male members of his retinue are exaggeratedly *masculine;* they parade disguised as satyrs. The flat-nosed mask with beard and animal ears conceals the wearer's face, but nothing hides the enormous erect leather phallus or the horse tail attached to his body. As displayed in these festivals, "the significance of the phallos is not procreative. . . . It is arousal for its own sake and also a symbol of the extraordinary."[39] Thus Dionysus represents not so much the feminine aspect of sexuality as sexuality for its own sake, a sexuality dedicated in the service of pleasure not power.

Vase paintings depict satyrs enthusiastically engaging in all those forms of sexuality deemed incompatible with respectable paiderastia—their penises are enormous (some satyrs even had two!), their erections dramatic (with the glans clearly exposed); they masturbate; they have anal intercourse; they make love lying down and in every imaginable position; they may be engaged with several partners simultaneously. As Dover says, "Satyrs were a godsend to artists who felt impelled to give expression to exuberant penile fantasies."[40]

That the satyr, though ostensibly a derided and mocked figure, represented something felt to be divine, immortal, is suggested by the honor paid Priapus, the Phrygian god of fertility, in Asia Minor—though he never attained much importance in Greece or Rome. An ugly satyrlike being with enormous genitals, Priapus, not surprisingly, was said to be a son of Aphrodite and Dionysus.

Also often associated with Dionysus, though actually an ancient Arcadian divinity, is Pan, the goat-god who represents the boundary between human and animal, the polis and the natural world. Like Dionysus, this ithyphallic god with the feet and horns of a goat was associated with natural, untamed sexuality, with those desires the civilized try to repress. Known as "the penetrator," he made love indiscriminantly with man and beast, male and female.

Evans honors Dionysus as the god "who evokes the emotional, nonrational aspects of human consciousness; asserts natural continuities between animal, human and divine; validates erotic pleasures as ends in themselves; and serves as a focus for aspirations and values preceding and contrary to the patriarchal revolution." He sees him as representing a challenge to the internalized homophobia of gay men, which may lead them to reject their own femininity.[41]

There are, as the Greeks saw, many homosexualities. Dionysus represents an Eros among men that may exalt the phallus—or do without it; a sexuality that celebrates instinctual pleasure and removes it from the context of power relationships. The worshiper of Dionysus does not fear ectasy—or submission.

ALL BUT ARES AND HADES

Except for Ares, the god of war, who had many affairs with divine and mortal women but never married, and Hades, the underworld god who emerged from his shadowy realm only once, to abduct Persephone, all the major Greek gods are represented as being erotically involved with men. (Ares, the epitome of an exaggeratedly aggressive masculinity, was viewed ambivalently by the Greeks, who respected his courage and strength but were appalled by his mindless bloodthirstiness. It is apparent that he in no way represents a Greek ideal; even the gods dislike him.)

One of the more elaborated tales involves Poseidon's courtship of Pelops. The story begins with Tantalus, a son of Zeus resentful of his mortal status. Having unsuccessfully sought to win immortality for himself by stealing the nectar and ambrosia that sustain the gods, he determines to trick them into eating flesh. He invites them to a feast at which he serves them a stew in which he has cooked the cut up pieces of his own son, Pelops. Demeter takes a bite of the shoulder portion, but the other gods almost immediately see through the trick and quickly restore Pelops to life (with an ivory shoulder). Poseidon was smitten by the beauty of the re-membered youth. As Pindar tells it:

> Son of Tantalos . . .
> . . . when your father summoned the gods
> to that stateliest feast at beloved Sipylos,
> and gave them to eat and received in turn,
> then he of the shining trident caught you up,
> his heart to desire broken, and with his horses and car of gold
> carried you up to the house of Zeus and his wide honor,
> where Ganymede at a later time
> came for the same desire in Zeus.

Unlike Zeus, Poseidon is not allowed to keep his beloved with him on Olympus. Their love, like the love of a human erastes and eremenos, belongs only to its brief allotted time. Pelops is sent back to earth:

> . . . they sent [Tantalos's] son
> back to the fleeting destiny of man's race.

But both Pelops and Poseidon remember the time when they were lovers:

> When at the time of life's blossoming
> the first beard came to darken his cheek,
> he thought on winning a bride ready at hand,
> Hippodameia, the glorious daughter of a king in Pisa.
> He walked alone in the darkness by the gray sea,
> invoking the lord of the heavy trident,
> and he appeared clear at his feet.

He spoke: "Look you, Poseidon, if you have had any joy of my love
and the Kyprian's sweet gifts, block the brazen spear
of Oinomaos, and give me the fleeter chariot
by Elis' river, and clothe me about in strength.
Thirteen suitors he has killed now, and ever
puts aside the marriage of his daughter. . . ."
He spoke, with words not wide of the mark.
The god, increasing his fame, gave him
a golden chariot and horses never weary with wings.[42]

The god's gift, the god's assistance in helping his former beloved win his bride, helps make this story of the love between a god and a mortal man fit almost perfectly the idealized pattern of paiderastia described in Chapter 9.

There are other myths that associate Hermes with Polydeuces, Asclepius with Hippolytus, Hephaestus with Peleus, Hypnus with Endymion.[43] None has cultic significance, some are clearly late literary inventions. They add little to our understanding of the deeper meanings Greek mythology discerns in same-sex love, though they confirm how naturally the Greeks assumed that their gods would practice it.

Though we will consider the Greek goddesses at greater length in Chapter 13, it might be worth noting here that two in particular, Aphrodite and Artemis, have been regarded as having a connection to male homoeroticism.

To differentiate the feminine from the mother is obviously an important task of male development. In terms of Greek mythology this would mean a turning away from the mother goddesses, Hera and Demeter: from Hera because she represents the demand that all a man's sexuality and feeling be lived within the conjugal relation; from Demeter not only because she represents the devouring mother of childhood, but also because in her realm men are viewed as either intruders or abductors.

Emancipation from the mother is facilitated by the motherless goddess of love, Aphrodite. This goddess, as we shall see when we discuss the *Symposium*, was regarded by the ancients as the divinity who blesses all love for love's sake, whether it is legitimate or adulterous, hetero- or homosexual. Indeed, because in her realm sexuality is distinguished from procreative responsibility and from social power, she is sometimes regarded as more sympathetic to love between men than to marital love.

In the ancient world Artemis was a goddess of women. There is some evidence that in medieval Europe she played an important role in the religion of the "faggots," the male homosexuals who were often burnt as heretics along with those women who were castigated as "witches"; and many of the contemporary gay men I know experience her as the deity to whom they feel closest. Artemis is honored for her commitment to her own integrity and her affirmation of same-sex bonds, for her attunement to the natural life of the wilderness and to her own instincts, for her rejection of patriarchal civilization and her ability to live outside of it. The nineteenth-century homosexual prophet Edward Carpenter put his vision of a goddess-inspired homosexuality this way:

> The meaning of the old religions will come back to him. On the high tops once more he will celebrate with naked dances the glory of the human form and the great procession of the stars, or greet the bright horn of the young moon which now after a hundred centuries comes back laden with such wondrous associations—all the yearnings and dreams and the wonderment of the generations of mankind—the worship of Astarte and Diana, of Isis or the Virgin Mary; once more in sacred groves will he reunite the passion and the delight of human love with his deepest feelings of the sanctity and beauty of Nature.[44]

·11·

SAME-SEX LOVE
IN THE AGE OF HEROES

As we turn to the myths that focus on the doings of mortal men in the long ago heroic age—a time conceived of as different from our own, as *illo tempore*, a time when human lives still had archetypal significance, a time the Greeks see as ending with those who fought at Troy—we discover that here, too, love among men plays an important role. The sexual element in that love is not made explicit in the Homeric epics, though later writers discover clues to its hidden presence. When the lyric poets of the classical period and Hellenistic writers retell the tales, they do so with considerably less reticence or discretion. On the other hand, there are no extant tragedies focused on homosexual love, although a lost trilogy by Aeschylus did take up the theme.[1]

The Greek ambivalence toward homosexual love may be suggested by the fact that, on the one hand, almost every part of Greece—except, strikingly, Athens—has its own founding tradition, and on the other, that the terms most commonly used in Athens to refer to the practice of paiderastia presented it as though it were a foreign custom: *lakonizein, khalkidizein, khiazein, siphniazein*—all, like "doing it in the Cretan way," derive from place-names outside of Attica.[2]

Mythical accounts of the first human to love a person of his own gender abound, confirming that same-sex love was recognized as an archetypal aspect of human life and suggesting that it was seen as having sacral significance. They also suggest, of course, that homosexuality is a cultural "invention" that was discovered at a discrete moment in time—like wine making, the cultivation of grain, or the institution of a particular religious ritual. Myths may attribute the innovation to a mortal culture-hero or to a god. Thus among such founders Sergent names Pelops and Hyacinthus, who were introduced to this form of love by the gods who loved them, and who on the other side of their initiation themselves come to be seen as initiators—

168

or, I think more accurately, as blessers of human unions between erastai and eremenoi.

HEROIC INITIATORS

More commonly, what the Greeks meant by naming someone as the human founder of homosexuality was that he had been the first to play the role of the lover, the erastes. In the myths about these figures who initiated not just a particular man but, through him, *men*, the typical hierarchal paiderastic pattern seems to obtain; but as we look more closely we see that invariably these myths seem to be about something going wrong, about some tragic element intervening. In his introduction to *The Heroes of the Greeks*, Kerenyi explains the difference between the mythology of the gods and the mythology of the heroes: it is of the very essence of the hero that he, unlike a god, will die. Thus his very immortality, in epic and cult, is "strangely combined with the shadow of mortality." The heroic mythology of Greece typically stresses the tragic realities of human life.[3] Not too surprisingly, then, failure and suffering will enter into these tales of heroic love.

We have already spoken of Thamyris, the Thracian bard who fell in love with Hyacinthus before Apollo (and, according to some sources, also with Hymenaeus and Narcissus). The one other story we know concerning him records that he became so proud of his reputation as a singer that he challenged the Muses to a competition. Of course, they won and in forfeit took away both his sight and his poetic gift. The two stories about the bard are more connected than might at first appear, for Hyacinthus is sometimes said to be the son of the Muse Clio, so in both cases Thamyris is trying to claim possession of something that by origin is theirs. We are not told that Thamyris was ever accepted as a lover by those whom he desired, only that he was their human suitor. At the heart of the stories about Thamyris is his *hubris*, his overconfident assertion of his own desire, his own potency. Dover tells us that there was in Attic law a specific offense called "hubris," which in the sexual sphere referred to the "shameless, importunate and headstrong" pursuit of another, that is, to sexual assault.[4] Thus Thamyris represents not the prototypical successful erastes, but the rejected lover, the one who is unaware of the feelings of those he pursues or of his own limitations. His love is a fantasy that exists in his own mind rather than in the real world.

Another legendary "founder" is Laius, the father of Oedipus. His story is related to the one we retold involving Poseidon and Pelops, for as a young man Laius spent time at the court of Pelops in Pisa and there fell in love with the king's beautiful son, Chrysippus. While teaching him to drive a chariot, Laius kidnapped the youth and fled with him to his own city, Thebes. There is obviously a kind of parallel between Poseidon's abduction of Pelops and Laius's abduction of his son, emphasized by the reappearance of the chariot theme; but, *pace* Sergent, the parallels serve to draw attention to the *differences*. Laius's deed came to be spoken of as "the crime of Laius"—not because his beloved was a man, not because of the homosexual aspect of his desire, but because he had violated the rules of hospitality, had seized Chrysippus without securing his father's permission and without winning the youth's consent.

In consequence, both Chrysippus and Laius come to tragic ends. To be taken thus by force is to have been robbed of one's manhood; one way or another, Chrysippus must by the logic of the myth die. The youth either kills himself in shame or is killed by his half brothers, Atreus and Thyestes, seeking to reclaim their family's honor. (I find uncompelling Sergent's assertion that his death is a "mystical" one and that Chrysippus is reborn as an appropriately initiated male in the persons of his half brothers.)[5]

Laius assumes the throne in Thebes and marries Jocasta, but he lives under a curse. He has been warned that if he has a son, that son will be his death. The point is clear: you, in essence, killed the son of Pelops; in retribution, your son will kill you. As we know, though Laius had a son, he sought to avert the prophecy by having Oedipus exposed at birth. Because the child's life was, unbeknownst to Laius, saved, Oedipus grew up and, all unconsciously, fulfilled the oracle. This is clearly not a myth that celebrates homosexuality, but one that shows what happens when the bond between father and son is dishonored. Rightly understood, the relation between erastes and eremenos is a continuation of the natural bond, not a violent supplantation. It is not surprising that the consequence of Laius's crime should be the radical disturbance of the relations between generations that is manifest in Oedipus's relationship to his mother/wife and to the daughters who are also his sisters, the sons who are also his brothers.

Orpheus, too, is sometimes named "the first man to love boys." We have already described his devastation at the second loss of Eurydice when, after having persuades Hades and Persephone to allow his bride to return to earth, he lost her by looking back to make sure she was still following behind. In the years that followed, Orpheus shrank from the love of women (though many desired him) and "preferred to centre his affections on boys of tender years, and to enjoy the brief spring and early flowering of their youth; he was the first to introduce this custom among the people of Thrace" (*Met.* 10.84–85).

As Ovid tells it, though grief-stricken, Orpheus still sings so beautifully that the very trees gather to hear his songs. He sings of Pygmalion and the power of art to give life, though his own art has failed to give him back the one life he treasures; he sings of women consumed by unlawful passion (like Myrrha obsessed with incestuous longing for her father), as though love inevitably wounds those it enters; he sings of gods who loved boys (and especially of his own father's love of Hyacinthus and Cyparissus), and tells how even the gods must suffer the death of their beloveds.

So absorbed is Orpheus in his singing that he does not notice the arrival of the maenads, who—calling, "See! Look here! Here is the man who scorns us!"—suddenly descend from the wooded hill and attack him with their spears. They kill and dismember him, but even after his death, as his severed head and his lyre float down the river, they utter a plaintive melody.

Many different reasons have been given for the maenads' attack. Perhaps these Dionysian women felt that Orpheus's narcissistic absorption in his own grief, his inability to see Eurydice as anything more than *his* beloved, affronted their sense of the independent reality of female existence. Perhaps this son of Apollo was seen as one who had failed to honor their god, Dionysus. But the most oft-adduced explanation is that their anger was fired by Orpheus's rejection of *them*, of women. Having lost Eurydice, the singer spurned all other women and turned instead to the love of boys. Congruent with this is that access to the shrine in Lesbos under which his head was said to be buried was reserved to men. W.K.C. Guthrie, suggesting that in some accounts Orpheus is "actively misogynist," hopes to make us see clearly that Orpheus was not an innocent victim nor killed in error like Hyacinthus. His death was a kind of ritual sacrifice, an appropriate atonement for his own deeds.[6] Again, this tale can hardly be seen as a simple affirmation of same-sex love. When such love is turned to because of disappointment in one's love for women, when it is motivated by anger, that anger will come back and destroy.

Since I have just spoken of the narcissistic aspects of Orpheus's love for Eurydice, this might be the appropriate place to consider the relevance of Narcissus himself to our exploration of same-sex love in Greek mythology. Sergent discusses an ancient version of the Narcissus story according to which a young man, Ameinias, fell in love with the exceptionally handsome youth who repeatedly refused his suit. One day Narcissus even sent his suitor a sword (a Freudian interpretation seems irresistible), with which

Ameinias then stabs himself in front of Narcissus's own house, "cursing his beloved as he dies." The sword was *not* what he longed to receive from his beloved. It was shortly after this that Narcissus saw his own reflection in the river and fell in love with it. When he realized the hopelessness of his self-infatuation, he killed himself and from his blood grew a narcissus plant.[7]

In Ovid's version (*Met.* 3:339–510) more attention is given to Narcissus's rejection of a *woman* who loves him, the nymph Echo. Having lost her voice because of Hera's impatience with her endless chattering, Echo has no way of directly communicating her love to Narcissus, but she secretly follows him everywhere. One day when he has accidentally been separated from his companions, he calls out, "Is there anyone here?" and she replies, "Here." Though all he actually hears are his own words echoed back, he is deceived by what he takes to be another's voice. When he calls, "Come here," the nymph hopefully approaches and flings her arms around him, but he violently pushes her off and flees. Here, as again later in the tale, Narcissus takes his own reflection, his reflected voice, for another's; but in this instance there *is* another and she he emphatically rejects.

But in Ovid, too, Narcissus has male admirers as well and he rejects their advances quite as proudly. Finally, one of these implores the gods, "May he himself fall in love with another, as we have done with him! May he too be unable to gain his loved one!"

Then follows that scene by the river where Narcissus falls in love with his own lovely reflection. Ovid shows plainly that the youth is unaware that he is enchanted by his own image. "Unwittingly, he desired himself, and was himself the object of his own approval, at once seeking and sought, himself kindling the flame with which he burned. . . . He did not know what he was looking at."

It is only when he discovers that what he had taken for another is himself that despair overtakes him. As Murray Stein observes, the moment of tragic realization comes when Narcissus sees through his illusion "and recognizes the projective quality of his love."[8] "O you woods," he cries, "has anyone ever felt a love more cruel. . . . That form which I see and love I cannot reach. . . . It is such a small thing that hinders our love. . . . Alas, I am myself the boy I see. I know it, my own reflection does not deceive me. . . . What should I do? Woo or be wooed?" Yet he still cannot pull himself away from the seductive image in the water. Slowly he wastes away and when they come to bury him, his body is nowhere to be found. Instead, they discover a lovely white narcissus flower. That Narcissus remains bound to his infatuation is powerfully communicated by Ovid when he tells us: "Even then, when he was received into the abode of the dead, he kept looking at himself in the waters of the Styx."

In the Persephone myth it is when the maiden reaches to pluck an especially beautiful narcissus that the ground opens and Hades appears to carry her away in his chariot to his underworld realm. *There* the plant seems to signify death but also sexual initiation and Persephone's leaving behind her identity as Demeter's daughter and discovering her own, that of underworld goddess. But in the Narcissus myth the plant seems to signify not the hero's transformation but rather his immortalization as one who plays both erastes and eremenos in a hermetically self-enclosed world. As Ovid tells it, the story is prefigured in its first line: Narcissus "had reached his sixteenth year and could be counted as at once boy and man." On the one hand, we might say that boy and man become so enamored of each other that no outward other has a chance. On the other, we might say Narcissus becomes caught *between* the two roles. For Narcissus—as his name, which derives from *narke*, lassitude, suggests—is passive, not in the so-called "feminine" sense of taking on a receptive, responsive rather than initiating role, but in a kind of unwillingness to take on any role, that of man or boy.

The myth of Narcissus is not just an account of a youth appropriately rejecting a particular suitor who fails to please him—but rejecting love as such. (There are obvious parallels to Hippolytus, who is punished by Aphrodite for his exclusive devotion to Artemis, his desire to avoid the entanglements of mortal love.) Eventually Narcissus feels real passion, but only for an image. The word Ovid uses, *umbra*, is the same "sad word" used for Eurydice's existence in Hades, a word referring to the shadowy existence of the dead.[9] In another tale this might signify deep, creative engagement with one's soul, a turning from the world of the literal to the world of the imagination. But Narcissus is not willing to relate to his image as image; he wants it to be the object he first took it to be. Narcissus belongs in our catalogue of homosexual lovers because his love is directed toward what he takes to be another youth, though it is in truth but a projection of himself. Even after learning the truth, he cannot reconcile himself to turn instead to an actual other.

THE BONDS OF MUTUAL LOVE

Thus far we have been considering myths that at least to some degree are shaped by the conventions of the initiatory paiderastic model. Heroic mythology, however, also offers us another pattern, one that celebrates non-initiatory mutual and permanent love between members of the same age cohort. Recognition of this alternative model has been somewhat occluded by the fact that in the ancient epics that celebrate such homoerotic bonds their sexual dimension is minimized, and that in later writings such relationships are reinterpreted so as to make them fit the erastes-eremenos ideal.

Thus Xenophon, who denies the sexual element in the most obvious example, the relation between Achilles and Patroclus, insists: "Homer portrays Achilles, so gloriously taking revenge for Patroclus' death not as his boyfriend but as his comrade. Orestes and Pylades, Theseus and Perithous and many other excellent demigods are praised in song not because they slept together but because they had the greatest admiration for one another and performed fine deeds."[10] Aeschines disagrees:

> Homer has many occasions to speak of Patroklos and Achilles; but he maintains silence on their eros and the specification of their bond (philia), judging that the extraordinary degree of their affection was obvious to sensitive hearers. There is a passage in which Achilles says . . . that he has unwillingly broken the promise he made to Patroklos' father . . . that he would bring him back safe [from] Troy. . . . It is obvious from this that it was through eros that he took charge of Patroklos.[11]

An extant fragment from a lost trilogy of Aeschylus presents Achilles addressing the dead Patroclus with words that explicitly evoke their former lovemaking: "And you felt no compunction for (my?) pure reverence of (your?) things—O, what an ill return you have made for so many kisses!" The next fragment has Achilles recalling "god-fearing intercourse with your thighs."[12]

In Plato's *Symposium* Phaedrus takes it for granted that Achilles and Patroclus were lovers but argues against Aeschylus that Achilles, not Patroclus, was the eremenos:

> I may say that Aeschylus has reversed the relations between them by referring to Patroclus as Achilles' darling, whereas Achilles, we know, was much handsomer than Patroclus or any of the heroes, and was besides still beardless and, as Homer says, by far the younger of the two. I make a point of this because, while in any case the gods display special admiration for the valor that springs from Love, they are even more amazed, delighted, and beneficent when the beloved shows such devotion to his lover, than when the lover does the same for his beloved. (*Symp.* 180a)

The very discussion about who played which role shows how poorly they fit the model—one was older, the other was clearly the more famous hero. Their relationship does not easily fit the pattern imposed on it by the later authors, who were so moved by Homer's account of their death-defying love. Granted that Homer does not explicitly present them as sexual lovers (and that good scholars disagree vehemently as to whether or not he nonetheless expected us to assume that they were), let us turn to Homer's account, which gives us as beautiful a depiction as any I know of two men not afraid to acknowledge the intense emotions they feel for each other, nor to put their commitment to each other at the very center of their lives.

As any Greek reader of Homer would have known, Achilles was a son of the sea goddess Thetis, who abandoned him when her husband intervened after catching her laying their child in the hearth embers so as to make him immortal like herself. The father then sent the boy to the wise, kindly centaur Cheiron (who had also helped to raise Jason, Asclepius, and Actaeon) to learn the skills of hunting and war. (Sergent, quite idiosyncratically I believe, suggests that Cheiron "presided over an educational program that included homosexual practises" and that "in some lost myth" he might have had positive, honorable sexual relations with his pupils.)[13] When Achilles returned to his father's court, Peleus put him under the charge of a visiting youth, Patroclus, who had been forced to flee his homeland after accidentally killing a playmate. The two soon became completely devoted to each other, and when Achilles, still a youth, was talked into going to fight in the Trojan War, Patroclus accompanied him.

A variant tradition has Thetis sending the youth to be reared at the court of Lycomedes. Because she knew it had been prophesied that her son would die if he went to Troy, she sought to hide him from Agamemnon's troop-assembling messengers. She persuaded the Aegean king to dress Achilles as a girl and to bring him up under the name of Pyrrha as one of his own daughters. Yet though Achilles spent these years of his youth disguised as a girl, it seems not to have affected him as it did Dionysus. There is nothing in the story to suggest that Achilles was brought in touch with some "feminine" side of himself (unless one wanted to so describe the extravagance of his emotional outbursts after Patroclus's death). For during the time of his seclusion in the women's quarters, although but fifteen, he managed to get one of Lycomedes' daughters pregnant, and all too easily fell for the trick by which Odysseus (sent to recruit him for the war) pierced his disguise. The wily Ithacan placed various feminine baubles along with a spear and shield on the porch of the palace. Tricked into thinking the island was being invaded, Achilles stripped off his dress and seized the weapons. Odysseus had no trouble persuading him to join the Greek forces.

On their way to Troy the Greek troops by mistake landed in Mysia, and during the ensuing battle with its inhabitants Patroclus was injured. A justly famous vase painting shows Achilles using the healing arts he had learned from Cheiron as he gently binds the wounds of his beloved companion. Later, when Patroclus is speared again at Troy, his wound is fatal; Achilles can cradle the dead body in his arms but cannot bring it back to life. It is Homer's moving account of that death and Achilles' response to it that made the bond between these two a model for Eros among men.

During the tenth year of the war Achilles resigns from the fighting, out of anger at Agamemnon for taking away Achilles' concubine, Briseis, in order to make up for the loss of his own. (Agamemnon had been forced to return his captive, the daughter of a priest of Apollo, so that Apollo would end the plague he had sent upon the Greek army.) Achilles' hope that the Greeks will discover that without him they are lost is realized. When the Trojans begin attacking the Greek ships, Patroclus who has also withdrawn from the war, appears before Achilles and weeps "warm tears, like a spring dark-running that down the face of a rock impassable drips in dim water." Achilles asks him:

> "Why then
> are you crying like some poor girl, Patroklos,
> who runs after her mother and begs to be picked up and carried,
> and clings to her dress, and holds her back when she tries to hurry,
> and gazes tearfully into her face, until she is picked up? (*Il.* 16.6–10)

Patroclus explains that he does not want to try to talk Achilles into rejoining the fighting but can't bear to see what is happening to their men. He begs Achilles to let him wear his armor "so perhaps the Trojans might think I am you, and give way from their attack" (*Il.* 16.40). Achilles agrees but warns his friend not to get carried away: "When you have driven them from the ships, come back" (*Il.* 16.87). And after his friend (wearing Achilles' corselet and helmet, and carrying his sword and shield) has gone, Achilles takes from the chest in his tent a beautiful goblet. Offering a libation to Zeus, he prays:

> Make brave the heart inside his breast . . .
> But when he has beaten back from the ships their clamorous onst,
> then let him come back to me . . . unwounded. (*Il.* 16.242–47)

But, of course, in the heat of battle Patroclus gets carried away and, exhilarated by the success lent him by Achilles' armor, keeps fighting long after the Trojans have been pushed back from the Greek fleet. Apollo himself intervenes to help the Trojans and makes it possible for Hector to kill "the gentle" Greek. The battle goes on as the two sides fight over Achilles' armor and Patroclus's body. Eventually Hector goes off proudly wearing the armor, but the Greeks have managed to recover the body. All this while, as Homer reminds us, Achilles knows nothing of what has happened.

When Nestor comes to tell him, he is devastated. He cannot help but cry out, "Yet I told him . . ." He pours dust over his face and tears at his hair. He cries to his mother, who reminds him how the war has proceeded just as he had wanted it to. To which he responds:

> But what pleasure is this to me, since my dear companion has perished,
> Patroklos, whom I loved beyond all other companions,
> as well as my own life. I have lost him. (*Il.* 18.80–83)

His own warm tears flow as he sees the corpse of "the man he had sent off before with horses and chariot into the fighting, who never again came home to be welcomed" (*Il.* 18.237–38).

> Peleus' son led the thronging chant of their lamentation,
> and laid his manslaughtering hands over the chest of his dear friend
> with outbursts of incessant grief. As some great bearded lion
> when some man, a deer hunter, has stolen his cubs away from him
> out of the close wood the lion comes back too late, and is anguished,
> and turns into many valleys quartering after the man's trail
> on the chance of finding him. (*Il.* 18.316–22)

Though Achilles had earlier hoped that they two alone might survive the slaughter (*Il.* 16.99), now he vows to kill his lover's killer, Hector, knowing that it is fated that Hector's death entails his own. If he and Patroclus cannot live together, then at least they can be together in death:

> Thus is it destiny for us both to stain the same soil . . .
> Seeing that is I, Patroklos, who follow you underground,
> I will not bury you till I bring to this place the armour
> and the head of Hektor. (*Il.* 18.329, 333–35)

Only a little later he addresses his dead lover again:

Now you lie here torn before me, and my heart goes starved
for meat and drink, though they are here beside me, by reason
of longing for you. There is nothing worse than this that I could suffer,
not even if I were to hear of the death of my father . . .
or the death of my dear son. (*Il.* 19.319–26)

I will not forget him, never so long as
I remain among the living and my knees have their spring beneath me.
And though the dead forget the dead in the house of Hades,
even there I shall remember my beloved companion. (*Il.* 22.386–90)

Achilles reenters the fighting in a fury of killing, as though with the death of Patroclus no other life has any value, and even the death of *every* Trojan would fail to pay for the death of Patroclus. Finally he accomplishes the death that matters most to him, the death of the one who killed Patroclus, the one who wears his own armor, Hector. Because he longs to defile Hector's body in every way he can imagine, he has it dragged by the feet around and around the walls of Troy, before the eyes of all of Hector's comrades and family. That night the shade of Patroclus comes to him in a dream:

I call upon you in sorrow, give me your hand; no longer
shall I come back from death, once you give me my rite of burning.
No longer shall you and I, alive, sit apart from our other companions
and make our plans. . . .
. . . There is one
more thing I will say, and ask of you, if you will obey me:
do not have my bones laid apart from yours, Achilleus,
but with them, just as we grew up together in your house. (*Il.* 23.75–84)

Achilles agrees, and then says:

But stand closer to me, and let us, if only for a little,
embrace, and take full satisfaction from the dirge of sorrow. (*Il.* 23.97–98)

His arms reach out but cannot take him, the spirit goes underground like vapor.

Achilles chooses a huge grave mound for Patroclus and himself and with much lamentation sets light to the funeral pyre of his dead beloved. He reminds his companions that his own bones are later to be laid with those of Patroclus in the same golden jar. After the elaborate funeral games

> only Achilleus
> wept still as he remembered his beloved companion, nor did sleep
> who subdues all come over him, but he tossed from one side to the other
> in longing for Patroklos, for his manhood and his great strength
> and all the actions he had seen to the end with him, and the hardships
> he had suffered. (*Il.* 24.3–8)

Apollo finds Achilles' grief extravagant:

> For a man must some day lose one who was even closer
> than this: a brother from the same womb, or a son. And yet
> he weeps for him and sorrows for him, and then it is over. (*Il.* 24.46–48)

Homer's Apollo, who is not the impassioned lover of youths that he becomes in later tradition, does not understand that for Achilles Patroclus was dearer than brother or son.

Even Achilles' mother grows impatient and suggests that perhaps it would help if Achilles found some woman to whom he might make love:

> My child, how long will you go on eating your heart out in sorrow
> and lamentation, and remember neither your food nor going
> to bed? It is a good thing even to lie with a woman in love. (*Il.* 24.128–31)

It is only when aged Priam bravely comes to ask Achilles to let him take his son Hector's body back to Troy for decent burial that Achilles begins to have some relief from his overwhelming grief as he sees it mirrored in Priam's and as the old man reminds him of the grief soon to overtake his own father. The two are able to mourn together:

> . . . the two remembered, as Priam sat huddled
> at the feet of Achilleus and wept close for manslaughtering Hektor
> and Achilleus wept now for his own father, now again
> for Patroklos. The sound of their mourning moved in the house. Then
> when great Achilleus had taken full satisfaction in sorrow
> and the passion for it had gone from his mind and body, thereafter
> he rose . . .
> and spoke to him. . . .
> Now you and I must remember our supper. (*Il.* 24.509–15, 601)

When Odysseus visits Hades during the course of his many-yeared voyage back to Ithaca, he sees Achilles and, close by his side, the soul of Patroclus (*Od.* 11.467–68).

This, clearly, is *the* story about mutual love between adult men given to us in Greek mythology. But there are others, and in those others as well it is clear that both partners are imagined as equally manly; there is no sense that one must play a feminine role.

Plutarch tells us that the male loves of Heracles are too numerous to mention. We shall consider only two: one, his relation to Hylas, follows what we have called the initiatory model; the other, to Iolaus, suggests the more egalitarian pattern.

Heracles, taken by his youthful beauty, kidnapped Hylas (after killing his father) and took him along on the Argonaut voyage. As an Alexandrian poet describes the relationship:

> We aren't the first
> to whom beauty seems beautiful,
> who are mortal and can't foresee
> the morrow. Even Amphitryon's
> bronze-hearted son, who withstood
> the savage lion, loved a boy—
> charming Hylas, whose hair hung down
> in curls. And like a father
> with his dear son, he taught him all the things
> which had made him a mighty man
> and famous. And he never left him
> . . . .
> That way the boy
> might grow the way he wanted him to,
> and yoked with him, attain
> the true measure of a man.[14]

During an island stop, Heracles thoughtlessly allows the youth to go off on his own to fetch water. The nymph of the spring falls in love with the lovely youth and pulls him down into the watery depths to live with her. Heracles searches for the boy to no avail and in the end has to leave the island without him. The paiderastic relationship between Heracles and Hylas comes to an end with a death or marriage, and as Sergent rightly claims in *some* of these tales these are equivalent endings—since both may signify the end of the eremenos phase in the boy's life.

The other myth involves Heracles' relation to Iolaus, the son of Heracles' mortal twin brother, Iphicles. The literary and artistic traditions report them as engaged together in the hunts for the Calydonian boar and Cerberus, in the killing of the Hydra, in the fights with Cycnus and Antaeus, and on the

Argonaut voyage. According to one tradition, Heracles gave Iolaus his own first wife, Megara, as a bride. Iolaus in his own right was a great charioteer, a famous warrior, a leader of a troop of youths. Although considerably younger than Heracles, and thus at the beginning of their relationship one who could appropriately be imagined as an eremenos, Iolaus stays close to Heracles throughout his life; and even after the older hero's death, when he is himself a white-haired old man, Iolaus successfully fights to protect Heracles' family against the great hero's lifelong opponent, Eurystheus.

What is most interesting about Iolaus is the rite that Plutarch reports was still in his time celebrated at the hero's tomb: the swearing of oaths between homosexual lovers. Although Sergent, in agreement with his central thesis, argues that these oaths were "declarations to the gods that the homosexual ritual had been completed" and indeed even surmises that the sexual union itself might have been consummated in the sacred place,[15] I find this highly doubtful. The sustained relationship between Heracles and Iolaus suggests to me that Iolaus's tomb would have served much more appropriately as a place where lovers might ask the gods to bless their commitment to each other, their hopes of an enduring union. Thomas Figueira describes the oaths made by lovers at this shrine as " 'matrimonial' in nature," meaning that the pledge of fidelity has the sanctity and force of a marriage vow.[16]

The tomb of the Dioscuri, Castor and Polydeuces, was another site to which lovers came to swear loyalty to each other, for though the twins were brothers not lovers, their devotion to each other even beyond death was seen as a model of dedicated love between two men. Perhaps the two tombs of Philolaus and Diocles—another pair of lovers who ended their days still together—served a similar purpose.

HERMAPHRODITES AND TRANSSEXUALS

Because from the Greek perspective love between two men, at least love that followed the paiderastic pattern, entailed one of them taking on a "feminine" role, it seems relevant also to consider their myths about persons who are *both* male and female or who have during their lifetimes on different occasions been male and female.

We might begin with Hermaphroditus. When this beautiful youth, the child (as his name suggests) of Hermes and Aphrodite, was fifteen, a nymph called Salmacis—the only nymph (according to Ovid) unknown to Artemis, a nymph without any interest in sport or hunting who was completely absorbed in beautifying herself—caught sight of him and immediately longed to possess him. Confused and embarrassed by her advances, Hermaphroditus asked her to leave him alone. But secretly she continued to follow him until one day she glimpsed him bathing naked. Quickly stripping off her own clothes, she plunged into the pool and began to caress and kiss him. She twined herself around him "like a serpent . . . like the ivy encircling tall tree trunks, or the squid which holds fast [its] prey." As the youth struggles to free himself, the nymph calls upon the gods, asking that the two never be separated.

> Her prayers found favor with the gods; for, as they lay together, their bodies were united and from being two people they became one. As when a gardener grafts a branch on a tree, and sees the two unite as they grow, and come to maturity together, so when their limbs met in that clinging embrace the nymph and the boy were no longer two, but a single form, possessed of a dual nature, which could not be called male or female, but seemed to be both at once and neither (*Met.* 4.285–380)

The youth is horrified at what has happened to him. Clearly, this is not a representation of an idealized joining together of the masculine and the feminine but of a monstrosity. Salmacis is a self-absorbed and needy female; she conquers by clinging. Hermaphroditus, too, is self-absorbed, irresponsibly naive and passive. A compellingly negative portrait of what Jung might call an anima-possessed man.

Another quite different hermaphroditic figure is Cybele. Though actually an ancient Phrygian mother goddess, Cybele was reported by the Greek traveler Pausanias to have come into the world when Zeus once long ago lay sleeping on Mount Dindymus. As he slept, the god had a wet dream. From the spot where his semen fell there emerged a strange creature with both male and female genitals. The other gods, frightened at its potential power, cut off the male organ. The castrated creature grew up to be the goddess Cybele (whom the Greeks sometimes identified with Rhea). Although she had no official place in the Greek pantheon, Cybele was widely worshiped in Greece as the leading representative of the ancient great Mother Goddess. The story of her hermaphroditic origin suggests Freud's vision of the primal mother as the phallic mother. That she was served by eunuchs, that she is herself in that sense castrating, also fits. To have *her* born of *Zeus* seems a reversal parallel to that which has Eve, mother of all living things, born of Adam—a sign of the fearfulness of female generativity, female self-sufficiency, to males.

The Greeks also had several traditions about men who at some time in their lives had been women. Ovid tells how Hera and Zeus once argued over whether men's or women's pleasure in lovemaking was the greater. They called on the ancient seer Tiresias to settle their playful disagreement for he had experienced both. Once as a youth he had come upon two serpents making love; upon striking them with his staff he was immediately turned into a woman. Eight years later he came upon the same sight, struck them again, and was returned to his masculine form. Tiresias told the divine pair that women had nine times as much pleasure as men, an answer that so infuriated Hera that she struck him blind. In recompense Zeus gave him the gift of foreseeing the future and a long life as well (*Met.* 3.322–50). Though the tales that emphasize Tiresias's prophetic insights in later years make no reference to these events of his youth, one could still play with the notion that some part of his wisdom derives from perspectives gained during the years he spent as a woman.

Ovid also tells us of Caenis, a beautiful maiden who had vehemently refused all her male suitors. One day Poseidon saw her walking on the beach and raped her. Afterward he told her that he would grant her any boon.

"The wrong I have suffered," she replied, "evokes the fervent wish that I may never be able to undergo such an injury again. Grant that I be not a woman, and you will have given me all." The last words were uttered in deeper tones: that voice could be taken for the voice of a man, as indeed it was. For already the god of the deep had granted Caenis' prayer, bestowing this further boon, that the man Caeneus should be proof against any wound. . . . Rejoicing in the god's gift, Caeneus departed, and spent his days in the pastimes men enjoy. (*Met.* 12.169–209)

Sergent sees this story as much like the tale that describes Achilles being reared as a girl. The girl Caenis who is raped by Poseidon is like an eremenos forced against his will to play a feminine role; in asking to be made a man Caenis thus achieves her rightful status.[17]

But if we read the tale as being about a *woman* (rather than an exploited eremenos), different interpretations suggest themselves. In this myth there is real recognition of the vulnerability of women and hints of how the violation of women that so often figures in tales based on heterosexual themes might turn women away from men—and toward women. There is also the possibility that what Caenis wants is not so much to be a male as to have access to powers and privileges her culture reserved to men—including the privilege of being an erotic *subject*, a desirer. These tales of rape suggest that women are more desired by men than desiring of them, that their desire might pull them elsewhere, toward those same objects men find desirable, others like themselves.

· 12 ·

WOMAN·LOVING WOMEN

As we turn now to consider how Greek mythology might deepen our understanding of women's love of women, we find ourselves having to deal with a new problematic—for, aside from Sappho's poetry, which we will consider separately, we have no written accounts by women of their own experience of such love or of its mythical representation. What we have directly available are *male* perspectives. Not too surprisingly, this means that the theme is addressed much more rarely; it will seem less important to men as well as more mysterious. Also the accounts we do have will communicate male fears and fantasies, guilt and longing—their surface denial of sexual gratification that is not phallus-centered, their deeper dread of women's original and originating power and self-sufficient independence of men. So some of what we learn from the Greek accounts of women's bonds with one another is yet more about male projection, hence about male psychology and male sexuality.

Yet it is possible to garner more than this, though we will have to rely more on extrapolation, empathy, imagination, than we have thus far in our study. By imaginative reconstruction we can discover something of what the tales and rituals may have meant to the women of the ancient world. We will also take more note than we have elsewhere of how the Greek traditions have stirred the vision and courage of women since then, particularly of our own contemporaries. Bachofen writes:

> There are two roads to knowledge—the longer, slower, more arduous road of rational combination and the shorter path of the imagination, traversed with the force and swiftness of electricity. Aroused by direct contact with the ancient remains, the imagination grasps the truth at one stroke, without intermediary links. The knowledge acquired in this second way is infinitely more living and colorful than the products of the understanding.[1]

This method has its dangers and limitations, as Bachofen's own employment of it makes amply evident. The leap from mythological truth to historical truth is often suspect, and even the leap to psychological truth requires that we try to be clear as to whether we are describing the psychology of the ancient Greeks or trying to explore our own (albeit recognizing the hermeneutical problematics inherent in the attempt to make such discriminations). I respect the importance of trying to distinguish the discovered from the invented—*and* believe taking the risk of the imaginative elaboration is justified by what it may yield: the gift of images that express the multidimensionality, the beauties and the terrors, of our own experince of loving women. It is easy to see, for example, how the Greek myths about the Amazons express male dread of female power, how they relate to infantile male separation experience; but we need not *reduce* the myths to that fear. I see the myths as overdetermined, as also signifying powerful female fantasies about women's bonds. If it weren't so, contemporary women would not have been so pulled to claim these stories as relevant to their own preherstory.

After assembling all the relevant myths we can find, we will try to understand what these betray about the consciously espoused values and more hidden fears of the men who tell them; but our real interest will be in discovering what in these myths might be relevant to *women* seeking to understand their own lives and those of their long ago foremothers. We have seen that the Greek myths about male love actually provide us with a much more complex version of that love than the paiderastic pattern socially sanctioned in classical Athens would have led us to expect; similarly, from the myths about women's love we may receive more about women's experience than at first seems likely. As Robin Morgan affirms:

> We *are* the myths. We are the Amazons, the Furies the
>   witches. We have never not been here. . . .
> There is something utterly familiar about us.
> We have been ourselves before.[2]

SELF-LOVING WOMEN

Much of Greek literature confirms the fear and awe inspired in men before strong-willed women who fight against male oppression—women such as Clytemnestra, Antigone, and Medea. These women do what they do *for themselves*, not out of conscious love of women. Yet in choosing themselves, in loving themselves, they are loving *woman*. Commitment to self is a commitment to a woman, as their contemporaries seem clearly to have understood. For these heroines are applauded by other women for acting on behalf of the dignity and honor of all women, and are castigated by men (and by some women) as mannish and unnatural.

In the first lines of Aeschylus's *Agamemnon*—although Clytemnestra will ironically call herself "a woman merely"—the Watchman speaks of her as having "male strength of heart." His words prepare us for a woman resolved to murder the long-absent husband who had killed her first husband and child before her eyes, who had then insisted on the sacrifice of their daughter, Iphigenia, and was now coming home from Troy with his captured concubine Cassandra. The play counterposes Clytemnestra against both her weak consort, Aegisthus, who "like a woman waited out the war at home," and her husband, Agamemnon, who protests that her welcome pampers him as though he were a woman.

According to Aeschylus, Cassandra is appalled by Clytemnestra's deed:

> No, this is daring when the female shall strike down
> the male. What can I call her and be right? What beast
> of loathing? Viper double-fanged, or Scylla witch? (*Ag.* 1231–33)[3]

But in Euripides' *Trojan Women* Cassandra acknowledges a secret kinship with Clytemnestra. She foresees her own complicity in bringing about Agamemnon's death: knowing that Clytemnestra, castigated for her own adultery, will not forgive his, she rejoices. Likewise Hecabe, the Trojan queen whose own family has been destroyed by Agamemnon, expresses awe at Clytemnestra's daring: "She would never do it!" These women feel themselves vindicated by Clytemnestra's daring.

In Sophocles' *Antigone* Antigone's determination to give her slain brother ritual burial despite Creon's decree that "the traitor's" corpse is to be left to the dogs evokes her sister's plea that she desist—"We must remember that we two are women"—and Creon's fearful acknowledgment, "I am no man and she the man instead if she can have this conquest without pain." Antigone herself even at one point uses the masculine "I" to refer to her resolve. Yet in her commitment to put familial bonds over civic obligation and the duty of honoring the dead over practical considerations, she is choosing values associated with the age-old matriarchal perspective over those of the patriarchal state. She voices specifically female feelings as she laments the virginity she will never lose, the children she will never bear, and she dies what is according to the conventions of Greek tragedy a "feminine" death, suicide by hanging. In the earlier events depicted in *Oedipus at Colonus* her father had praised her for displaying a manly loyalty her womanly brothers failed to match, but in this play Antigone receives no praise for her "masculine" strength of will (though Creon's son Haemon and his wife both end their lives in protest against the consequences of Creon's stubbornness in resisting her). Nevertheless, Sophocles has presented his character so as to win our admiration and pity, our own awe before a dedication both pure and frighteningly obsessive.

Euripides' *Medea* opens with the Nurse warning us:

> She is a fierce spirit:
> takes no insult lying down.
> I know her well. She frightens me:
> a dangerous woman, and
> anyone who crosses her
> will not easily sing a song of triumph. (*Med.* 38–45)

Medea herself reminds the women of Corinth how female courage and strength easily match that of men:

> We live safe at home, they say.
> *They* do battle with the spear.
> How superficial!
> I had rather stand my ground three times among the shields
> than face a childbirth once. (*Med.* 248–51)

As she confides to them her determination to pay back her husband for his deserting her to marry the Corinthian king's young daughter, they voice their respect and their hope that her courage presages a new era for women:

> One day the story will change:
> then shall the glory
> of women resound
> And reverence will come to the race of woman . . .
> The ballads of ages gone by
> that harped on the falseness
> Of women will cease to be sung.
> If only Apollo,
> Prince of the lyric, had put
> in *our* hearts the invention
> Of music and songs for the lyre,
> Wouldn't I then have raised
> up a feminine paean
> To answer the epics of men? (*Med.* 416–28)[4]

Those feminine paeans remained unwritten. We are not even certain whether Athenian matrons were allowed to attend the dramatic performances in which these women who refused to be passive were so powerfully represented. Yet to us they are heroines.

There were also mythological traditions about *groups* of women acting together against male domination: for instance, the fifty daughters of Danaus who killed their husbands on their wedding night rather than be forced into marriages not of their own choosing, and the Lemnian women who after neglecting the cult of Aphrodite were afflicted with so foul a smell that their husbands refused to sleep with them. In retaliation they murdered every man on their island and established an all-women's world. (The reference to their failure to pay Aphrodite due homage suggests that these women were already interested in more than the marriage bed *before* their husbands deserted them.)

In these myths there is always what Keuls calls a "strikebreaker,"[5] one woman who protects "her" man, as in the Danaid myth Hypermnestra spares her husband and among the Lemnians Hypsipyle spares her father. Whether it is the "spoilsports" or the others who are to be regarded as the heroines obviously depends on who is telling the tale. From a feminist perspective, these are tales of women bonding with one another against men. There is no indication that their bonds with one another are sexual; they are joined together in protesting not just against patriarchy in general terms, but against the *sexual* aspect of heterosexual domination.

The individual women considered above and these groups of women were so fearful to men in part because they evoked memories of more archaic female powers, the Gorgons and the Furies. The serpent-haired Gorgons were thought to be so hideous that to look upon them was to be turned to stone. Yet there are other traditions that Medusa at least was ravishingly beautiful, confirming Freud's intuition that the Medusa represents the awesomeness of the primal mother's sexuality. It seems almost inevitable that there would be a myth in which a male hero, Perseus, succeeds in killing the Gorgon and that the Greeks would want to imagine her energy, which cannot be destroyed, as amenable to transformation into the benign energies associated with Athena (who wears Medusa's severed head on her aegis). But for women, as May Sarton suggests in her poem "The Muse as Medusa," the Gorgons may signify the sources of their own lost creativity:

> I saw you once, Medusa; we were alone.
> I looked you straight in the cold eye, cold.
> I was not punished, was not turned to stone. . . .

I turn your face around. It is my face.
That frozen rage is what I must explore—
Oh secret, self-enclosed, and ravaged place!
This is the gift I thank Medusa for.[6]

In Aeschylus's *Eumenides*, when the priestess first catches sight of the Furies, she mistakes them for Gorgons: but these vengeful spirits are more ancient, more primitive still. The Erinyes were thought to have been conceived when the blood from Uranus's severed genitals fell on the earth, Gaia; their task was to uphold the sanctity of familial bonds and especially the debt owed by children to their mother. Because in their realm the most heinous of all crimes was matricide, they hound Orestes after his murder of Clytemnestra:

> Is there a man who does not fear
> this, does not shrink to hear
> how my place has been ordained,
> granted and given by destiny
> and god, absolute? Privilege
> primeval yet is mine, nor am I without place
> though it be underneath the ground. (*Eum.* 389–95)

In Aeschylus's drama their power is overcome by Apollo's and Athene's claim that only fathers parent, that mothers are but strangers who nurse the planted seed. The play concludes with the recognition that the Erinyes cannot be eliminated—coupled with a pious hope that they might be transformed into Eumenides, kindly assurers of the earth's fertility.

AMAZONS AND MAENADS

In the Greek mind the Gorgons, the Furies, and the Amazons were closely associated. In the *Eumenides* the defeat of the Furies, the pardon of Orestes' matricide, the definitive establishment of patriarchal rule—all happen at the very site where the Amazons long ago had set up camp during their siege of Athens:

> Here is the Hill of Ares, here the Amazons
> encamped and built their shelters when they came in arms
> for spite of Theseus, here they piled their rival towers
> to rise, new city, and dare his city long ago,

and slew their beasts for Ares. So this rock is named
from then the Hill of Ares. (*Eum.* 685–90)

The Amazons were associated with Ares, the god of war, because their queens were said to be daughters of Ares (their mother is most often identified as the nymph Otrere, but in some variant traditions as Harmonia, Ares' daughter by Aphrodite, or even as Aphrodite herself), but also because they were imagined as Ares-like women. The Greeks imagined the Amazons as a society composed entirely of women who threaten men and engage in war against them.

Their name was usually taken to signify "without a breast" and to refer to the legendary Amazon practice of searing off the right breast of their female children so as to enable them to become more proficient archers—although in visual representations Amazons are often shown with one breast bared but never with one missing. The name might also signify "opposed to man." Mary Daly playfully (and seriously) speaks of the *A-mazing* Amazon who breaks through the *maze* of patriarchal culture, the tracks/traps that lead nowhere, and commits herself to friendship and fidelity to women, who fights for her Self and other women.[7]

Amazon societies were not imagined as matriarchal in the sense of being mother-dominated but rather as women-only societies ruled by a group of sisters. They were believed to live out their sexuality mostly among themselves, though once a year they would seek out the men of neighboring tribes for intercourse, solely for the sake of reproduction. (Girl children were kept and raised; boys were either exposed or sent away.) These women were virgins in the sense of their self-sufficient independence of men, their resistance of any permanent bonds with men.

A favored subject for sculptural representation was the battle of Greeks against Amazons, often, as at the Parthenon, paired with a depiction of the battle gainst the Centaurs; the women and the creatures who were half horse/half man were evidently regarded as twin threats to male-dominated civilization. Their conquest was deemed evidence of patriarchal supremacy. As Bachofen puts it, "The rise of father right begins with the war against the Amazons."[8] A vase painting showing an Amazon aiming her spear at a naked Greek male's exposed genitals provides clear testimony to the nature of the threat these women were understood to embody.[9]

There are also tales showing many of the most celebrated Greek heroes testing their manhood against these fearsome female warriors—and (at least apparently) winning. After successfully killing the fire-breathing Chimaera, Bellerophon goes on to fight the Amazons; although ostensibly successful he fails to receive the promised reward. Heracles' ninth labor requires him to bring back the belt of Hippolyte, the Amazons' queen, to King Eurytheus's daughter. Though according to the story Hippolyte willingly agreed to give it to him, Hera (angry that the task should be so easily fulfilled) convinced the other Amazons that Heracles was kidnapping their queen. When they attacked his ship, he (imagining that Hippolyte had betrayed him) killed her and stole the belt. According to one version, Theseus accompanied Heracles on this venture; according to another, he and Pirithous undertook an independent campaign against the Amazons. One way or another Theseus was said to have taken an Amazon queen, either Hippolyte herself or her sister Antiope, back to Athens with him as his concubine. The Amazons followed in pursuit and engaged the Athenians in months of fierce battle, which ended only when the Amazons, their ranks severely depleted, agreed to a treaty mandating their withdrawal. The Athenians saw this as victory, even though the Amazons were *not* decisively defeated. (Among those killed was Theseus's captive, who before her death gave birth to his son, Hippolytus. This youth, though he never knew his mother, grew up as an ardent devotee of the Amazon's goddess Artemis.)

Still angry at the Greeks by the time of the Trojan War, the Amazons come to Troy after Hector's death to join the fight against the Greeks. Though Homer does not include this tale, others relate that Achilles killed their mighty warrior queen, Penthesilea, and then fell in love with her beautiful corpse—and perhaps even made love to it (though he kills Thersites for spreading the slander).

After describing Achilles' necrophiliac passion, Bachofen concludes: "What this signifies is that the woman willingly bows down to the man who gives her back her natural vocation. She realizes that not warfare against man but love and fertility are her calling. . . . The enemy's victory restores her true nature."[10] How bizarre, how perverted, how unrecognizably turned around this reinterpretation is. The stories are not about Amazons falling in love with heroes, but about these heroes seducing them, abducting them, raping them, stealing the belt that represents their virginity, their independence of men. To master them sexually is an essential part of challenging what is deemed their monstrous claim to live as self-sufficient women.

The Greeks themselves disagreed as to whether the Amazons were historical or purely mythological beings, but the persistence of the legends about these warrior women who lived at the far edge of the inhabited world is in no doubt and betrays the archetypal character of the belief. There is, however, disagreement about what the archetype signifies. Eva Keuls sees it as embodying *male* fear of the terrifying mother, Bachofen as a universal phenomenon expressing *female* response to an earlier degradation of women. He believes that originally women were simply the objects of casual male lust, entirely subject to superior masculine strength, and that the tales about matriarchies (with which he associated the Amazon mythologem) represent a memory of the beginnings of human society, the transition from nomadic to settled existence, from anarchy to law. He sees Amazon society as understandably based on a hostility to men, but values it only as an intermediary step to a society based on father-right, on the "spiritual" bond of monogamy rather than on hate.[11]

It is true that many besides Bachofen have imagined these fiercely brave and "manlike" women in "matriarchal" terms, though women attribute more durable value to mother-right than did he. Some female scholars have seen the Amazons as persistent remnants of early matriarchal societies, or as attempting to restore gynocracy in the face of the establishment of patriarchal rule—that is, as reacting against male domination. But I believe that Phyllis Chesler is right in seeing them as representing not mother-rule but sister-rule—an attempt by women themselves to form a woman-shaped society that is not based on the relation of daughters to the all-powerful mother but on sisterly relationships. As Chesler realizes, the rebellion of daughters is more problematical than that of sons, demanding "enormous energy, supreme self-denial, and great visionary ardor," for it represents an attempt to preserve many "matriarchal" values but to rebel against being defined by nature and tradition, by one's birth-giving capacity.[12]

Bachofen saw that there was some kind of inner connection between the Amazons and the Dionysian maenads. He believes that very soon after their initial exposure to the Dionysian cult the Amazons' "determined resistance to the new god shifted to an equally resolute devotion" testifying to "the power of a religion that satisfied sensual as well as transcendent needs," that validated the natural over the political.[13] He writes as though the situation were parallel to the tradition about the Amazon queen falling in love with her rapist/seducer Theseus, as though with the surrender to Dionysus the women are surrendering to the phallus.

But maenadic enthusiasm surely represents something different. The Amazons constituted a group of women who lived beyond civilization as a separate woman-only society; the maenads were envisioned as women who temporarily left their conjugal lives for a ritual period, during which they were free to release the energies ordinarily pent up. (It is consonant with this that ritualistic [that is, historical] maenadism—as opposed to the myths, which are older—was most important during the era of greatest sex polarization in Attica.)[14] The women leave their domestic responsibilities, their husbands, and their children to be with one another. Maenadic enthusiasm was not an individual experience but a communal one; the maenads become a temporary community, the *thiasos*. The god's appearances were called *epidemia*, they "spread like wildfire among women."[15] Other women, women not participating in the ritual, identify with those who are and band together to protect them from men. Plutarch tells of a roaming band of maenads losing their way and falling asleep, exhausted, in the center of a remote village. The local women surrounded the sleepers to protect them against sexual molestation.

The god is present but no man is. The maenads' ecstatic rites were clearly seen to have a sexual dimension:

> O let me come to Cyprus,
> island of Aphrodite,
> homes of the loves that cast
> their spells on the hearts of men.
> Or Paphos where the hundred-
> mouthed barbarian river
> brings ripeness without rain!
> To Perria, haunt of the Muses,
> and the holy hill of Olympus!
> O Bromius, take me there!
> There the lovely Graces go,
> and there Desire, and there
> the right is mine to worship
> as I please. (*Bacch.* 402–15)

But what they sought was not heterosexual intercourse; they repel the satyrs who approach them, they disappoint Pentheus's fantasies about their "shameless orgies." Their longing is to dance

> with bare feet the all night dances,
> tossing my head for joy . . .
> to dance for joy in the forest
> to dance where the darkness is deepest,
> where no man is. (*Bacch.* 863–64, 876–77)

In *The Bacchae* the Messenger discovers with surprise how "modestly and soberly" they lie asleep with exhaustion in the forest and describes their waking thus:

A lovely sight to see; all as one,
the old women and the young and the unmarried girls (*Bacch.* 693–94)

Even in *The Bacchae* the maenads become crazed and destructive only when they are intruded upon by men, when they discover the Messenger (and later Pentheus) spying on them; but, it is true, when their mysteries are profaned, fearful things happen.

As with the Eleusinian mysteries, we know little in detail about the maenadic rites. We know that the maenads are usually shown carrying a thrysus, a fennel stalk topped by a pine cone, which on vase paintings they sometimes aim at male genitals (much as the Amazons were imagined aiming their spears). I would agree with Keuls that this hardly suggests sexual longing for a male penis but rather aggression against this emblem of male power. We do not know what role the basket-hidden phalli, so prominently displayed in Dionysian processionals, might have played in their rites. Perhaps they used dildos to stimulate and gratify one another—as they explored a sexuality devoted to female pleasure. Or perhaps the presence of the dismembered god—the god without a phallus—served as an invitation to explore pleasures for which no substitute phallus is needed.

We know almost nothing of these mysteries except that they seem to have represented an initiation of women by women into women's own sexuality, into arousal for its own sake. The Dionysian initiation does not seem to have been a puberty ritual; the women participants were not unmarried virgins but wives, matrons—though within the *thiasos* such definitions did not apply.

In the Hellenistic version of the rituals depicted on the frescoes in the Villa of Mysteries at Pompeii the initiate was an adult though young woman, and the initiators were all women. This was definitely a *women's* mystery—but not a mother-daughter one. Nor Hall describes the "wanton" initiate as "a woman who is *wanting*. She does not want for a man, nor for a child" (italics mine). She is ready, open, for her own fulfillment. "The phallic presence is absolutely central, but there are no mortal men present. Only male figures that people the imagination: a paunchy satyr, pointy-eared Pan boys, and the God who, as Lord of Women, belongs wholly to them. . . . It is a way of saying that maleness has a critical intrapsychic role in a woman's passage." Thus Hall sees Dionysus as representing not husbands or male lovers but the woman's own inspiration, energy, capacity for a nonprocreative generativity—as making possible a very different initiation from the gentle, slow arousal of the emergence rites at Eleusis: an almost violent injection of spirit.

The source is not really outside herself, for it is represented as female energy, as instilled by a female angel with a whip.[16]

The maenads represent the truths about women that they can experience only apart from men. Not that these truths are simply sexual—but that the way to them is through knowing our bodies as our own and thus our souls as well, through ecstasy and not through dutiful obedience. The maenads found access to an entirely different value system that becomes available only when we separate ourselves from patriarchal constraint. As Jane Ellen Harrison saw, "The constant shift from physical to spiritual . . . is the essence of the religion of Dionysos."[17] The excesses associated with maenadic frenzy express what happens when women are cut off from access to their own sexuality, desire, and power—and from one another. The crazed maenads—those who initially resisted the god and their own instinctuality, who kill their own children, tear wild animals apart, eat raw flesh—reappear as the hysterics in Freud's consulting room (and more dramatically in Charcot's Salpietre). Greek men seem rightly to have seen the maenads as in many ways even *more* terrifying than the Amazons—for they live in their own midst.

They *are* terrifying—and not only to men. For they represent what is terrifying in ourselves, being in touch with our own raw instinct and its compulsive power—and the importance of accepting that instinct and what it leads us to as truly our own. As H.D. wrote:

> *What they did,*
> *they did for Dionysos,*
> *for ecstasy's sake:*
>
> now take the basket,
> think;
> think of the moment you count
> most foul in your life;
> conjure it,
> supplicate,
> pray to it.[18]

TALES OF INITIATION

There is no clear evidence that in ancient Greece pubertal girls were initiated into female sexuality and identity by older women in a way that

might parallel paiderastia—nor any unmistakable mythological representations of such initiation. Yet there are hints that Artemis might have been
associated with female initiation in a way that parallels her brother Apollo's
role with respect to male initiation.

Pausanias describes a tomb dedicated to Hyacinthus, which on one of its
sides depicts the dead hero and his sister Polyboea together being carried to
heaven by the gods. To Sergent this suggests that Polyboea is the female
equivalent of her brother, standing in much the same relation to Artemis that
he has vis-à-vis Apollo. Because Polyboea seems also to have been known as
Kore, as the paradigmatic maiden, Sergent also posits a connection between
her and Persephone (the goddess who was abducted by Hades and then
married him). Thus he speculates that Polyboea must, like Hyacinthus, have
gone through a homosexual initiation and then died—died as a maiden that
she might be reborn as a bride.[19] The difficulty is that Sergent bases his
whole argument on his conviction that there *"must"* have been a parallel
ritual and a parallel myth—so we can hardly use his account as evidence that
there *was*—much as we, too, may feel a kind of "must." Though we might
imagine Polyboea as the central figure in a myth answering to our longing,
we cannot say that the Greeks actually give us such a myth.

We do know, however, that girls were sent to Artemis's temple at Brauron
for an extended initiation just before they reached marriageable age. The
temple at Brauron was particularly associated with the myths surrounding
Iphigenia, a priestess of Artemis and also a by-form of the goddess.
Iphigenia was the young daughter of Clytemnestra and Agamemnon whose
sacrifice Artemis had required of the Greek troops stranded at Aulis on their
way to Troy, in atonement for their violation of her sacred precinct.
Agamemnon lured his daughter to Aulis by telling her and her mother that
she was to be wed there. Instead she was killed—although secretly Artemis
rescued her from the funeral pyre and conveyed her to Tauris, where
Iphigenia was installed as the priestess in charge of the bloody rites associated with Artemis at that particular shrine. Eventually the girl was rescued
by her brother, Orestes, and brought back to Greece. Brauron was thought
to be the site of her burial. Thus Iphigenia epitomizes the young girl just
before marriage, the stage of female life with which Artemis was most
intimately identified. Her death might be seen as analogous to that of
Hyacinthus. The goddess had chosen Iphigenia as her own; then she dies as a
maiden (as she also would have had the promised marriage to Achilles taken
place) and in some sense as a mortal—for the spiriting away from the
sacrificial altar is a kind of apotheosis.

Little has come down to us of what the girls sent to Brauron experienced.

We do not know if Artemis, the goddess involved with all the mysteries of female embodiment—menstruation, defloration, marriage, childbirth, death—was also imagined as the goddess who might initiate young girls into the mysteries of their own sexuality. Did the girls sacrifice their virginity to the virgin goddess—and thus keep it? That is, did they learn that their sexuality was their own, that it did not exist primarily for male gratification nor for producing children so that the ongoing life of the polis might be assured? We know that Greek girls sacrificed their childhood toys and their maidenly garb to Artemis as part of their marriage rites; this signified the sacrifice of their maidenhood, their farewell to the goddess. I believe it also signified a plea that the goddess not desert the bride, that she still be available to them in the pains and dangers particular to the new stage of female life upon which they were entering, especially in the risks associated with childbirth, and that she help them stay in touch with their real virginity, their in-oneself-ness, even as they become wives and mothers. (Keuls understands just the reverse; she sees the rites at Brauron as instilling in females subordination to males, accepting the pain and risk of childbirth as inevitable, the submission of marriage as their proper destiny.[20] This seems to me inconsonant with Artemis's clear identification with women and with the world outside the polis, the wilderness. Though it may be that by "giving" her virginity into the care of the goddess, a woman can feel it is still safe and so accept a submission that would otherwise be intolerable.)

The girls initiated at Brauron were known as "the bears of Artemis," a designation that suggests another important myth associated with the goddess, the one involving the nymph Callisto. "Nymph" refers both to the minor female deities of brook and forest who in mythology accompany Artemis in the forest and to "young women in their first encounter with love," particularly as they join together to dance at festivals in honor of the goddess. Thus nymphs are both myth and reality. Although, at least on the surface, these maidenly groups are more innocent and serene than the maenads, they represent another all-female community and one where male intrusion is met with violent response.[21] The maenads were married women during a "time off" from marriage spent in an all-women's world. The nymphs of reality were not-yet-married females enjoying their inviolate femininity in an all-female world. In both groups there is a clearly sexual ambience to the relationships among the women—though there is also a recognition that the maenads will return to their husbands, that the girls will become brides. The nymphs of mythology were dedicated to stay virgins, to stay true to the virginal goddess; but almost every myth about such a nymph describes her being pursued and raped by a god (or dying in the attempt to escape his pursuit). The commitment of women to women is represented as intolerable to men; that it might be represented as succeeding—even in myth—is therefore impermissible.

Callisto's name signifies that she was the "most beautiful" of all the nymphs, as she was also Artemis's favorite. One day, so the story goes, Zeus came upon this lovely creature alone in the forest, but though he desired her, he knew the graceful young huntress would not accept advances from a man. So he returned disguised as Artemis and was warmly welcomed. Callisto responded to his first kisses and his initial embrace but then drew back in horror when the god "betrayed himself by a shameful action." Ovid tells us that she fought him off with all her strength, "but what god is weaker than a girl?" Zeus had his way with her and left her with her shame and guilt—and pregnant, too, for it seems that gods are always potent, that every act of intercourse has issue. Although the other nymphs may have guessed what had happened by her painful dis-ease when she returned to join them, Artemis herself was slow to pick up on the clues. Until one day months later as Callisto hesitated to undress to join the others as they bathed, Artemis saw the clear-cut evidence and forthwith banished her from her company. All versions of the myth agree that Callisto was then transformed into a bear, although they disagree whether this was Hera's doing or Zeus's or a further act of retribution inflicted by Artemis herself (*Met.* 2.409–531).

The story suggests that Callisto had already been initiated by Artemis, that they were lovers—as witness Callisto's ready acceptance of intimacies she believes come from the goddess. It is her rape by Zeus that leads to her exclusion from Artemis's circle—and from humanity (for when transformed into a beast, though her mind remains unchanged, she is deprived of speech and cannot share her grief). This story powerfully communicates that in Artemis's world heterosexual initiation is violation.

Ovid tells one other story of a woman's love for a woman, a story that suggests how isolating, confusing, and terrifying such longing can be when there are no myths, no models, to follow. In the story of Caenis that we looked at in Chapter 11, the heroine prayed to become a man in order to escape from female vulnerability to male rape. The story of Iphis is very different, for here the heroine, Iphis, wants to be a male because she has fallen in love with another female and longs to be able to consummate that love.

The story begins with a poor Cretan peasant telling his pregnant wife that he hopes their child will be a son, for if they have a girl they will be forced to expose her. The man weeps no less bitterly than the woman, but remains adamant. The wife is in despair until the goddess Isis comes to her and, telling her not to worry, advises her that if she has a daughter, she should simply deceive her husband and raise her as a boy. The woman gave birth to a girl and reared her as the goddess had advised. All went well until, when Iphis turned thirteen, the father arranged a marriage with Ianthe, the most beautiful girl on Crete. The two had gone to school together and already loved each other. Ianthe was happy and looked forward to marrying the boy she already loved, but for Iphis things were more complicated:

> A girl herself, she was in love with one of her own kind, and could scarcely keep back her tears, as she said: "What is to be the end of this for me, caught as I am in the snare of a strange and unnatural kind of love, which none has known before? . . . No guardian, no precautions on the part of an anxious husband, no stern father keeps you from the embraces which you long to enjoy; the one you love does not refuse her favors when you ask. Still, she cannot be yours, nor can you be happy."

The mother, too, was in despair; she could not postpone the wedding forever. Finally the two went to the temple and the mother asked Isis to come to her aid again. As they walked home together, Iphis began to take longer strides, her features sharpened, she became a man. The wedding was held and "the boy Iphis gained his own Ianthe" (*Met.* 9.666–761).

From Ovid's perspective the story ends happily. We might be struck more by how it recognizes the love the two girls feel for each other and shows the confusion this engenders in Iphis, who does not know that women have ever before been drawn to women. She cannot imagine how such a love might be lived out—except by her becoming a man, being given a penis. The desire is acknowledged but not the possibility of fulfillment. One wonders what would have happened had the mother prayed to Artemis rather than Isis!

The tale of Iphis makes us acutely aware of the cost to women of the absence of myths about mortal, woman-loving women. Without stories, without models, the desire to love a woman like oneself is bewildering, frightening, and isolating. It presents a puzzle in which the only solution seems to be to cease to be a woman oneself, to become *other*—male—in order to love one like oneself.

· 13 ·

SAME-SEX LOVE
AMONG THE GODDESSES

When we turn to myths about divine females, we find that same-sex attachments play a more primary role. None of the goddesses, except perhaps Artemis, is represented as loving only others of her own sex, but all of them are involved with women in ways that illumine our own experience of same-sex love.

We might note that none of the goddesses is shown as fitting easily into the normative pattern of heterosexual relationship; *no* goddess is represented as a contented wife. As Burkert explains: "In the case of goddesses, the relation to sexuality is more difficult. Since the female role is generally described as passive, as being tamed, it accords ill with the role of [divinity]."[1] Even the one account we have of Hera (the only wife among the Olympian goddesses) and Zeus making love shows her taking the initiative, seducing him in order to divert his attention from the Trojan War. The particular powers associated with Artemis and Athene are correlated with their being untamed virgins. When goddesses are involved with mortal men, as Dover notes, they act like a male erastes with his eremenos—as witness Aphrodite's seduction of Anchises; Tithonus's abduction by Eos, goddess of dawn; and Endymion's by Selene, the moon goddess.[2] In relation to her male protégés, although there is nothing sexual in the relationship, Athene often assumes male disguise and figures like a wise erastes, mentoring and encouraging their youthful efforts.

Given the problematics inherent in the relationship between goddesses and males, it is not surprising that involvements with women should play so important a role in the myths concerning female deities. As we noted earlier, many contemporary lesbians reject the label "homosexual" in part because of the emphasis it implies on the explicitly sexual dimension, whereas they see emotional intimacy and sustained commitment, women's encouragement of one another's autonomy and creativity, as equally salient. If we were to look at the traditions about the Greek goddesses primarily for stories of overtly sexual connections with women, we would find little; but if what we are interested in is an illumination of the multidimensionality and diversity of the erotic relationships that exist between women, we will find much. The myths bring into view the beauty and power inherent in female bonds—and some of the darker, more fearful aspects as well.

THE RETURN TO THE MOTHER

Demeter is in Greek mythology clearly a woman-identified goddess. Having been separated from her own mother at birth when her father, Kronos, fearful that one of his children might grow up to overthrow him as he had overthrown his father, swallowed her, she seems to epitomize an idealization of mother love. She longs to have a daughter to whom she might give the love she herself never received. Representing a generation of goddesses who no longer had the parthenogenetic capacity of the original mother earth goddess, Gaia, Demeter cannot conceive without a male. Therefore she allows Zeus to father her child, but refuses him any participation in the child's rearing. Her daughter, Persephone, is to be hers alone and to be the object of all her love. Although it would go beyond the myth to say that Demeter *rapes* Zeus, who raped so many divine and mortal women, one could say that even in the myth *she* uses *him* (almost like a sperm bank). She also deliberately chooses her brother to be her lover, a male as like her as any she could find. She is a mother but emphatically not a wife; she chooses to be a single mother, solely responsible for her daughter's upbringing.

The bond between mother and daughter as Demeter and Persephone exemplify it is a bond of fusion—the intimate connection preceding the recognition of separate existence that we all imagine to have been there "in the beginning." Demeter hopes to maintain this closeness forever, to keep her daughter for herself—and seeks especially to protect their love from any male intruder. Almost inevitably, her daughter ends up being abducted by the male god of the underworld, Hades, and Demeter ends up devastated.

After her daughter's disappearance, Demeter is so overtaken by her grief and rage that she no longer attends to the growth of the grain on which all human life depends, but wanders desolate over the earth disguised as an old woman. During this time she spends an evening in the company of an aged dry nurse, Baubo (or, in some versions, Iambe), who succeeds even if only momentarily in getting the goddess to smile and even to laugh aloud. She does so by entertaining her with a lewd dance; she takes off her clothes, she spreads her legs, she displays her vulva. Long past her childbearing years, withered, wrinkled, and probably flabby, Baubo communicates her joy in her own body, her pride in her female organs, her conviction that her sexuality is *hers*, defined neither by the men who might once have desired her nor the children she may have borne. Conventional beauty, youth, reproductive capacity are all beside the point—she celebrates the pleasure her body can receive and give. The Greeks acknowledged that Baubo was a goddess, that the self-sufficient female sexuality she represents is a sacred reality. They depicted her seated on a pig with legs outspread, holding a ladder by which one might mount to the gods.

Demeter's laugh suggests that she catches on (if only for a moment) to Baubo's message that there is life, female life, even after one is no longer mother. It is that insight that prepares her to be able to accept a new relationship to Persephone after Zeus arranges for the maiden's return. For henceforward, Persephone will spend some time with her mother each year but some time away, in her own life, in the underworld realm that is now her domain. Demeter has been initiated into a mode of relationship that can tolerate separation and change—and into an understanding of self not dependent on the other. But to Greek women Demeter remains associated primarily with the love that flows between mothers and daughters and with the griefs and losses that seem to be an inevitable correlate of motherhood. (She is also the goddess of the cultivated grain and through her connection to Persephone associated with chthonic mysteries; but in those regards she was worshiped by men as well as women. We are interested particularly in her relation to women.)

During the Thesmophoria, the major ritual associated with Demeter alone (in contrast to the Eleusinian rites, where she and her daughter were worshiped together as "the Two Goddesses"), the women celebrated on their own at the expense of men with obscene exposure and mocking songs (called *Iambos*), which expressed their anatagonism toward men. The Thesmophoria was an extremely ancient festival; because men played no part in it and because of what Burkert calls "the natural conservatism of women," the ritual was preserved into late classical time in its archaic form and thus provides some of our best evidence of pre-Olympian religiosity. A late autumn festival, it undoubtedly had some agrarian function related to the sowing of crops, but it was much more important as a festival of women. The ritual was "liminal"—it represented a cultic inversion of everyday reality that paradoxically may have served to maintain everyday norms and structures. Thus this temporary dissolution of marital bonds may have strengthened marriage by providing a ritual outlet for expressing frustration, grief, and anger.

"At the core of the festival," says Burkert, "[is] the dissolution of the family, the separation of the sexes and the constitution of a society of women." For most women the Thesmophoria provided the only occasion when they could leave their family and home for three entire days and nights. Men were rigorously excluded from the ritual, as were children and (most scholars believe) virgins. "The absence of men gives a secret and uncanny quality to the festival."[3] Much about this gathering of women reminds us of the maenads. Herodotus's claim that the festival was brought to Greece by the Danaids, the husband-murdering sisters mentioned in Chapter 12, communicates the dread it inspired in men.

Sexual abstinence—that is, abstinence from intercourse with men—was demanded before and during the festival. On the first day pigs were sacrificed to commemorate the death/rape of Persephone (according to the myth, a herd of swine as well as the maiden were swallowed up in the chasm that appeared when the maiden plucked the narcissus) and then tossed down into a serpent-filled chamber. Later the rotten flesh (perhaps the remnants of the previous year's sacrifice) was brought up from the chasm and mixed with seed corn. In addition to its agrarian meaning, this part of the ritual served as a reminder of the inescapability of loss and grief. During the second day the women fasted; they sat on the ground in remembrance of grieving Demeter sitting on "the smileless stone" at Eleusis (on the day whose evening she would spend with Baubo) and shared their grief with one another. The women ate pomegranates, whose juice symbolized blood, whose fallen pips belonged to the dead. As Burkert says, they were occupied with blood and death. Their hostility to men is expressed in highly exaggerated form; there are even traditions attesting that the women castrated men who tried to spy on the festival. There was a real indulgence of obscenity and indecent speech (reminiscent of Baubo's self-delighting vulgarity). A late source reveals that the women worshiped a representation of the female pudenda and at least in Sicily cakes of this shape were baked and eaten.[4]

The ritual put considerable emphasis on sexuality and conception—but not on intercourse, not on the male role. At Eleusis, too (where Demeter and Persephone were worshiped together, and where the focus was on preparation for death rather than on coming to terms with one's life as a woman), the rites were somehow connected to conception and birth (there, as a symbol of ongoing life after death). But there, too, there is no hint of ritual intercourse having been part of the ceremonies.

The Thesmophoria provided women an opportunity to vent their anger against men, to share the difficulties and sorrows associated with their own experiences of motherhood—confident that Demeter, the grieving mother goddess, would empathize with and dignify their lot. The rite was one that encouraged abandonment—not only to anger and tribulation but to "obscenity" that is, to a self-indulgent sexuality. In the temple of the mother, all is permitted.

That licit transgression of boundaries relates closely to what I see as Demeter's most important signification with respect to same-sex love among women. For Demeter reminds us of a time when there were no boundaries, when lover and beloved were one. I believe that all close bonds between women inevitably conjure up memories and feelings associated with our first connection to a woman, the all-powerful mother of infancy. They remind us of a time in which one neither required the phallus nor rebelled against its power, when it was merely irrelevant. The *pull* to reexperience that bond of fusion, that sense of being totally loved, totally known, totally one with another—*and* the *fear* of reexperiencing that bond of fusion, of being swallowed up by a relationship, of losing one's own hard-won identity—enter powerfully into all woman-woman relationships. This does not mean that in a relationship between two women one partner will play the mother role, the other the daughter role; but rather that it is likely both will experience the profound longing to be *fully* embraced once again as by the mother of infancy—and the imperious need to break away. Much of the intensity, the emotional intimacy, women discover in one another comes from the Demeter-Persephone dimension of their bond. The particular beauty and power—and the particular danger and limitation—of love between women is here made manifest. For it is questionable whether this love really allows for personal relationship between two individuals, for what Buber called an I-Thou relationship. Certainly before Demeter loses Persephone she has allowed her no identity of her own; the daughter exists only as an extension of the mother.

The connection to the mother is always also a connection to one's own mysterious origins, and in this sense Demeter is also relevant to the particular power that the sexual dimension of women's love for one another may have. Because to enter another woman's vagina is to touch upon the whole mystery of one's own beginnings, it may seem for many women a more sacred experience than heterosexual intercourse (no matter how physically pleasurable) can provide. Even though women's lovemaking with women is not biologically connected to reproduction, experientially it touches on that mystery through a mutual return to and mutual departure from the gate of our origin. It may be that the cost of this aspect of lesbian intensity is the loneliness Demeter experiences, the necessary time of bereavement and separation required to support an I-Thou relationship exposed to this mystery.

REINTERPRETING MALE IDENTIFICATION

To bring Hera into a discussion of women's love of women may at first seem ridiculous—she is so clearly a goddess who focuses all her love on her husband, Zeus; a goddess who prides herself on her conjugal faithfulness. Passionately jealous of Zeus's infidelities, Hera is represented as actively persecuting his mistresses and their children. Her response to the early separation from their mother, Rhea, is utterly different from her sister's. Unlike Demeter, she seems to have learned from the years spent in her father's stomach to expect nurturance from men rather than women. Thus her female existence is lived in relation to her spouse; she lives defined by her marriage and its difficulties. Though she has children, that is almost incidental to her being a wife—she is never invoked as a mother. She seems not to like women—or being a woman—at all.

But that is the Hera of myth—Hera as men described her, the wife as experienced by husbands. As Burkert notes, the almost comic portrait of Hera in literature may be connected to the fact that "Hera does not willingly submit even to the strongest of gods, but remains a partner in her own right."[5] The passive role simply does not fit a goddess, which means, as we noted above, that none of the goddesses fits into the heterosexual model as the Greeks understood it. Each represents some form of protest against that model, each in some way represents the vision of a different kind of relationship.

Hera, as women worshiped her, as she functioned in her cult, was not the unhappy, frustrated, possessive wife of literature but a woman identified with all the longings, satisfactions, and difficulties of the wish for a permanent, committed primary relationship. Though she, too, is not immune to fusion longing and seems sometimes to have imagined that she really wants Zeus, marriage, to swallow her as her father had, unlike Demeter she is represented as actively engaged in a struggle for differentiation. One myth relates that eventually she gives up on Zeus, decides that he will never be the faithful husband of her dreams nor be able to provide the intimacy for which she yearns. She leaves him and makes her way to a magical spring in Argos that restores the virginity of women who bathe in it. Thus she recovers her in-oneself-ness and becomes someone who no longer looks to marriage for self-completion. On the other side of this she is ready for a different kind of relationship, one less dominated by the struggle for supremacy or by fantasies of possessing and being possessed.

Though in Hera's case she returns to Zeus but on a new basis, we could see the story as relevant to the life experience of "late-blooming lesbians," women who turn to primary relationships with women after discovering that heterosexual marriage does not answer their deepest needs. For what Hera seems most essentially to signify is not a sexual bond with men but a sustained and mutual bond with another: the gender of that other seems almost beside the point. The myth of Hera can bring into view the ways in which bonds between two women may be similar to the bond of heterosexual marriage, an analogy that has its virtues and its deficits. For the marriage model means not only loyalty and stability but often also—consciously or unconsciously—power-defined roles, the struggle over dominance and submission, a struggle that two women can also engage in. Hera's own obsession with socially sanctioned bonds and her cruelty toward unmarried mothers and illegitimate children may also serve as a reminder of how dependent the permanence of marriage is on social support, how difficult it is to maintain relationships in its absence.

Though women worshiped Hera as close to them in their own marital struggles, we need also to look directly at the many myths that relate her malevolent abuse of the women whom Zeus seduced or raped. (The difference seemed to be irrelevant to her.) That her anger was directed against these women rather than at Zeus suggests that it may have its origin in a feeling of unacknowledged anger at having been abandoned by her mother, that her relation to her female parent may play a much more powerful role in her life than she would acknowledge. Hera's apparent hatred of women may seem to have little to do with women who have chosen to love women, yet I see Hera as reminding us how persistent self-disparagement and disparagement of women are in the psyches of all women raised in a male-dominated world, irrespective of one's feminism or one's sexual preference. Homophobia, including fear and hatred of other women and of one's own female self, is no prerogative of the heterosexual.

What is really striking is the degree to which Hera's libidinal energy seems to be directed toward women. As I reflect on the many myths of Hera's persistent jealousy of the women with whom Zeus made love—Callisto and Semele, Alcmene and Io—I cannot help but think of Freud's notion that jealousy is a mask of homosexuality. Her attacks on Zeus's mistresses are the most active expression of her otherwise quite repressed sexuality. Hera is opposed not only to Demeter, who gives the bond to one's child the privileged place that Hera accords the bond to one's partner; she is also seen as struggling against Dionysus, who seeks to lure women from their marriage beds. For Hera is identified with bonding, not passion; from her perspective sexuality is dangerous. One may recall how upset she is with Tiresias for claiming that women get more pleasure from lovemaking than men. Aphrodite's warmth and grace may, as Hera knows, be a necessary element in any sustained relationship, but Hera is more concerned with how easily sexual desire moves us to betray our commitments.

Even more male-identified than Hera—on the surface, at least—is Pallas Athene, the goddess who could say:

> There is no mother anywhere who gave me birth
> and, but for marriage, I am always for the male
> with all my heart, and strongly on my father's side.
> (*Eum.* 736–38)

Born from Zeus's head, a goddess of war noted for her courage and self-sufficiency, her calm and collected reason, Athene is depicted as suspicious of sexual entanglement and emotional intensity, and as mentor and patron of such Greek heroes as Heracles, Perseus, and Bellerophon. She seems to deny her own femininity and to identify with these Gorgon- and Amazon-battling men.

That she might in any way be relevant to the self-understanding of women who love women seems—at first—preposterous. And yet we must recall that Athene was a *goddess;* that the Greeks saw her self-assurance and bravery, her practical wisdom, her gift for sustained friendship, not only as *divine* but also as *feminine* attributes. She serves as powerful testimony to a view of women as strong, active, and creative rather than as by definition passive and weak. By reminding us that such qualities are not *masculine* qualities but as much part of our own female being as our vulnerability, receptivity, openness to feeling, Athene may help us to recognize the obvious: that contemporary lesbian women who choose or are given the designation "butch" are fully, indeed quintessentially, *women*—not masculine, not men in women's bodies. Their refusal to be "femme"—to conform to conventional expectations about female dress and demeanor, body image or life-style—is a celebration of women's strength and their independence of male-defined values.

For though Athene may in patriarchal myth identify with her father, she is (as even those myths still let us see) to begin with the daughter of Metis, the goddess of wisdom, the goddess swallowed by Zeus from whom he acquired his own wisdom (*metis*.) So Athene has a mother, receives her own gifts from her—and yet refuses to identify with a mother swallowed up and silenced by the father, by patriarchy. She also refuses to *be* a mother, choosing virginity instead of maternity, cultural rather than reproductive creativity. (Athene is the goddess of the *polis*, the human community, and of the arts.) Here, too, she is highly relevant to those lesbians who refuse the traditional roles associated with our mothers and with motherhood.

The myths show that Athene is not only a goddess at ease in the company of men but also closely associated with women. She befriends and supports not only Odysseus but also Penelope and Nausicaa. She seems to spend her "off hours" in the company of other young maidens like herself: she is playing in the meadow with Persephone when Hades suddenly appears; when Tiresias unexpectedly comes upon her naked, she is bathing with her favorite nymph, Chariclo. Most important is her connection to Pallas, daughter of the sea god Triton, to whom Zeus entrusts his daughter's education. The girls become close friends and especially delight in the challenge of athletic competition with each other. One day when they are testing their skills at fencing, Athene inadvertantly kills her playmate. (The fault is Zeus's; he happens to look down to watch their sport and, mistakenly thinking his daughter threatened by her friend's thrust, intervenes and upsets the delicate balance of their parrying.) Grief-stricken, Athene makes a wooden statue of her friend (copies of which stand at the heart of her temples and represent Athene's protective care for the sanctity of her cities) and takes her name as part of her own. Pallas Athene is thus not only "the Twice Born" but twice woman, herself and the beloved friend of her childhood.

The parallels to some of the myths about Apollo and his beloveds are striking: the love between god and mortal, the inadvertent death so like Apollo's accidental killing of Hyacinthus, the later identification between the deity and the human. Yet there are significant differences, too: in the female example there is more equality and more mutuality. Athene's love of Pallas is love of another like herself—not love of her own younger self, nor love of a daughter or mother-surrogate. Her love has more of the quality of *philia*, that bond of friendship toward which men hoped their paiderastic Eros might develop. Athene's relationships with women do not emphasize sexuality, passion, or the renewal of infantile fusion, but close friendship. Her love is warm but not compulsive. As Walter Otto says, Athene is "goddess of the near"; she is available when we call upon her, not distant like Artemis but also not responsive to our longings for fusion as Demeter is.

Athene also wears on her aegis the severed head of the Gorgon Medusa, who represents the terrifying dark side of the feminine. Athene's own relation to this aspect of female energy is communicated by the fact that the animal most closely associated with her is a night-flying bird of prey, the owl. She is also a sister of Dionysus, Zeus's other "parthenogenetic" offspring (the quotes are intended to remind us of the ignored motherhood of Semele and Metis), and it is she who rescued her brother's heart as the Titans feasted on his dismembered body and brought it back to Zeus, so that Dionysus might be restored to life. It is not that Athene does not know passion—but that she has learned to express it in *her* way.

There are several Athene festivals reserved to girls and women. One, of which we know little, the mysterious nocturnal Arrhephoria, was connected to the initiation of young girls. The rite required that two such girls who had spent a year in service to the goddess (during which they lived in her precincts on the Acropolis) carry something deep underground and bring back something else. The hidden contents of the basket were in some way connected to the myth about the birth of Erichthonius, an ancient Attic king. Erichthonius was conceived when Athene repulsed Hephaestus's attempt to make love to her. The crippled god's excitement was too great for him to restrain; he ejaculated; his semen fell to the ground and impregnated the earth (Gaia). When the child was born, Athene put it into a chest, which she entrusted to the three daughters of King Cecrops with strict instructions not to look inside. Of course they did (or at least two did) and discovered within a snake coiled about the child. In punishment they were driven mad by Athene and killed themselves by jumping from the walls of the Acropolis. The chest or basket, the snake, the child, are obviously connected to sexuality. Just what the girls were to learn from participating in the rite we cannot say—except that it was an initiation by the goddess and her priestesses, by women, into the mysteries of female sexual identity.

The Skira was a special festival for women only, another of the rare occasions when they could leave their secluded quarters and assemble together. In celebrating this ritual they even left the city and took the road leading toward Eleusius. Their goal was a sanctuary dedicated to Demeter and Kore to which they conveyed a statue of Athene. There they, not the priests, took charge of the ceremony, of the purifications and sacrifices. This ritual of inversion—in which the city goddess left the city, in which women take power—was deeply unsettling to men, as evidenced by Aristophanes making this festival the setting for a scene depicting women plotting to seize political power.[6]

Bachofen is on to something when he says that in Athene "the warlike Amazonism of the old reappears in spiritual form."[7] Athene's friendly rivalry with Pallas is emblematic of a connection between women where women challenge one another to achieve, bless one another's creative accomplishments, encourage one another's power. Athene signifies relationships where the emphasis is not on the expanded narcissism of the dyad, not on what happens in "the between," but on the work women help one another do. Athene does not expect her protégés to accomplish tasks she imposes on them (as Hera imposes tasks on the heroes, like Heracles, associated with her) but subtly supports them in the realization of their own dreams.

ARTEMIS AND HER NYMPHS

Of all the goddesses, Artemis is most evidently one who models women's love of women. She shuns the world of men and spends her time in the wild; she refuses all association with men (except for her twin brother, Apollo, and their hunting companion, Orion). She spends her time alone or in the company of her nymphs, minor deities of brook and forest. She is both fearless huntress and kind nurse to orphaned or wounded beast. She was the goddess worshiped by the Amazons.

Her virginity, unlike Athene's, is a defiant claim that her sexuality is her own, not possessable by any man. When Actaeon comes upon her bathing, she turns him into a stag, which his own hounds then hunt and kill. Artemis can be decisive and cruel; she is as goal-directed as the arrows she shoots from her bow. Artemis feels no remorseful compunction over her treatment of Actaeon—unlike Athene, who struck Tiresias blind when he caught her bathing but in recompense awarded him the gift of prophecy, of second sight.

"The virginity of Artemis is not asexuality . . . but a peculiarly erotic and challenging ideal."[8] Artemis is not willing to hide her sexuality as Athene does—nor to yield it. She is not going to let herself be raped as her mother, Leto, was by Zeus; nor will she be co-opted into denying her sexuality so as to make things easier for the men who might feel desire for her. That is their problem, not hers. She is neither seductive toward men nor protective of them. She refuses to allow herself, her sexuality, to be defined by theirs. The passion of Artemis is not repressed like Hera's nor sublimated like Athene's nor lived out in relationships like Aphrodite's. Artemis is the Lady of the Wild Things—including the wildness within herself. Hers is a claimed, a chosen, wildness; a preference, not a given. She is goddess of the instinctual, not the rational or the civilized. Though Artemis chooses to live in the woods rather than on Olympus, she is not a primal earth goddess like Gaia but a goddess who lives *outside* civilization. What passion means in the realm of Artemis is unflinching knowledge of one's own savagery, instinctuality, bodily desires and responses. To know one's body, one's emotions, one's longings as one's own—that is Artemis.

Artemis is the goddess most intimately associated with female embodiment. She makes visible the sacral significance of those aspects of female experience connected to the particularities of female physiology: menstruation, conception, childbirth, nursing, menopause—and also the loss of virginity, female orgasm, marriage, and death. As we have already noted, there is no wedding without Artemis; each young bride calls upon her to ward off the dangers associated with this decisive turning point. Artemis is associated with maiden initiation and maiden sacrifice. Death and vulnerability are always nearby—marriage is one kind of death and menopause another; childbirth is always painful and often dangerous. Though Artemis is strong and decisive and sometimes cruel, she is solicitously tender toward the young and vulnerable, acutely sensitive to the paradoxical intertwining of strength and vulnerability in women's lives.

She is committed to women and her love for them clearly has a sexual dimension, as the story about Callisto makes clear. Callisto's unsurprised responsiveness to what she takes to be Artemis's embrace when Zeus begins to make love to her makes evident that the nymph considered physical contact with the goddess comfortable and familiar. Given Artemis's identification with the female body and with the instinctual, it would seem "off key" to try to transpose the relationship between her and the nymphs into a purely spiritual bond.

On the other hand, to understand this bond in primarily erotic terms is also to misunderstand Artemis, to confuse her with some other goddess. For whereas Athene is goddess of the near, the always available "friend," Artemis is "the goddess who comes from afar," a goddess who is essentially chaste, virginal, solitary—who does not give herself to any other, male or female. Whereas Aphrodite, the goddess of love, is herself in giving herself, Artemis is herself in her self-containment.

There is a kind of cruelty in Artemis, an unflinching single-minded commitment to her own integrity as a woman, her own self-sufficiency, that becomes evident in the many myths in which she disowns members of her retinue who were not strong enough to defend their own virginity, their selfhood—not only Callisto but also Britomartis, Arethusa, Taygete. Artemis does not say, "Choose me," or, "Choose women," but, "Choose yourself." She kills Coronis and Ariadne for betraying their divine lovers with mortal ones, for turning from Apollo to Ischys, from Dionysus to Theseus—because they have thereby in some profound sense betrayed themselves. Yet she supports Clytemnestra against Agamemnon—because Clyemnestra's adultery and her murder of her husband represent a redoubtable self-assertion. In Artemis's realm what the love of women most deeply signifies is the love of their womanly selves.

From Artemis's perspective sexual intimacy may be evasion, may be flight from self, may be flight from one's passion, may even be flight from the other, from the particular and fearful otherness of the other. Her refusal to give herself expresses her respect, not her rejection, of the other: "Be yourself, not mine." Her essential chastity expresses not frigidity but passion. She gives herself to her own passion, her own wildness—not to another.

THE SACRALITY OF SEXUALITY

What Artemis refuses to give, Aphrodite gives freely. To the degree that when we say "lesbian" we want to include as essential an explicitly erotic, physical, orgasmic dimension, we are imagining an Aphroditic lesbianism. It is in the sphere of Aphrodite that we learn to celebrate the particular modes of sexual gratification that women alone can give one another and can receive only from one another. The intensity of connection, the intimacy of touch, which come from knowing the other's body from one's deep knowledge of one's own, which come through discovering one's own body through one's exploration of another woman's; the joyful experiencing of a lovemaking whose pace is fully governed by female rhythms, whose climaxes are profoundly familiar—these are Aphrodite's gifts.

For Aphrodite is the goddess of all erotic love, all sensual pleasure, all delight in beauty. Though far more than a goddess of sexuality, she *is* that. Though Artemis may have been the goddess of the Amazons, Aphrodite was the goddess of Sappho. She blesses all lovemaking that is dedicated to mutual enjoyment (rather than to domination of another or to procreation)— whether marital or adulterous, heterosexual or homosexual, between men or between women. She is the goddess of poet and philosopher, as well as of courtesan and whore.

Aphrodite represents the ripe self-sufficiency of a female sexuality that is itself in being directed toward others. There are no accounts of Aphrodite losing her virginity, being initiated into sexuality by another, for it is fully her own. Yet she is herself in turning toward others; she represents the free giving and receiving and returning of love. She gives herself spontaneously but in response to her own desire; she cannot be possessed by another. Yet though she may take the active role with Anchises or Adonis, she can also be the receptive partner as with Ares. In her realm love generates love—not progeny, not permanent bonds, not art, but love. The Greeks saw Aphrodite as far more than a goddes of genital sexuality; her love had a cosmic dimension, was the source of all life, all renewal.

Aphrodite represents a particular mode of consciousness, a consciousness of feeling, one's own and the other's; not a consciousness *about* feelings and relationships but creative and responsible awareness *of* them. Aphroditic knowing is sensuous, concrete, delicate, attentive, feeling-toned. Truth in her realm means truth to genuine feeling, to desire, spontaneity, the moment. To really know what we are feeling now and to be led by that—not by habit or the past or another's expectation—that is Aphrodite's challenge. From her perspective we are most ourselves when led by our feelings—and when emotionally related to others.

Sappho and Plato, as we shall see, valued in Aphrodite her association with a love that is not just physical but is dedicated to the mutual encouragement and cultivation of a more subtle and mature consciousness. They imagine her in connection with a loving that is truly directed toward the other's being, a love directed toward *psyche*, soul—and because of this as perhaps *more* truly present in same-sex love than in heterosexual love, which especially among the Greeks was thought likely to be directed to physical reproduction.

Aphrodite thus represents a celebration of our own feelings, our own desires—the importance of knowing them, the rightness of acting on them. Though not specifically a goddess of women, she is a goddess who models women's affirmation of their own sexuality—as powerful, beautiful, and sacred. Of all the goddesses Aphrodite is the only one not ashamed to be seen unclothed, not shy of making love out in the open under the midday sun. Her own divine shamelessness may make us more aware of whatever shame we may feel about our way of loving—and help us move beyond it. A genuinely Aphroditic lesbianism could not be a closeted lesbianism. It could not be hidden out of fear of others nor could it be displayed to defy others; it could only be shown for what it is—a natural, unashamed loving.

But, of course, Aphrodite is also associated with the *dangers* of an understanding of love that focuses on its physical dimensions; for her own natural consciousness in loving is something we humans must learn, and seem to learn (the myths suggest) only through experience, only through suffering—only through loving. Initiation in Aphrodite's realm seems to come not through some established ritual, not by association in a designated community, but only through our actual engagements with particular others, only through the risk of exposing our feelings to them and opening ourselves to theirs, only through the risk of opening our body to another's touch and of entering the other's in turn—only in "the between."

The myths associated with Aphrodite are about all the dangers of promiscuous and obsessive loving, of incestuous desire and unnatural passion. They remind us of how much lesbians give up for the sake of their unconventional loving (the security, the familial blessings, perhaps children), as well as the dangers inherent in really giving ourselves to our love—the pain of unrequited love, of abandonment, of the ebbing of passion, of feeling frigid and cut off from feeling, or of being so taken over by our feeling that we neglect ourselves (what Artemis warns against) or our children and former mates (what Hera fears).

Above all—but this we will consider in the Epilogue—Aphrodite reminds us of the inescapable transience of all mortal bonds, of how all love means loss, of how the most difficult challenge of love is really to know that, from having lived it, and yet to be ready to love again.

The myths about women loving women help us see what deep human longings are expressed in such love: the longing to reexperience the total union with one another that we knew with our mothers "in the beginning," the longing for relationships free of that struggle for dominance so often characteristic of heterosexual bonds, the longing for permanent connections that are genuinely mutual and egalitarian, the longing to fully validate one's own female being and to celebrate that with others, the longing to be really true to one's own spontaneous feelings and desires, the longing to encourage another's creativity and find one's own inspired by it, the longing to deal with and overcome one's own misogyny and homophobia, the longing to become all one might be, the longing to be willing to give oneself to feelings of love and not to evade the feelings of loss but to go on, the longing to discover the rightful place in one's life of passion and sexuality, relationship and solitude.

The myths show these longings becoming conscious, being assuaged, being frustrated. They reveal the dark side of women's love as well as the light.

The Greek myths about same-sex love do not give us all that we long for; there is little in the way of mythological representation of fully mutual and reciprocal loving; of an easy, fluid exchange of active and passive roles; of lasting, committed relationships. But they give us something signally important: a simple acceptance that human love takes many forms, among them the love of members of one's own sex, and that this love itself has many faces, that same-sex Eros involves much more than literal sexuality.

The myths suggest that the pull to such love is part of all of us, that it an important part of our move into adult, gendered existence. They also communicate that there is a need for initiation or at least initiatory models and myths, that without them we go painfully astray. This means that the gods, and the older members of the community, carry responsibility for helping the young learn to know their own sexual desires and pleasures and how to live them creatively and responsibly.

We are not yet done with the Greeks. We need still to look at Sappho and Socrates, two figures who were viewed as paradigmatic initiators, who saw deeper dimensions of the inherited myths than any others had—and who themselves, although historical persons, became mythical figures in the imaginations of those whose lives and loving were touched by them.

·14·

SAPPHO

In Sappho's poetry we hear the voice of an individual woman—the earliest such voice whose words are available to us. Hers is the first extant testimony that comes to us directly from a woman—of what it is like to be a woman, of what it is like to experience love, of what women mean to one another.

It is astonishing that her voice is also almost the first of any, male or female, to describe inner feeling, to speak of the human soul as known from within, in the first person.

Her topic is love. Her poetry suggests that it is Aphrodite's entering into the self that brings awareness of being a self. Although there are a few references to other deities in Sappho's poetry, the primacy of her devotion to Aphrodite is undeniable—and sets her off from all other early Greek poets. The bond to *one* deity and the directness and intimacy of that bond is an important part of what gives her poetry—which communicates what it is like to experience the goddess at work in one's own soul—its unique power.

The innovative uniqueness of her vision suggests that such awareness might be more readily accessible to a woman than to men. Bruno Snell believes that Sappho's awareness of her *response* to Aphrodite's interventions—her feelings of *helplessness*, her recognition of *obstructed* love and *blocked* desire—made her aware of her personal feelings as *hers* in a way that was utterly new. "Sappho, impassioned and sick at heart, [experiences] a sensation of having approached to the very roots of her own being; she is favoured with a glimpse into the uncharted territory of the *soul*." What makes her most aware of this is the experience of inner conflict, of the simultaneous coexistence of contradictory feelings. Snell is particularly taken by Sappho's recognition that love can be both bitter and sweet at the same moment. "With her bold neologism 'bittersweet,' Sappho discovers the area of the soul and defines it as fundamentally distinct from the body." Snell continues:

In the expression of their private sentiments and demands the early lyrists try to reproduce those moments in which the individual is all of a sudden snatched out of the broad stream of life. . . . Such are the moments which furnish man with his first glimpse of the soul. This new personal soul is not yet by any means the foundation for all feelings and emotions; it is merely the source of the reactions which set in when the feelings are blocked. Love is not a passion which wells up from within but a gift of Aphrodite or Eros. Only the emotional discord released by unhappy love is truly personal.[1]

Sappho's "I" speaks to us directly from her poems. We know almost nothing of the *persons* who composed the great Greek epics, Homer and Hesiod, but "the first woman, Sappho . . . emerges through her poetry as a completely realized person."[2]

THE MYTH

Yet we know so little of her life. Scholars claim that the women in Lesbos of her era were given more education and allowed more freedom than women in Athens during the classical period, but they mostly deduce that from the evidence of Sappho's life. We cannot then turn around and use this conclusion to interpret the life.

She was born on Lesbos about 612 B.C.E. into a well-to-do family and may have spent some years in political exile in Sicily. She was married, at least for a time, and had a daughter. She was a respected poet and sure of her own fame. Younger women came from elsewhere to live in her company for a time and then returned to their homelands. We have no reliable image of her, though we know that she was called "beautiful Sappho" because of the beauty of her poetry and that the sculptors often represented her with the idealized features of Aphrodite. According to a Hellenistic tradition, Sappho ended her life by leaping from a cliff in despair over her unrequited love for handsome Phaon—an evident conflation of Sappho with Aphrodite (who leapt in love for Phaethon, Apollo's son), and a clear attempt to imply that Sappho *must* in the end have turned to the love of men.[3]

She was revered in the ancient world. Solon supposedly said that he wished only to learn a particular poem of Sappho's by heart and then die. Plato called her the tenth muse: "Some say there are nine Muses, but they're wrong. Look at Sappho of Lesbos; she makes ten."[4] Yet, only a little later, in the Middle Comedy of the fourth century and the New Comedy of Menander, she was mocked as a licentious, immoral figure.

The mythmaking about Sappho began early. She has served ever since as a kind of touchstone for attitudes toward creative and independent women and woman-identified women. Her love for women has been denied, castigated—and celebrated.

Eva Stigers reminds us how radically innovative Sappho was in her representation of a woman as an erotic *subject*. Because Greek culture, as we have so often already noted, did not permit women to assume the role of desirer vis-à-vis men, it may, Stigers suggests, have been almost inevitable that a poetry dedicated to the articulation of women's erotic impulse would represent that impulse as directed to other women.[5] Thus Stigers explains Sappho's emphasis on love among women as explicable on formal grounds and not *necessarily* revelatory of her own erotic orientation.

The poems present Sappho as associated with a circle of women companions to some of whom she was passionately attached and some of whom she regarded as rivals. In the nineteenth century she was most often viewed as having been a teacher in a girl's academy or the high priestess of a women's cult, a *thiasos*—a description put forward by scholars who valued her poetry and made her into a priestess to protect her from being seen as a lesbian seductress. But as more recent scholars have noted, the word *thiasos* does not appear in Sappho's poetry nor in ancient descriptions of her relationship to her circle. Instead Sappho used the word *hetairai* to speak of her companions, a term that connotes a close bond "in which one sleeps on another's bosom."[6]

In the twentieth century many scholars have accepted Denys Page's claim that Sappho's poetry records nothing but the personal loves and jealousies of Sappho and her companions and that there is absolutely no evidence of Sappho having had any public educational or religious role.[7] Page insists on the lesbian "inclination" that his predecessors had sought to deny (though he, too, seems to want to protest that she didn't *practice* it) and obviously believes that this acknowledgment implies no diminution of the power of the poetry. Yet he clearly views Sappho's women-oriented sexuality with some distaste.

To find readers who value Sappho's poetry *for* being lesbian—who suspect that its power might be intimately connected with its being written by a woman whose experience of love is lesbian and who is thus more attuned to attending to nuances of feeling, to celebrating physical love as a soul experience and to celebrating love as a fully mutual relationship—we must look elsewhere.

Though the word *thiasos* does not directly appear in any of the ancient testimonies concerning Sappho's Lesbos, many modern scholars continue to use it because they see it as communicating the religious bonds that connected Sappho and her companions. The poems—with their invocations of the goddess, their emphasis on the arrivals and departures of group members—communicate a ritual atmosphere. Some are clearly cult songs—*epithalamia,* wedding songs composed to be sung at marriage ceremonies. The intimacy of the poems is in some measure formulaic; the songs were composed in order to be shared with a group of listening women on informal (rather than formal) occasions.[8] Though much of Sappho's poetry is intensely personal, it is nonetheless about experiences that she assumes she shares with other women. It seems evident that Sappho played a central role in her group's gatherings. It seems likely that she taught the younger women with whom she associated music and poetry, and prepared them to dance and sing at the festivals in honor of Artemis and Aphrodite.

Bowra describes her group as a *moisopolon domos,* a school for those who cultivated the Muses:

> It was primarily concerned with the cult of Aphrodite and its members formed a *thiasos.* . . . The members of the *thiasos* were bound to each other and to their leader with ties of great strength and intimacy, and Maximus of Tyre was not far wrong when he compared the relations between Sappho and her pupils with those between Socrates and his disciples. But while Socrates held his young men together by his personal influence and the glamour he gave to the quest for truth, Sappho was bound to her maidens by ties which were at least half religious.[9]

Paul Friedrichs is convinced that there is excellent evidence for young women in many parts of ancient Greece forming groups where they received instruction in "dance, music, singing, the care and adornment of the body, and probably the lore and knowledge of sex and motherhood as well. . . . The main function of such groups was . . . to prepare girls for wedding and marriage, but the cultural, human, and often very personal bonds formed between the members and their leaders could be expected to continue and grow in later life." He sees the women's groups on Lesbos as representing an important cultural subgroup; while the worship of the larger Lesbian community was focused on Zeus, Hera, and Dionysus, the religious energy of Sappho's circle was dedicated to the Muses and to Aphrodite.[10]

Bagg, who sees Sappho as involved with the initiation of a young girl into female sensibility, speaks of Sappho "taking the girl's *emotional* education in hand."[11] Hallet believes Sappho's function consisted in instilling "sensual awareness and sexual self-esteem" in the young girls who came under her care and helping to make them aware that the emotional intimacy they were unlikely to receive from their husbands was available from other women. Thus she identifies Sappho as a teacher who initiated young girls into their own sensuality, but insists that this did not entail the practice of actual sexual intimacies. Her vision of Sappho is of a woman-identified woman who is not a lesbian.[12]

Others believe that ritualized initiatory homosexuality may have played an important role in Sappho's circle. They posit an initiation into female sexuality that would help prepare a young girl for marriage—like the initiation that we speculated in Chapter 13 might have been part of the Artemis cult at Brauron and as Bremmer and others have said was accepted practice in Sparta.[13] Segal notes that the forms of association that linked Sappho and her friends would naturally involve veneration of Aphrodite and the Muses and reminds us that "the presence of Aphrodite would not inhibit the physical expression among the members of this community."[14]

There can be no question that the "I" of the poems, Sappho's *persona*, expresses passionate attachment—to particular women, to Atthis, Gongyla, Anactoria, and to a circle of women:

> My feelings for you,
> my beautiful ones,
> will not change. (LP 47; Groden 20)[15]

And there is no way of knowing exactly how that "Sappho" is related to Sappho herself or how that passion was lived.

The disagreements were already present in the ancient world. In the *Tristia* (2.365) Ovid says: "What did Sappho of Lesbos teach but how to love maidens? Yet Sappho herself was safe," meaning (one would suppose) that she herself did not physically love them. Yet in his *Heroides* (21.200) Ovid has Sappho invoke "the daughters of Lesbos whom I have loved to my disgrace." Whereas one Hellenistic writer tells us: "Sappho's kisses would be sweet, sweet the embraces of her snowy thighs and sweet all her body. But her soul is of unyielding adamant. For her love stops at her lips and the rest she keeps virgin. And who can stand this? Perhaps one who could stand this could easily endure the thirst of Tantalos."[16] Another says: "Sappho was a whorish woman, love-crazy, who sang about her own licentiousness."[17]

Thus like a mythological figure Sappho serves as an object of many different projections about creative, self-affirming, avowedly sexual women—but as a historical figure she eludes our grasp. Therefore, when I speak of Sappho I mean the *persona* of the poems; and the degree to which *she* corresponds in her feelings and experience to the life of the seventh-century poet will be regarded as beside the point—as well as impossible to establish. That is, my attention will be given to the poet's imaginative projections of female emotions and sexuality, not necessarily to her actual experience. [18]

To find Sappho we have to look at the poems. They are available; she, apart from them, is not.

Horace, the Latin poet, wrote:

> The love still breathes, the flame is still alive that
> the Aiolian girl sang to her lyre. [19]

It seems likely that Sappho would not have been surprised by his praise:

> I have no complaint
>
> . . . dead, I
> won't be forgotten. (E 11; Barnard 100)

THE POETRY

To find Sappho we have to look at the poems. Most are love poems, passionate love poems. Most are directed to women.

As we turn to the poetry we want to discover what we can learn from it about love, about women's love, about women's love of women. Her voice comes to us from so long ago—this woman, the first woman whose name and words we know. She speaks to us about herself. She retells some ancient myths; she invokes an ancient deity—but she tells the myths because she believes they illumine *her* life and prays to the goddess as to an energy that enters her body and her soul and reveals her to herself.

We need to remember that our reading of Sappho's poetry is dependent on but a tiny fraction of her work and that much of the little of her writing that we do have consists of scanty fragments of poems. Of the more than five hundred poems, more than seven thousand lines, written by Sappho, about seven hundred intelligible lines (and only one intact poem) are available today. Much of it was deliberately destroyed when a fourth-century bishop of Constantinople ordered the burning of Sappho's poetry wherever it might be found because of its alleged immorality. Another public burning of her work was instigated by an eleventh-century pope. Much of her poetry was also lost in the fourth-century burning of the library at Alexandria, which destroyed so much of the Greek literature that had until then been preserved from Christian efforts at eradication. Thus we are lucky to have what little we do have; most of the extant verse was found buried in ancient textbooks of rhetoric as providing an example of some literary device or, more recently, discovered among mummy wrappings in Egyptian tombs.

Sappho's poetry falls into the tradition of true lyric; it was composed to be sung to the accompaniment of the lyre and of dancing. Most Greek lyrics were composed for cult occasions in honor of a particular deity. Lyric was seen as a medium for the expression of personal feeling and for the exaltation of the significance of the present moment. In lyric verse, though there might be reference to the same heroic exploits recounted in epic, the great deeds of the past are celebrated because of their relevance to the present. The ritual poem is intended to give the joy of the moment a kind of permanence.[20]

Some of Sappho's poems, especially the "wedding songs," were most likely composed for a formal ritual occasion. Most probably were not, though they have the *form* of cult songs. They directly address a divinity— almost always Aphrodite—as *you* (not as in the Homeric hymns of the older epic-bound tradition in which the deities are addressed in the third person). They use familiar epithets of the goddess and describe her parentage; they gratefully recall the deity's past services and invoke a present blessing, a new epiphany. They differ from formal cult songs in expressing Sappho's individual relation to the deity rather than the relation of the assembled group. Most are "personal records of personal experiences and expressions of personal emotions; their themes are never the attributes and adventures of the divinity invoked and the appeal for epiphany is not made on behalf of the community."[21]

Yet sometimes Sappho seems to invite Aphrodite to come to join a group of women who have assembled in a place they regard as sacred, though we may not be sure if the grove contains an actual temple or actual altars:

> Come to me here, from Crete,
> to this sacred temple of the lovely apple grove.
> Your altars are fragrant here with offerings of frankincense,
> and cool water rustles through the apple shoots.
>
> All the place is shadowed with roses
> and deep sleep slips down through the shimmering leaves . . .
> And here may you, Cypris, pour
> with graceful charm,
> your nectar, mixed with our festive rites,
> into these golden cups. (LP 2; Groden 4)

This is one of those poems that can be read as explicitly about lesbian sensuality and sexuality. The apple grove is certainly a secluded place where women gather apart from men. The apples, the nectar, the cups, may easily be understood as sexual images though the poem does not require such a reading.

More often Sappho addresses the goddess on behalf of her own personal and immediate suffering, not on some ritual occasion, not as a member of a group as the maenads might invoke Dionysus. In the *only* complete poem available to us, Sappho passionately invokes the goddess's presence:

> Richly-enthroned immortal Aphrodite, daughter of Zeus, weaver of wiles, I pray to you: break not my spirit, Lady, with heartache or anguish;
>
> But come here now, if ever in the past you heard my cry from afar, and marked it, and came, leaving your father's house,
>
> Your golden chariot yoked: sparrows beautiful and swift conveyed you, with rapid wings a-flutter, above the dark earth from heaven through the mid-air;
>
> And soon they would come, and, you, Fortunate, with a smile on your immortal face, asked what ails me now, and why I am calling now,
>
> And what in my heart's madness I most desire to have. "Whom now must I persuade to love you? Who wrongs you, Sappho?
>
> For if she flees, she shall soon pursue; and if she receives not gift, yet shall she give; and if she loves not, she shall soon love even against her will."
>
> Come to me now, also; and deliver me from cruel anxieties; fulfill everything my heart longs for. Be my comrade.
>
> (LP 1; Page 1, with some variations
based on Friedrichs, p. 124)

Though Sappho here addresses the goddess on her own behalf, the poem still embodies the magic incantatory power of ritual poetry. The emphatic repetition of *deute* (translated here as "now," sometimes as "again"); Sappho's twice-repeated "come *now*"; Aphrodite's "What *now*?" and "Why *now*?" and "Who *now*?"; and the thrice-repeated "if/then" pattern in the next to last stanza—all remind us how close Sappho's poetry still is to oral poetry, how related to gesture and magic. The litany of the physical signs of passion in some of the other poems (see especially LP 31, below) has the same incantatory effect. The poet's invocation of love brings us to experience both love and poetry as magical powers.[22]

Sappho's expectation of an epiphany to herself, an individual living in the historical present rather than in the heroic age of myth, is unprecedented in Greek poetry—so unprecedented that Page finds it almost impossible to know just how Sappho imagined the goddess might make her presence evident.[23] Others, including myself, feel that we know exactly what she means. The poem's image invokes the sparrows, but obviously Sappho is not expecting an outward visitation—it would not answer her plea. She is speaking of an inner experience, which is yet an experience of the goddess. As Friedrichs says, "Sappho's goddess is a projection of herself," and yet also a sacred power that takes her over.[24] Sappho sees Aphrodite as a "weaver of wiles," Eros as a "weaver of myths" (mythoplokon), as a poet like herself.[25]

One of the most powerful effects of the poem is its communication of the intimacy of Sappho's connection to Aphrodite. She is calling on the goddess to come *again* as she has come before. The goddess addresses her familiarly, by name. Sappho's recollection of the goddess's teasing reminder of how often Sappho has been through this before and of how it will turn around this time as it has in the past, gives Sappho a kind of consolatory distance from her distress—for obviously in one way it is Sappho herself who is speaking and smiling a little at herself. And yet (and here much of the power of the poem lies) we also feel—for now, it hurts; for now it is everything.

Several more fragmentary poems suggest that sometimes the goddess comes to Sappho in her dreams:

> Dream . . . black . . .
> you wander in and out when sleep . . .
> sweet god . . . (LP 63; Groden 39)

And:

> Cyprian, in my dream
> The folds of a purple
> kerchief shadowed
> your cheeks—the one
>
> Timas one time sent. (E 87; Barnard 21)

Again:

> Last night
>
> I dreamed that

you and I had
words: Cyprian (LP 134; Barnard 63)

How immediately present the goddess is; how directly Sappho addresses her.

Many other of Sappho's poems invoke Aphrodite's presence and aid. The poet's focused devotion to this one deity expresses her conviction that the most important dimension of human life falls within Aphrodite's domain. As Sappho freely admits, she sees love as the only real subject worthy of her poetry:

> There are those who say
> an array of horsemen,
> and others of marching men,
> and others of ships, is
> the most beautiful thing on the dark earth.
> But I say it is whatever one loves.
>
> It is very easy
> to show this to all:
> for Helen,
> by far the most beautiful of mortals,
> left her husband
> and sailed to Troy
> giving no thought at all
> to her child nor dear parents
> but was led . . .
> [by her love alone.]
>
> Now, far away, Anactoria
> comes to my mind.
> For I would rather watch her
> moving in her lovely way,
> and see her face, flashing radiant,
> than all the force of Lydian chariots
> and their infantry in full display of arms.
> (LP 16; Groden 7)

Valuing personal love above heroic glory separates Sappho not only from the epic tradition but from her only important lyric predecessor, Archilochus. The first woman poet is the first poet to give love this central place. Though she takes the figure of Helen from the epic tradition, she refuses to castigate her as the woman who betrayed her husband. Rather, she honors her as a woman strong enough to be led by love, by her own feeling. We may also note how easily Sappho shifts from Helen, a mythological figure whose life was shaped by her passionate love for a man, to her own personal experience, her love of a woman. She begins by saying that the most beautiful thing on earth is "whatever" one loves, but proceeds to the very specific "who" of her own love—a woman with a name. This woman is now far away, and the poem expresses Sappho's longing for her, yet it also communicates how Sappho's memory of her particular way of moving and of her radiant face brings her vividly, specifically, to mind.

Another poem about her delight in her daughter, in a few simple lines, again communicates the priority Sappho gives to personal relationship:

> I have a beautiful child
> whose body is like golden petals.
> She is my darling Cleis
> and I would not have for her
> all Lydia. (LP 132; Groden 80)

The Greeks saw Aphrodite as the cause of love and longing (and of the rivalry and jealousy that are love's other side). They believed that when the goddess "enters into" a person she creates a psychological state called *aphrodite*. The primary "work" of Aphrodite is desire, *himeros*, the physical hunger and its inseparable emotional correlates. Friedrichs believes they saw Aphrodite as associated with human *subjectivity* differently from any other deity, for her presence is not only a metaphor for underlying psychological phenomena but also evokes responsive feelings in us—sets *our* souls in motion. This, he believes, is why even Homer recognized her as the most potent of the goddesses.[26] But it is Sappho who really discovered this "subjective" dimension of the goddess.

In Sappho's poetry the goddess Aphrodite and her works, *aphrodite*, are complexly interfused. The closeness of Sappho's attention to physical and emotional states associated with erotic experience is perhaps most evident in what is sometimes called "the desire poem":

> Equal to the gods does he appear,
> that man who sits close by you,
> hears the sound of your sweet voice
> —intently near—
>
> and your delightful laughter. That sight,
> I swear, sets my heartbeat pounding:

the slightest glance at you puts my
speech to flight!

My tongue unhinges, a delicate
flame slips racing neath my skin,
I see nothing, am blinded, my ears
ring, pulsate

a cold sweat commands me, dread
grasps at my heart. More pallid
than grass, I appear to myself
nearly dead. (LP 31; Duban 51)

As we move beyond the first stanza, we soon realize that this poem is not really about the man whose closeness to the girl Sappho desires makes her jealous, nor even about the girl with the sweet voice and delightful laughter; it is about the feelings this scene (actual or imagined, the poem does not say) inspires in Sappho.[27] Again, there is a kind of detachment; it is because Sappho observes her feelings so attentively that she can describe them so precisely. Her symptoms, as she names them, are physical; yet we sense the inner experience of which they are the outward manifestation. Because in this poem we experience the inseparability of body and soul, the emotional devastation communicated in the simple declaration of the last line feels fully earned. As Friedrichs puts it, the poet's "body here becomes an icon for the myth of the inner life."[28]

In another poem Sappho expresses her experience of love's power to move her soul thus:

Without warning

As a whirlwind
swoops on an oak

Love shakes my heart. (LP 47; Barnard 44)

Many of the poems communicate her awareness of love's close association with painful experiences, loss and abandonment, unrequited love or jealousy:

Pain penetrates

Me drop
By drop. (E 17; Barnard 61)

We spoke earlier of a poem in which an absent beloved is made almost present through the poet's evocative recollection. But Sappho also knows well how painfully present love can be precisely in its absence:

> Tonight I've watched
>
> The moon and then
> the Pleiedes
> go down
>
> The night is now
> half-gone; youth
> goes; I am
>
> in bed alone. (E 111; Barnard 64)

Love makes her conscious of inner confusion and division:

> I don't know
> what
> to do: I am
> of two minds. (LP 51; Groden 30)

She can picture herself talking to herself:

> I said, Sappho
>
> Enough. Why
> try to move
> a hard heart? (E 93; Barnard 59)

Many have seen this ability to communicate multiple simultaneous points of view as lying at the heart of the power of Sappho's poetry. Her recognition of the ambivalence that is so often part of deep emotional experience is probably expressed most vividly in her reflections on love's bittersweetness—or, more accurately, its sweet bitterness:

> Eros once again limb-loosener whirls me
> sweetbitter, impossible to fight off, creature stealing up. (LP 130; Carson 3)

In this fragment Sappho once more invokes the familiarity of the experience that overwhelms her—again she uses that telling word *deute*, the "again."

Eros, like Aphrodite, is a god; he comes from without—and stirs her soul. Again the signs of his coming are physical: Eros is limb-loosening, melting. In response to his coming she feels both pleasure and pain, simultaneously. Love tastes both bitter and sweet at once on her tongue.[29]

Sappho's experience of love is a woman's experience, aroused primarily in response to the desirability of other women. Though the poems themselves suggest that (the persona) Sappho's desire for women did not make her immune to the desirability of men:

> Sweet mother,
> I cannot, I swear, do my weaving!
> I am broken in my desire for the boy,
> by the tender, supple Aphrodite. (LP 102; Groden 50)

To love women does not mean *not* loving men. Nor does Sappho see the impulse that pulls her to women as inherently different from the impulse that pulls women to desire men. She feels comfortable comparing love between women to Helen's desire for Paris, Andromache's for Hector, or Aphrodite's for Adonis. (As Friedrichs notes, her poetry "contains the first mention in Greek literature of the lover, Adonis.")[30] When she speaks of love between women and men, her emphasis falls on the woman's active desire, not her desirability to men.

The simple power of Sappho's confident acknowledgment of desire, of women's desire, comes across even in so simple a fragment as "I want and yearn" (LP 36; Groden 15).

Like most Greeks, she was drawn to physical beauty and regretted how aging affects the female body—particularly her own:

> All my flesh is wrinkled with age,
> my black hair has faded to white,
>
> my legs can no longer carry me,
> once nimble like a fawn's
>
> but what can I do?
> It cannot be undone?
>
> no more than can pink-armed Dawn
> not end in darkness on earth
>
> or keep her love for Tithonos. (LP 58, 21; Barnstone 1965, 93)

Her own desire, the poems suggest, was most often directed to women.
Many poems describe the beauty and desirability of another woman:

> and her feet she hid
> with the many-colored thongs
> they work so beautifully in Lydia. (LP 39; Groden 16)

And again:

> Be kind to me
>
> Gongyla; I ask only
> that you wear the cream
> white dress when you come
>
> Desire darts about your
> loveliness, drawn down in
> circling flight at the sight of it. (E 45; Barnard 93)

And again:

> I barely heard you,
> my darling;
>
> you came in your
> trim garments,
>
> and suddenly: beauty
> of your garments. (LP 62; Barnstone 1975, 91)

Some poems express Sappho's awareness of how, in relations among
women, the primary infantile bond between mothers and daughters is invoked. Several poems communicate her sense of the daughterliness of the
women who surround her; in one she sees herself as a daughter:

> Afraid of losing you
>
> I ran fluttering
> like a little girl
> after her mother. (LP 25; Barnard 54)

This intertwining of themes of sexuality and maternal love—of the divine
powers associated with Aphrodite and Demeter—may have been even more

shocking than Sappho's claim to be a woman who feels active sexual desire. Friedrichs believes it may be "one reason for the rage she has aroused in some minds for over two thousand years."[31] It is the particular character of love between women—the ways in which it differs from heterosexual love, the ways in which so much more is different than simply the choice of object—that make it so threatening, and so powerful.

The "Hymn to Aphrodite" (LP 1), in which Sappho mourns that another woman seems impervious to her, suggests how important to Sappho's understanding of love among women is the theme of reciprocity. The poem so unhesitatingly imagines how easily the pursued may become the pursuer, the recipient the giver. Because Sappho's model of love is not the erastes/eremenos model of domination/submission, she wants only love that is spontaneously given and she wants to be *desired*, not only esteemed. She doesn't ask Aphrodite to make the girl yield, but expresses her hope that the other woman might become aware of Sappho's attractiveness and become an initiator in turn. This image of loving expresses a profound recognition of how *alike* the one she desires is to herself and that what she wants from her is the *same* desire as that which stirs her own heart.[32]

Many of the poems are about *parthenia*, usually translated as "virginity" or "maidenhead"—which can refer to a social status, being unmarried, a physical state, having an intact hymen, or the hymen itself. Though some of these poems are marriage songs (and thus communicate that in Sappho's circle it was recognized that most of the girls *will* marry), they do not voice any simple celebration of the weddings about to take place; rather they indicate how much this transition represents an occasion for lamentation.

One, which vows resistance, begins:

It is time now

and ends:

O never! I shall be a virgin always. (E 157; Barnard 27)

Another is more accepting, and yet filled with regret:

Virginity O
my virginity!

Where will you
go when I lose
you?

> I'm off to
> a place I shall
> never come back
> from
>   Dear Bride!
> I shall never
> come back to you
>
> Never! (LP 114; Barnard 32)

And again:

> Why am I crying?
>
> Am I still sad
> because of my
> lost maidenhead? (E 159; Barnard 36)

There is disagreement about how explicit Sappho's allusions to female sexuality are. Friedrichs believes that the poet's perception expresses a female sexual responsiveness that is as attentive to emotional nuance as to physical sensation. He finds in her poems evocations of a sexuality that is slow and gentle in arousal and that is therefore appropriately rendered in "a more diffuse and symbolic poetic representation" than is true of much male erotic poetry. He suggests that Sappho may be experimenting with "a new women's language" and that "some of the fragments are unquestionably carnal and erotic."[33] Winkler finds much in the poems that is sexually explicit. He consistently reads "maidenhead" where others read "maiden"; he understands the "wings of love" as signifying the labia; he notes that *kleis* (which others have taken as the name of Sappho's daughter) might be an allusion to *kleitoris*, the clitoris. Yet he, too, agrees that we misread if we read "pornographically." These poems are not simply about physical, sexual experience. Sappho's "sacred landscape of the body is at the same time a statement about a more complete consciousness."[34]

Some of the poems seem clearly to lend themselves to a reading that focuses on women's sexuality:

> . . . like the sweet-apple
> that has reddened
> at the top of a tree,
> at the tip of the topmost bough,
> and the applepickers

missed it there—no, not missed, so much
as could not touch . . . (LP 105a; Groden 52)

Barnard called this one "Lament for a Maidenhead" (34). It seems so
evidently to be about women's sexuality and how inaccessible it is to men.
Winkler's reading, which sees the poem as specifically about male insensitivity to clitoral sexuality, accords with my own immediate understanding.

One wonders how much is being hinted at about the pain of penetration
and male violation of women's bodies in these lines:

> The groom who'll enter
> is as big as Ares—
> Far greater
> than a great big man. (LP 111; Groden 59)

And in these:

> . . . like the hyacinth
> which the shepherds in the mountains
> trample underfoot. (LP 105c; Groden 53)

How irresistible to compare those poems to another in which Sappho voices
her delight in the gentle lovemaking of women:

> I confess
>
> I love that
> which caresses
> me. (E 118; Barnard 6)

Other poems express the tenderness of female love:

> The gods bless you
>
> May you sleep then
> on some tender
> girl friend's breast. (E 128; Barnard 96)

And:

> When you come

You will lie down and
I shall lay out soft
pillows for your body. (LP 46; Barnstone 1965, 92)

Among the few longer fragments is a lovely poem about a woman who must leave Lesbos. Sappho tries to console her by beautifully gathering together for the departing woman recollections of their times together, offering them as memories they will always still have—though the poet, now remembering the separation as she writes, is herself disconsolate, and is perhaps trying to comfort herself with her own remembered words:

Honestly, I wish I were dead![35]

She was leaving me, tears in her eyes.

Much she said, this most of all:
"Ah, Sappho, what we've been through;
I swear, I leave not wanting to."

And I made this reply:
"Be on your way, yet remember me now
and again. You know how

we have cared for you.
If not I'd remind you
of joyous times which we once knew:

Of rosewreaths and crocus,
of violets you donned at my side,
necklace flower-tied

tossed round your gentle neck;
how you anointed yourself
with a queen's costly scent

and on yielding beds
gentle
desire

and no dance
no shrine   where
we two were not found." (LP 94; Duban 6)

The poem recollects a whole range of shared experience, including but not limited to moments of physical intimacy. It evokes memories of a shared private place—a fictional, poetic place. Nothing in this poem happens in the present; it speaks only of what has happened and what might.[36] Again, Winkler's reading highlights the sexual implications; his translation renders the last lines as "We explored every sacred place of the body—there was no place from which we held back."[37]

In another of the longer fragments Sappho consoles her sometimes rival, sometimes friend Atthis, saying that another departed friend still remembers them—with longing:

> My Atthis, although our dear Anaktoria
> lives in distant Sardis,
> she thinks of us constantly, and
>
> of the life we shared in days when for her
> you were a splendid goddess,
> and your singing gave her great joy.
>
> Now she shines among Lydian women as
> when the red-fingered moon
> rises after sunset, erasing
>
> stars around her . . .
>
> Now while our darling wanders she
> remembers lovely Atthis' love,
> and longing sinks deep in her breast.
>
> She cries loudly for us to come. (LP 96; Barnstone 1965, 22)

As so often in Sappho's poetry, love is seen as becoming visible through the pain to which it exposes us. The themes of loss and parting continually reappear. Love is marked by its transience. Death's presence is so often hinted at—and, though Sappho pushes it away, she knows it will not be dismissed:

> a desire to die
> has hold of me.
> and to see the shores of Acheron
> bedewed with lotus and . . . (LP 95; Groden 46)

Sappho's poetry expresses a woman's love for other women, her longing to be loved by them, her appreciation of the particular sweetness of woman-woman sensuality, her awareness of the bittersweetness, the pain, that openness to love's incursions brings into one's life.

For lesbian women (as the very choice of name says clearly), and especially for women poets, she has been *the* precursor, the foremother. For H.D. (the Imagist poet we discussed in Chapter 5) Sappho's fragments inspired her form—its precision, concision, and elliptical evocativeness—and encouraged her to risk naming the lesbian aspects of her own sexuality. In *Hymen* and *Helidora*, two collections of poems written in the early 1920s, at about the same time as the novels we discussed earlier, H.D. includes five poems based on some of the fragmentary remnants of Sappho's poetry. The fragments inspire "reanimation" as more finished poems might not have.[38] In one (based on a fragment in which Sappho bemoans a lover's infidelity: "thou flittest to Andromeda") H.D. invokes Aphrodite, that same "Lady of beauty" to whom so many of Sappho's poems are addressed:

> Lady of all beauty,
> I give you this:
> say I have offered small sacrifice,
> say I am unworthy of your touch,
> but say not:
> "she turned to some cold, calm god,
> silent, pitiful, in preference."
>
> Lady of all beauty,
> I give you this:
> say not:
> "she deserted my altar-step,
> the fire on my white hearth
> was too great,
> she fell back at my first glance."[39]

Inspired by Sappho's example, H.D. creates a poetic voice, an "I" through which she can name the "sweetbitterness" of her own experience of love.

·15·

PLATO: THE *SYMPOSIUM*

Perhaps the first thing we notice in moving from Sappho's lyric poetry to Plato's dialogues is the absence of the personal voice in Plato. His name appears in the dialogues rarely and even then only marginally; he never appears as a character with lines. Yet since Hesiod Greek writers had proudly used the personal "I"—not only lyric poets like Sappho but Parmenides and Heraclitus, Herodotus and Thucydides; even Xenophon includes himself in his accounts of the Socratic circle. But Plato is silent.

For all the many decades of his writing career he centers his work around the figure of his teacher Socrates. Not surprisingly, the relation between the two philosophers is complex and one about which scholars argue. The Socrates of Plato's dialogues is not identical with the historical Socrates, nor is he simply an invented character behind whom Plato hides—nor is it safe to assume that Plato's own thought is identical with that articulated by the Socrates of the dialogues.

As Paul Friedländer says, Plato's youthful acquaintance with Socrates seems to have been *the* "fateful encounter" of his life. If Plato had not been one of the young men like Charmides or Lysis or Alcibiades who found in Socrates someone "who turned his soul upside down," he might have become an author of tragedies like Agathon or a political figure of some consequence like his uncles—and Socrates might have been just one among the mass of Sophist teachers. But Plato met Socrates and saw in him a compelling model of a life devoted to *philo-sophia*, a passionate Eros directed toward wisdom. "The strength of this love and the transforming power of this unique personality combined to throw the young Plato out of the course for which he seemed to have been destined."[1]

We have already noted that the Athens of Plato was "a society completely filled with male love." In his writing Plato sought to introduce an understanding of Eros different from the assumptions of his contemporaries about paiderastia and also different from what was shown in the inherited mythology. To do this he created a new myth whose central figure was Socrates—represented not only as a teacher of Eros but as an embodiment of

237

Eros—and a new form of mythical representation, the philosophical dialogue. For in Plato's representation of him Socrates' interactions with the
young Athenian aristocrats who were his students, his conversations with
them, the homoerotic ambience of these encounters, was as important to
what made him *the* philosopher as the content of his teaching—and completely congruent with it. Socrates himself, as we shall see, was suspicious of
writing and believed that only words directly spoken to another have the
power to touch the soul. Plato invented a literary form that he hoped might
convey his teacher's erotic presence and draw us into the dialogue, thereby
awakening *our* Eros for wisdom.

It follows that we cannot understand Plato by trying to extract a philosophical doctrine from the dialogues—as most of us were taught to do in
school—*or* a "dialectical method." The dialogues *as a whole* communicate
the Platonic vision. Because Plato's Socrates taught that it is from the
interaction between the lover and the beloved that "the deepest insights
spring," we cannot even identify the meaning of the dialogues with Socrates'
speeches but must examine closely the complex interplay among the contributions to the discussion of all those participating.

Our focus will be on Eros—the one subject of which the always ironically
modest Socrates was willing to admit any knowledge. In the *Lysis* Socrates
announces: "Ignorant as I am in all other things, God gave me that power to
recognize one who loves and is loved" (204b). In the *Theages* he confesses:
"I know nothing about these lofty matters—how I wish that I did!—but as I
am always saying, I am quite ignorant in general save for one small subject:
the nature of love" (128b). His knowledge is experiential not just theoretical.
In Xenophon's *Symposium* he confides, "I can't think of a time when I
wasn't in love" (8.2).

Our focus will be on Eros, and more specifically on Eros among men.
Most scholars who have sought to articulate Plato's view of love have focused
less than I will on what I take to be more than a historical accident—that
when he spoke of love he spoke of male love directed to men (though they
would not dispute that such was the case). As was true of my reading of
Freud, my reading of Plato will discover in his texts a somewhat different
understanding than that usually attributed to him—an understanding whose
dominant theme is neither phallicism nor asceticism.

Plato's dialogues are full of allusions to Socrates' love of young men. At
the beginning of the *Protagoras* he is teased about his infatuation with
Alcibiades; in the *Charmides* he admits that "pretty well all youths of that
age seem beautiful to me" (154c) and continues: "Then I saw what was inside
his garments and I was aflame and beside myself" (155d). In the *Alcibiades*

he compares his love for Alcibiades to the divine ecstasy of Bacchic maenads. Such passages make evident Socrates' susceptibility to physical beauty and convey a taken for granted acceptance of his sensual responsiveness. Yet they also suggest that there is another beauty that stirs him even more deeply. Socrates declares that the nobility of Charmides' soul is even more important than the beauty of his face and body: "Before we see his body, should we not ask him to strip and show us his soul?" (154e). As the *Protagoras* unfolds, Socrates reveals that although Alcibiades was present, "I paid no heed to him. Indeed, I forgot him completely"—for there was someone *more* beautiful present, wise old Protagoras (309d). In the *Gorgias* he calls himself an erastes of both Alcibiades and philosophy and tells us that philosophy is a less capricious and unstable eremenos than Alcibiades (481d).

Although these stories about Socrates' infatuations are told in jest, they nevertheless communicate the strength of his responsiveness to physical beauty. They suggest that the sensual element, though "a steppingstone to a higher level," is nonetheless "a necessary steppingstone whose absence would make that higher level inaccessible."[2] In the *Symposium* Diotima *teaches* that one cannot omit the preliminary stage, the love of one body; in his representations of Socrates' interactions with his students, Plato *shows* how attainment of the higher level does not imply a simple negation of the starting point.

The dialogues also reveal that the relation between Socrates and the youths is not that typical between an erastes and a group of eremenoi. The *Charmides* ends with the beautiful boy threatening to rape the resistant philosopher (176b); in the *Alcibiades Major*, Alcibiades admits, "We shall in all likelihood reverse the usual pattern, Socrates, I taking your role and you mine" (135d). In the *Lysis* Socrates concludes, "It is necessary then for a genuine and not a pretended erastes to be loved by his boy" (222a), and in Xenophon's *Memorabilia* he says, "When I desire someone, I give the whole strength of my being to be loved by him in return for my love, to arouse longing in return for my longing, and to see my desire for companionship reciprocated by his desire" (II. 6.28). The roles are reversed, or perhaps erased; there is a novel emphasis on reciprocity. We begin to glimpse that there is a new myth about male-male love being introduced here.

We also begin to see that Eros itself is being understood in a different, more extended way. Philosophers are said to be erastai of being and truth, of understanding and knowledge. "Plato's language is designed to emphasize the active, restless character of the desire that is common to the passionate pederast and the aspiring philosopher," to show that philosophy begins in desire.[3] Socrates seeks to draw his students to participate in his own love for wisdom, for the soul, for the community. For the Platonic Socrates male love becomes the privileged path that leads to the growth of the soul, to creativity, and to the species of immortality available to humans.

The most fully elaborated explorations of Platonic Eros are to be found in two Middle Period dialogues, the *Symposium* and the *Phaedrus;* they bring to love among men a depth and beauty equivalent to what Sappho's poetry brings to love among women.

IN PRAISE OF LOVE

I have been intrigued for a long while by the role Diotima plays in Plato's *Symposium.* The setting of this dialogue is a banquet given by Agathon on the occasion of his having won the prize for tragedy in that year's competition. The men who are gathered together are old and close friends; several are recognized love pairs. They decide to take turns making speeches in praise of love. It soon becomes clear that for all of them the love most worthy of praise is love between men. Socrates' turn comes last. He begins by confiding that most of what he has to say will be but inadequate recapitulation of what he in turn had been taught by a Mantinean woman called Diotima. What is this unseen feminine presence doing there in the middle of that gathering of homosexual men?

The interweaving of the various speeches constitutes perhaps the most famous composition ever devoted to the inner meaning of love among men. What does Diotima communicate that would otherwise not be expressed? What are the "deepest mysteries" of love, which (Socrates tells us) she was not sure even he would be able to attain?

Despite my fascination with this question, I do not believe that we can reduce the meaning of this dialogue to Diotima's contribution. The setting within which it is introduced subtly qualifies and interprets her views. All the speeches play a role in helping us to understand what the deepest mysteries might be and why they might be so difficult to apprehend. Each is a necessary part of the way. Each represents a stage in the rite. Indeed, as I attempt to show, I believe Alcibiades' arrival, which follows after Socrates' speech, may represent the epiphany, the thing *shown,* as the whole event represents the transmutation of physical attraction into conversation, into poetry and philosophy, represents the thing *enacted,* and Diotima's teaching the thing *told.* Plato's retelling—the dialogue *we* have—like the conversation it re-presents (and creates), is also, I believe, intended to have initiatory power.

The form of the dialogue resembles one of those little Russian dolls that one opens up only to discover a smaller doll within and within that another and so on and on (or, less anachronistically, to use an image introduced by Alcibiades, one of those statues of Silenus that one opens up to find figures of the gods—to which he compares Socrates). Plato probably composed the dialogue around 380 B.C.E.; in it he purports to offer an account given at least twenty years earlier of an event that had occurred more than ten years earlier still.

What we are given is a repetition by Apollodorus, a young follower of Socrates, to an unnamed friend of a story he'd been pressed for by another young Athenian a few days earlier. His version is secondhand; he'd originally been told the story by someone who'd been present at the banquet itself as one of Socrates' most impassioned young admirers—then. For despite the current interest in the event, it had all happened years ago, "when you and I were in the nursery." And Diotima's conversations with Socrates were even then events of a long gone past.

The party has clearly already assumed mythic significance. The setting serves to communicate that at the time of the retelling (shortly before Socrates' own death in 399, perhaps at just about the time that the Athenians learned of Alcibiades' death in 404),[4] Socrates is still inspiring the love of young men like Apollodorus, and that they are fascinated with the details of their beloved teacher's life. They love him and want to know him. To know him includes knowing such tales; to retell them is to enact their love. Remembering the frame within which the dialogue is set may help us "read" Diotima's teaching about the stages of love more complexly than we might were we to ignore it.

The banquet itself is definitely established as having taken place in 416, the year of Agathon's victory—that is, just a year before the sacrilegious mutilation of the herms that we have already mentioned and Alcibiades' subsequent expulsion from Athens. The reader is expected to know, not only of Alcibiades' great beauty and promise, but also of his reckless wildness, so soon to be made publicly evident. The threat of violence associated with Alcibiades' appearance in this dialogue represents something real in his character.

A symposium is a drinking party; the banquet is in honor of Dionysus as well as of Eros—Dionysus, the god of theater, mysticism, love, and wine. Dionysus is present all along; he does not arrive with Alcibiades. The party is being held to celebrate an event that took place in Dionysus's theater the day before. When Socrates arrives and begins his mocking praise of Agathon, the other retorts, "Let Bacchus judge between us," suggesting that another dramatic competition is about to take place. Later, Socrates will tell us that Aristophanes' whole life has been devoted to Aphrodite and Dionysus.

But though they are initially gathered in honor of Dionysus, Eryximachus soon suggests (he says the idea really belongs to Phaedrus) that they spend the evening with each one present taking his turn to speak in praise of Eros—to which Socrates readily agrees for "love is the one thing in the world I understand" (177e). Eros is from the beginning present among them in many guises. In the *Protagoras* (whose dramatic date is some fifteen years earlier than that of the *Symposium*) Agathon had already been identified as the beloved of Pausanias; in Aristophanes' *Thesmorphoriazesae* (written in 411) he is mocked for never having moved beyond the eremenos stage. Here in the *Symposium* their friends' response to this long-term relationship is more complex; it is clearly accepted, perhaps even a little envied, and yet it also provokes teasing. Socrates, for example, pretends to be flirting with Agathon throughout the evening. Another relationship given recognition in several other of Plato's dialogues is that linking Phaedrus to the physician Eryximachus as his younger, respectful companion. At the time of the banquet Socrates is fifty-three, Alcibiades thirty-four; their relationship, too, as we shall see, has a long history.

These are the men who take turns responding to the question "What is love?" The asking is the practice. They search together, beget together, and though the contributions of some may be slight, sentimental, and conventional, nevertheless each builds on what the others have said. In other dialogues Socrates is engaged in focused interrogation of one or two youths or in a relatively formal debate with a famous Sophist; here he is meeting informally with a group of his peers, among whom are included two poets—as though this topic could not fully be explored without their participation. The insights grow out of the interaction, these people, this occasion. Even Diotima's discourse, supposedly told to Socrates long ago, is closely connected to what precedes.

Each speech is part of the way. Plato's view emerges only through an interaction in which Socrates' contribution is but one part.[5] Yet Socrates is not only one of the speakers but also in a sense the *object* of all the speaking. For they are all like rival suitors trying to impress him—the lover who is once again the beloved.

The first to speak is Phaedrus. His Eros is the cosmogonic god of Hesiod, "the ancient source of all our highest good," "the great giver of all goodness and happiness." Phaedrus takes it for granted that to speak of Eros is to speak of love among men; he accepts the conventional distinction between lover and beloved and emphasizes the social function of love in encouraging virtue and valor. Turning to mythical prototypes to illustrate what he takes to be the greatest proof of love—the offering of one's life for another—he praises the self-sacrifice of Alcestis and disparages Orpheus's unwillingness to join Eurydice in Hades. In honoring Achilles' resolve to be with Patroclus in death as even more commendable than Alcestis's dedication (because based on *philia*, friendship, rather than on *anteros*, responding love), he tries to impose the erastes-eremenos pattern on their bond. He disputes Aeschylus's conviction that Achilles was the lover, Patroclus the beloved—for, claims Phaedrus, everyone knows that Achilles was the more handsome. This disagreement about its application raises implicit questions about the adequacy of the conventional model. How well does it really describe the experience of those present? How well does it really correspond to our deepest intuitions about love? These questions will reemerge when Socrates begins to speak.

The next speaker, Pausanias, challenging Phaedrus's uncritical eulogy of love, reminds his friends that there are in reality two kinds of love: that deriving from the heavenly (Ouranian) Aphrodite and that engendered by her earthly counterpart, Aphrodite Pandemos. (Though he refers to a distinction they presumably all "know," Pausanias's description of the love associated with Aphrodite Pandemos as dedicated only to sensual pleasure and therefore directed indifferently to women and boys, and that associated with the Ouranian Aphrodite as "altogether male" and dedicated to the education of the soul of the beloved is actually an innovation—for Aphrodite Ourania was served in Corinth by prostitutes and Aphrodite Pandemos was the goddess as worshiped by the whole community. New myths are being created at this banquet.) By love Pausanias clearly means the active desire of a male lover. Despite the talk about Aphrodite, there is no acknowledgment of a truly feminine desire—though male love directed to bodily gratification is said to "partake of both male and female." Only love directed to males can be a desire of the soul.

Pausanias goes on to define the behavior of a worthy erastes in terms that commend his own enduring love for Agathon, as his friends plainly realize. (Whereas Phaedrus, himself still a youth, had argued that the gods value the devotion of an eremenos more highly than that of an erastes, for such love is a rarer accomplishment.) Pausanias questions love directed to yet-unformed youths; he honors the lover prepared to share his whole life with his beloved; he praises the lover's concern to share his wisdom and virtue. His speech emphasizes the distinctions between sensual and spiritual love, between worthy and unworthy love, between the lover's "wealth" and the beloved's "poverty." His speech—with its celebration of the spiritual and its denigration of the physical, with its focus on a rational morality—is almost a parody of what is often taken to be the "Platonic" view. He surely expects Socrates to applaud it.

Because Aristophanes is incapacitated by a fit of hiccups, Eryximachus speaks next. It seems appropriate that as the natural scientist among the banqueters he should return to the cosmogonic Eros introduced by Phaedrus and, moving beyond the realm of interpersonal relations focused on by both earlier speakers, describe how this god, who creates harmony between opposites, is active in the natural world, in religion, in music, and in his own art, medicine. Though he pretends to accept Pausanias's proposal that there are two Loves, his second cosmic principle, which aggravates the conflict between opposites, is in reality a kind of anti-Eros, reminiscent of the *Eris* (Strife) proposed by Empedocles as counterplayer to Eros.[6] His speech is prosaic and conventional and yet introduces themes to be picked up in Socrates' discourse.

Aristophanes, having recovered from his hiccups, now takes his turn. Into the mouth of the greatest of Athens' comic poets (who, as all his readers would recall, had mocked Socrates in his play *The Clouds* [423]) Plato puts the myth about the primordial "round people," which may well be the most widely remembered passage in the *Symposium*. He tells how these first humans came to challenge the authority of the gods and how Zeus, hoping to undermine their rebellion without destroying them, cut them in two ("just as one might slice an egg")—leaving "each half with a desperate yearning for the other" (191a). Though the images Aristophanes invents are undoubtedly humorous and some of his phrasing consummately flippant, like many readers over the centuries, I find this newly created myth deeply moving and believe it was meant to be. What Plato communicates here of the power of our conviction that we can be made whole only through relation to another, a particular other whom we recognize as uniquely *akin* (whereas Eryximachus had seen love as reconciling *opposites*), is not simply an understanding of love that Socrates will contest, but like Alcibiades' passionate utterance an important complement to Socrates' own discourse.

The comic tone may mask the radical criticism of the dominant conventions, may lead us to miss that Aristophanes is here acknowledging that the desire and pleasure felt by women and eremenoi is in principle no different from that of adult men. As Foucault notes, "His mythical tale upsets the generally accepted principle of dissymmetry of age, feelings, and behavior between the lover and the beloved"—and thus makes irrelevant the traditional moral focus on the issue of consent.[7] Though Aristophanes, like the other speakers, gives most attention to the desire of males for males, his tale makes clear that it is the same desire that animates the yearning of those sliced off from the original hermaphrodites (now heterosexually oriented men and women) and that also moves the women who are slices of the original female. (This, as we noted earlier, is the *only* reference outside of Sappho in classical literature to what we call lesbian love.) "What I am trying to say is this—that the happiness of the whole human race, women no less than men, is to be found in the consummation of our love, and in the healing of our dissevered nature by finding each his proper mate" (193c).

Aristophanes describes how in pity for the desperate longing of the severed pairs to be rolled back in one, Zeus moved their genitals so that they might at least have the solace of sexual intercourse and its momentary overcoming of the gulf between one human and another. But he also says that sexual desire is but a surrogate for a deeper longing, for "a something else to which they cannot put a name" (192c) but that is actually the return to their original state, a complete merging in an utter oneness—not just of bodies but of souls.

His tale, which communicates how our sexual need for another emanates from our sense of incompleteness, of being subject to a primal wound, reminds us of Freud and his recognition of our inexpungeable woundedness—as Aristophanes' emphasis on how all longing is really a longing to find again the lost first other reminds us of Freud's conviction that all later loves are but substitutes for our first love, our mother. Aristophanes gives us an account of love as directed to "entire beings, thoroughly embodied, with all their idiosyncrasies, flaws, and even faults. What makes them fall in love is a sudden swelling up of feelings of kinship and intimacy" directed to another "as a unique and irreplaceable whole."[8] Yet he also communicates how unlikely, how much a matter of chance, it is that we will, indeed, find our other half (and jokingly says that perhaps Pausanias and Agathon are among the lucky ones). So it is likely that most of us will always be driven by our desire—longing for a lost other, longing for an impossible fusion.

As Aristophanes presents love, the discovery of *the* other is an end in itself, the satisfaction of our deepest yearning, rather than what makes possible a mutually engaged upon higher pursuit. His tale offers no criteria for our choice of beloved beyond that powerful sense of recognition—neither physical beauty nor beauty of soul. The mysterious compulsive power of sexual attraction is beautifully rendered, but the moral choices involved in our erotic life are obscured and no recognition is given the creative energies that love may release.

After Aristophanes finishes, Socrates and Agathon engage in some good-natured jest before Agathon presents his speech. The pretty and sentimental lines Plato composes for the extraordinarily youthful winner of that year's prize in tragedy (commonly regarded as the greatest Greek tragic poet after Aeschylus, Sophocles, and Euripides) faithfully reproduce the aesthetic flourishes of his actual style. Though Agathon announces that *his* speech will extol the god himself and not focus on the blessings bestowed by him on humankind, his picture of the god comes strikingly close to being a self-portrait. As he invokes the other traditional mythological image of Eros, the one that sees him not as the oldest of the gods but as the youngest and most beautiful, we think of Agathon's own famous personal beauty. Though he celebrates Love's gentleness and righteousness, its temperance and valor, his real praise is reserved for Eros's creative genius. "Love is himself so divine a poet that he can kindle in the souls of others the poetic fire, for no matter what dull clay we seemed to be before, we are every one of us a poet when we are in love. . . . Do we not recognize that in every art and craft the artist and the craftsman who work under the direction of this same god achieve the brightest fame?" (196e, 197a).

When Agathon, with evident self-satisfaction, takes back his seat, Socrates ironically acknowledges his eloquence and observes that he had not realized earlier that the group had agreed to flatter rather than to praise the god of love, something he could not willingly undertake to do. "But I don't mind telling you the *truth* about Love, if you're interested, only if I do, I must tell it in my own way" (1996). Of course, those gathered all assure him that he should go ahead and make whatever kind of speech he likes.

DIOTIMA

Socrates begins by engaging Agathon in the kind of inquiry familiar from many of the early dialogues and pushes Agathon to agree that love is always directed toward something and furthermore always toward something lacking—which implies that if love desires the beautiful it must itself lack beauty. Having demonstrated his mastery in such dialectical interchange, he now proceeds to tell his friends about the lessons he'd been given "once upon a time, by a Mantinean woman called Diotima." (Like Apollodorus promising to retell Aristodemus's account of the Symposium as best he can, Socrates now promises to repeat Diotima's teaching as well as he can.)

Thus when it is time for Socrates to speak about the one topic he claims to know, he presents himself as an initiate and explicitly compares his relation to the priestess to Agathon's to him. Long ago, he says, he found himself occupying the position that the youths surrounding him now hold. Playfully he recalls Diotima's "almost professorial authority," the self-confidence with which she asserts, "Of course, I'm right," and his own ignorance, his eagerness for instruction, and his difficulty in keeping up with her arguments.

As Socrates rehearses Diotima's long-ago interrogation, he communicates that whatever he knows about love he learned through interchange—love can be learned only through love, only through a mutual searching. To speak of Eros, Socrates, too, has to tell us a story—a story of a teaching, an initiation.

For Diotima's language is that of the mystery religions. She is a priestess, not just a skillful dialectician. There are stages of initiation and there is a final revelation. As she says toward the end of her speech, "Whoever has been initiated so far in the mysteries of love and has viewed all these aspects of the beautiful in due succession is at last drawing near the final revelation" (211a).

Diotima, as I have already confessed, fascinates me. There is no evidence that she was a historical personage; she is Plato's invention. Even within the dialogue Diotima's evident familiarity with the earlier speeches (her mockery of the suggestion that "lovers are people looking for their other halves," her reinterpretation of the self-sacrificing devotion displayed by Alcestis and Achilles) reveals the playfulness of the conceit—and yet it is more than playful. To understand this dialogue and Plato's view of love between men requires that we understand why he brings this *female* teacher into the midst of this male gathering. Why is Socrates presented here—as in no other dialogue—as a mouthpiece through whom another announces her wisdom?

Perhaps in part as a device that permits the introduction of the familiar interrogative form within the set speech required by the symposium setting. Perhaps in part to acknowledge that the words Plato is here putting into the mouth of his teacher go beyond anything the historical Socrates had taught.[9] Perhaps because by putting the praise of paiderastia in a woman's mouth he would make it appear disinterested (as Pausanias's praise so clearly was not). Perhaps to prevent the implication that Socrates had once upon a time been initiated by a male erastes, thus suggesting an acceptance of Pausanias's valorization of the educative role of paiderastia.[10]

But I am persuaded that there is more to it than that. Diotima is and isn't Socrates, but there is a reason for his concealing himself behind a female mask. She serves as a kind of anima (to use Jung's term), as that in Socrates which gives him access to an understanding of love that has a distinctively feminine cast.[11]

Eros, Diotima informs Socrates, is not a god but rather a daimon, an intermediary between the divine and the human; and she tells him yet another tale of Eros's birth, which makes him the son of Poros and Penia,

Resource and Need. As she goes on to describe her unkempt and barefoot Eros, "a lifelong seeker after truth, an adept in sorcery, enchantment, and seduction" (203d), this (as Friedlander notes) is clearly "nobody but Socrates, even though the picture is ironically exaggerated."[12] Eros, as she describes him, "is never altogether in or out of need, and stands, moreover, midway between ignorance and truth" (204a).

She goes on then to acknowledge that Eros, like *poiesis*, has a more general and a narrower meaning—that as *poiesis* refers to all artistic creativity but more specifically to poetry, so Eros, though it includes every kind of longing for happiness, really signifies the longing for the good, longing for the good to be one's own forever.

Thus far the youthful Socrates, as he recalls their conversation, had had but little difficulty in following her. But then Diotima takes a leap that puzzles him—and that, I believe, Plato deliberately attributes to his female psychogogue. For Eros, as she goes on to describe its deepest manifestations, is presented very differently from the conventionally masculine ways of conceptualizing erotic experience reproduced in the earlier speeches. She identifies love with procreative activity—an understanding of love that the Greeks took to represent a feminine perspective. Women's nature, they believed, desires to give birth.[13]

The authentic aim of erotic desire, she tells him, is procreation. "To love is to bring forth upon the beautiful, both in body and in soul" (206b). Where Pausanias had clearly distinguished between the procreative heterosexual love and the spiritual love of paiderastia, Diotima now proposes that conceiving and giving birth is the true aim of love as such. Love is not a longing for the possession of the beautiful but for its conception and generation.

Diotima, as Halperin suggests, is an almost necessary invention; how else but through a woman could Plato introduce this unprecedented image of male pregnancy? The language of pregnancy—of fecundity, conception, gestation, birth giving, child rearing—this, Diotima asserts, is the privileged language to describe the true nature of Eros, of active male love. Thus she proposes a "feminine" dimension to male love very different from the celebration of "effeminate" passivity suggested in Agathon's speech—though her use of the language (as Halperin notes) is not exactly parallel to its usual employment. For here pregnancy is what causes love ("when the procreant is big with child, he is strangely stirred by the beautiful" [206d]) rather than being its consequence; the lover not the beloved conceives, and birth seems to be viewed as analogous to ejaculation.

Underlying her emphasis on procreative love is Diotima's conviction that love longs for the good to be its own *forever*. With all our longing for immortality, we are mortal creatures, and propagation "is the one deathless and eternal element in our mortality" (208b). The only way we can perpetuate ourselves is by leaving new life behind. Though in a sense accepting Aristophanes' description of the insatiability of love, Diotima goes on to suggest a way in which infinite longing may be appeased—not through possession but through creation. Thus the recognition of *death* lies at the heart of Diotima's teaching. Because of death (and our yearning to transcend it), Eros cannot mean simply gratification of self-fulfillment, but must mean new creation.

Such generativity may be expressed not only through literal procreation, by turning to women and conceiving children with them and together raising a family, but also through the turning to a young man of beautiful soul and undertaking his education. But as Diotima goes on to describe this homoerotic bond, it becomes clear that she has something quite different in mind from the educative paiderastia recommended by Pausanias. For she tells of the lover, through his association with his beloved, being finally "delivered" of his pregnancy. "And what is more, he and his beloved will help each other rear the issue of their love—and so the bond between them will be more binding, and their communion even more complete, than that which comes of bringing children up, because they have created something lovelier and less mortal than human seed" (209c). Thus it is not the erastes' love for an eremenos that is focal here, but their mutual co-creative love. As examples of such spiritual progeny she mentions the work of Greece's great poets and her lawgivers.

Diotima here is speaking of a mutual and reciprocal love. Plato's contemporaries would have accepted the notion that the aim of paiderastia is to move from an erotic hierarchical relationship to a more equal bond; but for that more mutual relationship between adult males they used a different word, *philia* (friendship), with different connotations. Diotima's use of Eros is radically innovative and actually undercuts the well-defined distinction between erastes and eremenos that all the other speakers (with the at least implicit exception of Aristophanes) had taken for granted. The image here is not of pursued and pursuer but of mutual responsiveness.

A loving in which one might be able to both give and receive pleasure at once was, again, a loving that the Greeks thought of as typically feminine. It was, you will remember, acceptable for women to enjoy the receptive role, and heterosexual intercourse was imagined to give pleasure to both partners simultaneously. Thus Plato here transposes the "kind of mutuality in eros familiar to women" into the erotic dynamics of male love.[14] In Diotima's model the lover and the beloved are both educated and transformed by Eros;

indeed, the distinction between the two is all but erased.[15] Nor is the love by which the beloved is moved simply "answering love"; both partners love in the same way. She even moves beyond Aristophanes' recognition that the same love may move both partners, in seeing that what they love is not each other but something that lies outside either, that which they have together brought to birth. The apprehension of beauty releases the power to create.

The move to a reciprocal model of love is possible because the love Diotima is describing does not involve physical consummation and therefore need not involve the penetration of one male's body by another, which the Greeks saw as so problematic. But from Diotima's perspective the avoidance of literal expression is not motivated by the need to honor the integrity of the eremenos but by the recognition on the part of both partners that that is not what they really want. Thus the roles are reversed—the beloved must learn to love, the lover teaches the renunciation of physical gratification and by modeling the beauty of his dedication of wisdom himself becomes the *object* of love.[16] This is thus a model of male love in which the phallus essentially disappears and through its disappearance makes possible an image of male-male love that is not polarizing.

Yet Diotima's insistence on calling the relationship she is describing "erotic" makes clear we should not move to too simplistic an understanding of "Platonic" love. The persistent reference to bodily metaphors suggests that they are not "only metaphors," that she sees real continuity—not radical disjunction—between embodied and spiritual love. Thus her position is very different from that voiced by Pausanias. The soul's love for the good and the beautiful is a passionate love, a knowing of the good that includes desire, that is anything but sterile cognition.

This is the point at which she tells Socrates that she is moving to the "deepest mysteries," which she is not certain he will be able to apprehend. She proceeds now to initiate him into the stages of love. "The candidate for this initiation cannot, if his efforts are to be rewarded," she says, "begin too early to devote himself to the beauties of the body" (210a). Thus, the necessary beginning point is appreciation of physical beauty. Nor is there any suggestion that such appreciation must be given up—only that one is not to stay stuck there, as though no other beauty existed. Instead, she lays out a series of stages, each of which depends on the other. The initiate comes to love a particular beautiful body and to enjoy the "noble discourse" to which his passion gives life. Beyond this he comes to recognize how little different one beautiful body is from another and to bring his love of a particular body into due proportion. The next stage is, of course, the recognition of how much more desirable is beauty of soul than beauty of body—which then opens him to recognize the beauty in laws and institutions, and in all kinds of knowledge, and leads him toward *philo-sophia*, the love of wisdom itself.

Having reached this stage, the initiate approaches the final revelation, which bursts upon him all at once as a wondrous vision (as in the Eleusinian mysteries, in which the culminating revelation was the disclosure of sacred symbols in a sudden blaze of light).[17] The *ecstasy* of that culminating epiphany lies at the very heart of Diotima's teaching. The real goal of the whole initiation is the *seeing* (as in the mysteries) of the "very soul of beauty"—not in any of its appearances, not as a face or hand, or even words or knowledge, but in itself, the beauty of which every beautiful thing partakes. Diotima here admits that this "universal beauty" is beyond words, inexpressible; it can only be "seen" by "inward sight," by the imagination, by intuition.

Again she insists that mounting this ladder, which begins with the response to one beautiful body, with "*prescribed* devotion to boyish beauties," is "the way, the only way, to approach, or be led toward the sanctuary of Love" (211c). (In the *Seventh Letter* [343e] Plato says that all of the stages must be "run through upward and downward.") Diotima expands the meaning of Eros in a way that reminds us of Freud's expansion of the meaning of sexuality. Just as Freud asserted that psychoanalysis stands or falls on the basis of the expansion of sexuality beyond heterosexual intercourse to include the nursing of the newborn child and the creative activity of the artistic genius, so Diotima says that true understanding of Eros means moving beyond its association with paiderastic relationship to the most profound experience of human life, the ecstatic experience of oneness with beauty itself—which is immortal as no particular beauty can be. Diotima intends the connections, the deposit of undertones.

She teaches how passion can enter into a relation to the nonpersonal. The sense of self-completion that Aristophanes said we hope to find in one another Diotima promises is really available in this mystical union. This vision is what makes human life worth living—and what frees one from the seductive power of "lads just ripening to manhood," of "the beauties that used to take your breath away" (211d).

But Diotima is not inviting us to some abstract realm of Ideas. Her last words, as Socrates recounts her teaching, are: "Remember, that it is only when he discerns beauty itself *through what makes it visible* that a man will be quickened by the true virtue. . . . And when he has brought forth and reared the perfect virtue, he shall be called the friend of god, and if ever it is given to man to put on immortality, it shall be given to him" (212a).

In Diotima's teaching, beauty and love (not truth and dialectic) are proposed as *the* way; our esthetic sensibility to physical beauty, our emotional responsivity, lead us on. "It is not exclusion of the body that characterizes true love in a fundamental way,"[18] but rather the shared recognition by two lovers that the other is not the aim of their love but rather the partner for the "bringing forth" to which she returns in her last words (which Cornford sees as hiding an allusion to "the language of the Sacred Marriage borrowed from the Eleusinian Mysteries").[19]

The most serious questions voiced about Diotima's teaching are those put forward by Gregory Vlastos in his important essay "The Individual as Object of Love in Plato's Dialogues."[20] Does she include in her vision any recognition of love directed to the particular other human person, not as an assemblage of beautiful parts but as a unique whole? Her visions of lovers engaged in the joint pursuit of beauty itself, a relation that is not reciprocal, seems to him to subsume the particularity of the other person. What Vlastos finds missing in her account is trust, forgiveness, tenderness, imaginative sympathy. Martha Nussbaum (who agrees with Vlastos) focuses on the important step in which Diotima recommends relaxing one's passion for a particular body, agreeing to "deem it of little or no importance"—which she believes is being recommended as a *therapy* that alters our way of looking at the world by "making the related the same, the irreplaceable, replaceable." For "Diotima connects the love of particulars with tension, excess, and servitude; the love of a qualitatively uniform 'sea' with health, freedom, and creativity." Her teaching removes us from vulnerable attachments and the conflict between them. When beauty itself is the object of our love, it is always available and we are freed from being slaves to passion and luck as we are in Aristophanes' myth.[21] But my reading of Diotima is different; it sees Diotima's teaching as warmer, more passionate, more accepting of desire and embodiment. And therefore my reading of the next part of the dialogue differs, too. For where Nussbaum sees radical discontinuity and challenge, I see a more subtle continuation and confirmation.

ALCIBIADES

When Socrates finishes his account of Diotima's teaching, all applaud except Aristophanes. Just as he is about to voice his objections, there is "all at once" a sudden knocking at the door, "followed by the notes of a flute and the sound of festive brawling," and Alcibiades enters, clearly drunk, "with a mass of ribbons and an enormous wreath of ivy and violets sprouting on his head"—the very image of a Bacchic devotee (212c,e).

As he enters the room and is welcomed, Socrates makes room for him on the couch. When Aristophanes notices by whom he's sitting, he exclaims: "Well, I'll be damned! You again, Socrates! So that's what you're up to, is it?—The same old game of lying in wait and popping out at me when I least expect it" (213b)—and proceeds to tease him for having managed to sit himself next to Agathon, the handsomest man in the room. Socrates laughingly protests: "It's a dreadful thing to be in love with Alcibiades. It's been the same ever since I fell in love with him. I've only got to look at anyone who's the least attractive, or say a single word to him, and he flies into a fit of jealous fury" (213d).

Remember, Socrates has just said that since receiving Diotima's instruction in the long-ago past, he has lived by that teaching and sought to bid others do the same. Thus his joking response implies that the love he acknowledges feeling for Alcibiades is part of *following* the path he has just been describing. The "all at once" of Alcibiades' appearance recalls the "all at once" of the final revelation, suggesting that the scene to follow will constitute a showing-forth of the hidden mysteries. Yet Plato's contemporaries would immediately remember Alcibiades as a *profaner* of the Eleusinian mysteries. No wonder readers ever since have argued about his role in the dialogue.

After having yet another drink and persuading Socrates to join him, Alcibiades is asked to make a speech, as the others have done, and Eryximachus suggests that he address his eulogy not to Eros but to Socrates. Thus, as Werner Jaeger puts it, "The long succession of encomia on Eros ends with an encomium on Sokrates," suggesting that "Sokrates is the embodiment of Eros."[22]

Alcibiades agrees and says, "I'm simply going to tell the truth" (reminding us of Socrates' promise to tell only the truth as he began his speech), and explicitly tells Socrates, "If I say a word that's not the solemn truth, I want you to stop me right away and tell me I'm a liar" (215a). Socrates' silence, his failure to challenge Alcibiades' account at any point, gives warrant to its claimed truthfulness.

Fully to understand this speech, as Plato would have expected his readers to, requires that we remember that Alcibiades was, indeed, a favorite of Socrates. This extraordinarily beautiful and brilliant young man had been loved by many who deserted him as it became clear how he would waste his youthful promise through ambition and recklessness. An early dialogue, the *Alcibiades Major,* "begins with the puzzling question of why, out of an entourage of lovers, only Socrates has remained loyal, and it concludes with the answer that only Socrates, among all others, has loved the youth himself (i.e., his soul)."[23] The others who had pursued Alcibiades abandoned him as "the flower of his youth began to fade"; it was just then that Socrates, who had long observed him, approached him for the first time." Socrates explains that until now his daimon had kept him away; "the god who has hitherto held me back now sends me to you." (We sense a connection between this daimon and the daimonic Eros of the *Symposium*.) The dialogue makes clear that though only Socrates had loved his soul, for him too, the attraction of Alcibiades' physical beauty had been a "necessary steppingstone whose absence would make that higher level inaccessible."[24] The dialogue reveals how initially annoyed Alcibiades was by Socrates' approach and how at its end Socrates' passion had engendered Alcibiades' answering love. Socrates says that his love for the younger man had "hatched the winged fruit of love." Yet the conversation Socrates initiated was not the typical erastes' praise of youthful beauty but instead praise of the polis and philosophy. The early dialogue already implies much that Diotima seeks to teach. It also confirms the truth of the story Alcibiades will tell.

Nussbaum speaks of Plato's "loving recreation of the speech of the other side"[25]—whereas I read Alcibiades' speech as the necessary complement to Diotima's discourse. Friedlander agrees:

> It is indispensable that after the path to the Forms has been shown, i.e., after clarification in words, there should follow a human-active movement revealing the nature of the goal. The pronouncements of the priestess could not be the end of the work. There had to be a concluding part in which the ascent to the heights would be depicted in the reality of actual life. The *Symposium* reaches its climax in the episode involving Alkibiades.[26]

I take this episode to function much as do the myths introduced at the climactic moment of some of the other dialogues (the *Republic*, for instance, and the *Phaedo*): it presents the truth that cannot be presented in the discursive mode. I'd go further, and suggest that the tragedy of Alcibiades from Plato's viewpoint is that he saw and understood Socrates' beauty more clearly than anyone else (except Plato himself—that he speaks *for* Plato in his eulogy), but was tragically flawed, so that he couldn't make his own the love devoted to wisdom and beauty that he glimpsed. Friedlander makes much the same point: "As far as Alkibiades' description of Socrates goes, could Plato have written anything like this without having experienced it in his own encounter with Socrates?"[27]

Alcibiades' speech takes a different form from that of any of the others. For one thing, he is drunk or nearly so, under the influence of Dionysus, exhibiting that god-inspired madness that we shall consider more fully in our chapter on the *Phaedrus,* but for which Diotima's emphasis on the passion inherent in true Eros has already prepared us. For another, he will, of course, be speaking of a *particular* love, his love for Socrates, not of Eros as such. And he will be telling the *history* of his love, not speaking of it in general terms—but then Socrates had told us the story of *his* initiation also. As Nussbaum notes, Alcibiades is telling a tale of "learning through suffering: *pathonata gnonai,* the maxim of tragedy."[28]

Alcibiades begins his eulogy with an image. He compares Socrates to the little Sileni statues (as we noted in our discussion of the structure of the dialogue's beginning) and to Marsyas the satyr. He says he means by the image to communicate Socrates' bewitching power, but clearly we are meant to remember that satyrs were noted for enjoying being anally penetrated, so that the confusion between the roles of erastes and eremenos that so much of Alcibiades' speech centers on is already introduced in the image.

Socrates' magic proceeds not from his music but from his simple unpoetic words, not from their eloquence but from *what* he says—which has the power, Alcibiades proclaims, to smite him "with a kind of sacred rage." The wild abandon Alcibiades had displayed on entering was due to Dionysus, but he tells us that Socrates has just the same effect on him. Socrates' words have the power to "turn my whole soul upside down," to make Alcibiades feel, as he says, that "I simply couldn't go on living the way I did" (216a).

As Alcibiades talks he calls upon the others (whom he names "fellow sufferers") to acknowledge the truth of his tale because of its correspondence with their own experience of Socrates. He says he's been "bitten in the heart, or the mind, or whatever you like to call it [and surely one of the points of the dialogue is the rightful conjunction of heart and mind] by Socrates' philosophy," as though by a poisonous snake that will not let go. "And looking round me, gentlemen, I see Phaedrus, and Agathon, and Eryximachus, and Pausanias, and Aristodemus, and Aristophanes, and all the rest of them—to say nothing of Socrates himself—and every one of you has had his taste of this philosophical *frenzy,* this *sacred rage.*" None present denies it, though invited to (218a, b).

In his portrait of his teacher Alcibiades emphasizes precisely all that is *unique,* particular about him. It is *through* this particularity that he sees *beyond* it. He speaks of feeling in response to Socrates "one thing I never felt with anybody else"; he says that Socrates is "the only man in the world" who can make him feel shame. For he acknowledges that there is something in himself that keeps him from fully responding, from dashing off "like a runaway *slave*" (216b). Toward the end of his speech he returns to this theme: "Personally I think the most amazing thing about him is the fact that he's absolutely unique; there's no one like him, and I don't believe there ever was" (221c).

He also says that he sees through Socrates, past the superficial admiration for beautiful boys to the deep inward sobriety and temperance. He claims to have at least once had access to that inner truth. "I don't know whether anybody else has ever opened him up"—note the sexual language—"when he's been being serious, and seen the little images inside, but I saw them once, and they looked so godlike, so golden, so beautiful, and so utterly amazing that there was nothing for it but to do exactly what he told me" (217a).

Reminding his "fellow drunks" that he has sworn to tell the truth, he tells of how, even when they were alone, Socrates would speak not "the sweet nothings that lovers whisper to their darlings" (217b) but just go on talking as he always did. More and more intrigued, Alcibiades finally resolved to ask "him to dinner, just as if I were the lover trying to seduce his beloved, instead of the other way round" (217c). Having talked him into staying the night, Alcibiades confides to him that he sees him as "the only lover I've ever had who's been really worthy of me," and that therefore he's decided that "it'd be just as absurd to refuse you *this* as anything else that belonged to me" (218d). But Socrates responds that if indeed Alcibiades recognizes how the beauty of an outwardly ugly philosopher outshines his own youthful beauty, then he should also realize that his offer is no bargain at all. Alcibiades, still hoping, crept under Socrates' mantle and slept through the night with this "godlike and extraordinary man" in his arms; but "when I got up the next morning I had no more *slept* with Socrates, within the meaning of the act, than if he'd been my father or elder brother" (219d).

When Alcibiades finishes, there is "a good deal of laughter at his frankness—especially as he seemed to be still in love with Socrates" (222c).

In Alcibiades' account of his relation to Socrates we see enacted that reversal of sexual roles described by Diotima. Alcibiades begins as an eremenos but finds himself taking on the erastes' role of pursuer. He has felt himself to be really seen by Socrates, in his soul, his personhood, as by no one else—which is so frightening he runs away and yet such a gift that he returns. He also wants to really know Socrates—to get inside—and imagines that the path to such intimacy would be intercourse. But indirectly and yet clearly, Alcibiades also shows that precisely what gives Socrates his power, what makes him unique, is that he doesn't yield to the opportunity for physical gratification (though he doesn't seem to object to falling asleep cuddled by the beautiful Alcibiades' body). He offers us the account of the "test" as the most telling revelation (the equivalent of Diotima's "final revelation"?) of who Socrates really is; but he had to experience Socrates' refusal of the proffered physical intimacy to "get" it. As Cornford says, "It is Socrates' 'indifference' which Plato is presenting as an instance—*the* instance—of the 'love' which finally emerges from the dialectic of the *Symposium*. But it is being presented with a delicacy so sure that there is not so much as a hint that the claim of Alcibiades' passion to the name of 'love' is being impugned."[29] (I can't help but see the abstinence that Freud requires of the analyst in responding to a patient's transference love as an expression of a love akin to that manifested here in Socrates. Socrates and Freud both seek to communicate that the real object of love lies elsewhere.) Or as Foucault says, "What Alcibiades discovers in the course of the famous 'test' is that Socrates is loved by [the youths] only to the extent that he is able to resist their seduction; which does not mean that he feels no love or desire for them, but that he is moved by the force of true love, and that he knows how truly to love the truth that must be loved."[30]

Socrates responds, not by contesting a word Alcibiades has spoken, but by acting as though he believes the whole point of his discourse was to interfere with Socrates' flirtation with Agathon. Just at that point the party is broken off by the entrance of a group of revelers; everyone gets drunk or leaves or falls asleep except for Agathon and Aristophanes and Socrates. Socrates tries to persuade the other two "that the same man might be capable of writing both tragedy and comedy" (223d). As, in my reading, Plato has shown himself doing here.

Nussbaum believes the dialogue leaves us having to choose between Diotima and Alcibiades; but I read Diotima (and the whole dialogue) differently. I see Dotima offering a more sensual, a more emotional, a more *human* teaching about Eros than Nussbaum sees—and consequently also find less tension between the Socrates of the *Symposium* and the Socrates of the *Phaedrus* than does she. She can recognize Plato's identification with the role assigned Phaedrus in the later dialogue but not his empathy with Alcibiades here. (Though Nussbaum recognizes that readers who take the dialogue form seriously may come to interpretations different from hers.)[31]

Different readings are no doubt shaped in part by coming to the texts with different questions. Because Nussbaum and most philosophers who have approached this dialogue are primarily concerned to apprehend Plato's moral views, they give a more central place to the logic of the philosophical arguments than do I. I have been reading in order to bring into view Plato's understanding of male love. I find in his writing clues to a new myth that goes beyond those he inherited and in significant ways enriches our understanding of the "deeper mysteries" of male love: a new myth perhaps particularly relevant in the age of AIDS—for it celebrates a love rooted in sensuality but not centered on orgasmic sexuality, and it is inspired by a recognition of death.

The myth is not fully adumbrated here in the *Symposium;* we must turn now to look at a slightly later dialogue, the *Phaedrus.*

·16·

PLATO:
THE *PHAEDRUS*

The most lyric exaltation of homoerotic love to be found in Greek prose (and, except for Sappho, in its poetry) is that contained in the dialogue to which Mary Renault's Laurie so often returns, the *Phaedrus*.[1]

For once Socrates finds himself outside the city's bounds in a landscape whose quiet beauty suggests to him that it must be consecrated to the nymphs—though his young companion, Phaedrus, remembers it as the scene of a famous mythical abduction. The setting seems to awaken in Socrates an uncharacteristically ecstatic poetry as he speaks to Phaedrus of love as a divine disturbance, a madness—a heaven-sent madness superior to man-made sanity.

This excursion is clearly meant to be understood as taking place well after the banquet in celebration of Agathon's victory, for there is an indirect allusion to the earlier occasion when Socrates teases Phaedrus for having been responsible for the deliverance of more speeches during his lifetime than almost anyone else. Yet settling on a date for the events represented in the dialogue is difficult, for the clues within the dialogue point to a time when the historical Phaedrus was not in Athens (he had been banished along with Alcibiades after the mutilation of the herms).[2] Thus we may be intended to recognize that the encounter does not occur in historical time—that Socrates' admission in the dialogue (with respect to his first speech) that "this story isn't true" may apply (in a literal sense) to the dialogue as a whole. As W.K.C. Guthrie says: "This singularly elaborate and beautiful setting is symbolic. Socrates is taken out of the surroundings which he never left. Within the limits of his dramatic art Plato could not have indicated more clearly that this poetic and inspired Socrates was not known to his habitual companions."[3]

It never happened. Socrates never left the city, never spoke in such impassioned poetry, never so fully celebrated the bond that unites life-long lovers. This is Plato's myth about a Socrates that never was, a myth,

259

Nussbaum suggests, that might express Plato's wish that his teacher "had been a little more mad," more truly exemplary of a fusion of clarity and passion, more fully open to a deep mutual love between teacher and pupil.[4]

At the time the dialogue supposedly took place, the beautiful youth who apparently inspired Socrates' effusion was not only not in Athens, he was nearly forty years old. So "Phaedrus" is not really Phaedrus either. In a sense he might be Alcibiades again, a fantasy Alcibiades who didn't succumb to ambition and impiety but stayed to become all that it had once seemed he might. In a sense he is Plato, who at that time was seventeen, newly introduced into Socrates' circle, and whom the later Plato now imagines as the recipient of a more intimate notice from Socrates than he had ever actually been offered. Nussbaum makes a powerful case for suggesting that in another sense he might be Dion of Syracuse (whose name, like Phaedrus's means "brilliant"), and that the image of a relationship based on complex passion and mutual respect, on shared devotion to the polis and philosophy, which lies at the center of the dialogue, might reflect what Plato, to his great wonder, had discovered to be true of his bond to Dion.[5] If this is so, Plato is subtly related to both participants in the dialogue; he is Phaedrus and also Socrates.

GOD-SENT MADNESS

Let us turn now to what transpires between his fictive Socrates and his equally fictive young companion. Socrates has agreed to accompany Phaedrus outside the city in order to have Phaedrus read to him a speech by a famous visiting Sophist arguing that an eremenos is better off surrendering to a dispassionate erastes than to one consumed by love. When Phaedrus finishes his recitation, Socrates says he is disappointed by its rhetoric and agrees to show how the same thesis might be argued more persuasively. Announcing that he will cover up his head so that he can rush through his speech "at top speed without looking at you and breaking down for shame" (237a), Socrates then delivers his own discourse on the unworthiness of a madly impassioned lover, emphasizing how such an erastes will seek to keep his eremenos docile and inferior, will protect him from exposure to manly exercise and divine philosophy, which might "make a real man of him," and will jealously insist on his isolation from friends and family—and then abandon him.

Having completed this part of the speech, Socrates says he sees no need to explicate the obvious other half, the eulogy of the clearheaded lover, and prepares to return to the city. But then, unexpectedly, he turns back to Phaedrus: "At the moment when I was about to cross the river, dear friend, there came to me my familiar divine sign—which always checks me when on the point of doing something or other—and all at once I seemed to hear a voice forbidding me to leave the spot until I had made atonement for some offence to heaven" (242c). He had suddenly realized that his speech, like that of Lysias, in forgetting that Eros was a god, the child of Aphrodite, was really blasphemous. Both speeches had treated Eros as though he were an evil thing—but a god, says Socrates, cannot be evil. So now Socrates must purify himself—by telling a true story to replace the false.

This speech, he tells Phaedrus, will be in the voice of Stesichorus, the poet who had atoned for his "defamation" of Helen by composing a more truthful palinode (though in actuality this "truth" was his own invention and the defamation the accepted truth). Plato introduces Stesichorus as a son of Euphemus ("reverent in speech") from the town of Himera ("desire"). The poetic conceit is not as elaborate as in the *Symposium*—Stesichorus does not become a figure in the dialogue as Diotima had—yet it prepares us for the lyric language and reverent tone of the passion-praising discourse that follows. (Socrates had already expressed to Phaedrus his appreciation of the "fair Sappho's" god-gifted praise of love.)

Lysias had commended a lover fully in control of himself, which means, Socrates now says, a lover closed to the gods. Socrates begins with some careful dialectical distinctions. The falsity in the earlier speeches, he claims, derived from their juxtaposing the mad lover to the one sound of mind and failing to recognize that there is more than one form of madness—that "in reality the greatest blessings come by way of madness, madness that is heaven-sent" (244b). Thus he discriminates between two forms of madness, profane and sacred, and within the latter distinguishes four forms: prophetic, mystical, poetic, and erotic. But one would have to be tone-deaf to the erotic poetry of Socrates' development of his theme, to the "madness" that animates it, to read it as a rhetorical exercise whose arguments we "get" by diagraming them. This is, as Friedlander says, the only dialogue in which Socrates himself is seized by the divine mania of mythopoeic inspiration; in other dialogues, he is the listener while others tell the mythical fables.[6]

Socrates compares the god-sent foresight of the prophetess at Delphi and the priestesses at Dodona with the sane prophets of his own day, who inquire into the future by means of birds and other signs, relying on the "purely human activity of thought" belonging to their own intelligence. This comparison suggests his hope that the image of love he will go on to introduce, though not yet a present reality, might be a god-sent vision of a future possibility. His invocation of the madness associated with religious initiation, with the Orphic cult and Dionysus, reminds us of the mysteries over which Diotima presided. Socrates' own susceptibility to poetic madness will soon be made manifest. This third form of madness, of which the Muses are the source, "seizes a tender, virgin soul and stimulates it to rapt passionate expression." Socrates warns Phaedrus that "if any man come to the gates of poetry without the madness of the Muses, persuaded that skill alone will make him a good poet," his works will be brought to naught (245a).

The highest form of madness is that associated with Eros and Aphrodite—erotic madness. Love is sent from heaven for the advantage of *both* lover and beloved. As Socrates' discourse unfolds, he will reveal Eros as the god of paiderastia—and of *philo-sophia*. The love of beauty and of wisdom are brought together, seen as one—as are real love and true rhetoric. The lover and philosopher are set above the poet, but like him seen as inspired by emotion and image. "This sort of madness is a gift of the gods, fraught with the highest bliss" (245c).

PSYCHE'S WINGS

To understand the role played by love in our lives, in the life of the human soul, requires (Socrates tells Phaedrus) that we begin by trying to characterize the nature of the psyche, its experiences and activities. We can start by reaffirming that the soul is self-moving and therefore is not born and does not die; but we soon discover the limitations of our apprehension and recognize that only a god could fully describe it. A human must rely on image, metaphor, and myth.

As Socrates then proceeds to do. His own discourse revolves around an image inspired by the traditional image of Eros as a winged god[7]—the soul, he suggests, is like "the union of powers in a team of winged steeds and their winged charioteer" (246a). As Socrates expands the image into a myth it becomes clear that the soul is indeed the *union* of powers, that it would be mistaken to confuse it with the charioteer (who represents cognition, or that aspect of the self, like Freud's *ich*, his *ego*, which those "sound of mind" might claim to be the whole)—for the charioteer without his horses is almost impotent, being dependent for his motion on their (emotional) energies. The steeds are not, in this image, the body but aspects of the soul. Our emotions and desires are part of our personhood. Though they may pull us in confusing, troublesome ways, our responsiveness to beauty, our aspiration toward the heavens, is an activity in which they and not only the charioteer participate.

The soul of the gods is described by the same image, but their task is easy, for both their horses are good and easily managed. With us humans, the task of the charioteer is more difficult, for his unruly horses are likely to pull in opposite directions. If he cannot control them, the soul will sink to earth, lose its wings, and there acquire a body and mortality. Such is the lot of all of us earthbound creatures; and in our embodied lives we easily forget the blessed vision we had access to when winged, when "whole and un-blemished," we were "all initiated into that mystery which is rightly ac-counted blessed beyond all others." But in our beginning, "pure was the light that shone around us and pure were we" (250c).

Though the soul is eager to regain its wings, doing so depends on how it orders its embodied life. After each life, the soul is judged and then assigned an appropriate reincarnation. Only those who honestly devote their lives to seeking after wisdom or "conjoin their passion for a loved one with that seeking" (249a)—and do so for three lifetimes—may hope to recover their wings. Such devotion to the search for wisdom, says Socrates, is inspired by remembrance of our former winged life and thus "approaches to the full vision of the perfect mysteries" (how closely that echoes Diotima). To the multitude, who do not understand that he is "possessed by a deity," one thus dedicated will be judged as being "out of his wits" (249d).

But it is just this possession that represents the fourth and best form of divine madness "both for him that has it and for him that shares therein" (249e), for both lover and beloved. Every human soul once had a vision of true being, but to be reminded of it by things here is not easy for most souls. (As Socrates describes the bliss-bringing light-filled vision, we cannot help but think again of the boy at his side whose name means "shining.") But there are some souls that, touched by the god's madness, by the love of beauty, are moved by earthly beauty to remember true beauty. He who is so moved is called a lover. Remembering, his wings begin to grow.

Beauty gives us embodied souls an access, otherwise unavailable, to the lost vision—for beauty is manifest to sense, to sight. Socrates believes that all humans have some responsiveness to beauty and assumes that the beauty that stirs us all most powerfully is personal beauty, the beauty of another human (rather than the beauty of a landscape such as the one that surrounds him and Phaedrus as they talk). But for those "whose vision of the mystery is long past," what is called beautiful here stirs no reverence—and they respond "like a four-footed beast" and surrender to physical desire (250e).

Then follows a beautiful passage in which Socrates describes the response to a "godlike face of bodily form" of one "fresh from the mystery":

> First there comes upon him a shuddering and a measure of that awe which the vision inspired, and then reverence at the sight of a god, and but for fear of being deemed a very madman he would offer sacrifice to his beloved, as to a holy image of deity. Next, with the passing of the shudder, a strange sweating and fever seizes him. For by reason of the stream of beauty entering in through his eyes there comes a warmth, whereby the soul's plumage is fostered, and with that warmth the roots of the wings are melted, which for long had been so hardened and closed up that nothing could grow; then as the nourishment is poured in, the stump of the wing swells and hastens to grow from the root over the whole substance of the soul, for aforetime the whole soul was furnished with wings. Meanwhile she throbs with ferment in every part, and even as a teething child feels an aching and pain in its gums when a tooth has just come through, so does the soul of him who is beginning to grow his wings feel a ferment and painful irritation. Wherefore as she gazes upon the boy's beauty, she admits a flood of particles streaming therefrom—that is why we speak of a "flood of passion"—whereby she is warmed and fostered; then has she respite from her anguish and is filled with joy. (251a–d)

Here we have moved far beyond allegory. The images are richly, associatively fused and communicate more than any interpretation can access.

The lover experiences the boy's beauty of a god-given gift. The stream of beauty that enters his eyes affects the *whole* soul, the sprouting wings belong to the whole soul (not only to the charioteer). The lover's response can only be expressed in images that derive from physical experience (and that may remind us of Sappho): he shudders and sweats, is warmed and melted, throbs with ferment. "The deep sensual response to a particular person's splendor, the emotions of love and awe, the intellectual aspiration that this love awakens—all of these flow together, so that the person feels no gap between thought and passion, but, instead, a melting unity of the entire personality."[8]

The images of melting warmth, of running water, of lush vegetal growth, recall the sylvan setting described at the beginning of the dialogue. The stump's swelling and rising growth clearly suggest male sexual responsiveness, a penis moving toward erection. But the passage also emphasizes the *lover's receptivity*—the beauty *enters* his soul like a *liquid* stream, is *poured* in; he is *warmed* and *melted*. The language suggests the sexual experience of women—or of the passive partner in male-male lovemaking.

(By faithfully recollecting that the word *psyche* is feminine, the translation's consistent reference to the soul in feminine pronouns helps us tune in to this undertone of meaning.)

Separation is almost unbearably painful; it means feeling the freshly watered openings dry up and close:

> But when she has been parted from him and become parched, the openings of those outlets at which the wings are sprouting dry up likewise and are closed, so that the wing's germ is barred off. And behind its bars, together with the flood aforesaid, it throbs like a fevered pulse, and pricks at its proper outlet, and thereat the whole soul round about is stung and goaded into anguish; howbeit she remembers the beauty of her beloved, and rejoices again. So between joy and anguish, she is distraught at being in such strange case, perplexed and frenzied; with madness upon her she can neither sleep by night nor keep still by day, but runs hither and thither, yearning for him in whom beauty dwells, if haply she may behold him. (251d,e)

When lover and beloved meet again, the liquid flowing in from the beloved releases the liquid pent up within the lover. Again the language is so sensual that it is hard to remember that Plato is speaking of souls rather than bodies: "At last she does behold him, and lets the flood flow in upon her, releasing the imprisoned waters; then she has refreshment and respite from her stings and suffering, and at that moment tastes a pleasure that is sweet beyond compare. Nor will she willingly give it up" (251e). The lover is, indeed, mad with love—even more ready himself to yield up all other relationships, all else he values, than the impugned lover of Socrates' "false" first discourse might have sought to make his beloved:

> Above all others does she esteem her beloved in his beauty; mother, brother, friends, she forgets them all. Nought does she reck of losing worldly possessions through neglect. All the rules of conduct, all the graces of life, of which aforetime she was proud, she now disdains, welcoming a slave's estate and any couch where she may be suffered to lie down close beside her darling, for besides her reverence for the possessor of beauty she has found in him the only physician for her grievous suffering (252a).

At this point Socrates turns to the actual boy who lies by his side on the bank of the river, for though Phaedrus is not really the beloved who inspires this praise of the soul's passion, he *is* his stand-in. "Hearken, fair boy to whom I speak," he says. "This is the experience that men term love" (252b).

THE MIRRORING OF LOVE

Socrates now turns his attention to the mutual affection that "arises through the madness inspired by love," the shared participation of "true lovers in the mystery rite" (253c). He imagines that long ago, before our souls fell to earth and lost their wings, each of us followed some particular god, Zeus perhaps, or Hera or Apollo, and that even now lovers seek to honor and copy the god in whose company they once were. The youths they choose to love are chosen on the model of this deity and worshiped as though an image of the god. They seek to foster in their beloveds the divine attributes they discern in him. "Every lover is fain that his beloved should be of a nature like to his own god" (253b) and his every act is aimed at that goal. To encourage this development in the other, of course, entails following up and developing "the traces within *themselves* of the nature of their own god" (253a). Thus the beloved is chosen because of his likeness, and through the ongoing relationship, lover and beloved are *both* transformed and both become more and more like the god they worship—and like each other.

But Socrates is interested in the beloved's love, not only the lover's, and wants to describe to Phaedrus how that love comes into being. Because he sees it as a *responsive* love, he must relate how the beloved first comes to experience his lover's love, which means reflecting further on the lover's own response to Eros's entry into his soul.

The appearance of Eros is a sacred event, an epiphany, which reveals to the lover the truth of his own being, the conflicting energies at work within. When the lover first feels warmth suffusing his whole soul, when he first feels the prickling of desire, the more hot-blooded, troublesome horse forces the soul to pull close to the beloved and speak to him of love's delights. At the last moment the charioteer—remembering the vision of divine beauty— succeeds in reining in his steeds and bringing them down on their haunches. Disappointed, the impetuous, wanton steed then abuses his companion and the driver as cowardly deserters and, neighing and pulling, compels them to return to the beloved and renew their offer. Again, and even more forcibly, the driver succeeds in holding back his horse. So it happens again and again until eventually the steed is tamed.

Here Socrates shows the real struggle that goes on in the lover's own soul, the power of his physical passion, its unabated vitality. The beloved's discernment of the honesty and integrity with which the lover engages this struggle is what leads him to realize that there can be no shame in responding to such a lover's advances. So he comes to welcome his suitor and take pleasure in his company; he comes to value this man "in whom there dwells a god" beyond all his other friends (255b).

As he allows his lover to come close, "that flowing stream, which Zeus, as the lover of Ganymede, called the 'flood of passion,' pours in upon the lover" (255c). But then something new happens—passion enters the soul of the beloved as well:

> Part of [the stream] is absorbed within [the lover], but when he can contain no more the rest flows away outside him, and as a breath of wind or an echo, rebounding from a smooth hard surface, goes back to its place of origin, even so the stream of beauty turns back and reenters the eyes of the fair beloved. And so by the natural channel it reaches his soul and gives it fresh vigor, watering the roots of the wings and quickening them to growth, whereby the soul of the beloved, in its turn, is filled with love (255c,d).

The beloved responds not just with gratitude and respect, not with *philia* but with Eros—a radical challenge to the conventions of Greek paiderastia.

We might reflect a little on this "mirroring." The allusion to Ganymede, the wine *pourer* of the gods, reminds us how Zeus was *drawn* to the beautiful youth and then *drew* him up to the heavens.[9] The erastes does not narcissistically project his own image on to the eremenos, does not love in him his own younger self. He sees in him an image of the divine, and when the youth then looks into his lover's eyes he sees there an image not of himself as such but of himself as his lover sees him. Only apparently in either case does the beauty emanate from the other; in truth it emanates from the god. Thus the mirroring is a transformative activity: in being seen by our lovers, in seeing them, we are changed, we come to know ourselves and them differently. The image also represents the lover as not only a beholder but as one who allows himself to become the object of vision to another. The passage recalls one from a much earlier dialogue, the *Alcibiades Major,* where Socrates and Alcibiades agree that had Apollo commanded us to *see* rather than to know ourselves, we would have had to use a mirror—and ideally the pupil of another's eye. "In order to see ourselves truly we have to see ourselves *seeing* . . . otherwise, we glimpse only a static image of ourselves and do not know ourselves as active, desiring, sentient beings. . . . Each lover grows wise by contemplating himself in the soul of his partner, discovering in this way the nature of the divinity within himself."[10]

Not surprisingly, the youth hardly knows what to make of his experience:

> So he loves, yet knows not what he loves; he does not understand, he cannot tell what has come upon him; like one that has caught a disease of the eye from

another, he cannot account for it, not realizing that his lover is as it were a mirror in which he beholds himself. And when the other is beside him, he shares his respite from anguish; when he is absent, he likewise shares his longing and being longed for, since he possesses that counterlove [responding love] which is the image of love, though he supposes it to be friendship rather than love, and calls it by that name. (255d, e)

Both lover and beloved actively love and joyfully receive. Socrates makes clear that the youth experiences not only loving feelings but physical *desire:* "He feels a desire—like the lover's, yet not as strong—to behold, to touch, to kiss him, to share his couch, and, now ere long the desire, as one might guess, leads to the act." (255e)

The youth's soul, like the lover's, is troubled by a hot-blooded steed, and in his soul, too, there is reverent resistance:

So when they lie side by side, the wanton horse of the lover's soul would have a word with the charioteer, claiming a little guerdon for his trouble. The like steed in the soul of the beloved, swelling with desire for he knows not what, embraces and kisses the lover, in grateful acknowledgment of all his kindness. And when they lie by one another, he is minded not to refuse to do his part in gratifying his lover's entreaties; yet his yokefellow in turn, being moved by reverence and heedfulness, joins with the driver in resisting. (256a)

Socrates affirms the fruits of such resistance: if the victory goes to the restraining elements, the pair's days on earth "will be blessed by happiness and concord" for they will have "won self-mastery and inward peace" (256b). When life is over, with wings recovered, they will have won the first of the three rounds that allow return to the heavenly realm. Clearly what Socrates is imagining here is a life-long relationship in which each makes "*simultaneous* and *reciprocal* though *independent* progress toward the contemplation of the Forms."[11] In which each, one might also say, helps the other prepare for death.

In this dialogue the particular beloved is the psychogogue. Socrates is speaking of a relationship that grows and develops through time, that acquires a history, in which the other is valued for himself not just as an instance of beauty. And this is as true of the beloved's regard for his lover as of the lover's regard for him. The relationship (as Nussbaum suggests) is here seen as having intrinsic and not only instrumental value; Eros is a *god* in this dialogue and not a *daimon*, an intermediary. "The best human life involves ongoing devotion to another individual."[12] Indeed, "it is now permissible," Halperin maintains, to speak of the lover and beloved as two lovers—although Plato himself as never so explicit—for they experience alike the passion of *eros*. Moreover, the interests of both lovers fully converge and so, in theory at least, neither is significantly subordinate to the other. As Socrates sets out to demonstrate in his celebrated palinode in the *Phaedrus*, eros affords an equal and identical benefit to both lover and beloved; through the madness of *eros* each is dear to the other, and thanks to *eros* each will have wings like the other's.[13]

Socrates acknowledges that the struggle is a persistent one, not easily finished with once and for all. (Plato himself, Friedlander says, "had to struggle incessantly for this very harmony, which he attributed ultimately to an act of grace on the part of the gods.").[14] As Socrates tells Phaedrus:

Mayhap in a careless hour, or when the wine is flowing, the wanton horses in their two souls will catch them off their guard, bring the pair together, and choosing that part which the multitude account blissful achieve their full desire. And this once done, they continue therein, albeit but rarely, seeing that their minds are not wholly set thereupon. Such a pair as this also are dear friends, but not so dear as that other pair, one to another, both in the time of their love and when that love is past, for they feel they exchanged the most binding pledges. (256c, d)

Even such a pair (not only those who remain celibate) participate in the blessings of the love that is touched by heaven-sent madness: "When death comes they quit the body wingless indeed, yet eager to be winged, and therefore they carry off no mean reward for their lover's madness . . . but shall walk together in a life of shining bliss, and be furnished in due time with like plumage the one to the other, because of their love" (256d, e).

Having acknowledged that this love, too, is given its power by the presence of the god, by the lovers' shared openness to divine madness, to passion, Socrates again directly addresses the youth by his side. "These then," he says, "are the blessings great and glorious which will come to you from [the impassioned] lover" (256e). He compares these blessings to the "niggardly" worldly benefits that the dispassionate lover praised by Lysias has to offer. As he began his "true" speech he had asked, "Where is that boy I was talking to? He must listen to me once more and not rush off to yield to his nonlover before he hears what I have to say." Phaedrus had answered, "Here he is, quite close beside you, whenever you want him" (243e). Clearly Socrates had hoped that his speech might touch the soul of the youth, might lead him to be willing to open himself to the transformative powers of the love that is touched with divine madness, rather than to choose the safe, calm love to which Lysias had beckoned.

Yet though Socrates is inspired to this eulogy of love by the easily impressed but eager youth, there is no pretense in the dialogue that the reciprocal love that Socrates has so eloquently described is realized between them. The boy hardly speaks; one is not sure how much of what Socrates has said he has even understood. Still, somehow his presence has helped Socrates to remember or imagine how a divinely inspired Eros might shape one's life, has helped beget (to return to Diotima's language) a beautiful speech—a speech that Socrates ends with a prayer to Eros in which he asks his forgiveness and favor.

The *Phaedrus* doesn't end here; indeed, it is but half over. Like the cicadas, Socrates and Phaedrus seem quite capable of forgetting to eat and drink, so engrossed are they in their talking. Time is suspended for them, as it is in a ritual.

The rest of the dialogue, however, will interest us less. The connections— as Socrates returns to the distinction between false speaking and true—to what has preceded are clear and important. It was obvious from the beginning of the dialogue that Socrates is persuaded of the integral connection between speech and love, logos and Eros. The insight itself was not new; even in ancient myth the goddess Peitho was associated with both rhetorical persuasion and the art of seduction.[15] Socrates' twist was to see philosophy as the highest form of both.

When finally they are ready to leave, Socrates suggests that they ought first offer a prayer to the divinities of the place (the only prayer in any of Plato's dialogues). "Dear Pan," he prays, "and all ye other gods that dwell in this place, grant that I may become fair within, and that such outward things as I may have may not war against the spirit within me" (279c). These few words gather together all the themes introduced in the course of the dialogue. The dedication invokes again the closeness to nature of the dialogue's opening. The address to Pan honors a god even more closely associated with instinctual, passionate love than Eros himself. The request for inner beauty by the notoriously ugly philosopher reminds us of the central place played by beauty in the life of the soul, and the plea for harmony between inner and outer recalls the struggle to bring peace between the opposing steeds.

Phaedrus tells him: "Make it a prayer for me, too. People who love each other have all things in common" (279c).

The ending is poignant, for we know that despite the beauty and passion of Socrates' speech in this dialogue, it did not really transform the life of the young man who lay by his side—nor did it persuade Plato's own contemporaries, for whom "his model of mutual erotic inspiration was apparently too alien."[16]

During the second life of the dialogue, which we have almost ignored, Socrates tells Phaedrus that the real defect of Lysias's speech and his own first one was that both were set pieces (in fact, Lysias's was written) rather than speech emerging out of intercourse, out of "the between." As he seeks to persuade Phaedrus of the importance of the direct contact between speaker and listener, of the specific address to a particular hearer who can ask for the filling in he needs, we cannot help but notice again how little Phaedrus has participated in the conversation and realize that there is something *odd* happening here. As Socrates contrasts the living speech of oral discourse where words lead to new words, to responsiveness and generativity, with the barren speech of written texts, we are inevitably reminded of ourselves as *readers* of a written account. Plato's dialogue has suddenly become self-reflexive in a way that irrevocably breaks the illusion. As Anne LeBeck recognizes, Plato's effect here is positively Brechtian![17] We are thrown back on ourselves, forced to recognize that this tale about true speech and true love, this tale woven of imagery and artifice, is directed to *us*.

We need, then, to try to discover how Plato's myth about love illumines our own understanding. He has given us a picture of a love relationship that grows and deepens over time. It begins with an intense response to physical beauty—and a resolution to live that response in a way that will encourage the growth of the souls of both lovers. From his culture's perspective—where penetration was seen as polarizing and demeaning—this meant abstention from physical gratification but full acknowledgment of the pull of physical desire. Where the assumptions about penetration are different and where the possibility of each partner in turn taking on the active and the receptive roles in physical intercourse is admitted, the injunction against literal fulfillment might seem less imperative. A deep engagement with Plato's thought at least allows us to consider this possibility.

What seems most important in Plato's myth is his celebration of love that is fully mutual—and that is truly dedicated to the inner growth and development of both participants. His account presents us, as none of the earlier Greek myths do, with an image of a love that grows and deepens over time, that is always vulnerable to challenge and change, and that recognizes that eventually we die. Loving comes to be seen as dedicated to the preparation for death.

In the face of death, as Freud, too, came to know, sexuality and love are transformed. In a sense all we have looked at thus far in this book has served to prepare us to consider what Freud and Plato and Greek mythology have to teach us about that transformation.

EPILOGUE

The Deepest Mystery

I began this book a year ago when a beloved friend came to tell me that he had AIDS. Now, as I am almost finished with its writing, an even closer friend came to share his diagnosis with me—as we prepared to go together to a young gay friend's funeral.

I spent yesterday with yet another beautiful young man who had come to me as his lover lay dying in the hospital—in a coma, long past any knowing, wasted away as though from Dachau. My visitor asked if we might sit in my hot tub together. He cried in my arms. I witnessed his pain and his anger, his refusal and his acceptance. His head lay nestled by my breast; his body twisted between my legs; for long periods he remained completely submerged in the water. He called me "Mother, Father, Sister, Brother." He called out to mother, lover, to death, and to renewal.

I thought of all the mothering he had done during the months his lover was dying. I thought of how he carries within him the knowledge that he, too, though now apparently so well, is likely to die, too soon, too painfully—and alone, with no one to nurse him as he nursed his beloved. I held him. I wept.

SEXUALITY AND AIDS

All through the writing of this book about same-sex love I have been haunted by the knowledge of how in my time so many of the men I love who love men are dying or are dead—because of their love. A whole generation, it sometimes seems. I understand as I never quite had before the feeling communicated in some of the poetry inspired by the First World War: the sense that a whole generation of youth had been wiped out.

I first heard of AIDS the day I came home from the trip around the world that I describe in my book on menopause.[1] A letter from a former student awaiting my return told me that his lover was dying and that he was ill. I am struck by how in every account of AIDS I have read there is an emphasis on the day when its reality became a personal reality, for when this happens the whole world seems changed. There is a "before" and an "after." Certainly this has been so for me. It is difficult to recall the innocence of that earlier time, the "before," and difficult sometimes to relate to those for whom this caesura does not exist. Given my history as a German Jew born just a few years before Hitler's accession to power, there is for me an almost inevitable analogy. I cannot help but feel that the discovery of this horror is like the discovery of the horror of what the Nazis really had in mind for the Jews. How on the other side of that realization the earlier innocence of assimilated Jews like my father seemed to belong to another life, another world.

Once known, AIDS is inescapable—at least for those whose friends are gay or who are gay themselves. It infects our whole community, not only those who are literally ill. We live surrounded by the dead, the dying, by death. At the memorial service from which I have just returned, the small group of us who had gathered to commemorate the friend just lost spoke informally of our love and our loss. How painful to hear so many young men, a generation younger than I, speak of how they now had more friends "on the other side" than on this and of their awareness of their own vulnerability.

"I don't know if I will live to finish this." So Paul Monette begins his memoir of his lover's battle with the disease.[2] As I read such accounts I am filled with a sense of my own unworthiness to address the issues that AIDS brings into view. My own relation to the disease is in some ways *still* relatively so distant. I have not yet had to watch the day-by-day deterioration of a closest other.

Yet when we first learned how many of the men I have been close to are infected, my own lover was filled with fears for me and for herself—and I have still not taken the test that might let me know whether I have been exposed to the virus or not. Either answer would be difficult to live with. I am not ready to die, but neither am I ready to know that I will escape—when so many I love will not. I feel I belong with the men I love, that I am one of them. I escaped from Germany before the concentration camps became death camps. I thought I already knew what it is to live with survivor guilt; now I wonder.

Worthy or not, prepared or not, one cannot today write about homosexuality and not write about AIDS. I know that AIDS is not a "homosexual disease," that many, in some places most, of those infected by it are not gay men, and that in some ways the relative affluence and communal esprit of the male homosexual world makes AIDS less devastating in that world than in the world of minority drug abusers. Like Ivan Karamazov, like Father Paneloux in Camus's *The Plague*, I am especially horrified by the image of babies infected even before birth. Nevertheless, AIDS has entered my life through its impact on the gay men I know.

I know that AIDS is not literally a sexual disease, that it is a blood-borne virus, not a venereal disease, that it has no intrinsic connection with sexual acts. Nevertheless, as I also know, it has been transmitted among the men I love through sexual contact and primarily through modes of sexual contact especially prevalent among gay men. I know they live with the knowledge that their lovemaking has also been a deathmaking.

I am also aware of the dangers in too closely identifying homosexuality with AIDS. There is so much more that is important about same-sex love than just that many who have practiced it have been exposed to this disease. Nevertheless, AIDS is today an inescapable presence in the gay world. To continue to find ways to celebrate gay sexuality, to reaffirm the hard-won self-affirmation and freedom of the too few years after Stonewall (the confrontation that serves to signify the beginnings of the gay liberation movement) before AIDS appeared, poses a formidable challenge.

As I read Monette's book I was aware of how increasingly important models from ancient Greece became for him and his lover, Roger, during Roger's last months. Monette refers to the bonds that come to exist between the sick and their care givers as having their "own sweet Platonic tang." When they go to the Getty Museum together, he and Roger are deeply moved by a grave relief of a warrior binding his beloved's wounds; the Greek image of the hero confronting death becomes their ideal. Monette writes that the wisdom that came to fill his lover taught him to understand what the Greeks meant by *sophrosyne:* an inner harmony of soul, a restraint not felt as restraint but as a reasonableness that issues in perfect freedom. "It struck me how Greek Roger's attitude was. . . . I still wanted Greece to be sunny and exalted, with white stone ruins and statutes of gods so perfectly human they breathed. Beauty was as far as I needed to go, and I wasn't equipped for the tragic design of fate." Toward the very end of Roger's life the two read Plato together: "August in my mind was mostly Plato. . . . When you have the time to read a little Plato, when the other half of you wants to do it as much as you do, nobody wastes a moment worrying that he's wasting time." They read the *Apology* and the *Phaedo*—"to see how a man of honor faces death without lies."[3]

Monette begins his book with an epigraph from Pindar: "Unsung the noblest deed will die." When he writes of a trip to Greece that he and Roger had taken before Roger's diagnosis, he reflects, "A gay man seeks his history in mythic fragments."[4] It is such fragments that I have sought to assemble and piece together here in this book, for I am deeply persuaded that it helps to have images. The Greeks—Plato, of course, but also the myths—and Freud and Jung give us images, not only the images of same-sex love considered in the earlier chapters of this book but also images of the painful, complex intertwining of Eros and death.

It helps to have images, analogues, metaphors. Of course, images and metaphors are also dangerous. They may encourage us to romanticize, to sentimentalize the tragic death of the young, to indulge in a morbid fascination with death—to forget this is an ugly disease that cruelly kills. They may promote a misunderstanding of the disease as a judgment, a punishment. They may strengthen a tendency to see it as "fate" and thus ignore or deny how many of its consequences might have been averted.[5]

I value Susan Sontag's reminder in *AIDS and Its Metaphors* of the inadequacies of many of the images most readily invoked.[6] She makes evident how the metaphor of "plague" connotes an exotic disease imported from *elsewhere* that infects a "tainted community," not just individuals. "The standard plague story is of inexorability, inescapability. . . . *All* succumb." The metaphor is typically not applied to such epidemics as influenza or polio, which strike the presumably "innocent," but only to those that afflict persons whose life-styles affront middle-class values, particularly middle-class sexual mores. The metaphor answers to a longing for interpretations that keep the disease distant, that keep the "us/them" difference in place; and yet it also communicates that "their" disease, through its easy transmissibility, now threatens the innocent. The metaphor implies judgment; it has an insidious capacity to make the sufferers themselves understand their suffering as punishment and to make those killed appear to be the cause of the disease.

Sontag shows how the focus on AIDS as a sexual disease and the consequent association of sexuality with suicide and murder are used as a way of making all sex seem dangerous. AIDS is then used as justification for a neoconservative condemnation of all sexual spontaneity and freedom.

Sontag also sees how the particular character of this virus—its long, patient latency—evokes apocalyptic rhetoric. It is seen as implacable, as representing an inevitable destruction that, although as yet invisible, has really already happened (as we fear may be true of our natural environment). It becomes entangled with fears of the greater disaster that we think both will and will not take place. Thus Sontag shows how the language with which we speak of AIDS associates it with humankind's deepest fears.

But that images may be misleading, inappropriate, does not mean we can do without them. There may be no fully adequate analogies. When Monette cries, "Nothing compares. That is something very important to understand about those on the moon of AIDS. Anything offered in comparison is a mockery to us. If hunger compares, or Hamburger Hill, or the carnal dying of Calcutta, that is for us to say,"[7] I think of how important it is to some to isolate the *Shoah* (the "Holocaust")[8] as an utterly unique event. Yet I have come to believe that it helps to consider how what happened in the Nazi's extermination camps illumines other genocidal acts and how they in turn illumine it; thereby all get seen more clearly. Still it remains important to attend to the specifics, to what is different, unique.

For the feelings and associations stirred up by AIDS are not inspired just by death but by a particular death.

That, in the gay world, AIDS has been a sexually transmitted disease cannot be evaded. Death has become associated with sex, not obsessive or meaningless sex—just sex. To live with the knowledge that the body, the penis, the semen, which were once a source of life-affirming pride, might be fatal to others; to live with the knowledge that an act of love may have brought death into one's body; to live with the knowledge that through an act of love one may have brought death to another—how does one live with such knowledge?

AIDS is killing young men—not just a rare, individual young man but a whole generation of gay men. Many, most, are *so* young, just entering the years of mature fulfillment. "We're all like 80 year olds," Monette says.[9] (Because it is a communal and not only an individual disease, the denial that so typically and naturally characterizes the initial response to a terminal illness has had disastrous consequences—as Randy Shilts has so convincingly shown[10]—in delaying the adoption of measures that can serve to slow its spread.) This sense that "all of us" are dying is among the most unbearable aspects of this illness.

It is also a singular characteristic of this disease that those who love and care for the ill are themselves so often at risk, and may be bound to those they nurse by a complex mixture of guilt and anger and fear. To care—to give all one's energy to caring for another—with no hope of curing, inflicts its particular costs. As does knowing of one's own susceptibility to the same harrowing death.[11]

The long period during which the virus may remain latent creates its own particular anxieties. The virus can live so long undetected. One can infect and be infected unknowingly. Adopting safe sex as soon as one has learned of the danger has proven no guarantee of immunity. One wonders and waits and worries.

The virus leaves one vulnerable to so many strange, exotic, disfiguring, isolating diseases; and to survive one of these scourges only opens one to the next. The person with AIDS is so extraordinarily susceptible to *any* infection to which he might be exposed—and yet has the experience of being treated as though he were the contagious one! And all this in a subculture where (even more than elsewhere in America) youth and beauty have been so highly prized.

How difficult not to feel oneself a "victim", passive and helpless before a disease that seems invariably to be terminal. How muster the courage to fight and to hope? Yet the kind of resignation to death that might seem wise in the octogenarian seems wildly inappropriate in the young.

The "trickiness" of the biology of the disease also has an impact. For the more the scientific community learns about this retrovirus, the more elusive a cure seems to become. How can this help but give the illness a mysterious aspect and heighten the sense of dread it provokes?

Indeed, everything seems heightened in the light of AIDS. It brings to the fore the stigmatization and isolation long associated with homosexuality—just as it had seemed that that might be lessening. It reactivates ambivalent feelings and dormant conflicts associated with unresolved "coming out," with repressed guilt about sexual identity. It triggers fears of abandonment and rejection, not only the fear of death.

There is, indeed, much that is specific and unique about AIDS; but it is also true that part of what underlies our terror and horror is that all of us in the modern Western world—gay and straight, women and men, even (albeit to a lesser degree) the economically disadvantaged and racially oppressed—have felt ourselves so immune from disfiguring illness, from early death. AIDS has meant coming to terms with limitations, with a finitude we had thought we might evade.

AIDS forces us to confront the death of the young and to look anew at the interrelation of love and death. Freud and Plato and the Greek myths are newly relevant because of their recognition that the power we attribute to sexuality is connected to our awareness of our finitude and mortality—and to our longing to transcend limitation and death. To affirm sexuality is to affirm the body—and bodies die.

LOVE AND DEATH

Freud and Plato both saw Eros and death as paired, as engaged in a strange dance: sometimes the two are in violent conflict with each other, sometimes almost blended into one. They saw the preparation for death as our most important and most demanding life task; they saw death to be what gives sex its sacred, numinous power.

During the First World War, and increasingly in the years that followed, death became a prominent theme in Freud's writing. As earlier he had focused on the costs of the repression of sexuality and the shortcomings of a too literal understanding of it, now he concerned himself with the repression of death and with persuading us to recognize death as a psychical, not only a biological, reality. There was much in his life to encourage this redirection: what the war itself revealed about our denied aggressivity and the power death has to enhance life's perceived significance, the death of a beloved daughter and a favorite grandson, his own cancer. But we should not exaggerate the novelty of this interest. We can discern its lineaments throughout his career.

As he told H.D., "My psychology is the basis for a very grave philosophy." And as she said of him, "Eros and death, these two were the chief subjects, indeed the only subjects of the Professor's eternal preoccupation."[12]

Early on Freud had rejected requests by Jung and others that for his expanded understanding of sexuality he choose some other name: psychical energy, for example. Yet in 1920 he himself begins to speak of Eros where before he would have said "sexuality." In the 1920 edition of *The Three Essays* he remarks on how closely the enlarged sexuality of psychoanalysis "coincides with the Eros of the divine Plato" (*SE* 7:134); in 1921 in *Group Psychology* he reaffirms his conviction that psychoanalysis's expanded understanding of love coincides exactly with Plato's Eros (*SE* 18:91); in 1925 he states: "What psychoanalysis called sexuality was by no means identical with the impulsion toward a union of the two sexes or towards producing a pleasurable sensation in the genitals; it had far more resemblance to the all-inclusive and all-preserving Eros of Plato's *Symposium*" (*SE* 21:210).

The meaning of this shift in language becomes evident in the seminal work published in 1920, *Beyond the Pleasure Principle*, the work in which Freud first introduced the death drive into his theory of drives. This part of Freud's thought is often neglected by psychoanalysts because it is not considered scientifically verifiable and because it is not believed to be clinically relevant. But for an understanding of Freud's *philosophy*, as Paul Ricoeur perceives, it is central.

The recognition of the power of death over our lives and the new honoring of Eros belong together. As Ricoeur (who refers to the "great upheaval" represented by *Beyond the Pleasure Principle*) puts it, "In face of death, the libido changes meaning and receives the mythical name of Eros." And: "Thantos reveals the meaning of Eros as the factor that resists death."[13]

Eros is for Freud the twin brother of death. Though his commentators, not he, speak of death as Thanatos, Freud, too, intends to communicate that he sees these two drives as primal powers, cosmological and not just psychological forces, energies that work on us and not just within us. Their polarity represents not a moral dichotomy but an often intensely dramatic antagonism. Neither is to be viewed as unambivalently evil—or good. They *are*, and we stand in inescapable relation to them.

We both fear and wish for death. Our fear is made manifest not only in our anxiety about our body's expiration but in our fears of the unknown, of being vulnerable, passive, "feminine"; of being abandoned, not loved, unloving. Death is not just end as *terminus* but end as *telos*, as goal. We wish for repetition, stasis, peace, permanence, resolution, completion. (Freud also understood how denial of the fear/wish issues in aggression: "If you die, I won't have to." And: "I do not wish my death, but yours.")

In his 1912 essay "The Theme of the Three Caskets" Freud spoke of the challenge to "choose death and make friends with the necessity of dying" (*SE* 12:291). The acceptance of death is a task: "*Si vis vitam, para mortem.* If you want to endure life, be prepared for death" (*SE* 10:37). But as the late works make clear, acceptance of death does not imply yielding to the wish to die. Acceptance is coming to terms with Ananke, necessity—and still loving life. "Resignation," the "possible wisdom" that Freud hints at in *Future of an Illusion,* is not the love of death but the love of life in spite of our death. It is against the death wish that Eros is aimed. Ricoeur sees Freud's philosophy as offering us this "delicate equilibrium"—or subtle conflict?—between lucidity free of illusion and the love of life."[14] When reality is accepted with resignation it becomes Ananke. Such a reconciliation, Ricoeur recognizes, "would be the victory of the love of the whole over my narcissism, my fear of dying, over the resurgence in me of childhood consolations."[15]

In *Beyond the Pleasure Principle* Freud returns to the myth Plato put in the mouth of Aristophanes in the *Symposium* (*SE* 18:57–58),[16] finding in it a confirmation of his own belief that there is a powerful longing at work in us to restore an earlier state of affairs, a longing that Freud in his essay calls the death drive.

Freud here also invokes the Eros of Plato's *Symposium* as identical with his own vision. In truth, Freud's Eros bears within it echoes of the Eros of Hesiod, of Empedocles, and of many of the speakers in the *Symposium*. The Eros of this essay and of *Civilization and Its Discontents* is the cosmogonic pre-Socratic eros, the primordial deity who holds all living things together, the creator and preserver of all things. But Freud is speaking also of Plato's Eros, for he has in mind the love we direct toward another's psyche (his *Seele*, his soul), a love that though not just of the body is yet continuous with body love. He believes that he shares with Plato the conviction that Eros, a shared love of the common good, is the basis for true community. He regards culture as dependent on libidinal attachments, on emotional connections—not as based only upon the rational containment of aggression. We want *and* resent society; it fulfills *and* frustrates. For Freud, as for Plato, there is a kind of "ladder" of love, a ladder we climb as we learn to move beyond love of our immediate family to an ever-widening circle—though for Freud love (albeit increasingly inclusive) is always still a particularized love, not the abstract love of all humankind. In *Civilization* Freud is particularly concerned to distinguish Eros from what he calls "oceanic feeling," from fusion. Such love he sees as regressive, as narcissism.

Freud's turn from sexuality to Eros is not a turn from the realm of the body to the spirit; it arises out of a deep contemplation of our embodiment and finitude, out of his reflections on the unavoidable discontents of civilization and the inevitability of death. *Civilization* issues in an invitation to participate in an erotic commitment to the extension of the communal bonds among men. Though Freud says he can offer us no consolation, he concludes by saying: "Now it is to be hoped that the other of the two heavenly powers, eternal Eros, will make an effort to assert himself in the struggle with his equally immortal adversary. But who can foresee with what success and with what results" (*SE* 21:145).

In "Analysis Terminable and Interminable," written in the last year of his life, Freud tells us that the most difficult of all human tasks is the overcoming of our fears (and he obviously sees them as linked) of femininity, of passivity, and of death. His recognition of the work involved in letting go of the heroic masculine stance brings to my mind Sophocles' lines about Oedipus's death after his many years of wandering exile. We might imagine that Freud, too, had in mind the aged Oedipus for whom

> the underworld
> opened in love the unlit door of earth
> For he was taken without lamentation
> illness or suffering; indeed his end
> was wonderful if ever mortal's was. (*Oed.* 1662–65)

For Freud had valiantly fought against the death threat posed by his own cancer until his mother died (when he himself was already seventy-four) and he at last felt it permissible to submit: "I was not allowed to die as long as she was alive and now I may."[17]

What we get from Freud is a sense of how sexuality leads us to recognize our identification with our bodies—and thus inescapably initiates us into our dying. We may turn to sex as an attempt to escape death (not only through reproduction but through transcendent ecstasy), but there is no escaping. Yet the connections with others that Eros opens us to provide what mitigation of death life allows us. In "Mourning and Melancholia" Freud acknowledges how difficult it is to dare to love again after the loss of a beloved—and how essential (*SE* 14:255). To live is to love. That is why it is Eros that must be paired with Death.

When Freud writes of Eros, of Eros and death, he has nothing specific to say about homosexuality; but his recognition of the intimate intertwining of love and death, his recognition of how in the face of death sex becomes love, is surely relevant to an understanding of how the bonds between gay men have been affected by AIDS.

Though Freud spoke powerfully on behalf of a more liberated sexuality, he never advocated a causal attitude toward sex. For him, as we noted above, sex (and death) were always numinous realities. He was always aware of how profoundly the unconscious "con-fuses" womb and tomb. He would understand our imagining the sexual transmission of AIDS as being like impregnating another with a seed of death. He would understand all our strange and fearful and beautiful fantasies—and their truth.

Some of the fantasies that AIDS may invoke in us are also reflected in Greek mythology.

We have already seen that there are many tales about same-sex love among men in Greek mythology, most of them tragic. This plurality means that this tradition offers us images for the many different, equally authentic, "archetypal" (we might say) modes of response to the deaths of lovers or their beloveds. I value this recognition for I have seen so many different responses among those I love. The first to die among those whom I have known well fought against his dying to the very end, trying every possible cure, seeking out every possible healer. Another, to the very end, shared the truth about what was really killing him with only a tiny circle of intimates, though many knew but were prevented by his silence from coming close. For yet another it was now as important to be "out" about his illness as it had earlier been to be open about his homosexuality. The first reminds me of Telephus, the son of Heracles wounded by Achilles, who persisted in seeking after the magical cure that might relieve him of his ever-festering wound; the last, of Achilles himself, determined that all should know of his grief as all had known of his love.

When I think of Greek myths that seem intimately connected to the trials of soul that AIDS imposes today, I turn immediately to Apollo. We have already noted how all the youths Apollo loved died young. I spoke earlier of my feeling that seeing these deaths, as Sergent does, only as a symbol of the boys moving into adult status was too simple. This understanding robbed the deaths of their poignancy, of their power to move us deeply. Who now reading Ovid's account of Apollo's grief over the death of Hyacinthus does not recognize it as a grief they have also felt? And if in any way one were to feel responsible for another's death, were to believe that one had unknowingly infected one's beloved, how different would that be from Apollo's guilt over the inadvertent slip of the discus? Apollo would have liked to die in place of Hyacinthus, but had to learn he could not. The myth does not explain; it does not console; it only offers us an image for our loss. It gives only what a myth *can* give.

I know that part of why Homer's account of the rage that overcame grieving Achilles, and of the power of his longing to join his beloved in death, moves me so deeply is how all too contemporary it feels.

I also sense how the myth of Zeus and Ganymede may have a new resonance among those who wish they had Zeus's power simply to bestow immortality on a mortal beloved, to have him for oneself forever or at least for longer than the dread disease allows.

This brings to mind another god, one not discussed earlier, Asclepius, the god of healing. The Greeks believed that this God underwent initiation into the Eleusinian cult because he had learned that human mortality cannot be evaded—though earlier he had sought with his healing powers to restore to life mortals he thought sent to Hades unjustly or too soon. He came to realize that though his gifts might serve to postpone a premature death, they could not avert death. Those who came to Epidaurus to be healed by the god learned that what he could give was simply the time needed to prepare for a death that *would* inevitably come. With AIDS, where at least at present we live knowing there is no cure, the hope for such a respite might lead us to a new honoring of this ancient god.

Dionysus and the rituals associated with his temple at Lerna suggest the possibility that the experience of homosexual submission, of being the receptive partner in intercourse, might in some mysterious way help prepare one for that reconciliation to death of which Freud speaks—though it may be very few young men for whom that, rather than active heroic struggle, would be the soul's choice, at least until the final hours of the struggle.

I also see in the Greek ethos surrounding paiderastia a new relevance, a relevance that has nothing to do with pederasty in the modern sense. For I discern among the gay men I know a new concern for the younger men just entering the homosexual world, a commitment to protect them, to educate them into safe ways of loving, to persuade them that one can still celebrate being gay. The men I am close to were already gay long before AIDS. How different it is for the young who enter homosexuality through this lens. Among the Greeks there was an expectation that a relationship initially based on Eros would become one based on *philia*, the mutual, caring love that friends feel for one another. This, too, has become an important reality today. How important bonds between former lovers have become in this time, when nursing the sick so often supplants erotic intercourse as the most valued work of love.

Even closer than the bond of sex, Plato affirms, is the bond of death. In my chapters on Plato I sought to show how he offers us an image of a love that grows out of a recognition of the inescapability of death and that is rooted in sensuality but not centered on orgasmic genital sexuality.

Though *his* reasons for avoiding a lovemaking that involves penile penetration may have little cogency today, there are *new* reasons. Thus Plato might be seen as offering encouragement to all the changes in sexual practice that love of life and love of others seem now to require. Monette writes so effectively of how "for all [his] loathing of the lies of straight religion as to love," he has come to agree that we "have to stop. . . . If everyone doesn't stop and face the calamity, hand in hand with the sick till it can't break through any more, then it will claim the millennium for its own."[18] How important to find ways to eroticize "safe sex," how necessary not to allow AIDS to issue in a denial of the beauty and power of Eros.

How important it also becomes, it seems to me, to find ways of honoring and celebrating some of the changes that have occurred in the homosexual world without denying the beauty of the 1960s and 1970s affirmation of gay sexuality. The heroism that many have shown, the compassionate care for others that many have exercised, the wisdom of a grateful appreciation of the gift of the most ordinary life-filled moment that many have come to, the deeper sense of truly constituting a community that many have experienced, the discovery of more permanent and more soul-oriented bonds that many have made—all these may be recognized as blessings, without our applauding the cause or denying the cost.[19] "Does anybody ever get taught these things by anything other than tragedy?" Monette asks.[20] One can still hope for an affirmative answer.

Among the "blessings" associated with AIDS I would include how it has helped break down some of the barriers of suspicion and misunderstanding that separated lesbians from gay men. AIDS has shown men as beautifully capable of a sensitivity and a dedication to nurturing others that ill accords with the stereotypes about the lack of fidelity and commitment among gay men that some lesbians once accepted. A new sense of a shared identification (as well as of a shared stigmatization) has begun to emerge. When the men burn out after tending one dying friend after another, lesbians have appeared to take on the nursing role. They have given blood when gay men feared that their blood was contaminated. They have given love when gay men's capacity to give was exhausted.

And, so the gay man who cried in my arms as his lover lay dying told me, lesbians are giving gay men something else as well, something just as important, by still making love freely and creatively and joyfully. Same-sex love encompasses so much more than sexuality—but sexual expression is among its most blessed gifts.

Seven Years Later

I wrote this book after a dear friend came to tell me that he had AIDS and that he had always hoped I might some day complete the study of Greek myths about love between men that I had begun seven years earlier and then laid aside. I wrote it in one summer, under the pressure of wanting to be able to put the book in his hands, for back then AIDS seemed like an imminent death sentence. He is still alive, still well.

Of course I also wrote it to celebrate and to try to understand more deeply my own involvement in same-sex love, my love for the woman with whom I was living. We are still together, still in love. Indeed, I am writing this on the anniversary of our first meeting fifteen years ago. We have spent the day remembering that first meeting, how I left it knowing I had met a woman I could fall in love with. We have also spoken of how little we could have known then of all these fifteen years have given us. How much we've each learned about the intimacy, the intensity, the mirroring, the encouragement of one another's work that may emerge in women's love of women. And of how that first meeting occurred in the innocent days just before the first news of AIDS.

So much both beautiful and painful has been shared between us in these intervening years. Our own experience has been so enriched by that of our many lesbian friends, especially the other lesbian couples who have shared their struggles with us. Our lives have also been profoundly marked by shared sorrow over the illnesses and deaths of gay men we love. We seem to have to keep coming to terms with AIDS. We go numb, and then suddenly a fresh assault overwhelms us almost as fully as did the very first one. We have lived through this together. These men are our brothers.

For a long time I resisted taking the HIV test because I could not bear to know whether I was infected or not. I wasn't ready to know that I might be marked for death nor was I ready to know that I had escaped when so many I love have not. Now I know and yet still feel I belong with the men I love, still feel myself one of them. Though I also feel survivor's guilt. Accepting such contradictory feelings seems to be part of what confrontation with this virus forces upon us. Both are true: I am a member of the tribe. I am not.

While writing this book I knew that I would have to write a final chapter about AIDS, about the ineluctable intertwining of love and death which AIDS puts before us so starkly, so inescapably. I could not avoid writing about it. The writing was difficult; I didn't finish the chapter until the rest of the book was already in galleys.

Yet then, seven years ago, I could still say, "My own relation to the disease is in some ways still relatively so distant. I have not yet had to watch the day by day deterioration of a closest other." But since then Philip, the second of the two gay men of whom I wrote in the Prologue, has died, as have also too many others whom I've loved very much. I find I have nothing now to add to what I wrote earlier about Freud or Jung, nothing more to say about the Greek understanding of same-sex love, but that I do need to affirm anew our need for myths and images, poems and stories to help us mourn, help us remember, help us praise.

I know how immeasurably my grieving for Philip has been both deepened and eased by the poems my partner River Malcolm wrote as he was dying. River could say what I didn't know how to say, saw clearly what I only glimpsed. In the years since I wrote the book I have found that the work of contemporary poets like Paul Monette, like Mark Doty, like Felice Picano, has been as important to me as the myths I evoked in the book. I have come to appreciate how sorely we need such poets (and by "poets" I mean not only those who write verse but all those who use words with love) because poets help us access the archetypal dimensions of this plague. They help us express how AIDS touches our souls as well as our bodies, how it affects the ways we see and touch and love one another, how it affects our intimacy and our sexuality. Poems and myths help us to express our bafflement and our hope, our anger and our love. They give us words which return us from the world of "them" to the world of "us."

I speak as a lover, as someone who has deeply loved men who have died or are dying, or who are living with AIDS. I speak as someone who also deeply loves words, language, metaphors, myths, stories, poetry. And who believes that language can heal. Not cure. Heal. To name the horror may help us come to terms with it—not erase it, but give it its place. I believe that words can help us become intimates of our experience, to get close to its actual, particular details. I believe that words can help us share our experience and share in another's. I have come to believe that providing access to images and words which have the power to nourish is one of *my* ways of caretaking.

As I've sought to feel my own feelings, to know the soul meaning of what I've experienced and witnessed, I've been fed by the words of others, by the memoirs, short stories, novels, poems composed in the last dozen years—most of them in the last few because it almost always takes poetry a while to catch up with experience. We need images to help us see, feel, acknowledge, share our anger, our grief, our fear, our guilt, our hope, our compassion—and to help us laugh, to find the humor even in the almost unspeakable. We can't go on if we can't be honest with ourselves about what's happening and how we feel about it. But often we can't feel it unless we're helped to. Borrowed words, remembered images and stories, may help us toward our own. Without words we are silent—silenced, passive, victims, the talked about—the other. With words we are speakers, subjects, agents, persons.

In his book *Dreaming with an Aids Patient*,[1] Robert Bosnak, a Jungian therapist, shows how much it helps to discover and honor our own images. His book makes visible how *eros* appears in the therapeutic relationship, how his encouragement enables Christopher, his patient, to attend to the images that appear in his dream, to make them part of his conscious imagining of his disease, so that they become part of the process whereby the soul struggles against the disease, is able to dialogue with it rather than letting it be a monster that has taken control.

Christopher's dreams show how his dreaming self knew of the disease's approach before he or Bosnak did: the very first dream they worked on introduced the theme of having to cross to the other side. Other images appear whose poignant meaning we can all recognize: not being able to find his place in a script, being sucked into a whirlpool, watching a car driving away without him, feeling the exhaustion of a long-distance runner. We learn how having the images, holding them, turning them over, wondering about them, helps Christopher fully experience his hopes, his fears, his life.

We are moved as we discover the therapist attending to his own images and how much his being able to help Christopher depends on his having honestly confronted them—so that he his not taken over by the hysterical mother in himself, or the omnipotent healer. We are stirred by how much Christopher in his last almost speechless days is nourished by Bosnak's coming to the hospital and reading to him from his dream journal, giving him back his own images. We are stunned when just before his death Christopher, who consciously remembers nothing of the Greek myth about Persephone, dreams of eating a pomegranate. Our own images, our own dreams, have so much capacity to teach us, to strengthen us, to deepen us.

But we need the poets, too. The poets are our shamans; they move into the world of images on our behalf. They are more gifted than most of us most of the time (perhaps especially in our waking lives) at finding just the right words, at escaping the cliché, the sentimental, at keeping their words loud and rude and strong and queer. Their fierceness of perception, their urgent, angry, tender acts of witnessing, their passionate optimism help us see, and unless we really see, we cannot accept, cannot love.

Poets help us see by their vivid naming. When confronted by a body wasted by the last stages of the disease, I inevitably remember River's poem, "Philip Fades":

> He grows grayer
> and more skeletal,
> though he glows
> remarkably
> with the haunting
> memory of his
> former beauty.
> Even strangers
> can see it.
> Gazing at him, it's as if
> I stand by
> watching vandals
> hammer away
> at Michelangelo's David.[2]

Poets help us find ways to support hope without colluding with denial, ways to affirm that in us which is still vital and alive. Poetry helps us to acknowledge our real feelings even if they don't accord with our politics, to accept the responses that are easy to own up and the ones that we're ashamed of but that do arise. By writing of these feelings poets give us a sense that we are companioned, seen, accepted even when we feel what we shouldn't. They help us remember that of course we can experience contradictory feelings at the same time—feel alive, vital, juicy *and* dry, barren, dying. We can feel ourselves in the middle of our life and close to its end. In a sense, we have to feel both.

Poets give us language to articulate the depth and complexity of our mourning. There is so much to mourn. The loss of youth, physical beauty, health. "We're all like 80 years olds," Monette writes. The loss of what might have been one's most productive years, the loss of a future, of the sense of having made an impact. The loss of a lover. The fear of further loss which cripples one's ability to risk loving again. The multiple losses that constitute loss of one's world.

Poets helps us express our anger—against church, government, the media, the drug establishment. The poetry inspired by AIDS is a poetry that can't help but have a political edge.

Poets offer us models of living and of facing death that are big enough, complex enough, diverse enough to do justice to the differences among us. They show us the harm done by trying to impose a single model that may prevent someone from dying *their* death. As in this poem by Mark Doty:

> She'd sit by the bed and say, *Annie,*
> *look for the light.* It was plain
> that Annie did not wish to be distracted
> by these instructions; she came to,
> though she was nearly gone then, and looked
> at our mother with what was almost certainly
>
> annoyance. *It's a white light,*
> Mom said, and this struck me
> as incredibly presumptuous, as if the light
> we'd all go into would be just the same.
> Maybe she wanted to give herself up
> to indigo, or red. If we can barely even speak
>
> to each other, living so separately,
> how can we all die the same.[3]

Poets remind us that death is rarely completion, that many die unreconciled—in denial, fear, anger—that that is part of what death *is,* an intrusion into life that is part of life.

I see poets as contemporary embodiments of the age-old figure of the wounded healer. That woundedness, illness, suffering are a prerequisite for taking on the role of healer is a truth recognized in the myths and rituals of traditional cultures throughout the world. It underlies the shamanic vision of the healer in Siberia, North America, Africa, and Australia. Everywhere we learn that initiation into healing comes through falling radically ill of a disease that often cannot be diagnosed and for which there seems to be no cure. Recovery comes only when the patients recognize the illness as a call, only when they agree to become healers. The woundedness is understood to signify an unusual sensitivity to the spirit world, the realm of visionary experience. The apprentice shamans must learn how to use their access to that realm, to channel their gifts and bring them into harmony with their culture's traditions. When others fall ill, the wounded healers re-enter the strange and terrifying otherworld to learn whom their patients have offended and what retribution they must make or how to recover their stolen soul.

The figure of the wounded healer is epitomized in Greek mythology by the centaur Cheiron, an immortal who suffered from an incurable, unremittingly painful wound and who precisely in consequence of his own woundedness became a consummate physician. The Greek god of healing, Asclepius, was taught his art by this centaur. As I noted in the Epilogue, Asclepius, the only god in Greek mythology to experience death, is a god who knows what it is to die. Though as a god his stay in Hades is only temporary, though as a god he can experience mortality without forfeiting his immortality, it is his own experience of vulnerability to death that makes him seem to the Greeks a god more kindly and more benevolent than any other.

I have a file of obituaries clipped from the *New York Times* of men whom I see as contemporary wounded healers: dancers, choreographers, playwrights, actors, novelists, essayists, journalists. Men whose own infection with AIDS has led them to use their creative gifts on behalf of fellow sufferers. Several of my own friends embody this archetype for me.

Paul Monette, of course, whose grief over Roger's death and a few years later over Stephen's, and his own long battle with AIDS, issued in what to my mind has been the most important literature inspired by AIDS: three novels, two books of memories, a volume of essays, two books of poetry. I came to know Paul shortly after the publication of my book. We were both speakers at a gay writer's conference. I had come to honor him; I was abashed by his praise of me. We met only a few other times. I visited him at his home just a few months before he died. We talked about shared loves, the Greek islands, Orcas Island where I live, poetry, books, mythology, teaching, and, above all, *writing*. We talked about the analogy between genre-breaking and gender-bending. We talked about so many things—AIDS and Sappho, divine rape and mystical ecstasy—it was as though we were high just on being together. But what I remember most is Paul saying that his deepest wish was to die pen in hand, as Dickens had.

I think of other friends, less well-known than Paul, who are just as truly wounded healers: Philip, whose last summer was devoted to his children, to giving them the opportunity to know that they had been strong enough to tend his dying and to bear his death. River's poem describes it beautifully:

> How strange to see you, Philip,
> changed by illness at last into
> someone I barely recognize,
> more like a picture from a
> magazine, an anonymous victim
> of AIDS or of famine, than
> your own particular person:
> the same hollow cheeks, the
> same angular legs, your skin
> abandoned by flesh, cringing
> against uncushioned bones.
>
> Before this, you'd always slip on
> long ample pants, a fresh shirt,
> dazzling blue—perhaps one we'd
> given to you—fool us into seeing
> the beautiful man you once were.
>
> Now you wear shorts, bland shirt,
> chin stubbled grey, as if to concede
> you can't masquerade, not today.
>
> Yet as soon as you speak of your
> children, your eyes spark, and beautiful
> Philip shines through.

> You tell how Ryan helps you to the
> bathroom when you can't walk alone,
> how Kyle gives you a bicycle horn
> for Father's Day, to rouse her out
> of deep sleep, as neither your cry,
> nor the loud clanging of a bell,
> have been able to do.
>
> For yourself, you might rather
> be dead. For your children, you
> live, hoping this hard work of
> helping reveals to them the sinew
> and muscle of love, the toughness
> you never required of them, which
> they'll need when you're gone.[4]

Andy, a 38-year-old physician who even just before his death was still the most zestful life-loving person I have known. Andy had become so sensitive to the beauty of this world that he was about to leave that an apricot sunset or a Botticelli Madonna would bring him to tears, tears of joy and appreciation. A physician all his adult life, he resigned from his position as an emergency room physician when he first fell ill and soon became nationally prominent as a doctor with AIDS actively involved with Act-Up, the gay rights protest group. In this unique role he worked to encourage other doctors to support its campaigns for accelerated AIDS research and for making the fruits of that research available and affordable. He put all his energy into serving as an intermediary between the physicians and researchers on the one hand and persons with AIDS on the other. He often told me that he believed that only in these last years was he doing what he felt he was born to do—fully using all his gifts, as a charismatic speaker and a compassionate physician. His wound and his healing were deeply intertwined. (When I think of Andy I cannot help but also remember sitting in the ICU waiting room with his parents, both Holocaust survivors, and having his father ask us, "How can God let such a beautiful young man die so young?" It stunned me that after Auschwitz one would still ask that question that way.)

After his diagnosis, another friend, Martin, an actor, a playwright, and a director, put his energies even more effectively than before into outrageous, in-your-face queer theater. A year or so after his death I dreamt of visiting him in New York. He was pleased to see me but said he had little time to talk, he was on his way to the dress rehearsal of a new performance piece. He invited me to come along, which I did, and gave me tickets for the next evening's opening night performance. When I arrived for the opening, I made my way to my second row seat and saw that the first row was filled by all the men I've loved who have died of AIDS—Paul and Philip and Andy and the too many others whose names you wouldn't recognize. I knew then that Martin is *there* (wherever "there" is) still helping others laugh at what is beyond tears.

Christine Downing
Orcas Island, Washington

Notes

Prologue: A Personal Foreword

1. In reading Mary Renault I have been impressed by how she really only found her own voice when she began writing through the personae of male homosexuals in the world of classical Greece—as though something in her *is* a gay male. Her attempts to write about twentieth-century lesbian experience (e.g., *The Middle Mist* [New York: William Morrow, 1945]) didn't quite work; she turned to the Greece of the *Symposium* and the *Phaedrus* as her ideal world, a world where same-sex love was accepted and valued, at least among men. Many of my male homosexual friends have also spoken to me of how convincing and how moving they find Yourcenar's account of Hadrian's love for Antinous in *Hadrian's Memoirs* (New York: Farrar, Straus and Giroux, 1954).

Neither Renault nor Yourcenar, as far as I know, have written about their relationship to their gay male protagonists. Colette, on the other hand, in *The Pure and the Impure* (New York: Farrar, Straus and Giroux, 1966), describes herself as a "mental hermaphrodite," an ambiguous mode of being unattractive to most heterosexual men who see relating to such a woman as representing a risk of homosexuality—but one that gives her access to a unique relation to homosexual men: "Up to now were they ever observed by any woman for the length of time they were observed by me? Ordinarily women—and let's say an ordinary woman—tries to entice a homosexual. Naturally she fails. She then decides she despises them. Or else—and the case is not rare—she wins a physical victory which gives her cause for pride: she has achieved a kind of brilliant advantage over him, but futile and misleading because she gives an exaggerated importance to external signs." Unlike the "ordinary woman," Colette sees herself as recognizing that "the antipathy of one sex for the other is not necessarily pathological," and therefore as understanding the "legitimacy" and "eternal character" of homosexuality (*Pure and Impure*, 141–47).

2. Fran Leibowitz, "The Impact of AIDS on the Artistic Community," *New York Times*, September 13, 1987, sec. H, p. 22.

3. See Arthur Evans, *Witchcraft and the Gay Counterculture* (Boston: Fag Rag Books, 1978), esp. chaps. 4–7; Mitch Walker, "Visionary Love: The Magickal Gay Spirit-Power," *Gay Sunshine* (Winter 1977).

4. Mary Daly, *Gyn/Ecology: The MetaEthics of Radical Feminism* (Boston: Beacon Press, 1978), 15.

5. Christine Downing, *The Goddess: Mythological Images of the Feminine* (New York: Crossroad, 1981), 3.

6. Christine Downing, *Journey through Menopause* (New York: Crossroad, 1988).

1. The Myth of Homosexuality

1. David M. Halperin, "One Hundred Years of Homosexuality," *Diacritics* 16, no. 2 (Summer 1986): 34–36, and the splendidly documented footnotes that were omitted from the published article but are available from Halperin at M.I.T.; Jeffrey Weeks, "Discourse, Desire and Sexual Deviance: Some Problems in a History of Homosexuality," in Kenneth Plummer, ed., *The Making of the Modern Homosexual* (Totowa, N.J.: Barnes and Noble, 1981), 76–111.

2. George Chauncey, "From Sexual Inversion to Homosexuality: Medicine and the Changing Conceptualization of Female Deviance," *Salmagundi*, nos. 88–89 (Fall 1982–Winter 1983): 119.

3. John Boswell, "Towards the Long View: Revolutions, Universals and Sexual Categories," *Salmagundi*, nos. 88–89 (Fall 1982–Winter 1983): 103–11.

4. Michel Foucault, *The History of Sexuality* (New York: Pantheon, 1978), 45.

5. Guy Hocquenghem, *Homosexual Desire* (London: Allison and Busby, 1978), 36.

6. Simone de Beauvoir, *The Second Sex* (New York: Bantam, 1961).

7. See Weeks, "Discourse," 98; and Annabel Faraday, "Liberating Lesbian Research," in Plummer, *Making*, 112–29.

8. Judith C. Brown, *Immodest Acts: The Life of a Lesbian Nun in Renaissance Italy* (New York: Oxford University Press, 1986), 6–20.

9. Lillian Faderman, *Surpassing the Love of Men* (New York: William Morrow, 1981), 18.

10. Daly, *Gyn/Ecology*, 26n.

11. Judy Grahn, *Another Mother Tongue: Gay Words, Gay Worlds* (Boston: Beacon, 1984), 105.

12. Don Clark, *Loving Someone Gay* (New York: New American Library, 1977), 3, 4; John Boswell, *Christianity, Social Tolerance, and Homosexuality* (Chicago: University of Chicago Press, 1980), 43–45.

2. Freud: The Personal Dimension

1. All quotations from Freud's writings unless otherwise noted are to *The Standard Edition of the Complete Psychological Works of Sigmund Freud*, translated under the general editorship of James Strachey (London: Hogarth Press, 1953–1974). References will be given in the text as *SE* with volume number followed by page number.

2. H.D. (Hilda Doolittle), *Tribute to Freud* (New York: McGraw-Hill, 1974), 146–47.

3. See the two dreams about his mother retold in *Interpretation*, both of which

invoke the theme of death (*SE* 4:204–6, 5:583–84), and his discussion of goddesses of love and death in "The Theme of the Three Caskets" (*SE* 12:298–301).

4. Quotations from Freud's letters to Fliess are from Jeffrey Moussaieff Masson, *The Complete Letters of Sigmund Freud to Wilhelm Fliess, 1887–1904* (Cambridge, Mass.: Harvard University Press, 1985). To facilitate consultation of the earlier abridged translation (Marie Bonaparte, Anna Freud, and Ernest Kris, eds., *The Origins of Psychoanalysis* [New York: Basic Books, 1954]), references in the text are given by date.

5. Erik Homburger Erikson, "The Dream Specimen of Psychoanalysis," *Journal of the American Psychoanalytic Association* 2 (1954): 5–56.

6. See Max Schur, *Freud: Living and Dying* (New York: International Universities Press, 1972), 86–89; and Jeffrey Moussaieff Masson, *The Assault on Truth* (New York: Penguin, 1985), chap. 3. The strength of Freud's determination to deny the acknowledgment of Fliess's guilt that the dream points to may also explain the fact that Freud, who shared so much with Fliess, wrote him on the very day he had this signally important dream but without mentioning it; nevertheless the central themes of the dream reappear in the letter that begins: "Daimonie, why don't you write? How are you? Don't you care at all any more about what I am doing? What is happening to the *nose, menstruation, labor pains,* neuroses, your dear wife and the budding little one?" (7/24/1895; italics mine). The salutation, never used elsewhere, beautifully expresses Freud's ambivalent relation to the friend he consciously defends, the friend who is both his "inspiring genius," his *daimon,* and a real source of trouble, a "demon."

7. Erikson, "Dream Specimen," 48.

8. Ibid., 49.

9. Quoted in Masson, *Assault,* 216, n. 17.

10. In this instance I have used the translation from the older, abridged version of the letters. Although Jeffrey Masson's recent unabridged edition allows us to trace the unfolding of the relationship much more closely, Masson's rendering of this first letter (which substitutes "relation" for "intercourse," "lead me" for "tempt me") obliterates the clearly sexual—though undoubtedly unconsciously so—connotations of Freud's German text.

11. When two sentences later Freud writes of having just bought Nietzsche "in whom I hope to find words for much that remains mute in me," one cannot help but wonder if Nietzsche is in some sense to serve as a replacement for Fliess.

12. Quoted in "Introduction" to Masson, *Letters,* 3.

13. Ibid., 4; Ernest Jones, *The Life and Work of Sigmund Freud* (New York: Basic Books, 1961), 2:92.

14. Quotations from the Freud/Jung correspondence are from William McGuire, ed., *The Freud/Jung Letters* (Princeton: Princeton University Press, 1974). References in the text are by letter number; e.g., 1F, 2J.

15. Jones, *Life and Work* 2:317. Another clue to the persistence of the memories of his relation to Fliess might be how often in Freud's writing sexual energy is represented as a flowing current—for in German *fliessen* means "to flow."

16. C. G. Jung, *Memories, Dreams, Reflections* (New York: Pantheon, 1963), 158–62.

17. My thanks to Eric Downing for this association.

18. Jones, *Life and Work*, 317.

19. Jung, *Memories*, 156.

3. Freud: The Theory

1. Ernest Jones, *Sigmund Freud: Four Centenary Addresses* (New York: Basic Books, 1956), 143.

2. W. H. Auden, "Thanksgiving for a Habitat," in *Collected Poems* (New York: Random House, 1976), 536.

3. Jacqueline Rose, "Introduction—II," in Juliet Mitchell and Jacqueline Rose, eds., *Feminine Sexuality: Jacques Lacan and the Ecole Freudienne* (New York, W. W. Norton, 1985), 40.

4. Juliet Mitchell, "Introduction—I," in Mitchell and Rose, *Sexuality*, 26.

5. The phrase is Paul Ricoeur's. See his *Freud and Philosophy* (New Haven: Yale University Press, 1970), esp. 3:2, 3.

6. For a good review of the "establishment" reading of Freud on this topic, cf. Robert M. Friedman, *The Psychoanalytic Review* 73, no. 4 (1986). See also Kenneth Lewes, *The Psychoanalytic Theory of Male Homosexuality* (New York: Simon and Schuster, 1988), which appeared just as this book was going to press. He begins with a short chapter on Freud; I mostly agree with his interpretation of Freud's theories about the etiology and dynamics of homosexual object-choice but often disagree with his assessment of Freud's own attitude toward "normal" and "perverse" sexuality. I applaud his account of how narrowly and rigidly psychoanalysts since Freud have reinterpreted homosexuality.

7. Steven Marcus, *Freud and the Culture of Psychoanalysis* (New York: W. W. Norton, 1984), 24.

8. Mitchell, "Introduction—I," in Mitchell and Rose, *Sexuality*, 11.

9. Rose, "Introduction—II," in Mitchell and Rose, *Sexuality*, 49.

10. Ernst L. Freud, ed., *Letters of Sigmund Freud* (New York: Basic Books, 1960), 423–24.

4. Freud: The Classic Cases

1. H. Nunberg and E. Federn, *Minutes of the Vienna Psychoanalytical Society* (New York: International Universities Press, 1975), 1:232.

2. This is the only case of Freud's for which such process notes are available. An abbreviated version of them is included as an appendix to Freud's case in the *Standard Edition*. Patrick J. Mahony was able to consult the full text at the Library of Congress while preparing his book *Freud and the Rat Man* (New Haven: Yale University Press, 1986). I have profited greatly from the fruits of his research.

3. Mahony, *Rat Man*, 159. Because at the time of this analysis Freud had not yet

recognized regression to sadistic anal eroticism as a characteristic feature of obsessional neurosis, this aspect of his patient's symptomology receives little attention in his theoretical discussion. Perhaps, as Mahony suggests, Freud disregarded it at least in part because of the furor aroused by the passages on anal sexuality in *The Three Essays;* evidence for the connection abounds in the process notes.

4. Ibid., 123.

5. Ibid., 106.

6. Ibid., 218. Mahony notes the exceptional disconnectedness of Freud's exposition in this case history and wonders if that might not be a manifestation of Freud's unconsciously mimicking the Rat Man's obsessional penchant for displacement.

7. Freud first had his attention drawn to the *Memoirs* by Jung, who was disappointed by Freud's use of them. Jung, characteristically, would have liked Freud to have focused more on the mythological parallels to Schreber's spontaneously created fantasies, to have seen in Schreber's images of giving birth to God's children evidence of his longings for spiritual creativity. He believed that the imputation of homosexual longings to Schreber revealed more about Freud's fantasies than about Schreber's.

8. William Niederland, who has uncovered much about Schreber's family history and biography not disclosed in the *Memoirs,* associates the onset of Schreber's illness with his having just received an important judicial appointment that required him to take on a male authority role; he suggests that this invitation to take the place of a father awakened Schreber's castration fantasies. This seems entirely compatible with Freud's interpretation of the case. See William G. Niederland, *The Schreber Case* (New York: Quadrangle, 1974), 41.

9. Freud seemed to have believed there was nothing particular in Schreber's early relationship that would explain his paranoia, although he acknowledged that the content of the delusions would be determined by the details of the father-son conflict, of which he knew nothing. Later researchers have discovered a good deal more. Schreber's father was not simply the benevolent physician dedicated to encouraging "the harmonious uphringing of the young" pictured by Freud. He was a widely known expert on child rearing who in his own family had usurped the maternal role and taken entire charge of his sons' upbringing. He sought to ensure that they would grow up free of weak or effeminate traits. His educational system emphasized coercion and obedience; he designed orthopedic apparatuses intended to ensure rigidly erect seating and perfect posture while sleeping that look like instruments of medieval torture. By his own admission he required "complete submission and passive surrender" of his own children. He believed that masturbation had to be prevented at all costs. He understood his "holy work" as designed to ensure a "better race." The detailed connections between the father's teaching and the son's delusions are striking. See Niederland, *Schreber,* 49–67.

10. Patrick J. Mahony, *Cries of the Wolf Man* (New York: International Universities Press, 1984), 42.

11. "The Memoirs of the Wolf-Man," in Muriel Gardner, ed., *The Wolf-Man by the Wolf-Man* (New York: Basic Books, 1971), 3–132.

12. Mahony, *Wolf Man,* 59, 119, and passim.

13. Ibid., 117.

14. In his 1919 essay "A Child Is Being Beaten," Freud discusses the masochistic and homosexual meanings of such fantasies (*SE* 17:198–200). This fits in with what strikes him here, that though the castration threat actually came from his female nurse, the Wolf Man (Freud insists) responded as though it came from the father, as though the archetypal (Freud says "phylogenetic") pattern supersedes the idiosyncratic historical reality (86).

15. Despite his emphasis on the Wolf Man's identification with his mother in the primal scene, as in most of Freud's case histories little is made of the patient's relation to his mother. (The personal factors associated with this avoidance will be considered in Chapter 5.) Some recent psychoanalytic interpretations of the case have seen the Wolf Man's maternal identification as its most salient feature. They highlight those moments in Freud's text where he discusses his patient's feelings for his mother, his sister, and his nurse. Though not denying the homosexuality, they explain it differently (see Mahony, *Wolf Man*, 141–42). Of course, they have the advantage of the theoretical formulations about the so-called "pre-Oedipal mother," which Freud first articulated a decade after he began his work with his most famous patient. (These formulations, too, we will look at in Chapter 5.)

5. Freud: Female Homosexuality

1. For the importance Freud attaches to the complex interplay between acceptance and disavowal, see my discussion of the Wolf Man case in Chapter 4 and *SE* 19:253.

2. See Dorothy Dinnerstein, *The Mermaid and the Minotaur* (New York: Harper and Row, 1977); Nancy Chodorow, *The Reproduction of Mothering* (Berkeley: University of California Press, 1978). Chodorow tends to simplify by assuming as *given* precisely what happens *through* gender formation: that girls will *identify* with mothers and see fathers as *objects*.

3. Catherine Clement, *The Weary Sons of Freud* (London: Verso, 1987), 91.

4. Karen Horney, *Feminist Psychology* (New York: W. W. Norton, 1967), 56. Horney acknowledges her indebtedness to Georg Simmel for the insight.

5. Dianne Hunter, "Hysteria, Psychoanalysis, and Feminism: The Case of Anna O.," in Shirley Nelson Garner et al., eds., *The Mother Tongue* (Ithaca: Cornell University Press, 1985), 79ff.

6. Sarah Kofman, *The Enigma of Woman* (Ithaca: Cornell University Press, 1985), 137.

7. James Hillman, *The Myth of Analysis* (Evanston, Ill.: Northwestern University Press, 1972), 271–87.

8. Peter Gay, *Freud: A Life for Our Time* (New York: W. W. Norton, 1988), 519.

9. See Juliet Mitchell, *Psychoanalysis and Feminism* (New York: Pantheon, 1974), esp. 401–6.

10. Gay, *Freud*, 505.

11. Kofman, *Enigma*, 137.

12. Ibid., 193.

13. Ibid., 192.

14. Eli Sagan, *Freud, Women, and Morality* (New York: Basic Books, 1988), 118.

15. Luce Irigaray, *Speculum of the Other Woman* (Ithaca: Cornell University Press, 1985), 99, 101.

16. Charles Bernheimer and Claire Kahane, eds., *In Dora's Case* (New York: Columbia University Press, 1985), 17.

17. Ibid., 27.

18. Gay, *Freud*, 430, 434.

19. Ibid., 438, 437.

20. Uwe Henrik Peters, *Anna Freud* (New York: Schocken Books, 1985), 41–47.

21. Gay, *Freud*, 441.

22. Peters, *Anna Freud*, 119–20.

23. In a review of Elisabeth Young-Bruehl's *Anna Freud* (New York: Summit Books, 1988) Walter Kendrick writes: "Ms. Young-Bruehl turns the 'sublimation' crank rather too often, repeatedly insisting that Anna Freud was chaste throughout her life, that she was, as Freud's close friend Marie Bonaparte called her, a 'vestal,' above all that she was not a homosexual. At least in Anna Freud's case, Ms. Young-Bruehl apparently believes that no sex life at all is preferable to a homosexual one. Sigmund Freud might not have agreed" (*New York Times Book Review*, October 16, 1988).

24. Susan Stanford Friedman, *Psyche Reborn: The Emergence of H.D.* (Bloomington: Indiana University Press, 1981), 5, 39, 303.

25. H.D. (Hilda Doolittle), *HERmione* (New York: New Directions, 1981), 211.

26. Friedman, *Psyche*, 35–49.

27. Uncollected, undated poem included in ibid., 47.

28. Norman N. Holland, "H.D. and the 'Blameless Physician,' " in Hendrik M. Ruitenbeek, ed., *Freud as We Knew Him* (Detroit: Wayne State University Press, 1973), 476–80.

29. H.D., *Tribute to Freud*, 146–47.

6. Jung: The Personal Dimension

1. Melvin Kettner, "Some Archetypal Themes in Male Homosexuality," *Professional Reports of the 15th Annual Joint Conference of Societies of Jungian Analysts of Northern and Southern California*, April 1967, 33–34. My thanks to the library of the C. G. Jung Institute, Los Angeles, for making this paper available to me.

2. Richard I. Evans, *Conversations with Carl Jung* (New York: Van Nostrand, 1964), 101. References to Carl Jung's autobiography, *Memories, Dreams, Reflections*, will be given in the text as *MDR*. References to Jung's *Collected Works* (Princeton: Princeton University Press, 1953–1979) will be given in the text as *CW* with volume number, followed by page (not paragraph) number.

3. Vincent Brome, *Jung: Man and Myth* (New York: Atheneum, 1981), 40–41.

4. Ibid., 31.

5. Eugene Monick, *Phallos: Sacred Image of the Masculine* (Toronto: Inner City Books, 1987), 96.

6. Nor Hall, *Those Women* (Dallas: Spring Publications, 1988), 55, 79, 80.

7. Marie Louise von Franz, *C. G. Jung: His Myth in Our Time* (New York: G. P. Putnam's Sons, 1975), 15–37.

8. Ibid., 35.

9. Monick, *Phallos*, 50, 74, 17, 62.

10. Hall, *Women*, 56.

11. Daniel C. Noel, "Veiled Kabir: C. G. Jung's Phallic Self-Image," *Spring* (1974): 229–30, 239.

12. Aniela Jaffe, "The Creative Phases in Jung's Life," *Spring* (1972): 163.

13. Monick, *Phallos*, 50–58.

14. Von Franz, *Myth*, 60.

15. Jaffe, "Phases," 169.

16. See Aldo Cartenuto, *A Secret Symmetry* (New York: Pantheon, 1982); Bruno Bettleheim, "Scandal in the Family," *New York Review of Books*, June 30, 1983.

17. See Ferne Jensen, ed., *C. G. Jung, Emma Jung and Toni Wolff: A Collection of Remembrances* (San Francisco: Analytical Psychology Club, 1982); Barbara Hannah, *Jung: His Life and Work* (New York: G. P. Putnam's Sons, 1976), 119–20 and passim.

18. Carl Jung, *Letters* (Princeton: Princeton University Press, 1973), 1:19, n. 8.

19. My thanks to Eric Downing for this association.

20. Brome, *Jung*, 92.

21. C. Jess Groesbeck, "The Analyst's Myth: Freud and Jung as Each Other's Analyst," *Quadrant* 13, no. 1 (1980): 33.

22. Jung continues with some puzzling ideas that he makes no attempt to contextualize or explain. He announces that the "removal of the moral stigma from homosexuality as a method of contraception is a cause to be promoted with the utmost energy" and concludes, "Because of our shortsightedness we fail to recognize the biological services rendered by homosexual seducers. Actually they should be credited with something of the sanctity of monks" (180J). How to reconcile this to the disgust Jung feels toward his own homosexual seducer, I do not know.

7. Jung: The Theory

1. The quotes are from Robert Fitzgerald's translation of Virgil's *Aeneid* (New York: Random House, 1983); *Aen.* 6.126–29, 7.312.

2. A 1952 revision of this work appears as CW 5 under the title *Symbols of Transformation;* it differs significantly from the original version, published as *The Psychology of the Unconscious* (New York: Moffat, Yard, 1919). I cite *Symbols* whenever possible since it is much more readily available; citations from *Psychology* are to passages omitted from the later edition. (It is sometimes difficult to date passages in Jung's writing because the editors have not dated paragraphs in the *Collected Works* nor always been careful to indicate omissions from earlier editions.)

3. Jung, *Psychology of the Unconscious,* 100.

4. Though Jung also recognizes that for the young there is a danger of being swamped by the unconscious: "Hidden beneath the hazardous mask of incest is the pull to original passivity, the danger of being devoured by the Terrible Mother" (*CW* 5:174).

5. The German equivalent of the Greek *psyche* is *Seele,* soul—the word used by Freud, which his English translators have obscured by rendering it as "mental structure" or "mental organization." See Bruno Bettelheim, *Freud and Man's Soul* (New York: Alfred A. Knopf, 1983).

6. Jung borrows the term *hermaphrodite* from alchemy but gives it a consistently psychical significance. June Singer proposes that we reserve "hermaphrodite" to refer to the physiological anomaly, use "bisexuality" to refer to a lack of clarity about gender identification made manifest at the level of interpersonal relationship, and "androgyny" to refer to the inner, psychical integration of masculine and feminine attributes. Thus she, even more than Jung, differentiates between biological, social or behavioral, and psychological reality, and reifies "masculinity" and "femininity" as "laid down by nature." Singer, *Androgyny,* 16–23, 193–94.

7. Jung also believes that the image of the hermaphrodite is ultimately inadequate because it remains dualistic; the union of love represented in the *hieros gamos* (the sacred marriage) may better communicate the goal for it "binds the opposites by love" (*CW* 16:197–98) as may the image of the son born from this union who "resolves the antagonisms of the parents" and symbolizes the emergence of something genuinely new (*CW* 14:29, 371).

8. My thanks to Howard Teich for directing me to these illustrations and Jung's discussions of them.

8. Jung: The Cases—Male and Female

1. C. G. Jung, *The Visions Seminars* (Zurich: Spring Publications, 1976), 1:212.

2. C. G. Jung, *Dream Analysis: Notes of the Seminar Given in 1928–1930* (Princeton: Princeton University Press, 1984), 170. Subsequent page references will be given in the text.

3. Jung, *Letters* 1:13–14.

4. In recent years this situation has been somewhat modified with the publication of the notes of the English Seminars Jung taught in 1928–30 *(Dream Analysis)* and in 1930–34 *(The Visions Seminars).* Each gives us Jung's analysis of an extended series of dreams with many references to the dreamer's life history and contemporary situation (along with many fascinating digressions). It nonetheless remains true that Jung never wrote or published a case history.

5. The account appears in *Two Essays on Analytical Psychology* (*CW* 7:100–109), a 1916 work prepared as an elaboration of a 1912 essay. As with many of Jung's writings, however, this work was considerably revised with each new edition, and the publishing apparatus of the *Collected Works* does not make it easy to establish

clearly the history of composition. This account was not included in the original edition; it was probably added in 1925.

6. Kettner, "Archetypal Themes," 33–58.

7. James Hillman, "Anima I," *Spring* (1973): 99.

8. James Hillman, "The Great Mother, Her Son, Her Hero and the Puer," in Pat Berry, ed., *Mothers and Fathers* (New York: Spring Publications, 1973), 81; *Myth of Analysis*, 15.

9. James Hillman, "Anima II," *Spring* (1974): 140.

10. James Hillman, ed., "Puer and Senex," in Hillman, ed., *Puer Papers* (Dallas: Spring Publications, 1979), 3–53.

11. Mitch Walker, "The Double," *Spring* (1976): 165–75.

12. Rafael Lopez-Pedrazo, *Hermes* (Dallas: Spring Publications, 1977), 77–79.

13. Thomas Moon, "The Faces of Mister Right: Archetypal Patterns in Gay Male Relationships," unpublished manuscript, 1980, p. 34.

14. Lopez-Pedrazo, *Hermes*, 77.

15. Addressing how Jungian theory might be revisioned from the perspective of female experience, many women, including Irene Claremont de Castillejo, Naomi Goldenberg, Estella Lauter, and Demaris Wehr, have raised serious questions about the adequacy of animus theory to do justice to the soul experience of women. Although they have not explicitly explored how an understanding of female psychology that recognizes that women, too, have anima might contribute to a theory about lesbianism, they have proposed that for women the relation to soul is more adequately viewed in same-sex than in contrasexual images. See de Castillejo, *Knowing Woman* (New York: Harper and Row, 1973); Naomi Goldenberg, *The Changing of the Gods* (Boston: Beacon Press, 1979); Estella Lauter and Carol Rupprecht, eds., *Feminist Archetypal Theory* (Knoxville: University of Tennessee Press, 1985); Demaris Wehr, *Jung and Feminism* (Boston: Beacon Press, 1987). In my own work I have explored how the sister archetype helps us toward an understanding of the archetypal dimensions of women's love of women—and, more peripherally, have also considered the analogous role played by the brother in male psychology. See Downing, *Psyche's Sisters* (New York: Harper and Row, 1988).

9. Demythologizing Greek Homosexuality

1. Mary Renault, *The Charioteer* (Cleveland: Meridian, 1961), 33, 214.

2. Harold Patzer, *Die griechische Knabenliebe* (Wiesbaden: Franz Steiner Verlag, 1982), 40.

3. Michel Foucault, *The Use of Pleasure* (New York: Vintage, 1986), 7n.

4. K. J. Dover, *Greek Homosexuality* (Cambridge, Mass.: Harvard University Press, 1978).

5. David M. Halperin, "Sexual Ethics and Technologies of the Self in Classical Greece," *American Journal of Philology* 107 (1986): 282.

6. Foucault, *Pleasure*, 41.

7. Halperin, "One Hundred Years," p. 39 and n. 30.

8. Ulrich von Wilamowitz-Moellendorff, *Der Glaube der Hellenen* (Basel: B. Schwabe, 1959), 1:157.

9. Eva C. Keuls, *The Reign of the Phallus* (New York: Harper and Row, 1985), 2.

10. Halperin notes that Artemidorus assumes that sexual images in dreams signify social events, not anything about the dreamer's sexual fantasies. See "One Hundred Years," 40.

11. Ibid., 39.

12. Keuls, *Phallus*, 82.

13. Foucault, *Pleasure*, 84.

14. Xenophon, *Symposium* 8.3 (I consulted J. S. Watson, trans., *Xenophon's Minor Works* [London: George Bell & Sons, 1884], 148–91); Foucault, *Pleasure*, 149–50, 202.

15. Halperin, "One Hundred Years," 40.

16. Foucault, *Pleasure*, 85.

17. Thorkil Vanggaard, *Phallos* (London: International Universities Press, 1972), 23.

18. All quotations from Plato unless otherwise noted are from Edith Hamilton and Huntingdon Cairns, *The Collected Dialogues of Plato* (Princeton: Princeton University Press, 1961). References will be given in the text with accepted abbreviations for the dialogues and by paragraph number.

19. Dover, *Homosexuality*, 82.

20. Foucault, *Pleasure*, pt.4, passim.

21. Dover, *Homosexuality*, 16.

22. Foucault, *Pleasure*, 223.

23. Vanggaard, *Phallos*, 67.

24. Halperin, "One Hundred Years," 44.

25. Xenophon, *Symposium* 8.18.

26. Dover, *Homosexuality*, 103.

27. Ibid., 87.

28. Ibid., 79, 137, 144.

29. Keuls, *Phallus*, 276.

30. Dover, *Homosexuality*, 87.

31. Ibid., 201–2.

32. Philip Slater, *The Glory of Hera* (Boston: Beacon Press, 1968), 59, 61.

33. George Devereux, "Greek Pseudo-Homosexuality and the 'Greek Miracle,'" *Symbolae Osloenses* 42 (1967): 78.

34. Keuls, *Phallus*, 275.

10. Same Sex Love among the Gods

1. See Downing, *The Goddess.*

2. Bernard Sergent, *Homosexuality in Greek Myth* (Boston: Beacon Press, 1986). I am also indebted to William G. Doty's unpublished paper "Male: Male Myths" (1977).

3. Sergent, *Homosexuality*, 16–20.

4. Ibid., 65 and passim.

5. Homer, *Iliad* 5.233, from the translation by Richard Lattimore (Chicago: University of Chicago Press, 1976). Subsequent references will be given in the text.

6. Charles Boer, trans., *The Homeric Hymns* (Chicago: Swallow Press, 1970), 80.

7. Dover, *Homosexuality*, 148–49.

8. Ovid, *Metamophoses*, 10.150–53, from the translation by Mary M. Innes (Baltimore: Penguin, 1975). Subsequent references will be given in the text.

9. Sergent, *Homosexuality*, 35; Sergent gives credit for this connection to Jan Bremmer, "An Enigmatic Indo-European Rite: Pederasty," *Arethusa* 13, no.2 (1980): 285.

10. Dover, *Homosexuality*, 93.

11. Keuls, *Phallus*, 287.

12. Monick, *Phallos*, 90.

13. Boer, *Hymns*, 80.

14. David Dukelow, "The Ganymede Archetype," Friends of Jung/San Diego, Seminar, January 1983.

15. Apollonius of Rhodes, *The Voyage of the Argo*, trans. E. V. Rie (New York: Penguin, 1985), 112.

16. Keuls, *Phallus*, 14.

17. Carl Kerenyi, *Apollo* (Dallas; Spring Publications, 1983), 24.

18. Carl Kerenyi, *The Gods of the Greeks* (London: Thames and Hudson, 1951), 139.

19. Walter Otto, *The Homeric Gods* (Boston: Beacon Press, 1964), 71–72.

20. Walter Burkert, *Greek Religion* (Cambridge, Mass.: Harvard University Press, 1985), 263, 144–45.

21. Sergent, *Homosexuality*, 107.

22. Ibid.

23. Ibid., 112.

24. Ibid., 108.

25. Otto, *Gods*, 61, 78.

26. Kerenyi, *Gods*, 139.

27. John Boardman and Eugenio LaRocca, *Eros in Greece* (New York: Erotic Art Book Society, 1975), 103. Zephyrus is shown on a red figure pot lying on Hyacinthus—evidently when the lover was a wind, this otherwise-avoided posture seemed irresistible!

28. Sergent, *Homosexuality*, 89; although my interpretation of the information from Pliny differs from Sergent's.

29. Ibid., 88.

30. Kerenyi, *Gods*, 140.

31. Burkert, *Religion*, 165.

32. I have taken Clement's account from Sergent, *Homosexuality*, 181.

33. Ibid., 187, 190.

34. Kerenyi, *Gods*, 273.

35. Burkert, *Religion*, 109.
36. Arthur Evans, *The God of Ecstasy* (New York: St. Martin's Press, 1988), 160.
37. Otto, *Gods*, 176.
38. Evans, *Ecstasy*, 28; see also Burkert, *Religion*, 291.
39. Burkert, *Religion*, 166.
40. Dover, *Homosexuality*, 131.
41. Evans, *Ecstasy*, 140, 179.
42. Richmond Lattimore, trans., *The Odes of Pindar* (Chicago: University of Chicago Press, 1947), 2–3.
43. For a complete listing, see Sergent, *Homosexuality*, 262ff.
44. Quoted in Evans, *Witchcraft*, 154.

11. Same-Sex Love in the Age of Heroes

1. Richmond Lattimore, "Introduction to *Rhesus*," in David Grene and Richmond Lattimore, eds., *The Complete Greek Tragedies*, 4 vols. (Chicago: University of Chicago Press, 1959–60), 4:82, n. 2.
2. Sergent, *Homosexuality*, 261.
3. Carl Kerenyi, *Heroes of the Greeks* (New York: Grove Press, 1962), 3, 13.
4. Dover, *Homosexuality*, 35–36.
5. Sergent, *Homosexuality*, 69.
6. W.K.C. Guthrie, *Orpheus and Greek Religion* (New York: W. W. Norton, 1966), 49, 53, 55.
7. Sergent, *Homosexuality*, 82.
8. Murray Stein, "Narcissus," *Spring* (1975): 75, 41.
9. Ibid., 55.
10. Xenophon, *Symposium* 8.31.
11. Quoted in Dover, *Homosexuality*, 53.
12. Quoted in ibid., 197.
13. Sergent, *Homosexuality*, 255.
14. Barriss Mills, trans., *The Idylls of Theokritos* (West Lafayette, Ind.: Purdue University Studies, 1963), 13.1–20.
15. Ibid., 151.
16. Thomas J. Figueira, "Initiation and Seduction: Two Recent Books on Greek Pederasty," *American Journal of Philology*, no. 107 (1986): 429.
17. Sergent, *Homosexuality*, 247–48.

12. Woman-Loving Women

1. J. J. Bachofen, *Myth, Religion, and Mother Right* (Princeton: Princeton University Press, 1967), 11–12.
2. Robin Morgan, "A Country Weekend," in *Going Too Far* (New York: Vintage, 1978), 142.
3. All citations of Greek tragedies unless otherwise noted will be from David

Grene and Richmond Lattimore, eds., *The Complete Greek Tragedies*, 4 vols. (Chicago: University of Chicago Press, 1959–60).

4. Paul Roche, trans., *Three Plays of Euripides: Alcestis, Medea, Bacchae* (New York: W. W. Norton, 1974).

5. Keuls, *Phallus*, 357.

6. May Sarton, *Collected Poems, 1930–1973* (New York: W. W. Norton, 1974), 332.

7. Daly, *Gyn/Ecology*, 2, 383; Mary Daly, *Webster's First New Intergalactic Wickedary of the English Language* (Boston: Beacon Press, 1987), 103, 211.

8. Bachofen, *Mother Right*, 154.

9. Keuls, *Phallus*, 4.

10. Bachofen, *Mother Right*, 136.

11. Ibid., 104–7, 131–39.

12. Phyllis Chesler, "The Amazon Legacy," in Charlene Spretnak, ed., *The Politics of Women's Sexuality* (Garden City, N.Y.: Anchor, Doubleday, 1982), 102.

13. Bachofen, *Mother Right*, 191, 102.

14. Burkert, *Religion*, 291.

15. Hall, *Those Women*, 21.

16. Ibid., 35, 53, 62, 74.

17. Jane Ellen Harrison, *Prolegomena to the Study of Greek Religion* (New York: Meridian, 1957), 453.

18. H.D., "At Eleusis" in *Collected Poems: 1912–1944* (New York: New Directions, 1983), 179–80.

19. Sergent, *Homosexuality*, 91–93.

20. Keuls, *Phallus*, 320.

21. Burkert, *Religion*, 151.

13. Same-Sex Love among the Goddesses

1. Burkert, *Religion*, 183.

2. Dover, *Homosexuality*, 172.

3. Burkert, *Religion*, 105.

4. Ibid., 242–46; Harrison, *Prolegomena*, 120–31.

5. Burkert, *Religion*, 132.

6. Ibid., 228–33.

7. Bachofen, *Mother Right*, 111.

8. Burkert, *Religion*, 150.

14. Sappho

1. Bruno Snell, *The Discovery of the Mind* (New York: Dover, 1982), 53, 54, 59, 60, 65.

2. Willis Barnstone, *Sappho: Lyrics in the Original Greek with Translations* (New York: New York University Press, 1965), xvii.

3. See Bonnie Zimmermann, "Is 'Chloe Liked Olivia' a Lesbian Plot?" *Women's Studies International Forum* 6, no. 2 (1983): 169–75.

4. Peter Jay, ed., *The Greek Anthology* (New York: Penguin, 1981), 47.

5. E. S. Stigers, "Sappho's Private World," *Women's Studies* 8 (1981): 47.

6. Paul Roche, *The Love Songs of Sappho* (New York: Meridian, 1966), xvi.

7. Denys Page, *Sappho and Alcaeus* (Oxford: Clarendon Press, 1955), 140–42.

8. Jack Winkler, "Gardens of Nymphs: Public and Private in Sappho's Lyrics," *Women's Studies* 8 (1981): 69.

9. C. M. Bowra, *Greek Lyric Poetry* (Oxford: Oxford University Press, 1967), 187ff.

10. Paul Friedrichs, *The Meaning of Aphrodite* (Chicago: University of Chicago Press, 1978), 109–10.

11. R. Bagg, "Love, Ceremony and Daydream in Sappho's Lyrics," *Arion* 3 (1964): 48.

12. J. P. Hallett, "Sappho and Her Social Context," *Signs* 4 (1979): 460–71.

13. Jeffrey M. Duban, *Ancient and Modern Images of Sappho* (New York: Press of America, 1983), 40; Bremmer, "Enigmatic Indo-European Rite," 292–98.

14. C. P. Segal, "Eros and Incantation: Sappho and Oral Poetry," *Arethusa* 7 (1974): 141.

15. References to translations of Sappho's poetry are included in the text. The LP numbers refer to E. Lobel and D. L. Page, *Poetarum Lesbiorum Fragmenta* (Oxford: Clarendon Press, 1968); the E numbers refer to J. M. Edmonds, *Lyra Graeca*, vol. 1 (Cambridge, Mass. Harvard University Press, 1958). I have consulted the following translations: Barnstone, *Sappho;* idem, *Greek Lyric Poetry* (New York: Schocken, 1975); Mary Barnard, *Sappho* (Berkeley: University of California Press, 1958); Guy Davenport, *Sappho* (Ann Arbor: University of Michigan Press, 1965); Duban, *Images of Sappho;* Suzy Q. Groden, *The Poems of Sappho* (Indianapolis: Bobbs-Merrill, 1966); Page, *Sappho and Alcaeus;* Roche, *The Love Songs of Sappho.*

16. "Testimonia," quoted in Barnstone, *Sappho*, 178.

17. Quoted in ibid., xxi.

18. Stigers, "Private World," 48.

19. Quoted in Barnstone, *Sappho*, 179.

20. Snell, *Discovery*, 44, 65.

21. Page, *Sappho and Alcaeus*, 42.

22. Anne Carson, *Eros: the Bittersweet* (Princeton: Princeton University Press, 1986), 118–19; Segal, "Oral Poetry," 139–41.

23. Page, *Sappho and Alcaeus*, 40.

24. Friedrichs, *Aphrodite*, 107–8.

25. Carson, *Eros*, 170.

26. Friedrichs, *Aphrodite*, 97–98.

27. Carson, *Eros*, 12–14.

28. Friedrichs, *Aphrodite*, 113.

29. Carson, *Eros*, 3–9.

30. Friedrichs, *Aphrodite*, 108.

31. Ibid., 109–10.
32. Stigers, "Private World," 53.
33. Friedrichs, *Aphrodite*, 114.
34. Winkler, "Nymphs," 83.
35. Translation of this line modified to correspond with other readings.
36. Stigers, "Private World," 58.
37. Winkler, "Nymphs," 84.
38. Rachel Blau DuPlessis, *H.D.: The Career of That Struggle* (Bloomington: Indiana University Press, 1986), 23.
39. H.D., "Fragment Forty-one," in *Collected Poems: 1912–1944*, 183.

15. Plato: The *Symposium*

1. Paul Friedlander, *Plato: An Introduction* (New York: Harper and Row, 1964), 127–30.
2. Ibid., 46–49.
3. David M. Halperin, "Plato and Erotic Receptivity," *Classical Antiquity* 3, no. 1 (1986): 71, 73.
4. Martha C. Nussbaum, *The Fragility of Goodness* (Cambridge: Cambridge University Press, 1986), 168–71.
5. R. A. Markus, "The Dialectic of Eros in Plato's Symposium," in Gregory Vlastos, ed., *Plato: A Collection of Critical Essays* (Garden City, N.Y.: Doubleday, 1971), 134.
6. In his 1938 essay "Analysis Terminable and Interminable" (*SE* 23:245–47), Freud acknowledges the connection between Empedocles' Eros and Eris and his own Love and Death.
7. Foucault, *Pleasure*, 232.
8. Nussbaum, *Goodness*, 173.
9. F. M. Cornford, "The Doctrine of Eros in Plato's Symposium," in Vlastos, *Critical Essays*, 125.
10. Dover, *Homosexuality*, 161.
11. See David M. Halperin, "Why Is Diotima a Woman?" 2, typescript of a paper to be included in David M. Halperin, John J. Winkler, and Froma I. Zeitlin, eds., *Before Sexuality: Structures of Erotic Experience in Ancient Mediterranean Societies* (Princeton: Princeton University Press, forthcoming), kindly sent me by Professor Halperin. I am delighted to have my understanding validated by so credible an authority.
12. Friedlander, *Introduction*, 174.
13. Halperin, "Diotima," 15–16, 13. It is true, of course, that Aeschylus proposed that women had no real role in generation, but in the medical texts of the classical world female orgasms are described as seed producing, and in the *Timaeus* (91) Plato speaks of the womb as a living animal passionately desirous of making children, which when it remains fruitless for a long time wanders all about the body producing all sorts of illness. (Though as Halperin points out, in actuality it is really

in males, where orgasm and seminal ejaculation are inseparable, that sexual pleasure and reproduction are inextricably entwined.)

14. Halperin, "Diotima," 24.

15. Halperin, "Erotic Receptivity," 68.

16. Foucault, *Pleasure*, 240.

17. Cornford, "Doctrine of Eros," 127.

18. Markus, "Dialectic of Eros," 141.

19. Cornford, "Doctrine of Eros," 127.

20. Gregory Vlastos, *Platonic Studies* (Princeton: Princeton University Press, 1981), 1–34.

21. Nussbaum, *Goodness*, 179.

22. Werner Jaeger, *Paideia* (New York: Oxford University Press, 1943), 2:196.

23. Paul Friedlander, *Plato: The Dialogues, Second and Third Periods* (Princeton: Princeton University Press, 1969), 227.

24. Friedlander, *Introduction*, 148–49.

25. Nussbaum, *Goodness*, 187.

26. Friedlander, *Dialogues, Second and Third Periods*, 28.

27. Friedlander, *Introduction*, 130.

28. Nussbaum, *Goodness*, 185.

29. Cornford, "Doctrine of Eros," 140.

30. Foucault, *Pleasure*, 241.

31. Nussbaum, *Goodness*, 198–99, 87.

16. Plato: The *Phaedrus*

1. Vlastos, *Platonic Studies*, 29.

2. Nussbaum, *Goodness*, 212.

3. W.K.C. Guthrie, *A History of Greek Philosophy* (Cambridge: Cambridge University Press, 1975), 4:397.

4. Nussbaum, *Goodness*, 232.

5. Ibid., 212, 229–32.

6. Friedlander, *Introduction*, 208.

7. Ibid., 194.

8. Nussbaum, *Goodness*, 216.

9. Anne LeBeck, "The Central Myth of Plato's *Phaedrus*," *Greek, Roman and Byzantine Studies* 13 (1972): 278.

10. Halperin, "Erotic Receptivity," 69, 70.

11. Ibid., 75.

12. Nussbaum, *Goodness*, 219.

13. Halperin, "Erotic Receptivity," 75–76.

14. Friedlander, *Dialogues, Second and Third Periods*, 240.

15. Carson, *Eros*, 108.

16. Halperin, "Erotic Receptivity," 70.

17. LeBeck, "Central Myth," 288.

Epilogue: The Deepest Mystery

1. Christine Downing, *Journey through Menopause.*

2. Paul Monette, *Borrowed Time: An AIDS Memoir* (New York: Harcourt, Brace, Jovanovich, 1988).

3. Ibid., 105, 220, 175, 298, 303.

4. Ibid., 31, 30.

5. See Randy Shilts, *And the Band Played On* (New York: St. Martin's Press, 1987), passim.

6. Susan Sontag, "AIDS and Its Metaphors," *New York Review of Books,* October 27, 1988, 89–99.

7. Monette, *Time,* 83.

8. See Bruno Bettelheim, "The Holocaust—One Generation Later," *Surviving and Other Essays* (New York: Random House, 1979), 91–93; Bettelheim's discussion makes clear how radically inappropriate, indeed sacrilegious, it is to apply the term *holocaust,* which refers to ancient rituals of a deeply religious nature, to the mass murders perpetrated by the Nazis in the death camps.

9. Monette, *Time,* 136.

10. Shilts, *Band,* passim.

11. Christopher Mead, "Homosexuality Beyond Disease," unpublished paper.

12. H.D., *Tribute to Freud,* 18, 103.

13. Paul Ricoeur, *Freud and Philosophy,* 256, 291.

14. Ibid., 337.

15. Ibid., 328.

16. Time time Freud recognizes (as he had failed to do in *The Three Essays*) that Aristophanes' tale was about variations in relation to the sexual drive's object and acknowledges that the views voiced cannot unequivocably be attributed to Plato himself, through he sees Plato as introducing the myth because he saw it as containing at least "an element of truth."

17. Jones, *Life and Work* 3 : 152–53.

18. Monette, *Time,* 44, 45.

19. Shilts, *Band,* 230, 356.

20. Monette, *Time,* 43.

Seven Years Later

1. Robert Bosnak, *Dreaming with an Aids Patient* (Boston: Shambala, 1989).

2. River Malcolm, "Philip Fades," *For Philip* (self-published, 1992), 6.

3. Mark Doty, "Bill's Story," from *My Alexandria* (Urbana: University of Illinois Press, 1993), 69. Used by permission of Mark Doty and the University of Illinois Press. "Bill's Story" also appears in *Poets for Life: Seventy-Six Poets Respond to AIDS,* edited by Michael Klein (New York: Crown, 1989), which includes many poems that exemplify the strengths I attribute to the poetry of AIDS.

4. River Malcolm, "Visiting Philip, June 1992," *For Philip,* 9–10.

Index

Also published by Continuum

Christine Downing
THE GODDESS
Mythological Images of the Feminine

"Highly recommended."
—Library Journal

"A must for those concerned with an experiential approach to religious studies, depth psychology, and above all the Goddess/es."
—Religious Studies Review

Gary David Comstock
UNREPENTANT, SELF-AFFIRMING, PRACTICING
Lesbian/Bisexual/Gay People within Organized Religion

"The most thorough, most documented description to date of lesbian/bisexual/gay people within organized religion. Backed up with hard data and rich personal experiences, he tells of the struggles of many Americans to gain religious acceptance. A timely and useful piece of research."
—Wade Clark Roof

Gary David Comstock and Susan E. Henking, Editors
QUE(E)RYING RELIGION
A Critical Anthology

The most important collection to date on the encounter between religious studies and lesbian/gay/queer studies, with major contributions by (among others) John Boswell, Judith Brown, George Chauncey, Christine Downing, Kenneth Dover, Will Roscoe, and Andrew Sullivan.

Kenneth R. Dutton
THE PERFECTIBLE BODY
The Western Ideal of Male Physical Development

"A readable and nuanced history of male body-building, from the ancient Greeks to today. . . . [Dutton's] scholarship is thorough, and his grasp of the issues broad and complex.
—Publisher's Weekly